ADVANCE PRAISE FOR

Native North American Authorship

"With dazzling breadth and depth, A. Robert Lee analyzes a rich spectrum of Native voices, some well-known, others less often heard, placing them in a medley of illuminating contexts. He writes of all genres with agility, in his own inimitable critical idiom. This valuable book crowns Lee's achievement in Native North American scholarship."

Cathy Covell Waegner, editor, *Mediating Indianness* (2015)

"This brilliant and highly engaging collection of essays by A. Robert Lee is the perfect companion for readers of Native North American poetry and prose who wish to go deeper: to discover, through close attention to text, ways in which each author's biographical and sociocultural influences have informed their own writings, and ways in which these writings have, collectively, shaped the various literary trends which contextualize them. The result of Lee's deft cross-referencing is a breathtaking *tour-de-force.*"

Ingrid Wendt, author of *Evensong* (2011)

"This book represents (in extraordinary breadth) a survey of Native American literary accomplishment over the now more than half-century since the inauguration of what has been called the Native American Renaissance. Using a close reading methodology it locates points of connection, both between the authors surveyed and also with their wider circle of literary and artistic contemporaries. It constitutes a strong argument for the rude health of Native American literatures as representing both continuation of tribal cultures into modernity and also difference from the settler society that surrounds them. It also represents an effort to understand the individual modalities of Indigenous experience, through an emphasis on the contradictory impulses of accommodation and resistance."

James Mackay, European University, Cyprus

Native North American Authorship

This book is part of the Peter Lang Humanities list.
Every volume is peer reviewed and meets
the highest quality standards for content and production.

PETER LANG
New York • Berlin • Brussels • Lausanne • Oxford

A. Robert Lee

Native North American Authorship

Text, Breath, Modernity

PETER LANG
New York • Berlin • Brussels • Lausanne • Oxford

Library of Congress Cataloging-in-Publication Control Number: 2022014457

Bibliographic information published by **Die Deutsche Nationalbibliothek**.
Die Deutsche Nationalbibliothek lists this publication in the "Deutsche Nationalbibliografie"; detailed bibliographic data are available on the Internet at http://dnb.d-nb.de/.

ISBN 978-1-4331-8845-9 (hardcover)
ISBN 978-1-63667-048-5 (paperback)
ISBN 978-1-4331-8865-7 (ebook pdf)
ISBN 978-1-4331-8866-4 (epub)
DOI 10.3726/b18420

Peter Lang Publishing, Inc., New York
80 Broad Street, 5th floor, New York, NY 10004
www.peterlang.com

Contents

Acknowledgments

My gratitude to writers of Native and First Nations heritage comes first.

Unreservedly.

To read the authorship of Native America and First Nations Canada is an enlightenment and always and at the same time a privilege. That remains the essential acknowledgment, especially venturing as a visitor into literary terrain an Atlantic away from my own origins.

I thank Gerald Vizenor for past friendship and for writings which have been of consequence in modern Native authorship. Latterly his views of empathy towards literature and good editorship could not have been more instructive. Our collaborations include *Shadow Distance: A Gerald Vizenor Reader* (1992), *Postindian Conversations* (1999), and *Loosening the Seams: Interpretations of Gerald Vizenor* (2000).

Other creative writers to whom I owe debts, whether in person or correspondence, notably include Louis Owens with whom I was working on a book of interviews provisionally entitled *Outside Shadow* at the time of his death in 2002.

I would also want to recognize the consequential poet who features in my *Salt Companion to Jim Barnes* (2009).

Much, too, is owed on my part to Native writer-scholars like Kimberly Blaeser, Betty Louise Bell, Robert F. Gish, Diane Glancy, Gordon Henry, Linda Hogan,

Carter Revard, Kathryn W. Stanley, Clifford E. Trafzer, Irene Vernon, Terry P. Wilson, Billy S. Stratton, Gary Strankman, and the late Patricia Clark Smith.

Debts to co-editors from the USA, Britain, Europe, Canada, Japan and Taiwan are likewise considerable: *Gerald Vizenor: Texts and Contexts* (2010), with Deborah Madsen, *The Native American Renaissance: Literary Imagination and Achievement* (2013), with Alan R. Velie, *Louis Owens: Writing Land and Legacy* (2019), with Joe Lockard, and *Ralph Salisbury, Transmotion*, Special Issue (2020), with James Mackay.

Equally it is a privilege to have contributed to *Transatlantc Voices: Interpretations of North American Literatures* (2007), *Survivance: Narratives of Native Presence* (2008), *Native Authenticity: Transnational Perspectives on Native American Literary Studies* (2010), *Aspects of Transnational and Indigenous Cultures* (2014), *Mediating Indianness* (2015), *The Routledge Companion to Native American Literature* (2016), *Native American Survivance, Memory, and Futurity* (2017), and *The Cambridge History of Native American Literature* (2020).

Across the international span the scholar list further includes Hans Bak, Elizabeth Bair, Helmbrecht Breinig, Susan Castillo, John G. Cawelti, Feng Pin-chia, John Gamber, Linda Lizut Helstern, Hsinya Huang, Elaine Jenner, Min Jung Kim, Arnold Krupat, Chris LaLonde, Iping Liang, Kenneth Lincoln, Tom Lynch, David Mogen, David L. Moore, David Murray, William H. New, Barry O'Connell, Yukiko Oshima, Simone Pellerin, Elvira Pulitano, Bernadette Rigal-Cellard, A. Lavonne Brown Ruoff, Colin Samson, David Stirrup, Rebecca Tillett, Cathy Covell Waegner, Ingrid Wendt, Hertha D. Sweet Wong and Shamoon Zamir.

Spain, my base this past decade, gives every reason to relish the creative good friendship of David Walton and Andy Sotiriou, together with that of Juan Antonio Súarez, Natalia Carbajosa and Estíbaliz Encarnación-Pinedo. In Valencia there has been the similar benefit of Carme Manuel Cuenca, Anna María Brigido Corrachán and Paul Scott Derrick. Madrid has meant especially Félix Martín Gutíerrez and Isabel Durán Giménez, and Barcelona, Gloria Montero and Jared Lubarsky.

I am grateful to the following journals for allowing my Native American literary-critical work into their pages: *American Book Review, Immigrants & Minorities, Journal of American Studies* (UK), *Konch Magazine, Modern Language Review, Studies in American Indian Literatures, Tamkang Review, Third Text, Transmotion,* and *Weber Studies.*

These and other writings arise from a career spent at the University of Kent, UK (1967–1996), and Nihon University, Tokyo (1997–2011). Equally it has been a major asset to have held frequent visiting appointments variously in the departments both of English and of Ethnic Studies at the University of Colorado and the University of California, Berkeley. Other year-long and summer teaching invitations have been essential, at Princeton University, University of Virginia, California State University, Northridge, Bryn Mawr College, University of Louisville, Northwestern University, University of Colorado, and University of New Mexico, together with a Newberry Library Summer Fellowship which allowed me access to their Native and Herman Melville holdings.

Subject position inevitably comes into consideration. I write as neither Native American nor, indeed, as any kind of American, but rather as a white Britisher albeit with a long university career teaching American Studies and Literature. Among many American literary interests has been the dynamics of multicultural imagination which I have sought to explore in studies like *Designs of Blackness: Mappings in the Literature and Culture of Afro-America* (1998, 25th Anniversary Edition, 2020), *Multicultural American Literature: Comparative Black, Native, Latino/a and Asian American Fictions* (2003) and *Modern American Counter Writing: Beats Outriders, Ethnics* (2010). These, and *Native American Writing* (2011) as the one multi-set alongside *African American Writing* (2013) and *US Latino/a Writing* (2014), intend reminders of the plurality of American literary voice. They also attest to how the multicultural has had to outflank well enough known exclusionist obstacles and so help the changing perception of American/Canadian literary canons.

Other debts.

A major thanks to Brian Donahue for the cover photography and appreciation of the Little Earth of United Tribes urban community in Minneapolis from where the images are taken.

An especial *xie-xie* to Lisa Yinwen Yu, both in Taiwan and the University of Arizona, for immense library and bibliographic help.

Philip Dunshea gave generous welcome at the outset for this book and has been hugely supportive throughout. My every appreciation.

As on previous occasions I thank Jacqueline Pavlovic at Peter Lang and the team at New Gen, most especially Charmitha Ashok (Production)

More personally, and infinitely to my good fortune, there has been Josefa Vivancos Hernández. Quite simply she has made this collection and its author possible.

Introduction: Text, Breath, Modernity

Native North American Authorship. You alight upon N. Scott Momaday's Kiowa-authored *House Made of Dawn* (1968) and enter a world of Native breakage and healing at once the wartime Pacific, postwar Los Angeles, and the mythic south-west pueblo called Walatowa. Turn to Louise Erdrich's Chippewa-Ojibwe *Love Medicine* (1984), teasingly poised between novel and story-cycle, and the fare is a dark-comic wheel of Upper Midwest mixed-blood dynasty. Read a line from the Acoma Pueblo writer Simon Ortiz's poem "Even the 'Indians' Believed" in his collection *Out There Somewhere* (2002) and you are faced with the query "Indians are made up?" Think First Nations Canada and a writer like Beth Brant (Bay of Quinte Mohawk), descendant of Chief Joseph Brant, and whose posthumous collection *A Generous Spirit* (2019) gives tribute to her gay and feminist life and the ancestry behind a poem like "For All My Grandmothers."

Whether non-Native, or even Native reader, you might well ask in good faith where you are located. In this regard, and at each first mention, I have given tribal affiliation – which is in no way to engage in the nag of controversies about blood quantum. That lies well beyond my credential. Rather, to meet the authorship of Momaday, Erdrich, Ortiz or Brant, and others of the literary generation of Leslie Marmon Silko (Laguna Pueblo), Gerald Vizenor (White Earth Chippewa-Ojibwe-Anishinaabe), James Welch (Blackfeet/A'aninin), Thomas King

(Cherokee), Joy Harjo (Muscogee-Creek) or Sherman Alexie (Coeur d'Alene), account needs to take on a range of forerunners and successors.

What historic pasts or sense of the present, what geographies, lie within the fashioning of these writings? Step back in time and Native American and Canada's First Nation literary-scriptural history generally has been agreed to start from the late eighteenth-century and early nineteenth-century. The Christian-convert evidentiary writing of Samson Occom (Mohegan), William Apess (Pequot) and the Canadian-born George Copway (Mississaugas Anishinaabe) supply usual pointers. Step forward to a contemporary sweep and you encounter a novel of Native urban life centered in Oakland through the dozen galleried voices of *There There* (2018) by Tommy Orange (Cheyenne-Arapaho); verse landscapes of inner spirit in *Dissolve* (2019) by Sherwin Bitsui (Diné/Navajo); a gay-themed New York city poem of selfhood's volatility amid welters of life and media information like *Feed* (2019) by Tommy Pico (Kumeyaay Viejas Reservation); or the trickster novel-trilogy launched with *Son of a Trickster* (2017) by the First Nations author Eden Robinson (Haisla-Heiltsuk). Early, late, or in-between, and however slow recognition, the texts aplenty are not to be denied.

Text. How, between then and now, to take full cognizance of these Native and First Nations writings, literary beginnings through to the writings published in the present Obama-Trump-Biden century? How as fully as possible to meet a tradition whose self-inscriptions run from codices and pictographs, through quill and page-print, to digitalization and global cybernetics? Whether one or many, genre or cross-genre, the texts at hand require attention as much to craft as vision, the sense of design as much as history.

Breath as part of the half-title for the book equally invites explanation. One helpful pointer is to be found in the poem "Turtle" by Linda Hogan (Chickasaw) in which the turtle becomes figuration in dreamed creation-story:

> I'm dreaming the old turtle back.
>
> He walks out of the water
> slow,
> that shell with the water on it
> the sun on it,
> dark as the wet trunks of hackberry trees.
>
> In water
> the world is breathing
> in the silt.

Calling Myself Home (1978)[1]

Hogan has her poem go on to situate her reader, Native and non-Native, among a spectrum of living things: fish, animals, eyes, women as birth-givers. The turtle, in any number of tribal-community figurations, serves as world-genesis avatar, the ancestral bearer of creation, its breath from under and then out of water carried into life's all-encompassing domain. "The world never leaves the Turtle's back" says Thomas King, Cherokee-heritaged, California-born but long resident in Canada, in *The Truth About Stories: A Native Narrative* (2003).[2] He, too, shares the trope, one of Native/First Nations creative breath and its continuance. At the same time, and in step with any number of compeers, King writes as a wholly modern author, well aware of debates as to textuality, the writer looking mirror-like over his or her or their own shoulder. Native/First Nations literal breath, so to say, elides cannily into Native/First Nations literary breath.

Modernity coequally needs its gloss. What indeed is it to write as modern for Native authors, whether reservation-centered or living in the cities? Arizona or Wisconsin or Oklahoma yield today's Indian Country but so, too, are there the Urban Indian domains of Los Angeles, Minneapolis or New York. What, to invoke Canada, has it meant to give new written idiom to First Nations experience, whether writers accorded governmental status or non-status and across the spectrum of Abenaki, Cree, Haida, Kwakiutl with discrete recognition of the Inuit and Métis populations, and yet again to life in the cities and across the provinces from Toronto to Vancouver?

Certainly Native/First Nations authorship has been adventuresome: urban and speculative fiction, ventures into new gothic and the postmodern, open-form verse, changing styles of life-writing, newly slanted story-cycle, two-spirit and LBTQI+ gendered texts, reflexive stage performance, and writings that might be called Native international.[3] Tommy Orange, in a 2021 interview with fellow debut contemporary David Heske Wanbli Weiden (Sicangu Lakota) whose *Winter Counts* (2020) itself makes new ground for a reservation crime and drugs thriller, offers the following observation about *There There*:

> I wanted the book to feel urban and have its characters reflect on urbanity, technology, and modernity as an act of resistance against all the ways we've been frozen in time.[4]

Text, Breath, Modernity. These each filter into the present study. They are meant as footholds, rungs.

***

Other perspectives bid for regard. In "A Discussion about Indian Affairs" Geary Hobson, contemporary writer-poet and Oklahoma professor of mixed Cherokee, Quapaw and Chickasaw descent, has his poem laconically ponder continuing gaps:

> She was a white woman
> from some little town
> in one of the Dakotas.
> "I've heard about Cherokees
> – everybody's heard about Cherokees –
> but I always thought Chickasaws
> were some made-up tribe –
> one that never existed –
> invented by someone like Al Capp,
> a word like 'Kickapoo,' you know?"
> "There's a Kickapoo tribe, too."
> I said. "Oh," she said,
> and having nothing more to say
> on the subject, said nothing.
> I wondered if we'd ever have
> anything to say to one another.[5]

"I wondered if we'd ever have anything to say to one another." What losses would be entailed were that always the case? To more immediate purpose, what writings would have gone un-read or risked continuing not to be so?

In the first part of her title-poem for the collection *Indian Singing in Twentieth Century America* (1990) Gail Tremblay, poet, visual artist, long a resident teacher in Evergreen State University, Washington, and whose New York lineage looks to both Onondaga-Micmac and French dynasty, has the issue revolve upon "two worlds" and upon who does, or does not, "explain[s] us":

> We wake; we wake the day,
> the light rising in us like the sun –
> our breath a prayer brushing
> against the feathers in our hands.
> We stumble out into streets;
> patterns of wires invented by strangers
> are strung between eye and sky,
> and we dance in two worlds,
> inevitable as seasons in one,

exotic curiosities in the other
which rushes headlong down highways,
watches us from car windows,
explains us to its children in words
that no one could ever make sense of. [6]

To these might readily be added Jim Barnes's "Contemporary American Literature," from his collection *The American Book of The Dead* (1982). A poet of Oklahoma-bred Choctaw ancestry, along with Anglo-Welsh roots, and long resident in Missouri and New Mexico, he brings an unflinching poignancy to the page:

For one thing, you can believe it:
the skin chewed soft enough to wear,
the bones hewn hard as a totem
from hemlock. It's a kind of scare-

crow that will follow you home nights.
You've seen it ragged against a field,
but you seldom think, at the time,
to get there it had to walk through hell.[7]

Native history, and much of the literature it has engendered, indeed carries the memory of walking through hell, be it on account of settler colonization, disease, removal, poverty, the cities, and axially, self-loss. But it also elicits Barnes's honoring tribute to powers of will, agency, the enduring creativity of life, art, story and word.

***

Native North American Authorship covers a full, yet at the same time still less than full, literary reach. Earlier texts I have been keen to recognize, but more focus, I perfectly acknowledge, falls on writing of the twentieth and now twenty-first century. The effect, it is to be hoped, gives nuance to the notion of a Native American Renaissance born of the 1960s and for which Momaday's *House Made of Dawn* famously emerges as landmark. Nor is it to resist cross-referencing of text or author, circle or rhizome over line.

By way of follow-on to this Introduction two sets of bearings come into view. "Native American Renaissance," Chapter 1, ponders the implications of the category, the undoubted efflorescence in names like Momaday, Silko, James Welch, Vizenor, or poets like Ortiz and Harjo. Necessarily, however, this phase of Native authorship needs to be contextualized. What comes before, acts of address and autobiography, earlier bodies of poetry like that of Jane Jackson Schoolcraft (Colville), interwar novels like those of D'Arcy McNickle (Cree-Métis, enrolled Salish-Flathead) and John Joseph Mathews (Osage), theatre, and literary journalism? What, in the wake of the Momaday era, has come since?

"Modern Life Writing," Chapter 2, takes stock of how individual self-telling emerges from within Native communal tradition, names variously political and literary writing from pioneer writing to the 1960s–1970s and its aftermath. Consideration of Momaday's close-worked lyrical *The Names: A Memoir* (1976) leads on to the comparable autobiography by Silko, Vizenor, Janet Campbell Hale (Coeur d'Alene), Carter Revard (Osage-Ponca), and Jim Barnes.

The modern novel enters consideration in Chapter 3 through *House Made of Dawn*, with accompanying address given to Momaday's *The Ancient Child* (1989) and *In the Presence of the Sun* (1992). Successively Chapters 4–9 interpret, one for one, individual authorships in the roster of Silko, Erdrich, Welch, Vizenor, Alexie and Owens (Choctaw-Cherokee-Irish). "Changing Points of Compass: The Novel 1990s-2020s," Chapter 10, gives focus to directions of narrative styling in different full-length Native/First Nations fiction from Linda Hogan and Thomas King to Eden Robinson and D. L. Birchfield (Choctaw). The texts under critique represent a range successively historical, neo-realist, woman-generational, coming of age, postmodern, and futurist or speculative. Native/First Nations short story, both anthology selections and a gallery of single-author collections, is annotated as working panorama in Chapter 11. Two case-names follow in Chapters 12 and 13, those of Diane Glancy (Cherokee) and Stephen Graham Jones (Blackfeet), the former's work often deceptively story-fragment, the latter's moving into *noir* and Science Fiction scenarios.

Poetry as spectrum receives purview in two main panels, Chapters 14 and 15, the contributing poets each given interpretation through a selected key collection. The first, women-authored and with remembrance as centering, opens from Joy Harjo, songwriter-musician as well as the author of *She Had Some Horses* (1983) and America's poet laureate in 2019, through to Kimberly Blaeser (Chippewa-Ojibwe) and her *Apprenticed to Justice* (2007). A number of single memory-poems by other same-generation poets add not just specificity but garland. The second explores the inflections of voice, closely tribal yet also reflective of modern city and township, in turn by Simon Ortiz, Ray Young Bear (Meskwaki) and Tommy Pico. Chapters 16, 17 and 18 develop mappings, overviews, for the poetry careers of Jim Barnes, Linda Hogan, and Ralph Salisbury (Cherokee-Shawnee). The epilogue seeks to deconstruct the wording of *Native North American Authorship*,

Native for remembered timeline, *North American* for cultural geographies, and *Authorship* for its relation to visual and cognate arts.

It may be best to say at the outset that across the chapters this study does not constitute literary history as such, but a convocation of readings, genres, authors. Cross-reference plays its part, even the use of a same text yet under different interpretative lights. In giving estimation, moreover, the accounts at hand seek to steer a balance between coverage and eye-on-the-page close readings. A number were initially written in response to different essay-collection and journal invitations. These have been considerably updated and rethreaded. Others are wholly new. Entering the expanse of this authorship is not to forget, or overlook, the condescension still to be met with in certain quarters of supposed margin as against mainstream.

***

Given the reclamation of past Native texts, and the emergence of each subsequent literary tier or wave, so Native-centered literary theory since the 1970s–1980s has kept pace. Critique has displayed its own complementary modernity. The so-called three Ws, Robert Warrior (Osage), Jace Weaver (Cherokee) and Craig C. Womack (Creek-Cherokee) pre-eminently come into the frame. Each, to one degree or another, embraces a nationalist aesthetic, yet one subtly resistant to exclusionism.

In both *Tribal Secrets: Recovering American Indian Tradition* (1995) and *The People and The Word: Reading Native Nonfiction* (2005) Warrior sets out his case for historic nation-situatedness and "intellectual sovereignty" in Native writing while not denying Euro-American input and hybridism. Rather he wants parity, an equality of independent lineage and diagnostic worth. For Weaver in *That the People Might Live: Native American Literatures and Native American Community* (1997), the issue centers on what he terms *communitism*, a bedrock of Native spirituality and value which also does not negate other participation or approach but insists upon discrete literary-cultural inheritance. Womack's *Red on Red: Native American Literary Separatism* (1999) and *Art as Performance, Story as Criticism: Reflections on Native Literary Aesthetics* (2009), while again decrying essentialism, even so argues for recognition of tribally created literary-cultural codings which not only cut across but contest usual western periodization or genre.

In their tri-authored *American Indian Literary Nationalism* (2006) Weaver, Womack and Warrior share interactive exchanges of diagnosis, again an insistence on the tilt towards tribal-centric critique. The move towards this kind of rootedness in tribe – though tribe as a term might better be replaced as sovereign nation – and its literary scripts also has ranking examples. Irvin Morris's *From the Glittering World: A Navajo Story* (1997) tracks creation story through the Navajo Long Walk to modern technology. The Cherokee scholar Daniel Heath Justice's *Our Fire Survives The Storm: A Cherokee Literary History* (2006) gives an account pinioned to theory. The thirty-plus prose and verse contributions to *The Diné Reader: An Anthology of Navajo Literature* (2021) reflect the literature at hand.

Key other interventions feature and spar. Gerald Vizenor's notion of *survivance* (early adumbrated in *Manifest Manners: Postindian Warriors of Survivance* 1994) has led to an aesthetic of Native authorship as newly enactive as well as given to remembrance of history. It has also drawn attention to the rights, even the necessity, of indigenous writers to draw on whatever wellsprings of interest or imagination they choose as against prescribed terrain. Elizabeth Cook-Lynn, Sioux scholar, novelist, and founder-editor of *Wicazo Sa Review*, and author of *Why I Can't Read Wallace Stegner and Other Essays* (1996) and *A Separate Country: Postcoloniality and American Indian Nations* (2011), issues a slap at precisely the kind of off-reservation this has produced with mixed-blood, often academia-based free range of viewpoint. She berates Vizenor and likewise Louis Owens, novelist, critic and the crafted essayist of *Mixedblood Messages: Literature, Film, Family, Place* (1998) and *I Hear the Train: Reflections, Inventions, Refractions* (2001), for imagining that postmodern/postindian style can have relevance for Native literary practice. On her reckoning tribal-centrism and "realism" has to be front and center of Native writing, its themes, its interpretation.

The arguments yet further circle. Paula Gunn Allen (Laguna, Sioux. with Scots and Lebanese ancestry) calls for gynocentric-feminist focus to Native culture and writing in *The Sacred Hoop: Restoring The Feminine in American Indian Traditions* (1986). David Treuer (Anishinaabe, Austrian-Jewish) in *Native American Fiction: A User's Manual* (2006) takes issue at the authenticity-identity axis from another angle, the notion that Native fiction is itself a fiction. He writes from discontent with how Native authorship has been corralled into agenda, program, nationalism, gender and identity politics, not to say judgment according to assumed rules of representation.

In Arnold Krupat the field looks to investigations like *The Voice in the Margin: Native American Literature and The Canon* (1989), *The Turn of the Native: Studies in Criticism and Culture* (1996), *Red Matters: Native American Studies* (2002) and *All That Remains: Varieties of Indigenous Expression* (2009). These seat Native authorship within a cosmopolitan or hybridist frame. He acknowledges literary indigeneity as specific yet of necessity profoundly cross-hatched with Euro-American and international practices of genre or assumed readership. Many of these lines of argument have a synopsis in Elvira Pulitano's *Towards a Native Critical Theory* (2003), much as she evidently favors the cosmopolitan over nationalist argument. Stock-taking has been actively under way, whether the advocacy of Robert Dale Parker's *The Invention of Native American Literature* (2002) or of Daniel Heath Justice's *Why Indigenous Literatures Matter* (2018).

Native and First Nations texts in Spanish and French, and even as there are calls for more publication in tribal languages, equally exert claim and respective study. The outcome overall, texts under one or another cultural custody or under several, confirm that long overdue interpretative debate has joined with an appetite unlikely to flag. It might even be said, with a certain irony, and whether a term like Native American Renaissance helps or hinders, there are grounds for thinking a renaissance in matters of theory has made its own entrance.

***

No one grand keypad or stencil prevails throughout this essay-collection but a number of lenses recur. Among them and of prime concern has to be compositional skill, symptomatically rhythm and sense of an ending in fiction, play of image and pattern in poetry, or the layers and folds of voice in life-writing. In each an axis especially falls upon the mirrors of memory, legacy within the now. This, however, is not to put aesthetics above anything else, some excessive nod to formalism, nor is it to sidestep "authenticity."

Life on reservation or reserve and each current having to do with identity, land and treaty rights, sovereignty, enrollment, intercultural mix, gender, wealth-gaps, health and cultural agency, all require recognition as participant themes. Demographics, likewise, require note that an estimated seven out of ten Native and First Nation populations live in cities, the interweave of family, schooling and college and employment (or un-employment) with the urban modernity of mobile phone, credit rating or commute.

Yet whichever the life, the history, being voiced, it is equally to examine how, and to what effect, the arising texts actually achieve interiority and scripting. Not every deserving name has been covered. The risk could be roll-call or catalog. *Native North American Authorship*, to re-emphasize, represents a selective body of literary interpretation, yet a sufficiency I hope to leave no doubt of the profits of imagination within the writings to which it attaches.

Notes

1 Linda Hogan, "Turtle," *Calling Myself Home*, Greenfield Center: Greenfield Review Press, 1978, 3.
2 Thomas King, *The Truth About Stories: A Native Narrative*, Minneapolis: University of Minnesota Press, 2008, 1.
3 For a helpful perspective, see Eric Gary Anderson, "Native American Horror, Fantasy and Speculative Fiction," in Melanie Benson Taylor, ed., *The Cambridge History of Native American Literature*, Cambridge and New York: Cambridge University Press, 2020, 431–46.
4 Tommy Orange in interview with David Haske Wanklin Weiden, Alta online, 2021.
5 Geary Hobson, "A Discussion about Indian Affairs," in Alan R. Velie, ed., *American Indian Literature: An Anthology*, Norman: University of Oklahoma Press, 2nd edition, 1991, 249–50.
6 Title poem in *Indian Singing in Twentieth Century America*, Corvallis: Calyx, 1990.
7 Jim Barnes, *On a Wing of the Sun: Three Volumes of Poetry*, 80.

Works Cited

Allen, Paul Gunn, *The Sacred Hoop: Recovering the Feminine in American Indian Traditions*, Boston: Beacon Press, 1986.

Barnes, Jim, *The American Book of the Dead*, Urbana: University of Illinois Press, 1982. Reprinted in *On a Wing of the Sun: Three Volumes of Poetry*, Urbana: University of Illinois Press, 2001.

Bitsui, Sherman, *Dissolve*, Port Townsend, Washington: Copper Canyon Press, 2018.

Blaeser, Kimberly, *Apprenticed to Justice*, Cambridge: Salt Publishing, 2007.

Brant, Beth, *A Generous Spirit*, ed. Janice Gould, Toronto: Inanna Publications, 2019.

Cook-Lynn, Elizabeth, *A Separate Country: Postcoloniality and American Indian Nations*, Lubbock: Texas Tech University Press, 2011.

_____, *Why I Can't Read Wallace Stegner and Other Essays: A Tribal Voice*, Madison: University of Wisconsin Press, 1996.

Erdrich, Louise, *Love Medicine*, New York: Henry Hold, 1984, expanded versions 1993, 2003.

Esther G. Belin et al, *The Diné Reader: An Anthology of Cherokee Literature*, Tucson University of Arizona Press, 2021.

Harjo, Joy, *She Had Some Horses*, New York: Thunder's Mouth Press, 1983.

Heath Justice, Daniel, *Why Indigenous Literatures Matter*, Waterloo, Ontario: Wilfred Laurier University Press, 2018.

_____, *Our Fire Survives the Storm: A Cherokee Literary History*, Minneapolis: University of Minnesota Press, 2006.

Hogan, Linda, *Calling Myself Home*, Greenfield Center: Greenfield Review Press, 1978.

King, Thomas, *The Truth About Stories: A Native Narrative*, Minneapolis: University of Minnesota Press, 2003.

Krupat, Arnold, *All That Remains: Varieties of Indigenous Expression*, Lincoln: University of Nebraska Press, 2009.

_____, *Red Matters: Native American Studies*, Philadelphia: University of Pennsylvania Press, 2002.

_____, *The Turn of the Native: Studies in Criticism and Culture*, Lincoln: University of Nebraska Press, 1996.

_____, *The Voice in the Margin: Native American Literature and the Canon*, Berkeley: University of California Press, 1989.

Momaday, N. Scott, *In the Presence of the Sun: Stories and Poems*, New York: St. Martin's Press, 1992.

_____, *The Ancient Child*, New York: Doubleday, 1989.

_____, *The Names: A Memoir*, Tucson: Sun Tracks/University of Arizona Press, 1976.

_____, *House Made of Dawn*, New York: Harper & Row, 1968.

Morris, Irvin, *From the Glittering World: A Navajo Story*, Norman: University of Oklahoma Press, 1997.

Orange, Tommy, *There There*, New York: Alfred Knopf, 2018.

Ortiz, Simon, *Out There Somewhere*, Tucson: University of Arizona Press, 2002.

Owens, Louis, *I Hear the Train: Reflections, Inventions, Refractions*, Norman: University of Oklahoma Press, 2001.

_____, *Mixedblood Messages: Literature, Film, Family, Place*, Norman: University of Oklahoma Press, 1998.

Parker, Robert Dale, *The Invention of Native American Literature*, Ithica: Cornell University Press, 2003.

Pico, Tommy, *Feed*, Portland: Tin House, 2019.

Pulitano, Elvira, *Towards a Native American Critical Theory*, Lincoln: University of Nebraska Press, 2003.

Robinson, *Son of a Trickster*, Toronto: Vintage Canada, 2017.

Standing Bear, Luther, *My People the Sioux*, ed. E.A. Brininstool, Boston: Houghton Mifflin, 1928, 1931; reprinted Lincoln: University of Nebraska Press, 1975, 2006.

_____, *My Indian Boyhood*, New York: Houghton, Mifflin, 1925.

Tremblay, Gayle, "Indian Singing in 20th Century America," *Indian Singing in 20th Century America*, Corvallis: Calyx Books, 1990.

Treuer, David, *Native American Fiction: A User's Manual*, Minneapolis: Greywolf Press, 2006.

Vizenor, Gerald, *Manifest Manners; Postindian Warriors of Survivance*, Hanover: Wesleyan University Press/University of New England Press, 1992.

Warrior, Robert Allen, *The People and the Word: Reading Native Nonfiction*. Minneapolis: University of Minnesota Press, 2005.

_____, *Tribal Secrets: Recovering American Indian Intellectual Traditions*, Minneapolis: University of Minnesota Press, 1995.

Weaver, *That The People Might Live: Native American Literatures and Native American Community*, New York: Oxford University Press, 1999.

Weaver, Jace, Womack, Craig C., Warrior, Robert Allen, eds., *American Indian Literary Nationalism*, Albuquerque: University of New Mexico Press, 2006.

Weiden, David Heska Wanbli, *Winter Counts*, New York: HarperCollins, 2020.

Womack, Craig, *Art as Performance, Story as Criticism: Reflections on Native American Aesthetics*, Norman: University of Oklahoma Press, 2009.

_____, *Red on Red: Native American Literary Separatism*, Minneapolis: University of Minnesota Press,1999.

Young Bear, Ray A., *Black Eagle Child: The Facepaint Narratives*, Iowa City: The University of Iowa Press, 1992.

Part I

Bearings

1 Native American Renaissance: Timelines, Texts

Contemporary Indian literature is not so much new, then, as regenerate: transitional continuities emerging from the old

Kenneth Lincoln, *Native American Renaissance* (1983)[1]

Native American Renaissance. As the term won currency fires were quick to ignite, even at times blaze. Did it mean that the undoubted efflorescence of Native American fiction, poetry, theatre, autobiography and discursive writing to have risen in the wake of N. Scott Momaday's Pulitzer-garlanded *House Made of Dawn* (1968) had no literary hinterland? Was this to propose a canon that risked under-recognizing antecedent Native authorship? However regarded, a label of celebratory recognition or an almost insouciant adaptation from the "renaissances" of seventeenth-century Europe or nineteenth-century America, not to mention the Harlem Renaissance, the designation has been little short of a jousting-ground, a stir to divides of opinion.

In Kenneth Lincoln's *Native American Renaissance* matters had a keystone. Oral storytelling, he argued, has to be given assiduous attention, its manifold subtleties of tribal story and ceremony. Black Elk, Oglala Sioux visionary and eventual Cody circus performer, offers a major point of reference (with recognition of John Neihardt's custodial maneuvering in *Black Elk Speaks*) – the past spoken, and then written into, the present. The then to date writings of Momaday, Silko, Welch and Ortiz required note. Burgeoning anthologies, the more so as the era moved into the 1980s, together with Native-centered journals, bore added witness. The upshot, on Lincoln's reckoning, marked literary-creative rebirth, a breakthrough in imagining. Admirers like Paula Gunn Allen were quick to pronounce a landmark at once timely and striking in eloquence. Others thought the sense of new dawn unpersuasive, artificial periodization. But whether praise or fault the phrase took hold.[2]

Forty years on, however, does the exponential growth of Native writing still fall under the term "renaissance"? Connectedly, given print or digital republication of pre-Momaday texts, can there be license to go on thinking these mere prologue?[3] No one seeks exaggeration. The quantity of early Native *writing* in English (which is to take full cognizance of early works in French and Spanish) remains relatively small. The quantity, by contrast, of Native writing since Momaday has been truly considerable. A number of the names in the assumed Renaissance rightly invite separate chapters, but so, too, does how they confirm the scriptural timeline begun at least two centuries earlier.

***

House Made of Dawn may well have ushered in the talk of a Native American Renaissance, in many ways a well-meant hurrah. But it also brought into play a sense of paradox, not to say vexation. Momaday himself has always acknowledged knowing little at the time of Native writing. Was this, again, to confirm some literary void? Could a Native text be modern? That his novel enlarged authorial space and possibility is incontrovertible. The triumph lies not just in Abel's "homing in" story, his existential recovery and re-centering.[4] It lies equally in design and configuration. Asian and Native war zones are shown to overlap. Pollen, vision, and day and night mythology build into a holding pattern. The text itself becomes reflexive fabling to bring salve, a pathway into both spiritual and physical health from broken history. The opening and closing acts of running so give wholly-to-purpose circularity equally to narrative dynamic as to human theme.

Other Native fiction close in time was not slow to confirm a growing sense of modernity. James Welch's *Winter in the Blood* (1974) explores, as though poised between dark dream and reality, the reeling and often dark-comic displacement of its unnamed Blackfeet protagonist within historic tribal as within township Montana. Leslie Marmon Silko's *Ceremony* (1977) tracks in both literal and mythic time the return of Tayo, damaged Pacific war returnee, to his Laguna-Keres roots. Gerald Vizenor's *Bearheart* (1978) works as visionary picaresque, Holy Fool mixed-blood pilgrims bound on their journey through a dystopian America depleted of both oil and moral balance. Louise Erdrich's *Love Medicine* (1984, revised 1993) gives her North Dakota Chippewa-Ojibwe dynasties a Faulknerian weave of past history, dense story-circles of kin, fracture, religion, sex, and potions. Thomas King's *Medicine River* (1990), set on an Alberta reserve, deploys ancestral trickster feints to capture the highly modern story of its photographer protagonist as he steers from non-status to community identity. Sherman Alexie's *Reservation Blues* (1995), in the voice of Thomas Builds-the-Fire, renders life and contradiction on the Coeur d'Alene/Spokane reservation as a satiric counter-mirror to settler and cavalry manifest destiny. This continuing roster, the novel's Native/First Nations subsequent junctures and departures, come under surveillance in a later chapter.

Poetry shares the time's extending realm. Momaday's own poetry, at strength in the elegiac title-piece of *Angle of Geese* (1974), gives itself to both literal and imagined corridors of time-space. Simon Ortiz's "Even the 'Indians' Believed" in *Out There Somewhere* (2002) wryly teases the presumption of "absent" indigenous populations ("Soon there were Indians all over the place. But mainly in the New World,/especially in America!"). His *from Sand Creek* (1981) memorializes the infamous 1864 massacre at the hands of the Third Colorado Cavalry, a text that in its double-column format links forward to Native military veteran PTSD damage in subsequent foreign wars from Korea to Vietnam.

Joy Harjo composes song-poetry seamed in contemporary Creek memory in *She Had Some Horses* (1983). Roberta Hill Whiteman's *Star Quilt* (1984) installs Oneida-influenced emblems of linen quilt and star into visions of the modern. Louise Erdrich's *Jacklight* (1984) resituates Chippewa-Ojibwe myth inside contemporary reservation homestead and school. Diane Glancy's *Iron Woman* (1990) calls up dual worlds, Cherokee and backcountry white, herself riven and yet gainful from both. Linda Hogan's *The Book of Medicines* (1993) might best be thought earth poems, time-now recognition of needed equilibrium for human, animal and all ecological life. Kimberley Blaeser's *Trailing You* (1994) alights on Chippewa-Ojibwe and white overlaps of memory, poetry's acts of naming as a route to understand and release past boundaries. Lucy Tapahonso's *Blue Horses Rush In* (1997), drawing intimately from her Navajo and Arizona origins, speaks in "Tsaile April Nights" of communal stories as "Warm, light circles." Her image points to the ways of tribal imagination but also to the interconnectedness of past and present worlds.

Modern and contemporary names much proliferate, Maurice Kenny (Mohawk-Seneca) and Duane Niatum (Klallam) to Mary TallMountain (Athabascan/Menominee) and nila northsun (Shoshone). Others, likewise, invite eye and acclaim, whether Ray Young Bear (Meskwaki), Adrian C. Louis (Lovelock Paiute), Wendy Rose (Hopi), Ofelia Zepeda (Tohono O'odom), Chrystos (Menominee) or Sherwin Bitsui. Once again no single "Indian" temper prevails as, in keeping, it has not done so in a yet subsequent gallery, the generation of California's Tommy Pico or Saskatchewan's Tenille Campbell (Dene/Metis). Momentum, always resistant to totalizing category, is not to be doubted.

Lincoln's volume for the most part leaves out Native theatre with its turn-about of the written into the spoken line. Lineage, yet once more, might step back into tribal chant and drum, whether to voice birth and death, the figuration of earth as sunrise and dark, Nature's season and the rites of re-generation. It might invoke Lynn Riggs's *Green Grow the Lilacs* (1931), one play of many from his hand, which with Rodgers and Hammerstein would metamorphose into the musical *Oklahoma!* (1943). Few names more resonate than that of Hanay Geiogamah, in works like the fast-change satire of *Foghorn* (1973) and a witty pantomimic chant like "The Scalp Dance." Under his watch was established the Native American Theater Ensemble (NATE) in 1972 as performance arena both for his own creative and directorial activities and for oncoming new talent.

The portfolio ranges energetically, whether the Spiderwoman feminist performance troupe, collections like D'Aponte Gisolfi's *Seventh Generation: An Anthology of Native American Plays* (1999), a dramatist like William S. Yellow Robe whose collection *Where The Pavement Ends* (2000) gives adroit eye to Rez and off-Rez identity politics, or critique as attentive as Christy Stanlake's *Native American Drama: A Critical Perspective* (2009) and Birgit Däwes's *Indigenous North American Drama: A Multivocal History* (2014). This spectrum suggests yet another way of situating Native texts, one that bridges actor's play-script and drama as belonging to the more inclusive roll-call of Native literary composition. A comparable venue lies in Native journalism, from founding journals like the *Cherokee Phoenix* (1828–1834) or White Earth, Minnesota's *The Progress* (1886–1889) through to contemporary publications like the Lakota *Indian Country Today*, New Mexico's *Gallup Independent*, Minnesota's *Native American Press/ Ojibwe News* or Washington's *Yakima Nation Review*.

***

National borders, those especially between the USA and Canada and the USA and Mexico, have long been sources of territorial contention. In English-language literary as in cartographic terms it would be almost impossible not to interconnect Native America and First Nations Canada. Where, then, does a so-called Native American Renaissance stand in relation to a First Nations Canadian Renaissance? *CanLit*, as it has been called, has grown increasingly diverse, the reflection of a nation on latest census figures 22% migrant and 5% indigenous. Cross-border voice, unbordering, has a notable instance in the work of Thomas King, California-born of mixed European and Cherokee family who has long held Canadian citizenship. His *All My Relations: An Anthology of Contemporary Canadian Native Fiction* (1992) remains an important marker.

First Nations authorship, however, has long shown longer historical straps, whether one steps back to George Copway (1818–1869), born into a Mississauga Chippewa-Ojibwe family in Ontario but resident for long periods in the USA, or to E. Pauline Johnson (1861–1913), Mohawk writer and stage performer born in the Six Nations reserve in Brantford, Ontario, to a cross-border family and the pioneer author of *Canadian Born* (1903) and the transcriptions from the Squamish in *Legends of Vancouver* (1911). In Frank Prewett, Iroquois-descended or as it has turned out maybe not, Canada has an Oxford-educated World War I soldier voice and the lover of Siegfried Sassoon who could write as though from an oddly spectatorial vantage-point "The Red-Man."[5]

A latter-day tranche would be negligent not to include Jeannette Armstrong's *Slash* (1985), that of a writer raised on the Penticton Indian Reserve in British Columbia and Canada's first-ever indigenous novel with its overlaps of Canadian and US sovereignty politics. Beth Brant's *Food and Spirits, Stories* (1991), by a writer of Mohawk descent, offers a sequence of eight pieces that address mother-daughter and like Gunn Allen and Chrystos lesbian intimacy. Métis fiction, mixed-blood writing, has classics in Beatrice Mosionier Culleton's *In Search of April Raintree* (1992) with its Winnepeg-set portrait of mixed-blood sisterhood, and Richard Van Camp's *The Lesser Blessed* (1996), a Dogrib coming-of-age story of abuse and murder, sex and religion. More Chippewa-Ojibwe humor, with Anishinaabe locutions in play, finds voice in Basil Johnston's Runyonesque story collection *Ojibway Tales: Moose Meat and Wild Rice* (1978, revised 1993). Tomson Highway's *Kiss of the Fur Queen* (1998), play and novel, unfolds its story of two Manitoba Cree brothers as part fact, part magic. This fantasticality might bear comparison with Gordon Henry's *The Light People* (1994) and its Chippewa-Ojibwe dream and vision story cycle, or A. A. Carr's *Eye Killers* (1995) with its Navajo vampire fable.

The range of fellow First Nations authorship has grown at pace. Lee Maracle (Salish, Cree) offers pioneer fact-fiction in *Bobbi Lee, Indian Rebel* (1975). Ruby Slipperjack (Fort Hope Chippewa-Ojibwe-Eabametoong) writes a Young Adult coming-of age classic in *Silent Words* (1992). Joseph Boyden (Métis, Irish-Scots), by contrast, in *Three Day Road* (2005) depicts World War I Cree soldiering, wound, and tribal recovery. Jeannette Armstrong (Okanagan) gives memorial verse-form to her British Columbia environment in *Breath Tracks* (1991). Beth Cuthand (Little Pine Cree) brings quest and her grandfather's horse-dance ceremony into the poetry of *Horse Dance to Emerald Mountain* (1987). Joanne Arnott

(Métis) exhibits her performance-verse flair in *Mother Time: Poems New and Selected* (2007).

Latest debut texts give fresh momentum. Natasha Kanapé Fontaine (Innu-French) writes *N'entre pas dans mon âme avec tes chaussures* (2012)/*Do Not Enter My Soul in Your Shoes* (2015) with its gypsy title and vivid choreographies of identity, body and environment. Terese Mariot Maillot's *Heart Berries* (2018) offers the laconic and telegraphic-styled British Columbia memoir of a troubled Seabird Island/Stó-ló upbringing shaped by premature motherhood, abuse and drugs. Tanya Tagaq Gillis's *Split Tooth* (2019), by an established Inuk-Arctic throat-singer, uses a cross-genre mix of fiction, folklore and visual illustration for her highly innovative autobiographical diary. [6] These first volumes, self-chronicle, poetries of place, translated slam poetry, give new impetus, First Nations Canada in changing voice.

***

A perspective increasingly better recognized obtains in LGBTI/Two Spirit Native and First Nations writing. This shift in awareness, and humanity, has its source not just in gender politics but a compendious body of writing again across the genres and with its own diverse foci and history. Maurice Kenny's 1970s essay "Tinselled Bucks: An Historical Study of Indian Homosexuality," written for the journal *Gay Sunshine*, adds text and context to his distinguished Mohawk-inflected writing like *Between Two Rivers: Selected Poems 1956-1984* (1987) and *Tekonwatoni, Molly Brant, 1735-1795* (1992). Paula Gunn Allen notably comes into the frame. *The Woman Who Owned the Shadows* (1983) gives web and spider framework to her novel of mixed-blood life and sexuality in the person of Ephanie Atencio. *The Sacred Hoop: Recovering the Feminine in American Indian Traditions* (1986) offers her benchmark gynocentric study and *Life is a Fatal Disease: Collected Poems 1962-1995* (1997) her flourish of same-sex intimacy.

The circle widens, whether the "Urban Indian" verse of Chrystos in *Not Vanishing* (1988) and *In Her I Am* (1993) with their envisioning of lesbian love and sexual pleasure, Craig S. Womack's Muskogee-Creek Oklahoma novel of sexual self-recognition and acceptance in *Drowning in Fire* (2001), or Qwo-Li Driskell's eclectic and inter-sexual *Asegi Stories: Cherokee Queer and Two-Spirit Memory* (2016). The authorship shows no de-acceleration. Janice Gould's collections *Earthquake Weather* (1996) through to *Seed* (2109) find their sources in her Koyang-k'auwi Maidu and same-sex identity. Tommy Pico's *Feed* (2019) signifies the latest in a verse tetralogy that calls up both reservation roots but also the city in flâneur-like and collagist form. The Saskatchewan-born Cree poet Arielle Twist's *Disintegrate/Dissociate* (2019) reflects her Nehiyaw or Two-Spirit identity in the mixed literary-form aesthetic of her verse. Joshua Whitehead's *full-metal indigiqueer* (2017) inscribes poems of gay indigeneity using highly reflexive internet landscapes by a writer of First Nations Cree and Peguis heritage. Max Wolf Valero (Kainai Blackfoot and Latinx), Canada-born transsexual and AIM activist, links gender and ethnicity in his volume *The Testosterone Files* (2006) and the film-work of *The Gendernauts* (1999).

In these lights would it not be appropriate to speak also of a gay Native/First Nations Renaissance? The indications are certainly there. *Living the Spirit: A Gay American Indian Anthology* (1988) and *Sovereign Erotics: A Collection of Two Spirit Literature* (2011) serves as multi-edited pioneer anthologies. Deborah Miranda (Ohlone-Costanoan Esselen), the poet of *Indian Cartography* (1999) and *Raised by Humans* (2015), brings a keenly gender-aware family perspective to her account of California Mission history in *Bad Indians: A Tribal Memoir* (2013). Lisa Tatonetti's *The Queerness of Native American Literature* (2014) explores how Kenny, Erdrich, Allen and Janice Gould serve as necessary torchbearers. The yet wider reach of global indigenous gay voice, from the Americas to those in Maori, Aboriginal and Samoan writing, has representation in an anthology like Kateri Akiwenzie-Damm's *Without Reservation: Indigenous Erotica* (2003).[7] Complementarity, indeed challenge, to heteronormative assumptions of canon is unmistakable.

***

To take on the authorship that leads to Momaday and his literary immediates in no way slights the passed-down and ongoing ways of tribal oral-performative legacy. For behind the emergence of all Native written word lies, always and inescapably, the vast, historic power of the spoken in all its manifestations of story, memory, recitation, humor, and vitally, speaker-listener relationship. Creation or "emergence" stories make for one kind of thesaurus, whether earthdiver, turtle, or twin-star and other stellar configurations. Trickster lure makes for another, rarely more so than Coyote in the figure of Nanabozho for the Chippewa-Ojibwe and other Algonquin peoples or Kumokums for the Medoc. His wiles, sexual and other lusts (in one version his hunger causes him to eat himself), have long made him shape-shifter and skin-walker. Other incarnations have him the world-creator figure for the Pawnee, Tohono O'odham or Crow, the death messenger for the Navajo. Connecting versions also hold, whether the Blue Jay, Hare, Wolverine, Dragonfly or Owl as usually the harbinger of sickness or demise.

Spoken lore, always adaptive to the one and another occasion, celebrates birth, sunrise, rain, good harvest, maize, rice, meat and food-stock. In almost all Native/First Nations tradition a right act of voice, as of ear, can make for cure against illness or grief, the psychic as much as physical restoration of self in the world. The beauteous Navajo Night Chant signifies one major instance. Prayer directed to the four points of the compass or wind, shaman utterance, even nicknames and tease, all build into the repertoire The range extends even to thought itself. In *Ceremony* (1977) Silko ingeniously so fuses Ts'its'tsinako or Thought-Woman into written text ("I'm telling you the story/she is thinking"). Spider, and its different tribal legends as Spider-woman, adds to this gendering as do Corn Woman and Serpent Woman and, to invoke the Silko of her Laguna-centered *Storyteller* (1981), the Keres-pueblo Yellow Woman or Kochininako story of female dreamer and her phantom lover.

Reference is needed, too, to other kinds of scriptural legacy. In the *Walam Olum*, the Lenape or Delaware Nation's "painted record," there exists a ribbon of historical pictograph and phrase. It endures as striking lexicon, early double-column codex. The US Constitution itself, written in 1787 and brought into force in 1789, has long been thought to shadow the accords for participatory democracy created by the Six Nation Confederacy of the Iroquois. There might be thought a unique adjunct to this legacy in the latter-day Navajo translation of the entire Bible, begun in the 1950s, spoken tribal language transposed to page at full scale.

This early trajectory into the printed and now digital page has increasingly been brought into better view.[8] A variety of voice has been clearly evident. Was it not William Apess, mixed-blood Pequot and a convert to Methodism, who in his *A Son of the Forest* (1812) delivered the following smack "I could not find the word 'Indian' in the Bible and therefore concluded it was a word imported for the purpose of degrading us"? In 1823 the scholar-leader and silversmith Sequoyah (1770–1843), known in English as George Guest, observed of his development of the Cherokee syllabary eventually published in 1835 "I thought it would be like catching a wild animal and taming it." "Talking leaves" was his memorable formulation.[9] When Luther Standing Bear, Oglala Lakota Sioux activist and among the first enrollees at the Carlisle Indian School, writes in *My People the Sioux* (1928) "It is my desire that all people know the truth about the first Americans and their relations with the United States Government" he clearly meant it to include by means of print.

In "A Short Narrative of My Life" (1768) by Samson Occom, Mohegan Presbyterian convert and minister, Native America likely has its first written text. The Christian true believer, he finds himself writing "I was born a Heathen and brought up in heathenism" and memorably celebrates his "saving conversion." Both spiritual call to arms and case-history of New England abuse of Native peoples, the 10-page script functions equally as knowing *literary* endeavor. Factual as may be, the account has its own shrewd imagining, self-history pitched as Bunyanesque parable. Comparably the *Life of Ma-ka-tai-me-she-kia-kiak (or Life of Blackhawk)* by the Sauk leader Black Hawk (1767–1838) bequeaths the remembrance of his role in the War of 1812 and the subsequent westward removal of his people but which comes out in 1833 translated by Antoine Le Claire and edited by the journalist J.B. Patterson. Spoken and then transcribed as may have been, it belongs alongside Occom's "Short Narrative" among the founding written chronicles. One can and should give mention to the 1820s sequence *Poor Sarah, or the Indian Woman*, from the pen of Elias Boudinot, Cherokee missionary and founder of the *Cherokee Phoenix*. At once often republished religious tract, a call to piety, it remains notable for having been translated in 1843 into the Cherokee syllabary and in a later Creek version.

The line of life-writing has won increasing appreciation. In *The Life, History, and Travels of Kah-ge-ga-bowh (George Copway)*, 1847, a work praised by Longfellow and Fenimore Cooper, Copway folds both his Chippewa-Ojibwe family and his Methodism into larger tribal interface and the Anishinaabe language itself. Sarah Winnemucca Hopkins (Northern Paiute) in *Life Among the Piutes: Their Wrongs and Claims* (1883) gives reflection to her background of Nevada reservation and activism in arguing for redress. Sioux legacy has voice in the writings of Zitkala-Sa/Gertrude Simmons Bonnin (Yankton Dakota) with her critique of assimilation in *Dreams, Poems, and the Sun Dance* (2001); the Santee Sioux Charles Eastman (tribal name Ohiyesa), medical doctor at Wounded Knee, in his account of negotiating the hybridity of being Native *and* American in *From the Deep Woods to Civilization: Chapters in the Autobiography of an Indian* (1918); and, to repeat the referencing, Luther Standing Bear in *My Indian Boyhood* (1925) and Black Elk in *Black Elk Speaks: Being the Life Story of a Holy Man of the Oglala Sioux* (1932). In the "telling" of these life-stories, wholly self-written or in collaboration, the note struck is not only one of history but the will to compositional imagining. A later tier of self-writing, its luminaries explored in Chapter 2, has added precisely to this double-thrust: life and fashioning.

Poetry draws from lineage that, by its very intonation and cadence, echoes spoken convention, a point wholly behind anthologies like Brian Swann's *Songs of the Sky: Versions of Native American Songs and Poems* (1985, 1993). Yet print poetry also has its own identifying history. The nineteenth-century notably yields the lyrics of Jane Johnson Schoolcraft (1800–1842), a number written in Anishinaabe, of which "On the Doric Rock, Lake Superior" bears her characteristic contemplative style. She has a near-spirit in Alexander Posey (1873–1908) whose Creek-themed nature verse has tended to overshadow his savvy Fus Fixico journal columns with their adept "Indian Country" satiric vignettes.

In the case of fiction Louis Owens in *Other Destinies: Understanding the American Indian Novel* (1992) justifiably gives the reminder that a scant nine or so Native-written novels saw print before 1968 with, thereafter, *la déluge.* Inaugural honors have usually been accorded to *The Life and Adventures of Joaquin Murieta, The Celebrated Mexican Bandit* (1854), by the Eastern Cherokee author John Rollin Ridge or under his tribal name Cheesquatalawny/Yellow Bird (1827–1867). Beyond its thief adventure and derring-do, however, even to a modern eye its pulp format, lies the subtler fable of land theft albeit Mexican and the making of "American" identity. Women's authorship, later commercially as well as critically triumphant in Erdrich and Silko, has its inaugurating marker in the recently recovered S. Alice Callahan's *Wynema: A Child of the Forest* (1891). Her Creek-Muscogee novel of interracial women's friendship between the full-blood Wynema Harjo and the white Dixie-raised Methodist Genevieve Weir, despite a certain inertness to the prose and dips into piety and domestic romance, includes reference to the Wounded Knee massacre in 1890 as but one ledger in the larger history that frames the story. These early literary entrances, however various in strength, leave moot any notion of early vacuum.[10]

***

It has become standard to speak of 1920s–1940s Native fiction, albeit a slim folder, to claim importance on two main counts, for its lien on "Indian" transition into the early twentieth-century and on mixed-blood lives. Precursors, certainly, were few, whether as always John Rollin Ridge's fact-fiction in *The Life and Adventures of Joaquín Murieta*, or Simon Pokagon's melodrama, likely co-authored, of Great Lakes Potawatomi family and the blights of drink in *O-gi-Mak-kee Mit-I-ki* (*Queen of the Woods*, 1899). Reception further complicates matters. Depression-era realism, as order of the day, whether by John Dos Passos, John Steinbeck, Richard Wright or James T. Farrell, much overshadowed fiction by Native authors. Retrospect, however, now speaks of forerunners to the generation of Momaday and beyond, an ambiguity on several counts. They have deserved better understanding.

For to construe the literary fiction involved risks under-attention not only to resources of idiom but their differences one from another. It has also meant omitting a name like Todd Downing (Choctaw), long a Mexico expert, who gave notice of his prowess as mystery-writer in a first novel like *Murder on Tour* (1933) with its Tex-Mex border setting and un-raveling of the killer by the customs agent

Hugh Rennert. A main text by each author proffers grounds for consideration both of overlaps and divergences.

Mourning Dove's *Cogewea* (1927), prior to the recovery of S. Alice Callahan's *Wynema*, long has featured as a Native historic first, that of the Salish-Okanogan and Colville woman author also known as Christine Quintasket and Christal. Birth in Canada, life and travel in the USA, whether hardworking fruit-picker when occasion required or the later anthropologist and activist, her career also underscores the dubiety of national First Nations/Native borders. The research into tribal storytelling behind collections like *Coyote Stories* (1933) and *Tales of the Okanogans* (post. 1976) meant frequent forays through the Pacific Northwest and British Columbia. These, too, may well have had a part in the slightly portentous full title: *CO-GE-WE-A, The Half-Blood, A Depiction of the Great Montana Cattle Range, By Hum-Ishu-Ma, "Mourning Dove."* Period western with ranch-hand cast and vernacular, horses and ridership, and the brace of a romance-triangle, the novel clearly risks formula. But the assets deserve not to be missed.

"I was contemplating the possibilities of becoming an authoress, of writing a book" (30). Cogewea's assertion to the H.B (Horseshoe Brand) foreman and her long-time suitor, Jim LaGrinder, gives more than passing touch of reflexivity. It asks how this mixed-blood Flathead granddaughter of the Salish elder Stemteemä, fierce but beauteous "plain's cowgirl" (45) and range-rider, will "write" her life in reality. Pulled between LaGrinder, fellow mixed-blood, and Alfred Densmore, white-genteel but ultimately villain Easterner after her cash and land, she might well think herself in the very romance she could be writing.

Deficits accrues, contrivances of plot and pattern. They include the defecting white father who has left to find Yukon gold, Densmore as *Shoyohpee* or white man to whom Salish custom must be explained, and the horse races in which as "squaw" Cogewea is denied the first place she has won both by white then full-blood competitors. Stemteemä's warning fable of a Flathead tribeswoman, Green-blanket Feet betrayed by her white spouse, or the trick elopement of Cogewea and Densmore and her being balked of her cash and last-minute rescue by LaGrinder, veer close enough to melodrama. But Mourning Dove also does better, allowing that her editor Lucullus V. McWhorter had a hand in shaping the text and supplying the glossary.

The novel manages unsentimental insights into "the sunset of a closing era" (37), the abrasion of "two fires, the Red and the White" (37) with Cogewea positioned midway in ancestry, passion, and the larger backdrop of a changing occupation of the West. Tribal dance, Cogewea's original language of Okanagan, comparative versions of deity, tobacco, marriage ceremony, land use as against land ownership, all elicit commentary whether or not that belongs to the author speaking through her main figure. Observations frequently possess bite, even acidity.

"The Indian Bureau was a blighting curse" (144) runs one judgment. The nearby Blackfeet, "a once virile, self-supporting people" have been reduced to "a pitiful, diseased remnant" (145). Nations have been dispossessed by the "luring voice" of white intruders (243), whether Black Robe Jesuits, fur trappers, buffalo trophy-killers, or those seeking sexual and marriage partners. In Cogewea's marriage to Jim mixed-blood status continues in defiance of either-or race category. Mourning Dove has her remain mediating witness-participant to the Flathead Valley landscape, the Rockies, the as yet un-ended racial dynamic of the west.

Likely the two best-known ensuing novels belong to John Joseph Mathews, and D'Arcy McNickle. Mathews's *Sundown* (1934) takes its setting from Oklahoma's turn-of-the-century boom and white-speculator finagling of the Dawes allotment policy and arising Osage intra-tribal division. "He shall be a challenge to the disintegration of his people."[11] So Mathews has John Windzer, Osage mixed-blood father, envisage the destiny of the son he has parented with his full-blood wife and who he will call Chal for Challenge. In Chal, at once Osage legatee yet eventual Jazz-era profligate, Mathews creates a figure who inwardly regrets even as he accedes to the very process of his own mixed-blood doubling. The one story, moreover, shadows the still larger historic overlap and its fractures between tribal and white America through the oil that has led to their new-found economic compact. In these respects, among others, the novel justly can be thought to serve as a benchmark.

Infancy, horsemanship, High School, University, sexual encounter, enlistment as airman in the World War I Signal Corps, Europe, and return to home township of Kihekah with Chal's inherited oil and family monies, Mathews gives in almost granular detail. Equally he depicts Oklahoma as an intimate ecology of prairie, creek, coyote and other animal and bird life to be seen under Osage understanding of land and cosmos. The arrival of "black oil derricks" (62), and the order of life they portend, supplies the contrast. This degree of specificity, much of it drawn from Mathews's own life, has been known to arouse complaint of a kind of Sinclair Lewis surfeit, too great a drag on the novel's fluency. Likely in some degree it carries over from the history Mathews published as *Wah'Kon-Tah: The Osage and the White Man's Road* (1932). But that is not to detract from the larger gain, the dilemma embodied in Chal of meeting the ways of American modernity – ownership, technology – without enduring cost to Osage and other tribal heritage.

The novel, to be sure, has its pivot in Chal, his augmenting sense of being "filled with a vague but insistent yearning for something" (152). Dreams and contemplation have him imagining himself the Osage horseman-warrior, dancer, the ancestral prairie and hill-dweller. At different times, boy or adult, he attaches himself in fantasy to red-tailed hawk, coyote, bear, owl and eagle. Reality, however, puts him in a world in which "Osages and Osage oil were national news" (243), its accusing symptom an "oil-polluted pool of water" (251). Mathews keeps the contrasts clear enough with Chal in his veerings figured as both witness and participant.

Sundown's sequence of incident works to precisely this end. The opening apostrophe to the sacred "god of the great Osages" with its "fantastic play of lightning and thunder" (1) sounds a warning against the arriving industrialism of "the Reservation of Oil and Gas" (8). While he revels in Osage-animate sight and sound of prairie or creek ("he wanted to sing and dance....with deep reverence" 73) he despairs of one time full-blood companions like Sun-on-his-Wings, an eventual alcoholic. Much as he respects Running Elk and the other full bloods he voices reprimand at their "acting like Indians" (94). He, like they, recognizes pejorative naming as Blanket Indians, Big Hills Skin Indians (92). Yet on his own reckoning the Osage, for all that he thinks back in envy at their best years, "he had begun to believe was backward and uncivilized" (177).

The rest of the novel's inventory likewise reflects contradiction. In the Agency schoolroom of Miss Hoover, Easterner and Quaker, Cal retreats into outward silence even as for her part she publishes romanticized "Indian" vignettes. In college he fancies himself the beau to the whitest of co-ed belles, Blo, only and indicatively to see in the mirror the reflection of his brown skin. The college crowd he takes to witness Ponca "Indian dancing" (253) signifies serious ritual viewed through drink-laden tourism ("the girls said it was romantic" 216). His flights as Air Cadet Windzer can be models of piloting, "translucent wings" (217), and especially at night-time when he take his plane on visits to his wealthy lover Lou Kerry to whom he describes himself as "Spanish," but they also remind him of the avian grace he once relished in the flight of birds above prairie Oklahoma.

Alignments of these and related kinds give the novel its very shape. Drinking, lethargy, parties, consort with the tribal spiritual vision he is reminded of through the words of Watching Eagle, Road Man and Elder, in the Sweat Lodge Ceremony. His mother, full-blood, will speak Osage while he, like his "mixed" progressive father likely killed at the hands of either white townspeople resistant to Osage bids for equity, or even his fellow Osage themselves for compromise with dispossession of land, operates in English. The two languages reflect not merely tongue but of history. Chal is said not "to know what to do with himself" (262), to wish being "far away," and in a last scene to fantasize himself the maybe latter-day orator or Harvard Law School alumnus (311). The irony of having become "a man among civilized men" (230) – "this civilization was here now" (236) – permeates *Sundown*, Mathews's cautionary tale of worlds at damaging cost looped one into the other.[12]

For McNickle in *The Surrounded* (1936) personal and cultural divides are signaled in Sniél-emen and St. Xavier as two western Montana place-names, Salish and European, together with the "Indian settlement" after Allotment. In the life of Archilde Leon, son of Spanish-born ranch father Max Leon and full-blood mother Catherine Wolf ("Catherine Le Loup"), the novel seeks to give representation of mixed-blood identity at the interface of power through the 1890s-and-after apportioned, or rather mis-apportioned, to settler and Native. "Max did not know what to make of Archilde" (107) comments the novel. The eldest son back from school and work in Portland, educated beyond his ten siblings, child artist and then musician, he is designated "civilized" yet full of "uneasy feeling" (62), heir to Salish writ yet belonging to "a new time" (108). The city has been one challenge. Yet "This, his home, was a strange country" (120). At every turn the novel acts expansively on his discomfiture.

What is Archilde to think himself? What are we? The title does instructive full duty. Whatever the evident eventfulness of plotline or the invocation of Salish elders and tradition, surroundedness snares both himself and those around him. The Salish suffer duresse, full of historical memory yet depleted for the future. Generational circles of family clash. Indian School inflicts shadow with only rarest rays of light. Black robe Jesuits, white Indian traders, the Indian Agent, sheriff, a mixed-blood female lover, all enter as though players in a preordained drama. Double-murder, with to follow mountain search and capture, becomes the dénouement. Above all, Archilde's splits of lineage, together with each personal and cultural borderland in their making, leave little option except final self-resignation as the emblematically handcuffed co-accused.

The human action of the novel, to McNickle's imaginative credit, ends in this perfect irresolution, the author's unwillingness to allow the snap ending, each contradiction tidied or resolved. To this end *The Surrounded* reads rich in contrasts of detail. Archilde has made a living as a fiddle player, no inappropriate metaphor for how he will assume domain on the Leon estate after Max's death. "An Indian boy...belonged with his people" (2) thinks Catherine of the son who has returned but cannot belong. She, in shifting turns, is resident in a hut separate from her husband's ranch-house, in young womanhood the readiest convert to Jesuit Catholicism ("faithful Catherine" 22) yet who will she will become the returnee to Salish rites as she moves towards her demise ("No priest" is her demand 259). Max has a Mediterranean skin tone darker than many Salish and can aver "he had never seen a red Indian" (42).

In Modeste, the blind Salish ancient, and the Summer Dance over which he presides as the clans gather, ritual is both kept alive but seen by Archilde as out-of-time. The younger brother Louis, horse-thief, in his flight to the hills and having shot a female deer can claim, in his own unintended irony, "We're Indians, and we're free of game laws" (125). Elise La Rose, Archilde's lover, may well give him passion, needed sexual exhilaration, but will implicate him in the murder of the sheriff just as his mother does so by axe-murdering the Game Warden and helping bury his body. The boy nephews, Mike and Narcisse, at one point skip return to Indian School to "play Indians" in the woods to become under Archilde's monitoring eye and not unlike himself shadow dancers as it were.

Each white authority figure adds to the encirclement. Sheriff Quigley ("He was a sheriff out of the Old West" 114) is seen as threat, "sinister" governance personified. Father Crepilloux, missionary priest and friend to Max, edges into old age under the Grand Illusion of messianic rescuer of lost souls. George Moser, trader, all outward bonhomie (especially to Max) is in the game for profit and his wife's respectability at whatever the cost to the Salish ("Moser was up to his neck in land" 31). Horace Parker, Indian Agent, assumes a Great White Father role, ambiguous paternalism, at once seeming benefactor to Archilde but eventual lead member of the search and capture party. These circlings, Native, European, American, and their pathway into Archilde's literal arrest, define *The Surrounded.* McNickle's achievement is to keep his novel active, even dynamic, throughout, *huis clos* but also turning wheel.

Two further novels from the 1930s to 1940s, the one seeming-historical, the other inclined towards myth, add focus. *The Singing Bird: A Cherokee Novel* by John Milton Oskison (Cherokee), set in the 1820–1865 period of Cherokee removal and the Civil War, missionary intrusion, and the role played by Sequoyah and the quest for Cherokee "sacred symbols," though written in the 1930s and unpublished in its own time approaches fiction of fact. *The Man Who Killed the Deer: A Novel of Pueblo Indian Life* (1942) by Frank Waters (Cheyenne) furnishes a richly imaged narrative of its protagonist's rite of passage from Indian School and the vexed Anglo-Pueblo interface into home nation at America's turn of the century. Both center also in memorable imagined personages, respectively Oskison's Ellen Wear as flighty, selfish but sexually sovereign Native woman, and Waters's Martiniano as Taos/Puebloan returnee initially caught out by a white forest ranger for shooting the deer but then put to find his balance of ritual and modernity.

***

Whether or not Native American and First Nations Renaissance does good or less good service as a signifier, two decades into the present century there can be no assuming prior vacancy. Nor, from interwar to the 1960s, was there silence. Lynn Riggs, besides *Green Grow the Lilacs*, has further theatre success with *The Cherokee Night* (written 1932, produced 1936). Will Rogers, cowboy humorist, aviator, author, and born into the Cherokee Nation ("absorbed Indian" was a typical aphorism he repeated), produces a barrage of radio and film scripts into the 1930s and then beyond along with his *Autobiography* published posthumously in 1949. Ella Cara Deloria (Yankton-Standing Rock Sioux), bilingual anthropologist, writes *Waterlily* early in the 1940s yet unpublished until 1988, an insider-informed story of mother-daughter relationship, Sioux kin and custom, and told against the backdrop of smallpox and sun-dance. Mathews writes *Talking to the Moon* (1945), his Thoreauvian memoir of season and landscape in Osage country. D'Arcy McNickle writes *Runner in the Sun: A Story of Indian Maize* (1954), his fable of pre-Conquest coming of age and leadership. Carlos Castaneda writes *The Teachings of Don Juan: A Yaqui Way of Knowledge* (1968), his controversial best-seller of peyote shamanism and spiritual exploration.

Reminders of these and the literary inventory they comprise come in several forms. Silko gives one kind of implied retrospect when in 1977 she attests "Writing a novel was a ceremony for me to stay sane."[13] Tommy Orange observes in *There There* "We didn't have last names before they came. When they decided to keep track of us, last names were given to us, just like the name *Indian* was given to us."[14] Stephen Graham Jones, prolific virtuoso of an array of popular culture story-texts and especially of the crafted modern/postmodern novel *Ledfeather* (2008), suggests something of the perspective. Writing in 2017 he observes:

> The Native American Renaissance…was a great and essential and transformative movement without even meaning to be a movement, but that was a different generation, with different issues. You're not resisting falling dead off the back of a horse anymore. You're not resisting people wanting to call you Billy Jack. You're not resisting the invisibility that comes from colonial mythmaking so much as you're resisting the voicelessness that comes from commodification. What you're resisting is headdresses on Reebok shirts….think about it: if you do stand up and try to fight for the same things those Native American Renaissance writers were fighting for, then you're pretty much saying they didn't make any headway, that American Indian literature hasn't made much progress.[15]

Progress, in truth, has been made, hugely, widely. Writings from before the Momaday generation join those of its own time and in its wake. The poet-critic and novelist Erika Wurth (Apache-Chickasaw-Cherokee) in "The Fourth Wave" argues for Native poetry as four interconnecting sequences, the latest the generation embracing names like Sherwin Bitsui (Navajo), Santee Frazier (Cherokee), and herself on the basis of the verse collection *Indian Trains* (2007). The newer voices make for pluralities as ready in quantity as idiom. However the Native American Renaissance is now to be regarded, platform through which to view past authorship, literary coming-of-age, or point of departure for the future, it continues to signify. It does so, however, the more so when seen as one stage or indeed "wave" in a literary continuum beyond the single timeslot, place, gender or typology.

Notes

1 Kenneth Lincoln, *Native American Renaissance*, Berkeley: University of California Press, 1983, 8.

2 Lincoln has hit back at negative critique with some energy. See Kenneth Lincoln, "Tribal Renaissance," in Alan R. Velie and A. Robert Lee, eds., *The Native American Renaissance: Literary Imagination and Achievement*, Norman: University of Oklahoma Press, 2013, 330–51. In *Native American Renaissance* he had also insisted that his study "is neither anthropology nor literary criticism, strictly speaking, but a hybrid" (9).

3 Thomas King usefully summarizes the point: "The magic of Native literature – as with other literatures – is not the themes of the stories – identity, loss, ceremony, community, maturation, home – it is in the way meaning is refracted by cosmology, the way understanding is shaped by cultural paradigms." *The Truth About Stories: A Native Narrative*, Minneapolis: University of Minnesota Press, 2013, 112. See also Franchot Ballinger, *Living Sideways: Tricksters in American Oral Traditions*, Norman: University of Oklahoma Press, 1998.

4 "Homing in" has long passed into familiar usage. See William Bevis, "Native American Novels: Homing in," in Brian Swann and Arnold Krupat, eds., *Recovering the Word: Essays in Native American Literature*, Berkeley: University of California Press, 1987, 580–620.

5 For an informed recent estimate see Joy Porter, *Trauma, Primitivism and the First World War: The Making of Frank Prewett*, New York and London: Bloomsbury, 2021.

6 For earlier overviews see Penny Petrone, *Native Literature in Canada: From the Oral Tradition to the Present*, Toronto: Oxford University Press, 1990, and Thomas King,

Cheryl Calver, and William Beynon, eds., *The Native in Literature: Canadian and Comparative Perspectives*, Oakville, Ontario; ECW Press, 1987.

7 See also Brian Joseph Gilley, *Becoming Two-Spirit: Gay Identity and Social Acceptance in Indian Country*, Lincoln: University of Nebraska Press, 2006.

8 For a now dated but still wholly useful overview see A. Lavonne Brown Ruoff, "American Indian Authors, 1774-1899," in Andrew Wiget, ed., *Critical Essays on Native American Literature*, Boston: G.K. Hall, 1985.

9 The phrase, not inappropriately, has won considerable ongoing currency, See, for instance, Craig Lesley, ed., *Talking Leaves: Contemporary Native American Short Stories*, New York: Bantam Doubleday Bell, 1991.

10 A restorative study in this respect is to be found in Colin Calloway, *The World Turned Upside Down: Indian Voices From Early America*, New York: St. Martin's Press, Bedford Books, 1994.

11 John Joseph Mathews, *Sundown*, New York: Longmans, Green & Company, 1934. Reprinted Norman: University of Oklahoma Press, 1988, 4. Page references are to this edition.

12 Louis Owens argues that the closing images of nestlings, a mother robin and a grasshopper serve as natural tokens of hope, new life. That may be right but if so it hardly assuages the downward slope of Chal's misgivings. See *Other Destinies: Understanding the American Indian Novel*, Norman: University of Oklahoma Press, 1992, 59.

13 Leslie Marmon Silko, "Stories andTheir Tellers," Interview with Dexter Fisher, 1977, 24. *Conversations with Leslie Marmon Silko*, ed., Ellen L. Arnold, Jackson: University Press of Mississippi, 2000.

14 Tommy Orange, *There There*, New York: Alfred A. Knopf, 2018, "Last Names."

15 Stephen Graham Jones, "Letter to a Just-Starting-Out Indian Writer – and Maybe to Myself," in Billy J. Stratton, ed., *The Fiction of Stephen Graham Jones: A Critical Companion*, Albuquerque: University of New Mexico Press, 2017, xi.

Works Cited

Akiwenzie-Damm, Kateri, ed., *Without Reservation: Indigenous Erotica*, Wiarton, Ontario: Kegedonce Press, 2003.

Alexie, Sherman, *Reservation Blues*, New York: Atlantic Monthly Press, 1995.

Allen, Paula Gunn, *The Sacred Hoop: Recovering the Feminine in American Indian Traditions*, Boston: Beacon Press, 1997.

_____, *Life is a Fatal Disease: Collected Poems 1962-1995*, Albuquerque: West End Press, 1997.

_____, *The Woman Who Owned the Shadows*, San Francisco: Spinsters Ink, 1986.

Apess, William, *A Son of the Forest: The Experience of William Apess, a Native of the Forest Comprising a Notice of the Pequot Tribe of Indians, Written by Himself*, New York: published by the author, 1829, 1831.

Armstrong, Jeannette, *Breath Tracks*, Vancouver: Williams-Wallace, Theytus, 1991.

_____, *Slash*, Penticton, British Columbia. Theytus, 1985.

Arnott, Joanne, *Mother Time: Poems New and Selected*, Vancouver: Ronsdale Press, 2007.

Barnes, Jim, *On Native Grounds: Memoirs and Impressions*, Norman: University of Oklahoma Press, 1997.

Bear, Luther Standing, *My People, the Sioux*, ed. E.A. Brininstool, Boston: Houghton Mifflin, 1928, 1931. Reprinted Lincoln; University of Nebraska Press, 1975.

Bevis, William, "Native American novels: Homing in," in Brian Swann and Arnold Krupat, eds., *Recovering the Word: Essays in Native American Literature*, Berkeley: University of California Press, 1987.

Black Elk, with John Neihardt, *Black Elk Speaks: Being the Life Story of a Holy Man of the Oglala Sioux*, 1932, reprinted Lincoln: University of Nebraska Press, 1961.

Blackhawk, *Autobiography of Ma-Ka-Tai-Me-She-Kia-Kiak, or Black Hawk, Embracing the Traditions of his Nation, Various Wars In Which He Has Been Engaged, and His Account of the Cause and General History of the Black Hawk War of 1832, His Surrender, and Travels Through the United States. Also Life, Death and Burial of the Old Chief, Together with a History of the Black Hawk* War, J.B. Patterson, Oquawka, Illinois, 1833. Reprint 1882.

Blaeser, Kimberly, *Trailing You*, New York: Greenfield Review Press, 1994.

Boyden, Joseph, *Three Day Road*, Toronto: Penguin, 2005.

Brant, Beth, *Food & Spirits: Stories*, Ithica: Firebrand Books, 1991.

Callahan, S. Alice, *Wynema: A Child of the Forest*, Chicago: Smith, 1891; reprinted Lincoln: University of Nebraska Press, 1997.

Carr, A.A., *Eye Killers*, Norman: University of Oklahoma Press, 1995.

Castaneda, Carlos, *The Teachings of Don Juan: A Yaqui Way of Knowing*, Berkeley: University of California Press, 1968.

Chrystos, *In Her I Am*, Vancouver: Press Gang, 1993.

_____, *Not Vanishing*, Vancouver: Press Gang, 1988.

Cook-Lynn, Elizabeth, *Why I Can't Read Wallace Stegner and Other Essays: A Tribal Voice*, Madison: University of Wisconsin Press, 1996.

Copway, George, *The Life, History, and Travels of Kah-ge-ga-bowh (Geroge Copwa)*, Albany: Weed and Parsons, 1847.

Cuthand, Beth, *Horse Dace to Emerald Mountain*, Penicton, British Columbia: Theytus, 1987.

Däwes, Birgit, *Indigenous North American Drama: A Multivocal History*, Albany: State University of New York Press, 2014.

Deloria, Philip, *Indians in Unexpected Places*, Lawrence: University of Kansas Press, 2004.

Deloria, Vine, *Custer Died for Your Sins: An Indian Manifesto*, New York: Macmillan, 1969.

Downing, Todd, *Murder on Tour*, New York: G.P. Putnam's Sons, 1934.

Driskell, Qwo-Li, *Cherokee Queer and Two-Spirit Memory*, Tucson: University of Arizona Press, 2016.

Driskell, Qwo-Li, Justice, Daniel Heath, Miranda, Deborah and Tatonetti, Lisa, eds., *Sovereign Erotics: A Collection of Two-Spirit Literature*, Tucson: University of Arizona Press, 2011.

Eastman, Charles A. (Ohiyesa), *From the Deep Woods to Civilization: Chapters in the Autobiography of an Indian*, Boston: Little Brown, 1916.

Erdrich Louise, *Love Medicine*, New York: Henry Holt, 1984; expanded version, 1993.

_____, *Jacklight*, New York: Henry Holt, 1984.

Fontaine, Natasha Kanapé, *N'entre pas dans mon âme avec tes chaussures*, Montréal: Editions Mémoire d'Encrier, 2012. *Do Not Enter My Soul in your Shoes*, Toronto: Mawenzi House, 2015.

Geiogamah, Hanay, *New Native American Drama: There Plays by Hanay Geiogamah (Body Indian, Foghorn, and 49)*, Norman: University of Oklahoma Press, 1980.

_____ and Darby, Jaye T., eds., *Stories of Our Way: An Anthology of American Indian Plays*, Los Angeles: UCLA American Indian Studies Center, 1998.

Gilroy, Paul, *The Black Atlantic: Modernity and Double Consciousness*, London: Verso, 1993, Cambridge: Harvard University Press, 1995.

Glancy, Diane, *American Gypsy: Six Native American Plays*, Norman: University of Oklahoma Press, 2002.

_____, *War Cries, A Collection of Nine Plays*, Duluth: Holy Cow! Press, 1997.

_____, *Iron Woman*, Minneapolis: New Rivers Press, 1990.

Gould, Janice, *Seed*, Sequim, Washington: Headmistress Press, 2019.

_____, *Earthquake Weather*, Tucson: University of Arizona Press, 1996.

Hale, Janet Campbell, *Bloodlines: Odyssey of a Native Daughter*, New York: Random House, 1993.

Harjo, Joy, *She Had Some Horses*, New York: Thunder's Mouth Press, 1983.

Henry, Gordon D., *The Light People*, Norman: University of Oklahoma Press, 1994.

Highway, Tomson, *Kiss of the Fur Queen*, Toronto: Doubleday Canada, 1998.

Hogan, Linda, The *Woman Who Watches Over The World: A Native Memoir*, New York: W.W. Norton, 2001.

_____, *The Book of Medicines*, Minneapolis: Coffee House Press, 1993.

Hopkins, Sarah Winnemucca, *Life Among the Piutes: Their Wrongs and Claims*, Boston: Cupples, Upham. 1883; reprinted Bishop, California: Chalfont, Sierra Media, 1969.

Johnson, Basil, *Ojibway Tales: Moose Meat and Wild Rice*, Toronto: McClelland & Stewart, 1978. Reprinted Lincoln: University of Nebraska Press, 1993.

Johnson, E. Pauline, *Legends of Vancouver*, Vancouver: G.S. Forsyth, 1913.

_____, *Canadian Born*, Toronto: G.N. Morang, 1911.:

Jones, Stephen Graham, "Letter to a Just-Starting-Out Indian Writer – And Maybe to Myself," in Billy J. Stratton, ed., *The Fiction of Stephen Graham Jones: A Critical Companion*, Albuquerque: University of New Mexico Press, 2017.

_____, *Ledfeather*, Norman: Fiction Collective 2, 2008.

Kenny, Maurice, *Tekonwatoni: Molly Brant, 1735-1795*, Fredonia: White Pine Press, 1992.

_____, *Between Two Rivers: Selected Poems, 1954-1984*, Fredonia: White Pine Press, 1987.

_____, "Tinselled Bucks: An Historical Study of Indian Homosexuality," *Gay Sunshine: A Journal of Gay Liberation*, 1975–6. Reprinted in Will Roscoe, ed., *Living the Spirit: A Gay American Indian Anthology*, 15–31, New York: St Martin's Press, 1988.

King, Thomas, *The Truth About Stories (A Native Narrative)*, Minneapolis: University of Minnesota Press, 2008.

_____ (ed), *All My Relations: An Anthology of Cotemporary Canadian Native Fiction*, Toronto: McCelland and Stewart, 1990, Norman: University of Oklahoma Press, 1992.

_____, *Medicine River*, New York: New York: Viking, 1990.

Krupat, Arnold, and Swann, Brian, eds., *Native American Autobiography: An Anthology*, Madison: University of Wisconsin Press, 1994.

Lincoln, Kenneth, *Native American Renaissance*, Berkeley: University of California Press, 1983.

Maillot, Terese Marie, *Heart Berries*, Berkeley: Counterpoint, 2018.

Maracle, Lee, *Bobbi Lee, Indian Rebel*, Richmond, Vancouver: LSM Information Centre, 1975.

Mathews, John Joseph, *Talking to the Moon*, Chicago: University of Chicago Press, 1945.

_____, *Sundown*, London and New York: Longmans, Green and Co., 1934.

McNickle, D'Arcy, *Runner in the Sun: A Story of Indian Maize*, New York: Henry Holt, 1954.

_____, *The Surrounded*, New York: Dodd, Mead & Co., 1936.

Means, Russell, *Where White Men Fear to Tread*, New York: St. Martin's Press, 1995.

Miranda, Deborah, *Raised by Humans*, Sylmar: Tia Chucha Press, 2015.

_____, *Bad Indians: A tribal Memoir*, Berkeley: Heyday Press, 2013.

_____, *Indian Cartography*, New York: Greenfield Review Press, 1999.

Momaday, N. Scott, *The Names: A Memoir*. New York: Harper & Row, 1976.

_____, *Angle of Geese*, Boston: D.R. Godine, 1974.

_____, *House Made of Dawn*, New York: Harper & Row, 1968.

Mourning Dove, *Cogewea, the Half-Blood: Given Through Sho-Powtan: A Depiction of the Great Montana Cattle Range*, Boston: Four Seas, 1927; reprinted Lincoln: University of Nebraska Press, 1981.

Occom, Samuel, "A Short Narrative of my Life," 1962. Reprinted in Bernd Peyer, ed. *The Elders Wrote: An Anthology of Early Prose by North American Indians, 1968-1931*, Berlin: Dietrich Reimer, 1982.

Orange, Tommy, *There, There*, New York: Alfred A, Knopf, 2018.

Ortiz, Simon, *From Sand Creek*, New York: Thunder Mouth's Press, 1981.

Oskison, John Milton, *The Singing Bird: A Cherokee Novel* (post), Norman: University of Oklahoma Press, 2007.

_____, *Brothers Three*, New York: MacMillan, 1935.

Owens, Louis, *Other Destinies: Understanding the American Indian Novel*, Norman: University of Oklahoma Press, 1993.

Penn, William, ed., *As We Are Now: Mixblood Essays on Race and Identity*, Berkeley: University of California Press, 1998.

Pico, Tommy, *Feed*, Portland: Tin House Books, 2019.

Revard, Carter, *Winning the Dust Bowl*, Tucson: University of Arizona Press, 2001.

_____, *Family Matters, Tribal Affairs*, Tucson: University of Arizona Press, 1998.

Ridge, John Rollin (Yellow Bird), *The Life and Adventures of Joaquin Murieta, The Celebrated California Bandit*, 1854; reprinted Norman: University of Oklahoma Press, 1977.

Riggs, Lynn, ed. Jace Weaver, *The Cherokee Night and Other Plays*, Norman: University of Oklahoma Press, 2003.

_____, *Green Grow the Lilacs*, New York and London: S. French, 1932, Richard Rodgers and Oscar Hammerstein, *Oklahoma! A Musical*, New York: Random House, 1943.

Rogers, Will, *The Autobiography of Will Rogers*, ed. Donald Day, Boston: Houghton Mifflin, 1949.
Roscoe, Will, ed., *Living the Spirit: A Gay American Indian Anthology*, New York: St. Martin's Press, 1988.
Schoolcraft, Jane Johnson (Bamewawagezhikaquay), *The Sound the Stars Make Rushing Through the Sky: The Writings of Jane Johnson Schoolcraft*, ed. Robert Dale Parker, Philadelphia: University of Pennsylvania Press, 2006.
Sequoyah (George Gist), *Cherokee Alphabet*, Boston: Pendleton's Lithography, 1835.
Silko, Leslie Marmon, *Storyteller*, New York: Arcade/Little, Brown and Company, 1981.
_____, *Ceremony*, New York: Viking Press, 1977.
Slipperjack, Ruby, *Silent Words*, Saskatoon: Fifth House, 1992.
Standing Bear, Luther, *My Indian Boyhood*, New York: Houghton, Mifflin, 1925. Reprinted Lincoln. University of Nebraska Press, 1988.
Stanlake, Christy, *Native American Drama: A Critical Interpretation*, New York: Cambridge University Press, 2009.
Swann, Brian, ed., *Songs of the Sky: Versions of Native American Songs and Poems*, np. Four Zoas Night House Press, 1975. Reprinted Amherst: University of Massachusetts Press, 1993.
Swann, Brian, and Krupat, Arnold, eds., *I Tell You Now: Autobiographical Essays by Native American Writers*. Lincoln: University of Nebraska Press, 1987.
Tapahonso, Luci, *Blues Houses Rush In: Poems and Stories*, Tucson: University of Arizona Press, 1997.
Tatonetti, Lisa, *The Queerness of Native American Literature*, Minneapolis: University of Minnesota Press, 2014.
Tremblay, Gail, *Indians Singing in the 20th Century*, Corvallis: Calyx, 1990.
Twist, Arielle, *Disintegrate/Dissociate*, Vancouver: Arsenal Pulp Press, 2019.
Van Camp, Richard, *The Lesser Blessed*, Vancouver: Douglas & McIntire, 1996.
Vizenor, Gerald, *Interior Landscapes: Autobiographical Myths and Metaphors*, Minneapolis: University of Minnesota Press, 1990.
_____, *Bearheart*, Minneapolis: Truck Press, 1978. Originally titled *Darkness in Saint Lewis Bearheart.*
Waters, Frank, *The Man Who Killed the Deer*, Chicago: Sage, 1942; reprinted Swallow/University of Ohio Press, 1989.
Weaver, Jace, *Red Atlantic: American Indigenes and the Making of the Modern World, 1000-1927* Chapel Hill, University of North Carolina Press, 2014.
Welch, James, *Winter in the Blood*, New York Harper & Row, 1974.
Whiteman, Roberta Hill, *Star Quilt*, Duluth: Holy Cow! Press, 1996.
Whitehead, Joshua, *Full.Metal Indigiqueer*, Vancouver: Talonbooks, 2017.
Winnemucca Hopkins, Sarah, *Life Among the Piutes: Their Wrongs and Claims*, Boston: Cupples Upham, 1883.
Womack, Craig S., *Drowning in Fire*, Tucson: University of Arizona Press, 2001.
Wurth, Erika T., "The Fourth Wave," *Waxwing*, 7, 2016.
_____, *Indian Trains*, Albuquerque: West End Press, 2007.
Yellow Robe, William S., *Where the Pavement Ends: Five Native American Plays*, Norman: University of Oklahoma Press, 2000.

Zitkala-sa/Zitkala-sha/Red Bird (Gertrude Simmons Bonnin), *Dreams, Poems and the Sun Dance Opera*, Lincoln: University of Nebraska Press, 2001.

2

Modern Native Life Writing: Telling You Now

> Every writer is forced to rely, at some point, on the imagination. The skill with which he can do that determines his success as a writer. I can take credit for setting down those Kiowa stories in English, in *The Way to Rainy Mountain*, but I didn't invent them. The imagination that informs those stories is really not mine…It's an ancestral imagination. It's important to understand that dimension. But in the secondary materials and in that third voice, which is personal reminiscence, I brought my own imagination to bear.
>
> N. Scott Momaday, *Ancestral Voice* (1989)[1]

> There are stories that take seven days to tell. There are other stories that take you all your life.
>
> Diane Glancy, *The West Pole* (1997)[2]

> Something strange appears when we look at certain autobiographies of Indian people: the notion of identity, of how the individual is related to the world, people, self, differs from what we see in "Euro-American" autobiography.
>
> Carter Revard, *Family Matters, Tribal Affairs* (1998)[3]

Native American life-writing has long come accoutred in contention. How much, how little, is first-person authorship entitled to reveal of ceremony, spirituality, origin myths, clan naming and custom? Is there a risk of vaunting self-identity above shared larger genealogy, the betrayal of tribal-community etiquette? Oral tradition, the governance of the spoken word, is axiomatic in Native tradition. Yet how writerly, not to say readerly, is a Native author allowed to be? If an estimated more than two-thirds of Native Americans now live in the townships or cities, be it by choice or by historic BIA termination and relocation policies, how to balance duty to tribal rite of passage or origins or homeland with, in an increasingly deployed term and in all its pluses and minuses, urban-cosmopolitan (not to say international) modernity?

It can little surprise that Native autobiography since N. Scott Momaday's *The Way to Rainy Mountain* (1969), and its follow-up replete in sepia visuals in

The Names: A Memoir (1976), has been a spate. In giving attention both to the kinds of modern life-writing, and to a number of its highlights like those of Momaday himself, Leslie Marmon Silko, Gerald Vizenor, Janet Campbell Hale, Carter Revard and Jim Barnes, the emphasis again falls upon the qualities of imagination, textual caché, within each.[4]

If written Native autobiography has its beginnings in the Christian-conversion texts of Samuel Occom, William Apess and George Copway, memorial threads as it were, those since Momaday have utterly diversified the legacy. Not only has that meant full-length prose narrative, albeit often with insets of corroborative poem or photograph, but full-length mixed prose-poetry composition and few more consequential than Ray Young Bear's *Black Eagle Child: The Facepaint Narratives* (1992). Issues of interpretation and status have been quick to arise, especially as to whether any one Native voice can be assumed to carry representative, or synecdochic, weight, the single figural voice speaking for the many.

Were one to seek the busy expansion of Native autobiography anthologies do every service. Few have done so more than those under the editorships and co-editors of Arnold Krupat and Brian Swann in *I Tell You Now: Autobiographical Essays by Native American Writers* (1987, Mary TallMountain to Joy Harjo), *Native American Autobiography: An Anthology* (1994, Occom to Vizenor), or *Here First: Autobiographical Essays by Native American Writers* (2000, Sherman Alexie to Ofelia Zepeda). "Collective memoir" is the phrasing given these essay-chapters, apt observance for so encompassing a diversity of Native first-person voice.

As We Are Now: Mixblood Essays on Race and Identity (1997), under the editorship of the novelist William Penn, adds to the variation of gallery. Penn himself writes from Nez Perce and Osage ancestry, though some Osage have questioned this, plied into likely Quaker-Pennsylvania family. Among other chapters Craig S. Womack's Creek and Cherokee self-portrait ("Howling at the Moon") delineates his two-spirit identity, a gay Native selfhood. For Kim Blaeser in "On Mapping and Urban Shamans" with its rumination on her Chippewa-Ojibwe-German background there is the contrast between her upbringing at Minnesota's White Earth Reservation as against Chicago as metropolis and her Newberry Library Fellowship. Inez Petersen (Quinault, Danish) takes a sally at identification and mis-identification by dint of family legacy and blue eyes in "What Part Moon."

For Elizabeth Cook-Lynn, be the domain fiction or verse as much as autobiography, and as she develops her views in *Why I Can't Read Wallace Stegner and Other Essays: A Tribal Voice* (1996), *New Indians, Old Wars* (2007) and her editorials in *Wicazo Sa Review*, the desideratum calls for autobiographical and other texts to be rigorously tribal-centric and pledged to speak overwhelmingly to historical redress and the restoration of sovereignty. She places herself firmly, and self-evidentially, inside this ideological stance.

Paula Gunn Allen, especially in *The Sacred Hoop: Recovering the Feminine in American Indian Traditions* (1986), gives accent to gynocentrism, the voicing of Native women's power of life-bearing and spiritual connection. She especially highlights Leslie Marmon Silko for the Laguna Pueblo "war-zone" storying of *Ceremony* (1977), and Wendy Rose for, as she sees it, the sweet-and-sour verse of her mixed Hopi-Miwok-European womanhood in *The Halfbreed Chronicles and Other Poems* (1985). In each of these and the other texts she explores, she discerns the myriad reflections of her own life.

In the case of Louis Owens, the syncretism of his background feeds imaginatively through the various life-writings of discursive collections like *Mixedblood Messages: Literature, Film, Family, Place* (1998) and *I Hear the Train: Reflections, Inventions, Refractions* (2001). That Owens was under way at his death with a whole book of interviews provisionally titled *Outside Shadow* leaves undisclosed the yet fuller curvature of his complex mixed-blood life from Dixie indigence to California writer-professorship.[5]

The roster of modern Native autobiography approaches a plenitude, the span variously political, regional, gendered, even professorial.[6] Reservation leadership and AIM pan-tribalism equally have engendered their own share of life writing, albeit often co-authored. Wilma Mankiller's *Mankiller: A Chief and Her People* (1993) tells the Cherokee history behind her career as activist and community social worker. Ladonna Harris's *Ladonna Harris: A Comanche Life* (2001) gives the Oklahoma portrait of a life's politics and marriage to Fred Harris as Senator and presidential candidate. Russell Means's *Where White Men Fear to Tread* (1995) and Dennis Banks's *Ojibwa Warrior* (2004), with their memorialization not only of the activism that led to AIM's founding in 1968 and the 1973 occupation of Wounded Knee, but their itineraries of BIA schooling, reservation life, FBI surveillance (in Banks's case his eleven years of being a fugitive), and respective drink afflictions, marriages and family.

Tribal spectrum has notable manifestations. In *The Blue Jay's Dance: A Birth Year* (1995) Louise Erdrich inscribes a Connecticut-farm year, her poetic diarygraph of nature, birthing and mothering, the writer's life, and then marriage to Michael Dorris. It has a companion volume in *Books and Islands in Ojibwe Country* (2003), meditative journey-writing under National Geographic auspices around the Minnesota-Ontario border in company with a baby daughter and with eye to habitat, rock-painting and Anishinaabe speech and culture. In *The Turquoise Ledge: A Memoir* (2010), successor volume to *Storyteller*, Leslie Marmon

Silko deploys the Tucson mountain-range as grounding, earth's spirit, for exploration of her genealogical Laguna, Mexican and European braiding together with acute probes into Native slavery and the Southwest's ecology threatened by atomic testing. Other origins are to be met in Beverly Hungry Wolf's life within Blackfoot gynocracy in *The Ways of My Grandmothers* (1980) or a First Nations Cree self-portrait like Jane Willis's *Genieish: An Indian Girlhood* (1973).

Many mixed-blood lives transposed to the page disclose self-fissure, often hauntingly troubled personal trauma. Yet they also signal the gains of self-recomposition, writing's pathways to recovery. Maria Campbell's *Halfbreed* (1973), the Vancouver-set chronicle of a Métis drift-life at the margins of racism, drugs and prostitution, gives these breakages recuperative framing. Vincent L. Mendoza unfolds a Creek-Mexican ancestry and life before and after Vietnam in *Son of Two Bloods* (1996) in which he moves towards the necessary sense of his own center. Tiffany Midge's *Outlaws, Renegades and Saints: Diary of a Mixed-Up Half-breed* (1996) takes the form of verse autobiography for her hard-lived Sioux and city legacy, a work of movement from self-breakage into what on first view might well have been unlikely self-possession. Linda Hogan in *The Woman Who Watches Over the World: A Native Memoir* (2001) writes the redemptive Chickasaw chronicle of illicit early love, alcoholism, injury, and her mothering adoption of two Lakota sisters.

Collaborative or "as told to" writings, with footfalls in an early 1930s landmark like *Black Elk Speaks* as the sayings of an Oglala Sioux elder under the editorial rearranging of John Neihardt, has met with different kinds of continuance and from time to time contention. Who exactly wrote what? Subsequent co-written volumes likewise have met with doubts. *Lame Deer. Seeker of Visions: The Life of a Sioux Medicine Man* (1972), with Richard Erdoes, even so offers a Lakota self-narrative seemingly spontaneous in its visionary memories of rite into manhood, BIA schooling, the death of his same-name grandfather in the Miles cavalry attack of 1877, the Ghost and Dun Dances, and for all his personal drift, eventual rise to medicine man. Mary Crow Dog's *Lakota Woman* (1990), again with Richard Erdoes, reads unyieldingly in its account of abused girlhood, boarding school, reservation drugs and drinking, and AIM marriage and politics with Leonard Crow Dog.[7] Greg Sarris's *Keeping Slug Woman Alive: A Holistic Approach to Indian Texts* (1993) pivots the other way, virtual if not actual autobiography in the guise of an essay-sequence as to his adoptive California upbringing under the guidance of the Cache Creek Pomo weaver-medicine woman Mabel McKay.

In her chapbook, *Claiming Breath* (1992), Diane Glancy, who describes herself as of "Arkansas backhill culture mixed with Cherokee heritage,"[8] imagistically formulates yet another style of first-person voice, hybrid yet perfectly whole as to its operating terms and conditions:

> I want to explore my memories & their relational aspects to the present. I was born between 2 heritages & I want to explore that empty space, that place-between-two-places, that walk-in-2-worlds. I want to do it in a new way.[9]

She, like Momaday, Silko, Vizenor, Janet Campbell Hale, Carter Revard and Jim Barnes, puts the literary imagination as much as factuality to the fore. The stance signals astute awareness of the authorial poetics, even ventriloquism, at work.

From the outset, and then increasingly, Native self-writing has steered an unusual double-path. How far can the writer simply assume rights of self-story? How far is there obligation, the self as synecdoche, to carry the voice of a larger Native identity? The issues persist even as they get subsumed into the text being composed. But whether under the rubric of "true story" or the altogether more oblique remit of autofiction and other forms of literary self-in-the-mirror, Native lineaged autobiography continues to extend parameters.

***

Whichever pathway is to be allowed into Momaday's life-writing, his Kiowa origins and its creation story, Navajo and Pueblo upbringing, or sense of the Southwest as iconographic, there can be no doubt as to his conscious reference to imagination. In his celebrated 1970 essay "The Man Made of Words," in an account of a meteor storm in 1833 as an abiding disaster omen to the Kiowa, he gives a succinct touchstone as to how fact and the act of imagination fuse in the process of story-making:

> Do you see what happens when the imagination is superimposed upon the historical event? It becomes a story. The whole piece becomes more deeply invested with meaning.[10]

The Names, the second of his autobiographies, is yet more explicit in underscoring the modern narrator-self in conjuncture with tribal-specific ways of disclosure. At one level the story follows a clear enough chronological line: the Momaday born of Kiowa father and part-Cherokee mother, raised on Navajo and Jemez Pueblo reservations where his parents were teachers and artists, and the eventual Stanford PhD. At another, however, it works in the impress of spoken tradition:

> In general my narrative is an autobiographical account. Specifically it is an act of imagination. When I turn my mind to my early life, it is the imaginative part of it

> that comes first and irresistibly into reach, and of that part I take hold. This is one way to tell a story. In this instance it is my way, and it is the way of my people.[11]

The Way to Rainy Mountain anticipates the doubling. Momaday highlights his own life journey against that of the Kiowa people from Montana to Oklahoma, the latter told as a series of twenty-four triads: personal history, family history, calendar history, and tribal-mythic history. The outcome is one of contending, yet brilliantly complementary, runs of narrative. Something analogous happens in *The Names*, his own "isolated, yet fragmented and confused, images" (61) played against the journey he undertakes to Tsoai, Wyoming's Devils Tower (literally *Tso-aa* or rock-tree in Kiowa) in quest of beginnings and heritage. However literal the sweep of New Mexico, Oklahoma, Arizona and the Dakotas as Indian Country, or of the lives and family played out within their sound and sight as locale, he could not more insist on, for him, their inwardly memorial and visionary resonance. Imagining, or "reflections" (161) as he calls them, takes on special force throughout *The Names.*

He so speaks of his closing journey to *Tso-ai* (in his spelling) as implicating him in a double response: "I saw with my own eyes and with the eyes of my own mind" (167). A better reflexive marker would be hard to invoke. For each phase of *The Names* works in precisely this manner, the present-day actual with the past-time actual, the present-day imaginary with the past-time mythical. Time, place, tribe, origin, genealogy: Momaday has each deftly circle round, and into, the other, within the one coordinated autobiographical disclosure.[12]

First there is the summoning of his mixed genealogy. For his paternal Kiowa people he begins from their creation myth as the Kwuda who emerged from a hollow log, itself to become the motif also at the close of *The Names* – "a fallen tree, the hollow log there in the thin crust of ice" (167). The remembrance to follow includes his naming ceremony as Tsoai-talee by Pohd-lohk, step-great-grandfather; the life of Mammedaty, his horseman grandfather buried at Rainy Mountain Cemetery; and his father Huan-toa, or Alfred Morris Mammedaty, caught on the cusp of prior tribal and modern 1920s life, wanderer, teacher, and watercolorist (and who would use Al Momaday as his *nom de peinture*). His maternal Cherokee-white line he invokes through his beauteous mother Natachee, her grandmother Natachee and the marriage into the Galyan-Scott-McMillan dynasty with its different roots in Anglo and Scots-Irish Appalachia and Cajun Louisiana. This signifies family as literal mosaic, fragment and photograph, yet also, and more fugitively, as fictions of, and in, memory.

It leads him to call up the last Kiowa sun dance in 1887; life in Navajo country or *Dine bikeyah* in the 1930s; his white grandfather, Theodore Scott, photographed at Fort Sam Houston playing the banjo of his hill forbears; and Jemez Day School as among his "most vivid and deeply cherished memories" (117–18). Each, along with the references-back to Kiowa tribal devastation brought on by smallpox in 1839–1840 and measles in 1892, or his childhood sense of query to the point of near bafflement as to "'how to be a Kiowa Indian" (101), or his first horse with its harking back to the Kiowa as a horse culture and its change of visual line for him ("I had a different view of the world" 155), provokes a reach into fact but also as a call to imagination ("I lay the page aside, I imagine" 93).

Landscape, equally, is made subject to these double auspices, a Southwest at once actuality and yet vision, the one given time and yet always a species of metatime. Whether Jemez Pueblo, or Gallup in New Mexico with its iconic Route 66, or Rainy Mountain and its cemetery or, en route to the Kiowa homeland, *Tso-ai*, the literal topography takes on its own imagist wrap, an implied immanence to township, mesa, desert and horizon. The account of Monument Valley works typically, landscape if in shape and timeline best accommodated in Navajo then whose perfect linguistic fit Momaday seeks to emulate in his own prose:

> The valley is vast. When you look out over it, it does not occur to you that there is an end to it. You see the monoliths that stand in space, and you imagine that you have come upon eternity. They do not appear to exist in time. You think: I see that time comes to an end on this side of the rock, and on the other side there is nothing forever. I believe that only in *dine bizaad*, the Navajo language, which is endless, can this place be described, or even indicated in its true character. Just there is the center of an intricate geology, a whole and unique landscape which includes Utah, Colorado, Arizona, and New Mexico. The most brilliant colors in the earth are there, I believe, and the most extraordinary land forms – and surely the coldest, clearest air, which is run through with pure light. (68-9)

The sustained imagining of the Southwest's geology, its time, air and light, as of the tribal and family lineages it has hosted and which are shown to have been bound into, and around, the name Navarre Scott Momaday, gives *The Names* its distinction. The self is imagined as having been absorbed into the non-self of landscape, natural chronology, optics, temperature, even language, not to say the hollow log of Kiowa origins and the lives that have been lived in its footfalls. It makes for autobiography simply luminous in the telling.

***

In a 1986 interview Leslie Marmon Silko gives her version of the place of story in Laguna community life and tradition:

> The key to understanding storytellers and storytelling at Laguna Pueblo is to realize that you grow up not just being aware of narrative and making a story or seeing a story in what happens to you and what goes on all around you all the time, but just being appreciative and delighted in narrative exchanges.[13]

If the observation holds for spoken storytelling, that of live mouth and ear, so it can be said to have been adapted to written script. *Storyteller* (1981), certainly, could not better be thought Silko's individual endeavor to shadow these spoken "narrative exchanges," the text as enactive text-and-image, a composite of story, poem, song, and photography shaped into cyclical life writing.

Silko acknowledges at the outset her own paradox of *writing* oral heritage through the figure of Aunt Susie, protectress, Carlisle educated teacher, and archivist of Laguna life and family:

> This is the way Aunt Susie told the story.
> She had certain phrases, certain distinctive words
> she used in her telling.
> I write when I still hear
> her voice as she tells the story. (7)

Oral-written, the speaking voice overheard as it were, makes a perfect point of entry. Each component text within a text, to include the unfolding line of visual work, speaks in equal weight with the other, interactive and simultaneous voice yet none unduly more privileged than the other.

The pattern is established at the outset. Aunt Susie herself, and Great Grandma A'mooh and Grandpa Hank, speak as though live, a continuum, to which Silko supplies a species of gloss in interlocutions like "Storyteller" (17–32) and "Storytelling" (94–98). The point is made explicit in "The Storyteller's Escape" (247–53):

> With these stories of ours
> we can escape almost anything
> with these stories we will survive. (247)

Silko's white Marmon family is given equal play alongside her Laguna family, rarely more touchingly than in the story of Grandpa Marmon's refusal to bow to anti-Indian prejudice in an Albuquerque hotel ("These are my sons" he tells the manager in a proud show of paternity 17). Real-life history weaves into poem-chronicle or legend throughout. Aunt Susie's story of the drowned children who become butterflies (7–15) offers an opening instance. The Yellow Woman episode (54–62) gives a story of present-day love told as coyote myth. The episode of the golden feathered rooster which Silko unfolds in a letter to the poet James Wright develops into a wonderfully Aesopian story (226–7). Likewise the comic-absurd story "Uncle Tony's Goat" (171–6) Silko retells from the Acoma poet Simon Ortiz.

The actual includes references back into history: "Grandpa Stagner had a wagon and team and water drilling rig. He traveled all over New Mexico drilling wells" (88). It can summon the near-contemporary, like the police encounter and racism in "Tony's Story" (123–29). It can be personal memory as when the author remembers an encounter with a bear: "When I was thirteen I carried an old 30–30 we borrowed from George Pearl (77–8)." The mythic can be a Pueblo creation story ("The world was already complete/even without white people./There was everything/including witchery"' 130); a vignette of tricksterism ("One time/Old Woman Ck'o'yo's/son came in/from Redleaf town...He asked the people/ 'You people want to learn some magic?"'111–21); a Mexican-Pueblo courtship told as coyote fable ("Coyote holds a full house in his hand," 257–65); a corn fertility parable ("The Go-Wa-Peu-Zi Song" 158); or a Spider Woman sexual drama of love and fate ("Estoy-eh-Muut and The Kunideeyahs" 140–54).

Silko also extends her range beyond the pueblo ("The hills and mesas around Laguna/were a second home to my father..." 160). She writes in a letter to Lawson F. Inada in September 1975, "The purple asters are growing in wide fields around the rocks past Mesita clear to the Sedillo Grant" (170). Centered on Laguna pueblo life as may be, *Storyteller* also has no shortage of allusion to Hopi, Navajo, Sioux and Apache culture, typically the opening image of "a tall Hopi basket" with its inlaid woven grasshopper or Hummingbird Man (1) and "A Geronimo Story" (212–23) as the near mythic cavalry pursuit and escape version of the legendary Apache fighter yet also magical and holy deer-whisperer.

Throughout Silko keeps her reader-listener aware of the protocols in play. Introducing a Laguna-Keres myth to do with Acoma place she issues a reminder of how story, tribally, is by necessity a shared circle and consent:

> The Laguna People
> always begin their stories
> with "humma-hah":

> that means "long ago."
> And the ones who are listening
> say "aaaa-eh" (38)

Yet, equally, she reserves her own margin to adapt, transform, collate, as imaginative form requires and as, in fact, oral tradition itself has always allowed:

> I know Aunt Susie and Aunt Alice would tell me stories they had told me before but with changes in details or descriptions. The story was the important thing and little changes here and there were really part of the story. There were even stories about the different versions of the stories and how they imagined these differing versions came to be. (227)

This could virtually also serve as *Storyteller*'s prospectus, Silko's authorial guidance as to the interaction of oral and written, Native-spoken and Native-scriptural, in the delivery of her own self-telling.

***

Gerald Vizenor has long pitched for a trickster aesthetic of voice, subversive of received assumptions as to Native "identity" and in his life-writings tactically playing the self-aware author. Rarely has that more been on display than in his autobiography and its very titling as *Interior Landscapes; Autobiographical Myths and Metaphors* (1990). Native, and in particular Chippewa-Ojibwe city tricksterism, so can align with reflexive textual and postmodern circling from his own acknowledged readings in Derrida and Baudrillard.

The full page opening black and white photograph offers "Clement Vizenor and son Gerald, in Minneapolis, 1936." As an image of parent and child affection, it looks replete. Smiling, open shirted, a father in fedora holds his two year old in protective arms. The boy, bright eyed, wrapped, although the subject of the camera, appears to be monitoring its very action. Behind them lie piled up bricks and two stern, crumbling houses, one with a curtained window. The picture, however, contains more than a few dark hints of prophecy.

First, Clement Vizenor, "crane descendant" (3) and "reservation-born mixed-blood in dark clothes" (22), Chippewa-Ojibwe house painter and ladies man from White Earth, Minnesota, within a year would be found murdered with his throat cut on another Minneapolis street. Police left the murder an "unsolved," a brawl perhaps, or a jilted husband's revenge, at any rate one more "Indian" who had got himself killed and bequeathed himself only in name. Fatherless, his son would be quickly deposited with relatives, or fostered out, by his feckless yet eventually three times married Swedish American mother, Laverne Lydia Peterson. It was a young life that was far from protected, despite the benign intervention of his feisty, irascible Anishinaabe grandmother, Alice Beaulieu, herself, in trickster mode, to enlist his aid in persuading a blind younger man of her enduring physical beauty and to become her husband. Vizenor's self-authoring, in life, as later in script, becomes as much necessity as calling.

That process finds its life-shape as he evolves from Minneapolis "mixed-blood fosterling" to Native American writer-professor, from the Boy Scout who camps on grounds "stolen from tribal people by the federal government" (62) to adult enrolled member of the Chippewa-Ojibwe White Earth Reservation. Throughout all of *Interior Landscapes* he emphasizes yet further paradox: the GI sent to Korea, and by chance of having a name at the end of the alphabet assigned to a unit in Camp Chitose, Japan, transmutes from soldier into author ("Mount Fuji over my typewriter...my liberation was the military in Japan" 128); the mixed-blood Native American who fantasizes a new life as a re-incarnated Lafcadio Hearn; and the returnee soldier who, on demobilization, studies for a technical qualification at New York University but who, after Asian areas studies at Minnesota University, becomes successively city activist, journalist, then professor at Bemidji, the University of Minnesota, Santa Cruz, Oklahoma, Berkeley, and in due course the University of New Mexico, and one of the most published writers in the Native literary canon.

The other kind of self-authoring finds its shape in the "Vizenor" of his books. The classroom Minnesota youngster who dreamed up Erdubbs MacChurbs as his *alter ego* storyteller, and an early manifestation of his taste for baroque naming, has become one of the most voluble of Native authors. A literary output of well over thirty volumes accrues to his name. This, and each other paradox, *Interior Landscapes* makes into the one narrative spectrum, a present of interacting pasts.

The span runs from "Families of the Crane," with its allusion to Anishinaabe-named clan systems, through to "Honor Your Partners," partly a credo of Vizenor's own postmodern improvisations and tactics, and partly an account of the violent, and far from communitarian, threats against him from AIM members for having dared criticize their politics of Red Power as radical chic. The twenty nine "autobiographical myths and metaphors," or first-person fictions, each dated yet gapped one from another, serve as interfoliations, discrete yet at the same time complementary panels of memory.

Not inappropriately he sees himself early on in the Earthdiver role of Anishinaabe Creation myth, a postmodern Earthdiver, however, as likely to call upon a Eudora Welty, Michel Tournier, Primo Levi, William Scheick or Michel Foucault all of whom supply prefatory quotations, as upon tribal legends of Nanabozho, generic begetter of the Anishinaabe. This tribal cum postmodern blend, in fact, becomes the very hallmark of *Interior Landscapes.* A reference to Ishi, last of the Yahi, eventually the residential maker of museum artifacts in San Francisco, foreshadows his own academic tenure at Berkeley. Anishinaabe legacies of Nature, pictographs carved on bark, he connects to his lifelong taste for the dynamic stillness of haiku and for Matsuo Basho as haiku master. He ponders another kind of connection between Hollywood and "The Indian" in recalling that his mother, a frequenter of Depression-era movies, fell for his handsome mixed-blood father because of a resemblance to George Raft. His father's death likewise calls up an overlap of two worlds: "Clement William must have misremembered that tribal web of protection when he moved to the cities from White Earth Reservation" (26).

One-time classroom day dreaming finds its army counterpart when he tells a none too interested officer in Japan "I want to be a writer" (126). As he moves into authorship, so he finds himself more and more authored by his own truest subject: Native America in all its historic mixed-blood windings. Patronizing white school authorities metamorphose into "the new fur traders" (185), a nice reference back to an ancestry which calls up his own *métis* or French Canadian Chippewa-Ojibwe mixed family, the Vézinas, whose name was mis-transcribed into Vizenor by a then Indian Agent. Vizenor's own "trickster signature" (263) as storyteller, two centuries on, might well be thought a textual making good. In the National Guard he thinks himself "a mixedblood featherweight" (80), his boxing that of a kind of shadow tribal warrior. "Death Song for a Rodent," a vignette of his remorse on shooting a squirrel, again suggests linkage between past and present, the modern hunter in disregard of woodland etiquette.

As journalist his purview widens to include reporting the suicide of a twelve year old Dakota Sioux boy, Dane White, also inadequately parented, and then detained in a prison cell for school truancy; the murder trial of Thomas James White Hawk, a killer for sure yet, on Vizenor's long held reckoning, also a victim of "cultural schizophrenia" (289); and, in "Avengers at Wounded Knee," his keen understanding of the Seventh U.S. Cavalry's massacre of Big Foot and his Minneconjou Sioux (nearly 300 in all) at South Dakota's Wounded Knee Creek in 1890, and yet, at the same time, his un-pious take on the Dennis Banks style of warrior bravura during the 1973 protest with its drugs, guns and even limousine service which he calls "a revolutionary tribal caravan" (237). He re-creates his own haunting by skinwalkers or tribal poltergeists, in a Santa Fe room where, previously unknown to him, there have been painful deaths. He also recalls an article he once wrote for the *Minneapolis Tribune* which indicts a University of

Minnesota archaeological dig as tribal desecration. With just the right working blend of seriousness, yet trickster provocation, he proposes a "federal bone court to hear the natural rights of buried human bones" (258).

These interfolding domains of Native and white, city and reservation, America and Japan, street and campus, amount to a life remembered always as simultaneity and yet contradiction. In this they take their cue from an observation by N. Scott Momaday, his greatly admired co-spirit: "Story-telling," he quotes from Momaday's address to the First Convocation of American Indian Scholars, is "a process in which man invests and preserves himself in the context of ideas."[14]

The point holds exactly for Vizenor's own "survival trickeries on the border" (73). He indicts fixed categories of "Indian" as Hollywood or TV silhouette, or as social science case study, or, perhaps above all, as prime exhibit in the annals of victimry. *Interior Landscapes* unravels a life consciously imagined in all its contradance: self-possession as textual process, Native modernity from out of Native ancestralism, city from reservation, Indian, in the term Vizenor has made his own, as postindian.[15]

***

In opening *Bloodlines: Odyssey of a Native Daughter* with a familiar dedication, "For All My Relations," Janet Campbell Hale speaks ancestrally, for a Native tie into history. Two insets follow, first the memory of a village Coeur d'Alene raven prophecy as to the arrival of three Black Robes ("By then everybody knew who the terrible enemy was" xv), then a turtle clan dream of rejoined family despite having been "stepped on, broken into a million little pieces" (xxxi). Throughout the life-account that follows these Native flows and contra-flows are plaited into a personal focus, a balance-sheet of loss and gain, scar and healing. Hale indicts mainstream racism but also gives unblinkered recognition to Native miscreancy. Each can be said to represent how she develops her own version of Momaday's "being what we imagine."

At an immediate level *Bloodlines* could not more be portraiture of life caught within poverty, the marred childhood of a hostile mother and often absentee father, alcohol, disruptive flits ("twenty-one schools in three states" 34), the marital violence of her second marriage ("I was absolutely destitute, staying not at a battered wife's shelter but at a welfare hotel" 80), and vulnerable single-mother struggles of food-stamps and tenancy ("We had to move again – this time to a ratty suite above Mission and South Van Ness" 100). Itinerancy, son in tow, means townships and cities across California, Washington, Idaho and Oregon and from Tijuana to Vancouver. Eventual Berkeley and UC Davis education yield a pathway into self-possession, and with it fulfillment of the aborning urge to written word long presaged in her childhood poetry and stories and which eventually secures different visiting writer-professor academic berths.

The set-backs, even the intermittent returns to Yakima reservation in Wapato, Washington, underline her sense of the irony of a heritage whose Coeur d'Alene name translates from the French as "heart of steel" (145) as does the history of the name Campbell anglicized, and so appropriated, as a version of her great-grandfather's name of Cole-man-née (170). Even so, Hale makes her own counter-appropriation not only in *Bloodlines* but her novel, *The Jailing of Cecelia Capture* (1985), which shares a fair degree of autobiographical material. The outcome is a life told to its own commanding rhythm, Hale's self-aware authorial lens. However much seeming straight-from-the-heart-chronicle (it has received praise as oral narrative) it actually draws upon a savvy sense of design, the alignments and contrasts of an author-autobiographer always shrewdly in control. The eight "autobiographical essays" (xxii) are so to be seen as orchestration, each panel a monitoring time-present adroitly folded into time-past.

It is in this respect that *Bloodlines* as autobiographical text gives every grounds to Hale's observation "real life comes into play only insofar as it can serve the purpose of art" (15). An early sequence she titles "Autobiography in Fiction" brackets childhood first doodlings in "three Big Chief tablets" to the "much later...writer of novels" (4), even imagining what it would be to invent a persona called Julia whose life shadows her own. Julia, too, is to be seen as mixed-blood, aging, given a drink problem, with a brother in Vietnam, and finally confronted with her mother's hospital frailty even as her own daughter grows out of girlhood. To good purpose the text speaks of "fiction tapestry" (11), "fiction and fact" (12), "re-arrangements" (12), as if to underline awareness of the account's scripting, its deliberateness of imaginative pattern. It makes a perfect route-marker, working rules-of-the-game, for how the autobiography unfolds, the protocols that have gone into its writing and which by implication hold for its reading.

Like Maxine Hong Kingston's *China Men* (1980), *Bloodlines* does a subtle trade in historical family. The mother's setbacks ("We're so poor, Mom and me, so damned poor" 30) play against her un-maternal capacity to demean Hale ("a master, an absolute master of verbal abuse" 60). The Coeur d'Alene and Kootenay legacies turn and re-turn, mother, father, sisters, in-laws, the promised but never delivered tribal help, the memory of being cruelly excluded from a family July 4th, and her own final call to mothering of her own illness-shrunken mother ("My mom is gone. In the end there are no resolutions. Only an end" 86). The few respites achieved in childhood and adolescence transition into her being "a young welfare mother" (96), belted in the eye by her second husband, and then both amazed and hushed by the family at the discovery of being descended also from Dr. John McLoughlin, "Father of Oregon" (139). The image of the Chippewa wife of this touted Irish American pioneer is foisted on the young Janet as a model of what it is to be a "good Indian" – meaning compliant, "white," and whose marriage, together with McLoughlin himself as both great man yet un-exemplary in his treatment of extended family, she researches on a Newberry Library fellowship in 1984. Excavating this genealogy re-enforces her resolve to contest all versions of the "good Indian" ("I didn't care to be a good Indian" 113). McLoughlin, and his role in her history, she further delineates through Gram Sullivan, shared descendant and kinswoman and as Hale imagines her – her story, even her facial appearance – a species of persona, herself mirrored in earlier incarnation.

A speaking tour takes Hale to Bear Paw, Montana, where she conjures into being her own Coeur d'Alene grandmother's unwitting part in the flight of Chief Joseph and his Nez Percé in 1877. In imagination, she writes, "I saw her, my grandmother" (152). The two stories elide, her grandmother's, her own, even the detail of seeing where the anti-Indian bullets of racists have nicked the memorial plaque of Joseph's surrender. A 1992 visit to the Coeur d'Alene reservation in Idaho ("I live in New York with my third husband" 163) reminds of her father's Coyote stories but also his random and sometimes drink-fueled mistreatment of her. The remembered fantasy of a childhood ideal Native homeland contrasts with the actuality of "my poor, transient childhood" (186). Back in Spokane she sees (but leaves un-named) the film *Thunderheart*, the 1992 Michael Apted/Val Kilmer screen story of a part-Sioux FBI agent set down to solve murder in tribal South Dakota. "On the rez he learns Who He Is" (187) she observes laconically, with capital letters for emphasis. It points both to her own hard-fought intimacies of Native legacy and a latest "Indian" story-line she dubs "action-packed and full of clichés" (187). Among Native-authored autobiographies *Bloodlines* assumes a rare niche in imagining the gaps between the two.

***

The ebullience of Carter Revard's poetry and essay-work equally suffuses his autobiographical writing, the two volumes given over to a life-span from childhood in his Osage-Ponca 1930s Oklahoma Dust Bowl dynasty and through to Emeritus Professorship of medieval literature and linguistics at Washington University, Missouri. His prolegomena, "To The Reader," in *Winning the Dust Bowl*, gives off indicative density:

> This book tells of growing up in a mixed-blood family of Indian and Irish and Scotch-Irish folks…It moves from Oklahoma to Oxford to the Isle of Skye, to Jerusalem, Paris, and the Isle of Patmos, to Knossos, Bellagio, St. Louis, Cahokia Mounds, and California. These are stories of Poncas and Osages, of the American Indian Movement and urban Indian centers. Some are powwow stories, some Oxford fables; some talk of racing greyhounds and stealing watermelons, others of bootlegging and bankrobbing. (xiii)

Revard rarely delivers less than the full menu. The contributions to *Family Matters, Tribal Affairs* read in kind with *Winning the Dust Bowl*, albeit allowing that the latter assumes more of a collagist styling as interstitial verse, photography, and diary. His different speculative panels possess their own winning variety, Oklahoma land-and-oil politics to Old English prosody, growing deafness and memories of sound to Las Vegas as neon kitsch. The sum translates into life-writing always busy but not at the expense of aplomb.

Each major increment of Revard's history gets its accord starting from Pawhuska, Osage capital and his Oklahoma Indian Agency birthplace. Revard hardly shies from acknowledgment of a life fed by learning, books, libraries, and an eventual creative and scholarly repertoire of his own. Early Buck Creek country-schoolhouse learning and a University of Tulsa scholarship leads into his Oxford Rhodes Scholarship and Yale Ph.D followed by several decades of academic life in St. Louis. Much as the portraiture necessarily includes the campus, library holdings of fabliaux and manuscript, it also moves well beyond the professorial cv. *Family Matters, Tribal Affairs* vows "a community of words on Indian ground" (x). *Winning the Dust Bowl* speaks of placing "a meadow…of history and autobiography" around poems that look out to "people, places, and happenings from 1931 to the present" (xiii). The use of meadow as image astutely points beyond academia.

The Oklahoma dynasty in which "there was always plenty of trouble and strife" (*Family Matters*, 11) gives a further nonacademic touchstone. Early in life he is required to give carcass feeds and dawn exercise to greyhounds owned by the Kendall family who employ him in occasional work. Teenagery is "full of miserable moments" (63), boy-consciousness, smallness in competitive sport. His recollections step back, a touch Bonny and Clyde-ishly, to both bootlegging relatives and Uncle Carter Jump's parole after an attempted bank robbery. A key figure is Aunt Jewell, Ponca matriarch, whose subtle ancestral humanity and ministrations he eulogizes in the poem "An Eagle Nation." His Osage "Thunder-ceremony" naming as Nom-peh-wah-the he invokes with pride, the very touchstone of heritage. His recognition of AIM and the significance of the Wounded Knee/Pine Ridge Occupation in 1973 bespeaks a politics far from those of any university. To be factored in is the plethora of overseas travel, the UK of the Cotswolds and Hebrides, the Mediterranean of Lake Como and rural Greece, and his own ongoing activism at the St. Louis-based American Indian Center of Mid-America (AICMA). Throughout, and in splashes of color, there is the relish of animal and avian life, coyotes and birdsong, interests imaginatively further developed in a body of later verse addressed to jurassic and related evolutionary genetics.

This abundance, however, is carefully framed, each volume unfettered by mere chronology. In this respect, *Family Matters* can typically engage in a reverse "Columbus discovers map" ("Report to the Nation: Repossessing Europe"), with the author positioned as scriptural Coyote – *Special Agent Washazhe No. 2,230.* With just an echo of Mark Twain, Revard guys Europe as high civilization, a seeming "report" on new-old territory to mirror the colonialism that seized Native lands in the Americas. In "How Columbus Fell from the Sky and Lighted up Two Continents" he ponders "Columbianism" as discovery myth in the contexts of both Osage and Navajo creation myth and Milton's *Paradise Lost*, the writer-scholar's reach into paratextual flourish.

Winning the Dust Bowl opts as much for autobiographical commentary as history, each poem indeed glossed for occasion and context. "Training Greyhounds" so balances the account of hard-chore kennel work with a verse racetrack story. The seven-part "Indian Survival" links Osage-Ponca cultural and sovereignty history to each particularizing poem. Coyote fare underwrites the Ponca nation's un-vanished continuance as expressed in a closing poem like "After Sand Creek," with its allusion to tribal song: "*We recognize that song. It's one that we still sing*" (203). Revard's best forte, throughout, lies in bringing to the hinterlands of his life a considerable poetics.

***

The subtitle to Jim Barnes's *On Native Ground: Memoirs and Impressions* lends the working key, memory as theatre given a poet's tuning – his "inland sky" as he engagingly calls it in one of the inter-foliated poems (37). Like Revard, Barnes has lived a life of teaching and books and yet also of pursuits far beyond. His east Oklahoma birth in 1933 to a family at once Anglo-Welsh and Choctaw finds definition in the hard-scrub landscape of LeFlore County's Fourche Maline bottoms and Holson Creek hills. Childhood and World War II coming-of-age takes its place inside topography of smallholding, tenant share-cropping, animals, fish and birdlife, arrowheads, bones and petroglyphs.

Chafed, a touch stir-crazed, he steps west in 1951–1959 to lumberjack in Oregon before college study both in Oklahoma and Arkansas. Thereafter, he becomes the professor-author and writer-in-residence at Truman State University (cofounding *The Chariton Review*) with a late stint at Brigham Young, and with intervening writing and translation fellowships in Bellagio, Lausanne, Paris and Munich. This trajectory of "Indian Country" Oklahoma, Northwest logging and Missouri classroom, Europe as repository of Homeric Greece, *Rinascimento* Italy, a France of Baudelaire, the Impressionists and Picasso through to the latter-day Metro – together with French Switzerland and Bavaria's Villa Walberta – he makes over into formidably elegiac narrative.

Not the least of his "memoirs and impressions," reflexively one might say, lies in setting forth desiderata for "the art of making" – "irony," "vantage point," "tone" – qualities he suggests, to take the writing "beyond subject" (235) and "against pretentious self-absorption" (191). In part this is the poet speaking, in part the seasoned magazine editor. His own autobiography acts on these prompts to a tee: contemplative ("The Fourche Maline River and Holson Creek flow through much of what I have written" 3), honed ("I fell in love with the art of writing twenty years before I knew what had afflicted me" 49), and elegiac yet without saccharin ("I was raised in Choctaw country...and count myself one-eighth *Chahta*. I was raised on the language and foods, practically all that was left us then of the culture" 117).

Choctaw and related seams supply history, and also image, throughout *On Native Ground*, whether mounds, bones, trails, arrowheads, or even books ("I am reading Angie Debo's *The Rise of the Choctaw Republic* [of] when the Choctaw Nation was struggling for national autonomy" 97). But they do so also within each other domain: the still larger "Great Southwest" (115), the sumptuous Cascades and alluvial Willamette Valley (though he writes "I knew, finally, that I would not find in Oregon what I had left Oklahoma for" 134), together with the Paris that stirs his poetry, *le midi*, the Montreux of authors as divergent as Hemingway, Rousseau, Dostoevsky and Rilke, and the Bellagio where by Lake Como and the castles his imagination summons Pliny and Dante.

In other words Barnes gives simultaneous place to "Indian Country," the America of Oklahoma and the Pacific Northwest, and the Europe of cultural encounter and voyage. All play their part in forging the remembered "geography," past and present, of the self so adroitly summoned in *On Native Ground*, itself as Barnes fully acknowledges its own further act of self-authorship. This goes a long way in giving his autobiography its measure, a Native-heritaged writer bound into mixed Choctaw family origins yet however wholly alert to the one signature then unwilling to let that be all-defining. His stance as author, moreover, invites controversy:

> There have been many, many anthologies...to tell us just who are the American Indian writers, just who this and who that, along with pedigree...But we must not be misled. The writer is first a writer, second a Native American, a black, a Chicano. (122)

Such may not be a prospectus to win over all hearts and minds.[16] But it speaks to, and from, a conviction as to the exigency of imagination in all consequential domains of authorship.

On Native Ground, assuredly, works to act upon Barnes's own sense of the need for exactitude of word, image, craft. From the opening vignette of hearing the roar of a mountain lion as an Oklahoma five-year old to his return to the Sommerville family plot in 1995, there can be no doubt of how readily he himself makes each serve the contour of his life. Whether telling the blacksmith's Choctaw story of "how crow got black" (19), the "Indian" iconography of Deadman's Trail (70), shopping in otherwise historic Bellagio ("It is a tourist town, with tourist prices...Even a mixed-blood from Oklahoma can tell that" 169), or a fond visit to Gertrude Stein's Rue de Fleurus (209), there is the contemplative verve, the formidable lyricism. Furthermore, and indicative of the whole, his travels beyond Oklahoma in no way diminish attachment to origins of family, inheritance, place. "Wherever I go," he observes in typical mode, "it seems I never get too far from home but what I am reminded of it" (259).

***

Momaday's construing of *The Names* as "an act of imagination," like his dictum "We are what we imagine" in the much-celebrated 1970 essay "The Man Made of Words," provides the most apposite of sightlines not only for his own but almost all autobiography.[17] Inevitably this entails a degree, often very large, of reflexivity, the transcript from life endemically given to signaling its own process of composition. Even those autobiographies of American selves already greatly public and so assumedly agreed, be it Benjamin Franklin, Henry Adams, Henry James or Gertrude Stein, in fact do not disguise their own circling awareness of the identity being magicked on to the page. Richard Poirier's diagnosis of "the performing self," at once "self-discovering" and "self-watching," wholly applies.[18]

In Native autobiography, however, another self-tier presses, that of at the same time *un-writing* an identity-category of "Indian" long installed as shadow, harlequinade. To write, to compose, any one Native self, and beyond wrangles about tribal-communal fealty over the "western" desideratum of the singly disclosed self, is to write against simulacrum, the preemptive myth that has passed into history as "Indian identity." But amid the stories told, and the encircling issues of identity, oral-scriptural inheritance, settler colonialism, family, reservation and city, sovereignty, and protocols of appraisal, it is hard not to be struck by the emphasis on imagination – precisely Momaday's bringing "my own imagination to bear."

From another angle Susan Sontag, in her Preface to Roland Barthes's *Writing Degree Zero*, offers the greatly useful general reminder that "the choices made by the writer always face in *two* directions: towards society and towards the nature of literature itself."[19] It may be that a celebrated French semiotician, not to say an equally celebrated American admirer like Sontag, would be the last to come to mind in an account of Native American autobiography. But the point being made strikes a right chord.

These texts, "literary" autobiographies without wishing to prejudice matters, indubitably carry their sense of history – tribal-existential and self-existential. But they equally exhibit, indeed depend upon, a force of telling, their efficacy as design, self-inscriptive voice, and always, imagination. It is in this respect, as in the lives and the ambit of "Indian" history, culture, or region they seek to encode, that they make their wholly indelible contribution.

Notes

1 *Ancestral Voice: Conversations with N. Scott Momaday*, ed., Charles L, Woodward, Lincoln: University of Nebraska Press, 1989, 57.

2 Diane Glancy, *The West Pole*, Minneapolis: University of Minnesota Press, 1997, 70. Cited also in Thomas King, *The Truth About Stories: A Native Narrative*, Minneapolis: University of Minneapolis Press, 2003, 122.

3 Carter Revard, *Family Matters, Tribal Affairs*, Tucson: University of Arizona Press, 1998, 126.

4 N. Scott Momaday, *The Way to Rainy Mountain*, Albuquerque: University of New Mexico Press, 1969; *The Names: A Memoir.* New York: Harper & Row, 1976.

5 The first chapter of *Shadow Distances*, "Louis Owens in interview with A. Robert Lee," is published in Jacquelyn Kilpatrick, ed., *Louis Owens. Literary Reflections on His Life and Work*, Norman: University of Oklahoma Press, 2004, 20–52.

6 Key historical mappings of Native life-writing, early to modern, include Hertha Dawn, *Sending My Heart Back Across the Years: Tradition and Innovation in Native*

American Autobiography, New York: Oxford University Press, 1992, and "Native American Life Writing," in Joy Porter and Kenneth M. Roemer, eds., *The Cambridge Companion to Native American Literature*, New York: Cambridge University Press, 2005, 125–44; Kendall Johnson, "Imagining Self and Community in American Indian Autobiography," in Eric Cheyfitz, ed., *The Columbia Guide to Native American Indian Literatures of the United States*, New York: Columbia University Press, 357–409; David Murray, *Forked Tongues: Speech, Writing, & Representation in North American Indian Texts*, Bloomington: Indiana University Press, 1991; David Bumble III, *American Indian Autobiography*, Berkeley: University of California Press, 1988; David Murray, "Authenticity and Text in American Indian, Hispanic and Asian Autobiography," in A. Robert Lee, ed., *First Person Singular: Studies in American Autobiography*, London: Vision Press, 1988, 177–97 and "From Speech to Text: The Making of American Indian Autobiographies," in Ian F.A. Bell and D.K. Adams, eds., *American Literary Landscapes: The Fiction and the Fact*, London: Vision Press, 1988; Arnold Krupat, *For Those Who Come After: A Study of Native American Autobiography*, Berkeley: University of California Press, 1985; Gretchen Bataille and Kathleen Sands, eds., *American Indian Women Telling Their Lives*, Lincoln: University of Nebraska Press, 1984; and David Bumble III, *An Annotated Bibliography of American Indian and Eskimo Autobiographies*, Lincoln: University of Nebraska Press, 1981.

7 In *Indian Killler* (1996) Sherman Alexie has one of his characters, Marie Polatkin, excoriate these "white" Indian texts as more cultural appropriation than acts of self-owned authentic Native voice.

8 Diane Glancy, *Claiming Breath*, Lincoln: University of Nebraska Press, 1992. 22.

9 *Claiming Breath*, 4.

10 N. Scott Momaday, "The Man Made of Words," Rupert Cosco, ed., *Indian Voices: The First Convocation of American Indian Scholars*, San Francisco: Indian Historian Press, 1970, 49–84.

11 This is taken from Momaday's italicized frontispiece to *The Names: A Memoir*, New York: Harper & Row, 1976.

12 Hertha Dawn Wong gives a perceptive account of the cyclic journey, and structure, within *The Names*: "The narrative movement of the work is from the mythical past to the Kiowa-personal to the imaginary mythical past reimagined in the present. This process parallels the very nature of autobiographical activity in which one filters past experience into the present moment. At the same time, the focus shifts from tribal to family to individual back to the family and tribal." *Sending My Heart Back Across the Years: Tradition and Innovation in Native American Autobiography*, New York: Oxford University Press, 1992, 177.

13 Kim Barnes, "A Leslie Marmon Silko Interview," *The Journal of Ethnic Studies*, Vol. 13, Winter 1986, 83–105.

14 N. Scott Momaday, "The Man Made of Words," *Indian Voices*, 1970.

15 The term postindian and the view of Native legacy it encodes is explored in Gerald Vizenor and A. Robert Lee, *Postindian Conversations*, Lincoln: University of Nebraska Press, 1999.

16 One writer to whom this would appeal, however, is David Treuer in his battling *Native American Fiction: A User's Manual*, Minneapolis: University of Minnesota Press, 2006.

17 N. Scott Momaday, *Indian Voices*, 1970.

18 Richard Poirier, *The Performing Self: Compositions and Decompositions in the Languages of Contemporary Life*, New York: Oxford University Press, 1971, xiii.

19 Barthes, Roland, *Le Degré Zéro de l'Écriture suivi de Nouveaux Essais Critiques*, Paris: Editions du Seuil, 1953. *Writing Degree* Zero, New York: Hill and Wang, 1968, Trans. Annette Lavers and Colin Smith. Preface by Susan Sontag, xiv.

Works Cited

Allen, Paula Gunn, *The Sacred Hoop: Recovering the Feminine in American Indian Tradition*, Boston: Beacon Press, 1986.

Apess, William, *A Son of the Forest: The Experience of William Apess, a Native of the Forest. Comprising a Notice of the Pequot Tribe of Indians, Written by Himself*, New York: Published by the author, 1829, 1831. A Son of the Forest and Other Writings, ed., Barry O'Connell, Amherst: University of Massachusetts Press, 1997.

Banks, Dennis, with Richard Erdoes, *Ojibwa Warrior*, Norman: University of Oklahoma Press, 2004.

Barnes, Jim, *On Native Grounds: Memoirs and Impressions*, Norman: University of Oklahoma Press, 1977.

Campbell Hale, Janet, *Bloodlines: Odyssey of a Native Daughter*, New York: Random House, 1993.

Castañeda, Carlos, *Teachings of Don Juan: A Yaqui Way of Knowledge*, Berkeley: University of California Press, 1968.

Cody, Iron Eyes, *My Life as a Hollywood Indian*, New York: Everest House, 1982.

Cook-Lynn, Elizabeth, *New Indians, Old Wars*, Urbana: University of Illinois Press, 2007.

_____, *Why I Can't Read Wallace Stegner and Other Essays: A Tribal Voice*, Madison: University of Wisconsin Press, 1996.

Copway. George, George, *The Life, History, and Travels of Kah-ge-ga-bowh (George Copwa)*, Albany: Weed and Parsons, 1847.

Cosco, Robert, ed. *Indian Voices: The First Convocation of American Indian Scholars*, San Francisco: The Indian Historian Press, 1970.

Crow Dog, Mary, with Richard Erdoes, *Lakota Woman*, New York: Grove Weidenfeld, 1990.

Erdrich, Louise, *Books and Islands in Ojibwe Country*, Washington, D.C.: National Geographic Society, 2003.

_____, *The Blue Jay's Dance: A Birth Year*, New York: HarperCollins, 1995.

Glancy, Diane, *The West Pole*, Minneapolis: University of Minnesota Press, 1997.

_____, *Claiming Breath*, Lincoln: University of Nebraska Press, 1992.

Hale, Janet Campbell, *Bloodlines: Odyssey of a Native Daughter*, New York: Random House, 1993.

Harris, LaDonna, *LaDonna Harris: A Comanche Life*, Lincoln: University of Nebraska Press, 2001.

Hogan, Linda, *The Woman Who Watches Over the World: A Native Memoir*, New York: W.W. Norton, 2001.

Hungry Wolf, Beverly, *The Ways of My Grandmothers*, New York: William Morrow, 1980.

Krupat, Arnold, ed., *Native American Autobiography: An Anthology*, Madison: University of Wisconsin Press, 1994.

Krupat, Arnold, and Swann, Brian, eds., *Here First: Autobiographical Essays by Native American Writers*, New York: Modern library, 2000.

Mankiller, Wilma, with Michael Wallis, *Mankiller: A Chief Among Her People*, New York: St Martin's Press, 1993.

Means, Russell, *Where White Men Fear to Tread*, New York: St Martin's Press, 1995.

Midge, Tiffany, *Outlaws, Renegades and Saints: Diary of a Mixed-Up Half-breed*, Greenfield Center, NY: Greenfield Review Press, 1996.

Momaday, N. Scott, *The Names; A Memoir*, New York: Harper & Row, 1976.

_____, *The Way to Rainy Mountain*, Albuquerque: The University of Arizona Press, 1969.

Occom, Samuel, "A Short Narrative of my Life," 1962. Reprinted in Bernd Peyer, ed., *The Elders Wrote: An Anthology of Early Prose by North American Indians, 1968-1931*, Berlin: Dietrich Reimer, 1982.

Owens, Louis, *I Hear the Train: Reflections, Inventions, Refractions*, Norman: University of Oklahoma Press, 2001.

_____, *Mixedblood Messages: Literature, Film, Family, Place*, Norman: University of Oklahoma Press 1998.

Penn, William, ed., *As We Are Now: Mixblood Essays on Race and Identity*, Berkeley: University of California Press, 1997.

Revard, Carter, *Winning the Dust Bowl*, Tucson: University of Arizona Press, 2001.

_____, *Family Matters, Tribal Affairs*, Tucson: University of Arizona Press, 1998.

Rose, Wendy, *The Halfbreed Chronicles and Other Poems*, Los Angeles: West End Press, 1985.

Sarris, Greg, *Keeping Slug Woman Alive: A Holistic Approach to Indian Texts*, Berkeley: University of California Press, 1993.

Silko, Lesley Marmon, *The Turquoise Ledge: A Memoir*, New York Viking, 2010.

_____, *Storyteller*, New York: Arcade/ Little Brown/Arcade, 1981.

_____, *Ceremony*, New York, Viking Press, 1977.

Swann, Brian, and Krupat, Arnold, eds., *I Tell You Now: Autobiographical Essays by Native American Writers*, Lincoln: University of Nebraska Press, 1987.

Vizenor, Gerald, *Interior Landscapes: Autobiographical Myths and Metaphors*, Minneapolis: University of Minnesota Press, 1990.

Vizenor, Gerald, and A. Robert Lee, *Postindian Conversations*, Lincoln: University of Nebraska Press, 1999.

Weaver, Jace, Womack Craig S., and Warrior, Robert, eds., *American Indian Literary Nationalism*, Albuquerque: University of New Mexico Press, 2001.

Willis, Jane, *Geniesh: An Indian Girlhood*, Tonrnot: New Press, 1973.

Woodward, Charles, ed., *Ancestral Voice: Conversations with N. Scott Momaday*, Lincoln: University of Nebraska Press, 1989.

Young Bear, Ray, *Black Eagle Child: The Facepaint Narratives*, Iowa City: University of Iowa Press, 1992.

Part II

Novel

3

Wordwalker: N. Scott Momaday Tryptich

"Wordwalker" is a term that I used to describe myself in a lecture I gave a couple of years ago. That was a very interesting idea to me...That term seems to me to suggest someone who makes his way on the basis of words, and it also has the connotation of migrant and migration, which is an important part of the Kiowa tradition. Wordwalker.

N. Scott Momaday (1989)[1]

If Native authorship has been accorded any one canonical name it is generally agreed to rest with N. Scott Momaday. This, it can be said immediately, involves no small irony: a writer from the once assumed literary margin but on the basis of *House Made of Dawn* (1968), and in its wake the life-writing of *The Way to Rainy Mountain* (1969) and *The Names: A Memoir* (1976), given huge headline standing. Almost by rote he has come to be thought the herald-founder of the Native American Renaissance, however controversial the categorization. Both at the time of the novel's publication, as subsequently, the further ambiguities were quick to gather. Somehow, as though by literary parthenogenesis, there had emerged an author and a text unique in American fiction: Native, a novel unaccommodating of stereotype, and not the least, as modern in narrative as ancestral in tribal allusion. No matter the prior authorship to which Momaday himself was heir, be it spoken or inscriptive, could claim a lineage actually far older than colonial New England or Virginia and in their wake the frontier settlement of America.

After all, was not the "Indian" portfolio sufficiently addressed by Cooper or Twain, and always each and every continuing popular-culture and screen manifestation? To follow in the 1970s, and not a little controversial on grounds of cultural appropriation, had there not been bestsellers like the Leaphorn/Chee

Navajo Tribal Police detective fiction of Tony Hillerman?[2] Did not the decade of the 1960s have its agreed fiction reading in, say, Harper Lee's *To Kill a Mocking Bird* (1960), James Baldwin's *Another Country* (1962) or Saul Bellow's *Herzog* (1964), with Kerouac's *On The Road* (1957) as the era's just prior road-novel landmark? Matters grew the more raveled in the case of *House Made of Dawn*. There could be no doubt of tribal-spoken Pueblo and Kiowa sources yet at the same time it evidently displayed savvy western-modernist credentials.

Who, it was to be asked, exactly was Momaday? Academia knew him to be the Stanford PhD with a thesis on the New England Transcendentalist and sonneteer Frederick Goddard Tuckerman, and then a university career of three subsequent decades. That would see him hold teaching posts at the University of California Berkeley and Santa Barbara, the University of New Mexico, the University of Arizona, with a visiting six months at Moscow State University. As novelist and poet what sources of Native experience was he drawing upon and then transposing into narrative? Momaday's autobiographical Kiowa mythographies supply one answer. The versification of *Angle of Geese and Other Poems* (1974), and of the collections that have followed through to *Again The Far Morning: New and Selected Poems* (2011) and *Earth Keeper: Reflections on the American Land* (2020), give another. Nor is this to overlook his tribally inflected work for children such as *Circle of Wonder: A Native Christmas Story* (1994) and *Four Arrows & Magpie: A Kiowa Story* (2006). Momaday's range includes the play-script *The Indolent Boys* first staged in 1994, and his discursive hand has its well-known outlet in *The Man Made of Words: Essays, Stories, Passages* (1998), never least the title piece with its emphasis on "the force of language" and "ecology, storytelling and the imagination."[3]

The immediate emphasis in this chapter, however, falls upon three prime texts in the Momaday oeuvre. Each offers a "modern" text but given both memorial and tactical Navajo, Kiowa, and other story-filtering. For Momaday folds into each different composition legacies of Native cultural practice, whether tribal storytelling with its spontaneity of invention as itself the story, or creation myth, or cosmology, or fabling of bear, season, land and weather. He does so, moreover, with rare virtuosity, the situating of modern Native worlds in terms of each continuing stock of community history and in not a few cases language. *House Made of Dawn*, *The Ancient Child* (1989) and *In The Presence of the Sun* (1992) not only confirm his self-nomination as "wordwalker," and in the last of these three also line-drawing artist, but his indicative verve.

***

"He had lost his place. He had been long ago at the centre, had known where he was, had lost his way, had wandered to the end of the earth, was even now reeling at the edge of the void" (104). On appearance *House Made of Dawn* seemed for many the definitive portrait of worlds in collision, Native and Euro-American, Laguna New Mexico and modern California, with the World War II Pacific and Pueblo "Indian Country" juxtaposed as two kinds of American war-zone. But where Abel indeed could be said to embody "Indian history," a casualty of conflict both outer and inner, was there not a risk of casebook victimhood, sentimentality? Nothing could have done greater injustice. For Momaday had put on offer a wholly larger grasp, the wider and deeper American history given its own inflection of voice.

The story-line, the career of Abel in his lost alcoholic displacement, can too easily be thought linear, chronological and western. The trajectory involves his unknown father and deaths of his mother and brother Vidal of TB, his battle trauma from World War II, the return to Jemez Pueblo (Walatowa or Village of the Bear as originally called), and the drinking, prison sentence for murder, drift and injury in Los Angeles, and final return to the pueblo. The novel even goes so far as to date its sections, 1945 through to 1952, a time-present which at the same time elides into time-past for Abel, his grandfather, Francisco, and his Los Angeles friends, the Navajo Ben Benally, and the white social worker Milly. For Father Olguin, who lives in the pueblo, it is chronology which summons the nineteenth-century through the journal of his clerical predecessor Father Nicolás who, unclerically, was father to Francisco.

This same trajectory, however, Momaday puts under the auspices signaled in the Laguna Pueblo words *Dypaloh* and *Qtsedaba* for a beginning and end of story as based in the oral-aural nexus of speaker and listener. In this Abel's dis-equilibrium, and his slow-won advance into recovery, is given in terms at once circular, spatial and Native-ceremonial, and which avail themselves not only of Laguna but, inter-tribally, of Navajo and Kiowa tradition. It is also in this respect that the opening and final scenes of running, the "house of dawn" mythology itself, the linked pollen, kiva, katsina and corn allusion, hold greatest importance, the signatures of a Native centering of the world. *House Made of Dawn*, thereby, transforms into the very thing of its own plotline, a fiction about, and yet at the same time itself the enactment of, Abel's healing. Throughout each of the novel's four sections Momaday keeps this weave in full imaginative play.

In "The Longhair" Francisco, ailing in leg as may be, embodies a lived con-trast to his grandson, at one with his multiple heritages of ethnicity (Laguna-Navajo-Tanoan-white), belief (he believes the solar as well as Catholic calendar), land ("an intricate patchwork of arbors and gardens" 5), and language (he chants Laguna and Spanish en route to the bus to collect Abel), as against Abel's self-fissure, his drunken return. Abel's flashback to the eagle-catching ceremony, and his unceremonial killing of the female bird, presages his own severance. In the relationship with Angela St. John he is reduced to sex-primitive, silenced "other" and "non-being" (37). The "old rhythm of the tongue" (58) eludes him. He can make no creation song, no "right words" (59). It is in this state of verbal, as much as existential, dispossession that he kills the albino, a figure of scaled lips and writhing tongue: this is a bar-fight in one way, yet, and as Father Olguin equally recognizes, Abel's vision of witchery, whiteness as in the view of Melville's Ahab both evil and blank.

"The Priest of the Sun" and "The Night Chanter" work likewise. Abel, newly released from prison, cannot hold a job, has his hands and body near broken by the cop Martinez, finds himself caught amid different kinds of attributed Indianness. In John Big Bluff Tosamah he encounters an urban trickster and cynic and yet also Kiowa fond memorialist of Rainy Mountain. Witness to a peyote cult, a circle of real and false believers, he also wins new strength from Benally's "Beautyway" and "Night Chant" as songs of Navajo/Diné healing. Where the Albino embodies whiteness as serpentine male malignancy, Millie gives him whiteness as love, an affirming feminine presence. It has justly been said often that *House Made of Dawn*, itself the translation of a Navajo phrase, not only invokes the healing "Night Chant" but actually makes it into the very rationale of the novel overall.

Abel so is put to negotiate competing worlds, a remembered Laguna order of festival, deity, ceremony, as against, typically, a law-court as the instrument of white America ("Word by word these men were disposing of him in language" 102). The stasis of his drinking contrasts with the ceremony of running, his broken hands with the repaired body, his whitened prison cell with the multicolor of Jemez Pueblo and its surrounds. In a World War II battlefield, in the face of guns, noise and an oncoming tank, he has danced a Native dance of disorder. In the Pueblo, however slow his rewakening, he re-enters the dance of Laguna time-space and health. This contrapuntal movement, one of un-balance played against balance, gives *House Made of Dawn* its unique dynamic, the circling and fine spun energy of its drama.

"The Dawn Runner" draws these seemingly divergent lines into a circular, dynamic whole. Francisco dies, Abel inherits his spirit. The grandfather's deathbed words, again an overlap of Spanish and Laguna, balance against Abel's "nothing to say" (195). "*The great organic calendar*" (198) reassumes its place: Abel takes care to provide Francisco with both a Native and Christian burial. Father Olguin, in shock, broaches understanding of Abel's double-world. Abel's last act of running, his body ritualized by ash, his mind singing "*House made of pollen, house made of dawn*" (212), and amid "canyon, mountains and the sky" (212), supplies the novel's perfect "ending." The dancer becomes the dance. Motion leads no longer away from, but towards, centeredness. Momaday has his novel exactly enact this process, its theme but also its form, with word-walking just the right cover-term.

***

Although it carries Momaday's ongoing skills of fable *The Ancient Child* has rarely met the acclaim given *House Made of Dawn*. That may in part have to do with the syndrome of second novel, or the market's pre-emptive one "ethnic" novel at a time. But either way it underplays the text's assured weave of modern Portrait of the Artist with ancestral Navajo and Kiowa legend. The alliance of Locke Setman, acclaimed San Francisco painter of middle years but long severed from his Kiowa origins, and Grey, emerging Navajo-Kiowa medicine woman in her twenties, might have gestured towards ready-made romance or homing-in. In the event Momaday's paired life-stories amount to wholly subtler narration, at once panel and collage, the modernity of a modern Native artist framed contrapuntally in dream vision. The upshot is lattice, spiral, story once again its own encirclement of mirrors.

Two prime narratives so overlap and fuse. In the one a species of psychodrama holds. For all his success ("he enjoyed celebrity" 37) Set undergoes augmenting disbelief in his art as in his terms of existence. Creative misdirection, a sense of absent world view, takes him to the point of near-death sickness. The arduous path to recovery from "numbness, a kind of paralysis" (215) will shadow the Kiowa and Piegen boy-bear myths, brother to the seven sisters, the child who came and went before metamorphosing into stellar constellation. It will involve him in a final vision quest, his unmasking into authentic self. The rooms of Set's existence, accordingly, give geometry to his evolving stages of consciousness as much as physical wellness. They include his Beach Street studio in San Francisco, the series of Manhattan and Paris art galleries, Oklahoma City's Will Rogers airport, hotel and hospital rooms, and the Navajo hogan he will finally share with Grey. Each acts a staging-post, as it were, in Momaday's sequence of the interaction for Set of modern and ancestral life. In her transition from near androgynous girl into mature medicine woman, Grey negotiates a shared evolution of identity. She acts as nurse and legatee to Set's dying ancestress Kope-mah and early girl companion to the winningly named *anciano* Worcester Meat. Horsewoman of plain and rodeo she rides the incongruously named Dog with the kinetic flair of her forerunners. In fantasy ("haunted by her reveries" 228), she sees herself as Billy the Kid's white-dressed lover, and even muse, a relationship she makes over into the chapbook which reflexively becomes part of Momaday's text. The bearer of the medicine bundle from Kope-mah that holds the clues to Set's destiny, she will become the mother-to-be of their child when they journey deep into the tribal southwest plains and color of Oklahoma and Lukachuka, Arizona. As in the case of Set, Momaday portrays her life as though to be understood liminally, lived always at the border of truth to fact and truth to dream.

Throughout the contributing folds involved in bringing Set and Grey together and locating the significance of their union, the novel works at a pace suitably unhurried. A busy surround of people and event, even so, adds density, a poetry, to the story. The telegram from Milo Mottlemare, mixed-blood preacher, that summons Set to Saddle Mountain, Oklahoma, and tells him to notify his (actually deceased) artist-father Cate who he remembers knew of "octopuses, whales, and bears" (57) and whose grave he will visit, opens into a network both dynastic and immediate. "He knew of no Grandmother Kopemah…all he had of his forebears was a sediment in his memory" (51) plays against "At forty he was in the first rank of American artists, and he was in danger of losing his soul" (36). The novel makes a ready triumph of bringing these domains into relationship, Set's West Coast gallery success as against the release of fuller imagination under tribal bear rebirth.

Time present is thereby shown to have obscured his very making. Set's adoptive other father, Bent Sandridge, also an artist, will die, leaving Set to doubly re-father himself. His love affair with Lola Bourne, warm, initially full of moral support, will yield to love and considerable erotica with Grey. Art auction sales and purchases though his agent-manager Jason give increasingly sour patina to the celebrity write-ups. Each remembrance, whether the Peter and Paul orphanage, tutoring by Sister Stella Francesca, fascination with the Ursa Major, and the career begun with his first charcoal, supplies the prologue. Yet for all the talent, as Momaday traces out Set's life, his art has become expressions of distemper, hooded, dark images of haunt.

In Grey, and Navajo-Kiowa history and land, lies the re-sourcing of creative selfhood. Momaday tells this not as some ready-made formula but in his own careful alternations of story, interposed prose poems, and conjoined swathes of metaphor. To this end he moves contrapuntally. Ts-oai bear legend oscillates with Billy the Kid fable. Grey's sexual revenge on her brute white farmboy pursuer Dwight Dicks contrasts with her intimacy with Set. The reading by which

Grey further en-words her world, and which spans the Gettysburg address, the psalms, Wallace Stevens, Joyce, and the Shakespeare of *Romeo and Juliet*, throws its light on the oral Navajo stories of her childhood. Set's final act of running, in kind with that of Abel in *House Made of Dawn*, contrasts with the stasis that has immobilized his art. Snippets from the Navajo language and Mexican Spanish give variation, and implicit narrative challenge, to the novel's English.

Indian Country, however, most supplies Momaday with his underlying lodestone, the land's restorative complexity of shape and color symbiotically stored in Native consciousness. Set approaches this recognition as he watches through his plane window:

> Coming down out of the clouds towards Oklahoma City, Set thought of puzzles. He gazed upon the immensity of red and green and yellow geometry – rectangles, triangles, squares, jigsawn shapes. The geometry rolled on forever to the skyline. Oh, but there, he thought, look; here is exception and redemption, a redeeming disorder, the opposing aesthetic of the wilderness – the green belts slashing through the boxes like limbs of lightning, like sawteeth and scythes. It was a country of rivers and creeks, prairies and plains. (57)

Momaday clearly implies the earth's turn as Art on its own terms, living ecology, a pathway into vision, and specifically the necessary taproot for Set. The styling of the passage yields symptomatic Momaday, his poet's iconographic eye, and which has notable continuance in his latter-day meditation *Earth Keeper: Reflections on the American Land* (2020).

One of the several key reflexive markers for *The Ancient Child* is struck in Book 2 of the quartet which makes up the novel in which Set looks into his studio mirror. He tries to decipher how art, his own but, by way of larger example, the prints of Hokusai and of the cave-engravers in Lascaux, have gone about the creation of image. His interior monologue speaks implicitly to Momaday's own picturing of art's alchemy, literary or visual:

> On the skylight an intermittent play of colors from the streetlamps and the traffic lights and the cars below, and the caroms of rain, each drop exploding into color, not now: there are stains, deep and indefinite, in the flashes of yellow, white, blue, green, orange, red light. And I want to believe that there are real forms there, unique, intricate forms straightly related to a deep field of receding grounds, one after another, ranging to a black infinity, the definite forms of definite things, the very things I cannot comprehend by other means (134).

To find his "definite form of definite things" Set will need to reach his own center, beyond self-dispossession, or metropolitan fame, or the glitz of art-speak and commerce. In Grey he will incrementally find and share that center, earth and body, all in the novel's presiding metaphor his hitherto absent Native bear-self's full creativity. Momaday does not actually intrude himself into the narrative but it would be hard not to hear a degree of authorial footfall.

Scholarship has done conscientious excavation of the bear framing in *The Ancient Child* as it has the Billy the Kid materials. Both come into play as far from anthropology or literal historical portrait. For the novel, start to end, is about two kinds of medicines: those of existence and art, Set and Grey as bound in passage to imaginative as to physical health. Whether American city life or Navajo-Kiowa fable, Set's palette or Grey's chapbook, Momaday can again be said to have written a novel adroitly the refraction of its own plot. The intricacies are several but there can be little doubt of the successful ply of both, the yet another unique impress of his word-walking.

***

A shared impetus holds for *In the Presence of the Sun*, Momaday's collection of poetry previous and new, his reworked fugue on the Billy the Kid sequence from *The Ancient Child*, and "A Gathering of Shields" as prose-and-visual vignettes for the iconography of different tribal signatures. Each has accompaniment in his ink and graphite washes, variously bears, buffalo, heads (his own included) and the shield sequence. The whole can justly be considered a selective imagist treasury, verse, story, soliloquy, chapbook, ekphrasis, epigram, line drawings, a thirty-year span of work and published in the 1990s that both holds up its own lantern and at the same time throws light on the career launched with *House Made of Dawn* and the autobiographies of *The Way to Rainy Mountain* and *The Names: A Memoir.*

Citing Emily Dickinson's "This is my letter to the world" he speaks in his Preface of his birthright attraction to "Tanoan, Athabascan, Spanish and English words" (xviii), a thesaurus most especially to include the *Diné bizaad* and Kiowa language of his mixed parental heritage. He also remembers his father's canvas work "which proceeds from rock paintings to hide paintings to ledgerbook drawings to modern art" (xix) along with the cubist and modernist turn of Spain's Pablo Picasso, Germany's Emile Nolde and Georg Baselitz, and Britain's Francis Bacon. The attestation that "The poems and stories, the drawings…express my spirit fairly I believe" (xx) offers no more, and no less, than the exact truth, perfect guidance into *In the Presence of the Sun.*

Perhaps inevitably two bear drawings give the gateway into the poetry, both conveying kinetic crouch, force, and yet the repose of old age. Both, too, Momaday renders as studiedly impressionist in the way they are limned. "The Bear" (3) as follow-on poem shares in temperament, the last years of one of Nature's own warrior forces of Nature. This is the bear of "somnolence," "outworn valor," almost "dimensionless." Viewed as it were "in the windless noon's hot glare" it carries scar from a bear trap, pained withers, limbs now crooked. The last stanza moves into In Memoriam:

> Then he is gone, whole,
> without urgency, from sight,
> as buzzards control,
> imperceptibly, their flight. (3)

It would be hard to miss the sense of participant intimacy, the speaker's immersion in the cyclic passage of bear and buzzard, the time of the natural order. The lines convey acceptance but also respect, an admiring grasp of the animal's "fact of courage," its cycle now completed and yet its forever un-lost example.

"Angle of Geese" (21) rightly takes hold as one of Momaday's best-known poems, a eulogy, an epiphany. The funeral of a friend's firstborn child and the "lag" of words to say anything adequate coalesces with the remembrance of his own November hunt and killing in childhood of a flying goose. The bird's power of body and symmetry, its "great shape," has labored, then fallen, and so become "quit of hope and hurt." What remains is "motionless gaze," the bird's removal from time's "dark distant flurry" yet somehow still hauntingly "alert." The speaker's poignant nexus of the two deaths, his contemplative aligning of child and bird framed by "the pale angel of time," offers an instance of Momaday at his most affecting.

The accompanying choice of Momaday's other previously published poems, along with their companion drawings, give reminders of the same redoubtable acuity of observation. "Comparatives" (5) invokes live "sunlit sea," "the drift of fronds," and "wind on waves" with a netted "fish upon the planks," in all, the one day's sight. But then the poem remembers an inland sea's "fossil fish" at once "rude in the rock" and "forever." The ripples of waters play against ancient petrification as another of the oldest of cycles. "Headwaters" (19) summons the Kiowa creation story of hollow log as tribal birth-canal. Looked upon at noon and in "the intermountain plain" it exhibits a custodial single insect and moss. Beneath any apparent stasis, however, waters nourish roots and brim into its stalks. They act as though "archaic force," headwaters as life-source at once "wild and welling." Momaday keeps his imagery tacit, the immediate local sighting also Nature's irrigational code of life.

The poems yet more explicitly Native-referenced give voice to memory, celebration, art. "The Delight Song of Tsoai-talee" (16) written under Momaday's own Kiowa name, assumes form as celebratory life-pattern in imagery from "a feather on the bright sky" to the "an angle of geese in the winter sky," the beauty of earth to that of his wife-lover Tsen-tainte. "Sun Dance Shield" (17) anticipates the later shield sequence, the Plains ceremony of self-power and medicine given its heraldry ("My life is in this shield"). "The Gourd Dancer" (22–3) memorializes Mammedaty, Kiowa dynastic ancestor, dreamer ("he dreamed of dreaming"), dancer ("old processions and returns"), honored horseman ("the reins in Mammetaty's hands"), and progenitor always for those like Momaday himself "who imagine him in his name."

"The Strange and True Story of My Life with Billy the Kid," told in the first person and a re-versioning of that penned by Grey in *The Ancient Child*, assumes the form of a 21-sequence self-diary, cameos of one of the American west's presiding legends. In "A Word on Billy the Kid" Momaday mentions "facts," however difficult he acknowledges them to establish and with the proviso "All else of what follows is imagined; nonetheless it is so" (43). The opening panel has the speaker at Jemez Pueblo, New Mexico, in 1946, witness to Navajos full of dignity and song arriving for the feast of San Diego. As the "wider world" beckons, "Billy the Kid was with me on most of these adventures" (47). The pitch is at one and the same time historic, dates and place real enough, but also a companionship imagined as though in fable or fantasy.

The verse pieces immediately following envisage Billy in lullaby ("Sleep, Billy, Billy" 48), Billy in boyhood ("already…he resembles himself in death" 49), and Billy under his birth name of Henry McCarty the witness to his mother's remarriage ("Henry imagines marriage,/The remorse and agonies of age" 50). Each ensuing piece negotiates the reality-dream boundary. "The Man in Black" relates a ghost-like meeting with "colorless" Billy dedicated only to "his own mean and exclusive survival" (51) and the prelude to "the strange and true story of my life with Billy the Kid" (52).

Subsequent poems see Billy the "fossil" (53), "coyote" (54), "whoremonger" (55), the "desperado…of felonies and broken hearts" (57), a figure of kindness who against habit can share "a plug of tobacco" (59), and the devotee of the nun Sister Blandina who visits him "at the jail in Santa Fe" (62). "Billy Fixes a Bully in His Gaze" gives witness to "the only man I have ever known in whose eyes there was no expression whatsoever" (63). "Billy the Kid, the Departure of His Soul, 14 July 1881" hears, as it were, Pat Garrett's shot, Billy to be resurrected "in dark," and "in thought" ("And you appear/And are indefinite" 67). The penultimate verse sees Billy "dead" and yet "He was always here" (68), and in the last of the verses encased in "Death and Death's dog, Time" (69). One might, for comparison, think of the Ned Kelley of Sydney Nolan's paintings, he and Billy two actual yet always fantastical outlaw avatars of American frontier and Australian outback.

"A Gathering of Shields," Plains shields to be precise each made of hardened bison hide and easily portable, signify as Momaday explains "medicine," "a unique work of art," "warrior ideal," "mask," "story," "language," "meditations that make a round of life" (74–5). His page's drawings and vignettes so work as sixteen paired styles of locution to express these ends, each shield discrete, each engendered by tribal-mythic, family or historical event. Momaday's compositions make for memorable semantics as to how the tribes, their menfolk at least, have messaged themselves to the world.

"The Shattered Sky Shield" (77), which opens, re-pictures a likely meteor storm of 1833 and as envisaged by the tribesman Give Him Back. "The Shield of Two Dreams" (107), which closes, joins daughter and father dreams, Dark Water's of the "rhythm of a running horse" and Green Shirt's of "a shield with owl feathers." Both these shields bespeak "story," picture and word in parable-like juncture. The same holds throughout. "The Shield That Came Back" (79), its drawing a fan of scissortail feathers, is matched in its story of lost fan but enduring shield. "Bote-talee's Shield" (83) combines Spider Woman drawing and legend into a shared glyph. "The Shield That Was Brought Down from Tsoai" (105) recounts how Many Dogs traded eight favorite horses with Dragonfly for "a famous shield" imagined to have been brought down from the sacred Kiowa landmark of Ts-oai. In the parallel of "rock tree" visual image and story vignette Momaday can be said to give the exact instance of his own literary shield-art.

The "New Poems" sequence reflects Momaday in untiring form. Wry erotica and population control enter the brief "Planned Parenthood" (112). Dorothy Parker wit marks a piece like "The Death of Beauty" ("She dies a beauty of repute,/Her other virtues in dispute" 112). A city dweller fantasizes returned prairie beasts in the major thoroughfare of San Francisco's Pacific Heights ("One bull, animal representation nation of the sun,/he dreams back for the brink of his hunter's heart" 119). "Scaffold Bear" (133) summons ursine myth, the speaker's sleep vision of a mutilated bear yet which still "speaks" ("I am at home to bears"). It has Momaday's signature written indelibly into its lines.

In "At Risk" (143), the last of the choices, Momaday reflects upon his writer's calling, his life's attraction to "words," "intricate etymologies," the confusions of "soul" and "time." Haunted by the dance of "ancient animals" and by "my face in the mirror of masks," he or his persona attests "there was I." It makes a necessary credo for himself as wordwalker through the galleries of novel, poetry, life-writing, essay, and the entire wider body of his writings that has been his career. Momaday, however, faces not just himself, the I am what I am. The deep wells of tribal and intercultural history that he brings to his writings give invitation to the reader, and especially those not of Native provenance, to learn from the gallery gathered in *In the Presence of the Sun*.

Notes

1 *Ancestral Voice: Conversations with N. Scott Momaday*, ed., Charles L. Woodward, Lincoln: University of Nebraska Press, 1989, 149.
2 The Hillerman series was launched with *The Blessing Way* (1970) and extends through eighteen or so thrillers to *The Shape Shifter* (2006).
3 N. Scott Momaday, "The Man Made of Words," Reprinted as separate essay in Abraham Chapman, ed., *American Indian Literature*, New York: New American Library, 96–110, and A. Robert Lee, ed., *Native American Writing*, Vol. 1, New York and Tokyo: Routledge/Edition Synapse, 2011, 27–39.

Works Cited

Baldwin, James, *Another Country*, New York: Dial Press, 1962.
Bellow, Saul, *Herzog*, New York: Viking Press, 1964.
Kerouac, Jack, *On the Road*, New York: Viking Press, 1957.
Lee, Harper, *To Kill a Mocking Bird*, Philadelphia: J.B. Lippincott, 1960.
Momaday, N. Scott, *Earth Keeper: Reflections on the American Land*, New York: Harper, 2020.
_____, *Again the Far Morning: New and Selected Poems*, Albuquerque: University of New Mexico Press, 2011.
_____, *Four Arrows & Magpie: A Kiowa Story*, Tulsa: Hawk Publishing Group, 2006.
_____, *In the Bear's House*, New York: St. Martin's Press, 1999a.
_____, *Circle of Wonder: A Native American Christmas Story*, Albuquerque: University of New Mexico Press, 1999b.
_____, *The Man Made of Words: Essays, Stories, Passages*, New York: St. Martin's Press, 1998.
_____, *In the Presence of the Sun: Stories and Poems*, New York: St. Martin's Press, 1992.
_____, *The Ancient Child*, New York: Doubleday, 1989
_____, *The Names: A Memoir*, Tucson: Sun Tracks/The University of Arizona Press, 1976.

______, *Angle of Geese*, Boston: D.R. Godine, 1974.
______, *The Way to Rainy Mountain*, Albuquerque: University of New Mexico Press, 1969.
______, *House Made of Dawn*, New York: Harper & Row, 1968.

4

The Full House in Her Hand: Leslie Marmon Silko

I have a naive faith that somehow, at some time, all the stories in me will get told.

Letter to James Wright (1979)[1]

I write to find out things I don't know. I write to find out what my unconscious knows but I don't know.

Interview (1994)[2]

Coordinates for Silko's novels can rightly draw upon *Storyteller* (1981) as a point of departure. Was not this consequential collage, deftest fusion of Laguna Pueblo family memory, verse, photography, song, and fable? Yet however sourced from actual puebloan life was it not also a species of composite fiction replete with stories-within-story? The title piece, "Storyteller" (17–32), told as the jail memoir of a Yupik village woman, in fact draws attention to how the act of story itself becomes in equal part the story. "Storytelling" (94–8), ostensibly a wife's account to her ex-husband-to-be and of the lover who fathered her twin children during his ten-month absence, takes form from the mythic legend of "Buffalo Man." It makes for a sharp-witted case of how the one story implies but never wholly discloses the whole story. "Storyteller's Escape" (247–53), poem-sequence, shades Grandmother A'moo'ooh's spoken trickster tale of life and death into Silko's own paginated telling of the story. Silko has long shown familiarity with these kinds of reflexive manoeuvre and rarely more so than when grounded in Laguna and other tribal ways of spoken storytelling.

Each of the accompanying story components in *Storyteller* works similarly. "Yellow Woman" (54–62) offers a *kachina* or mountain-spirit love dream in verse of a young Native woman's sexual awakening and at the same time reflects how the imagination edits and re-factualizes human event. "Uncle Tony's Goat"

(171–76), which she attributes to Simon Ortiz, with its story of a rogue and considerably priapic billy-goat, edges towards animal kingdom myth. "Coyote Holds a Full House in His Hand" (257–65) retells a racy seduction episode, again a story told at the threshold of fact and dream, Mexican and Pueblo in one location yet night-time erotica and fantasy in another. The subtleties of each, the ingenuity of sequence and composition, supply a template for how Silko orchestrates the longer run of her fiction, in sequence *Ceremony* (1977), *Almanac of the Dead* (1991), *Gardens in the Dunes* (1997), and the novella *Oceanstory* (2011).

***

"Ts'its'tsi'nako, Thought Woman...is sitting in her room thinking of a story now/I'm telling you the story/she is thinking."[3] The prefatory verse in *Ceremony* quite exactly offers the rationale both of and for her novel. The account of Tayo as damaged World War II returnee, as mixed-blood, and as linked into the Laguna reservation drought and the nearby Los Alamos atomic tests, could not imply a more evident contemporaneity. Throughout, however, and within the sunrise to sundown frame, Silko grounds her novel in, and make it parallel with, Laguna-Keres story: creation myth, witchery, sickness, vision quest, and healing. This sustained interaction, a double fiction doubly told, deservedly has won the novel a center-place within Native American fiction.

The intertextual link to *House Made of Dawn* has been much noted. But Silko's novel is, and remains, wholly her own, a narrative about "ceremony" yet, reflexively, itself that self-same ceremony. At the opening Tayo's "humid dreams of black night" (5), his "fever voices" (6), and specifically the Pacific jungle killing of his uncle, Josiah, and cousin Rocky, along with Japanese soldiery, are said to be tangled up "like colored threads from old Grandma's wicker sewing basket" (6). At the close, and after the war-veteran deaths of Harley and Pinkie, and the banishment of Emo, yet also Tayo's restoration from the "battle fatigue" (31) which has caused him repeatedly to drink and vomit, Old Grandma observes "It seems like I already heard these stories before...only thing is, the names sound different" (260). This reiteration Silko tells in terms of Tayo's literal return to Laguna, yet also of his return to a sustaining myth-world, a cosmos which coheres.

In this his life-passage takes him through the encounters with key healing medicine figures. Ku'oosh starts the process with his herbs, bundles and "old dialect." Josiah's paramour, Night Swan, part-Mexican dancer of flamenco, prophetess, and herself an incarnation of Thought Woman, gives him love and a vision of the pathway to recovery. The Navajo healer Betonie, who updates the ceremonies with his telephone books and like, recenters him through sand painting, prayer-stick, ritual cut, and the five hoops, and sends him on to find the missing spotted cattle. The healer-lover Ts'eh Montaño, an incarnation of Yellow Woman and companion to the Mountain Lion Man, gives him power to resist further "witchery," whether his own (the refusal to kill Emo) or that visited on, and perpetuated by, the white world. He regains, however slowly or at cost, his tongue (early described as "the carcass of a tiny rodent" 15) and his body, and finally, enters the kiva as himself newborn medicine man, for the moment at least, both the healed and healer.

In situating Tayo's story within each legend of Corn and Reed Woman, Ck'o'yo and other tricksters, Hummingbird, Pollen Boy, and their spirit company, Silko unravels a story both actual and ethnomythic. Her protagonist's war-zones, abroad, at home, or in figures of drift like Emo or the Apache-Ute woman Helen Jean from Towac reservation, she tells as wholly specific in time and place. Yet it is a place synchronous with, and to be understood through, a tribal vision of the world. Illness and cure, whether of Tayo, or more generally of postwar Laguna itself, is told throughout *Ceremony* as literal, yet also as though the shadow-act of the "fifth world" (68).

In the one the terms are those of Philippines killing, post-traumatic disorder with would-be "white" hospital treatment, bars, the barbed wire fencing of the land (Tayo's quest for the lost cattle is set against such fencing), drought, and ultimately, the atomic bomb. In the other they are those of Pa'caya'nyi's bad magic (46–9) or the mythical witch gathering ("It was Indian witchery that made white people in the first place" 132), against which the deities of sun, cloud, corn, and water provide good stories and tribal ceremonies of health. In depicting Tayo's course, from death-in-life ("He was tired of fighting off the dreams and the voices" 26) to his own sunrise, Silko writes a one yet multiple fiction and, near faultlessly, with a command of style to match

***

No Silko novel more exhibits the will to multiple story-telling than *Almanac of the Dead* (1991), her resolutely hemispheric text of the Americas. For it envisages nothing less than the restoration of historic landscape, the reassertion of indigenous custody through a risen people's army of a borderless, brown, nature-respecting human order in despite of all European (and Euro-American) cooption. In this respect Tucson, the American Southwest, acts as the novel's geo-historical center, a place-name originally meaning "plentiful fresh water…in Papago," yet where the city has "built its largest sewage treatment plant…next to the river." [4] Sewage, corruption, people and territories despoiled, underwrite the novel. This is the Americas as broken history, dysfunctions of caste and family, modernity as glut. Tucson itself is designated a "city of thieves" (610).

According to the passed-down Mayan Almanac of the Dead, however, actually a Book of Life, there is the prophecy of a reversal, a taking back of the land. This will find form in an eventual south-to-north indigenous alliance ("The prophecies said gradually all traces of Europeans in America would disappear and, at last, the people would retake the land" 631–2). Silko, even so, offers no reductive white-brown cultural binary, a too-ready blame narrative. Her vision remains one of the Americas historically forged of myriad nomenclatures and genealogies, be they indigenous, Euro-white, north and south American, military or corporate.

The novel, to this end, sets its narrative register as one of politics, crime and betrayal. Guns and cocaine rule. Oil, uranium mining and like excavation have left the land scarred. The CIA operates unchecked. Regimes run from Cuban revolutionary schools to police and army video torture pornography. Hollywood and TV Hotline Indians appear in the media. Selective imaging of Chiapas-like insurrection implies a controlled media. Real estate is endlessly finagled. The human organ trade lurks. Marxism and Capitalism vie, the one all plots and assassination, the other consumer frenzy. Either way, tribal dispossession continues. Above all the writ is war large and small ("War had been declared the first day the Spaniards set foot on Native American soil, and the same war had been going on ever since: the war was for the continents called the Americas" 133).

The upshot, its more than seventy characters, ply of plot-lines, and compendium of indigenous sites whether Arizona, New Mexico, Mexico, Central America, Alaska, New Orleans or Las Vegas, and desert, city or jungle, could not more aspire to be the eco-epic *de nos jours*. Silko unhesitatingly makes use of Yaqui, Navajo, Laguna, Hopi, Cherokee, Seminole, Mayan, and Inca tradition. She invokes the Aztecs as original blood sacrifice sorcerers who caused tribal peoples to flee north. The novel's inventory reworks Native snake creator-gods and paired twin mythology (Lecha and Zeta as heiresses to the almanac, Tacho and El Feo as leaders of the coming insurrection guided by macaw spirits). Shamanism prevails, or as Comrade Angelita, tribal revolutionary, observes "The ancestors's spirits speak in dreams. We wait. We simply wait for the earth's natural forces already set loose, the exploding, fierce energy of all the dead slaves and dead ancestors haunting the Americas" 518). Other gods enter the reckoning, not just Quetzacoatl, but the African and Haiti-to-New Orleans ancestor godheads of Damballah, Ogoun and Eursulie.

Opinion, predictably, has varied. Silko over-reaches, her novel too crowded, or hectoring, or damagingly under-edited. Admirers speak of rare brilliance, the New World as indeed a very old world, replete in its own wisdom of populations and languages. The novel, even as it fills out its tapestry of fissure and self-loss, its show of multiple sexual desire or damage, so bears the promise of a redemptive better world of the Americas than that preyed on by the modern raptors of both capitalism and communism. Within the novel the almanac supplies the banner of resistance, a complex prophecy, a codex. Born down across five hundred years and weathered by time and transport, and annotated by the grandmother Yoeme and others before her, its deciphering remains incomplete. Literally its "horse-gut parchment" (570) has been part eaten by starving fugitives at one point. That it is given by the psychic Lecha to the coke-addicted Seese, searching for her kidnapped infant son, to transfer to computer files, implies unfinished history, a text of life still to be fulfilled.

To this end Silko can list past tribal and slave insurrections. Spanish *encomienda* and Dixie plantation labor give departure-points. The role of the Seminoles with Andrew Jackson in his victory at the Battle of New Orleans and unedifying expulsion to the west-of-the-Mississippi Indian Territory that becomes Oklahoma acts as symptomatic historic irony. Geronimo and Wovoka, Wounded Knee, the Navajo code-speakers in World War II, and the recent indigenous rebellions in Guatemala, El Salvador and Peru, all bespeak a Native trajectory. The novel's proliferating strings of story and cause-and-effect builds, almost headily, into the one holding narrative.

Each contributing folder of characters and action is so conceived to work as the narrative subsequent to the original Death Dog rule across the Americas. Lecha as psychic and Zeta as smuggler serve as inaugural voices. Seese becomes adoptee amanuensis for the almanac. The Tucson desert ranch with its family of Ferro, Jamey, Paulie and their dogs and companions might be time's outpost, a remnant tribal colony. Seese's connection through her stolen child Monte into the David-Eric-Beaufrey-Serlo gay circuit, the latter with his monied search for *sangre pura* eugenics with body parts supplied by Trigg, throws a morbid light on both death cult photography, the raising of children, and race and gender purity.

In the Max, Leah and Sonny Blue imbroglio, New York mafia crime is brought south to the country golf world of Arizona, another layer of corruption. The figure of Menardo, self-denying mestizo and global insurance entrepreneur, his affair with the greatly mis-named Alegria, his half-membership of Arizona's power-elite El Grupo, his willing collusion in the CIA arms operation, and his farcical death on being shot through a supposed bullet-proof vest by his chauffeur-spy Tacho (a not so veiled allusion to the 1890s Ghost Dance and imagined immunity from bullets), supplies both truth to history and pastiche. The Angelita La Escapía-Bartolemeo axis nicely undermines Cuban-style Marxism as solution

("The Indians couldn't care less about international Marxism; all they wanted was to retake their land from the white man" 326).

In Sterling, initially banned by the Laguna for breaking tribal community protocol and showing their sacred stone snake to a film-crew, the novel has its conciliator and returnee. As he makes his way out of Tucson, the very vortex of historic ill, he encounters the pueblo's new giant snake ("The snake was looking south, in the direction from which the twin brothers and the people would come" 763). On Silko's part this is the novel as hemispheric vision, mythic while sedimented in the historic, the Americas as vast ecological landscape nurtured against odds in the lives of its original populations.

***

Gardens in the Dunes, if not entirely as expansive as *Almanac of the Dead*, runs close both in density of recreated historical period and recourse to indigenous as against colonial-settler understanding of the earth. The Ghost Dance 1890s as Native chronology rather than simply "white" frontier marks the epoch. Interstate Arizona-California, Riverside County and the Colorado River, Long Island's Oyster Bay, Guatemala, England, Italy and Corsica, with the garden as coordinating metaphor of female creative principle and growth, give contrasting but linked locales. Silko's trellised strings of story, her dialectic of environmental cycle as against capitalist appetite, remains as keen as always. The fashioning involved, sequence for sequence, rightly has been thought the equal of any ranking Victorian novel.

For across the different lines of story Silko builds a theater of competing civilizations. In the remnant Sand Lizard "desert Indians," the female line of eleven-year old Indigo and her sibling Sister Salt, and the "Mama" who has been obliged to flee and Grandmother Fleet as wise-woman, she provides the one dynasty. Hattie Abbott, born of the New York Abbots, Harvard theology student turned down for her heretical Gnostic-feminist doctoral thesis, and wife to her unaffecting and ultimately corrupt botanist spouse Edward Palmer, serves to provide the other. Around them, whether the American Southwest, Latin America or Europe, Silko evolves a fable of colonization, gynocentric myth, and both literally and figuratively "roots, seeds and leaves" as against ever encroaching eco-damage.[5] The upshot is multi-narrative with its center in the loss and yet pathway into cure of planetary ill-health, be it desecration of the Amazon rain forest for profit from rubber, botanical specimen-hunting, the Colorado dam, or the blighted mining of gold and other minerals. It makes for formidable story-tapestry, formidable story-reading.

From departure points in Sand Lizard tribal life, its holistic rounds of food and craft, and the snowfall and peyote-driven sight of Wovoka, Native revivalist Messiah as equal in significance as Christianity's Jesus, the novel gives its convex mirror to Indigo and her family and those who populate the history around them. "Indian Wars," however inappropriate the label, coexist with other kinds of frontier predation ("For years and years, the U.S. soldiers chased Mormons when they weren't chasing Indians").[6] History turns live with Indigo's highjack to be sent to Indian School and would-be adoption by Hattie. That story, with its escapes and journeying to England and Italy, is told in attentive detail as is that of Sister Salt as Sister Salt in her survival through money-making as launderer, beer-maker, and guiltless sex-worker at the camp building the Parker Canyon Dam from the Colorado river. The presiding image, however, is signaled in the novel's title, one of "garden," Native or Edenic, saved or compromised, and as against the earth as "research laboratory."

Silko works a full paradigm. The alimentary resources of the dunes, its terraced plant and harvested edibles, the herbs and pools, the avian, snake and floral life, identify Indigo's lived round. The cornucopia of the Guatemala jungles where Edward on Pará river expedition seeks orchid and other exotica he sees as little more than a fusion of heart of darkness and scientific workshop. The manicured estate of the Abbots with its family Masque of the Blue Garden is seen to have artificialized natural bloom and pattern. England's Kew Gardens can be both pleasure-garden and yet agri-museum. In the environs of Bristol and Bath, behind the Roman and Regency heritage and under the redoubtable watch of Aunt Bronwyn as a kind of English medicine-woman, Hattie and Indigo contemplate Arthurian-Celtic matrilinear spirals and symbols in the garden statuary. Italy yields "the gardens of Tuscany" (294) and "Great Mother" vulva-flowers, and the conviction voiced by Professoressa Laura whom they visit in Genoa that "seeds may be among the greatest travellers of all" (293). Corsica's Cervione, with its rare lemon-groves and from whose smuggled grafts Edward plans to make a fortune out of *citrus medica*, becomes another site of both beauty and theft. These all, community and Native husbandry as against the waste brought on by the imperatives of cash profit, Silko seams into the one sweep of narrative.

The novel in no way eases in ambiguity as it works towards its close. The storying, on the return to America, takes Indigo back into the intimacy of desert, canyon and river even as it is threatened with land-grab and destructive flood engineering. She travels again with her monkey, named Linnaeus in ironic taxonomy, and her parrot with its equally ironic spectrum name of Rainbow, yet remains under threat. Edward dies of fever yet Sister Salt, by contrast, bears the new life of her baby. Hattie, whatever her intended good will towards the Native world, suffers sleepwalking and rape at the hands of Native men and finally steps back to Europe's gardens. Other contrary filaments likewise contribute.

The Australian confidence-man Dr. Gates abuses both the earth in his fake minerals-scheme and his misdiagnosis of Edward as patient. The Paiute-Chemehuevi sisters, Maytha and Vedna, who befriend Sister Salt, if at one time held in custody by Apache Indian police, outwit capture and become canny gardener-provisioners before finally joining Indigo and Sister Salt in their sand dune commune. The black chef Big Candy and his boss Wiley find their cash profits from the engineering camp, which emblematically as well as literally they bury beneath the earth, stolen by the revolutionary Native-Mexican trickster woman Delena with her dog circus and its lead money-sniffing dog. Indigo and Sister Salt, dispossessed initially of each other, believers in Wovoka, circle back by will and cunning to their dynastic female domain of the sand dunes. In her final scene Silko has a young (and wholly un-diabolic) successor snake drink from the pool which waters their habitat, harbinger of breath and continuance. The ending thereby challenges closure, be it tribal life-history whatever the odds, and reflexively, the very chronicle that tells that history.

***

"Prayer to the Pacific," one of the verse sequences in *Storyteller*, images the Asia to California ocean in terms of "moving blue water/Big as the myth of origin" across which "Indians came riding…carried by giant sea turtles."[7] It might readily supply the frame for *Oceanstory*, Silko's novella set against the Pacific of mythic birth waters and "devastating power" for the Tohono O'odham and other Sonoran tribes. As mirror or current it gives its reflection to a wholly modern story of what might justifiably be called domestic *noir*. Foremost, that involves the unsettled relationship of the un-named Pueblo-born woman freelance writer and daughter of BIA teacher parents who voices her times with her Algerian-born partner, himself known only as X in their move from truck-stop Tucson to residence at the sea-edge (Puerto Z) of Mexico's Baja California Peninsula.

History and place encircle the relationship. Silko dips back poetically to the geological plate-formations beneath the Pacific and to the sea's botany of multiple tides, almost surreal seaweed species (one exotically named ocean's scrotums), driftwood, painterly shells, and the "walking dunes" which reformat the beach and their houses. She invokes not only the Tohono O'odham and Yoeme or Yaqui but the ancestral Comcaac people and their fraught bouts of resistance to Spanish governorship and Catholic-mission intrusion.

The scenario, however, indeed is also modernity: shady Mexican real estate deals, the hint of a connection to 9–11 (X once fueled up a truck driven by Mohammed Atta and gets paranoid that he is being watched by CIA operatives), middle class Mexican and American villa-life, and illegal prize-rooster fighting which brings in rich Argentine punters. The Iraq War is being reported on TV. Despite plentiful tequila and hard liquor, cocaine is a wedding-party drug of choice and bales of trafficked marijuana wash up on shore. Other voices enter in a multicultural spectrum, from New Orleans and Algeria (X's mother), from Cuba (the "bad brother"), and to the relief of the narrator, X plans to leave with the Korean wife of an entrepreneur from Seoul who has made serious money marketing puffer fish. In the event X will be killed in a jeep crash.

The momentum Silko keeps at well-judged pace. Wild dogs break into the rooster cages being held by X, one savagery for another, shrieks and blood, feathers and fangs. By contrast when the narrator falls into the ocean from X's skiff as they race to an emergency and which has been holed by her own bullets previously fired at the dogs, she keeps afloat – as fits pacifically and dream-like – clinging to an island of bulbous seaweed before fishermen rescue her. An ocean, different in kind, gives the story its last image and even as the narrator has returned to Tucson, one of New Orleans tidal flood in which X's mother has died. *Oceanstory*, the fusion of water theme and text, a fable of keeping afloat in the face of death, works as yet another kind of Silko full hand from all her stories within.

Notes

1 Leslie Marmon Silko to James Wright, November 5, 1979, ed. Anne Wright, *The Delicacy and Strength of Lace, Letters*, Saint Paul: Graywolf Press, 1986, 90.

2 Stephen Pett, "An Interview with Leslie Marmon Silko," *Short Story*, 2.2., 91–95. Reprinted in Ellen L. Arnold, ed. *Conversations with Lesley Marmon Silko*, Jackson. University Press of Mississippi, 2000, 114.

3 Leslie Marmon Silko, *Ceremony*, New York; Viking Press, Preface.

4 Leslie Marmon Silko, *Almanac of the Dead*, Simon and Schuster, 1991, 190, 189.

5 Leslie Marmon Silko, *Gardens in the Dunes*, New York: Simon and Schuster, 40. For a well-informed perspective see Joni Adamson, "Gardens in the Desert: Migration, Diaspora and Food Sovereignty in the Work of North American Women Writers," in Hsinya Huang and Clara Shu-Chun Change, *Aspects of Transnational and Indigenous Cultures*, Newcastle upon Tyne: Cambridge Scholars Press, 2014, 47–69.

6 *Gardens in the Dunes*, 40.

7 *Storyteller*, 179.

Works Cited

Silko, Leslie Marmon, *Oceanstory*, Odyssey Editions: E-Book, 2011.

_____, *Gardens in the Dunes*, New York: Simon and Schuster, 1999.

_____, *Almanac of the Dead*, New York: Simon and Schuster, 1991.

_____, *Storyteller*, New York: Little Brown/Arcade, in arrangement with Seaver Books, 1981.

_____, *Ceremony*, New York: Viking Press, 1977.

Silko, Leslie Marmon, and James Wright, *The Delicacy and Strength of Lace, Letters*, Saint Paul: Graywolf Press, 1986.

5

Web and House: Later Erdrich, Earlier Erdrich

Meeting up is always complicated in Ojibwe country, and never seems to happen when it was planned.

Louise Erdrich, *Books & Islands in Ojibwe Country* (2003)[1]

Publication of *The Night Watchman* (2020), with *The Sentence* (2021) shortly to follow, leaves no room to doubt Louise Erdrich's stamina, not to say invention. These two novels may well draw from different eras, the one her own grandparental 1950s Turtle Mountain Chippewa-Ojibwe history, and the other, contemporary Minneapolis with her own bookstore Birchbark Books and a ghost for company.[2] Notwithstanding, they share, and assuredly extend, the established Erdrich signature, the complex threads of story, the pull of ancestral habitat through to modern reservation and the ravels of bloodline and dynasty. Faulkner's celebrated phrase of mythical kingdom for his Chickasaw-named Yoknapatawpha fiction continues to apply, in Erdrich's case the Upper Midwest world of the Chippewa Nation and its plaits into Euro-American settler arrival. [3]

The Night Watchman, for its part, invites full estimation, winner of a deserved Pulitzer in 2021. At the same time the novel offers a podium from which to take stock of the stellar literary career that precedes. For since the outset Erdrich has been able to startle, even compel, her very first novel, *The Beet Queen* (1986), quick to win for her Philip Roth's accolade as "the most interesting new novelist to have appeared in years."[4] The almost twenty novels and story-collections since that debut have justifiably gone on to establish her at the Native and American-at-large literary forefront, abetted by her discursive and travel work of which

Book & Islands in Ojibwe Country offers a prime example, the children's writing beginning from *Grandmother's Pigeon* (1996), and the poetry inaugurated with *Jacklight* (1984) and *Baptism of Desire* (1989).

Chippewa-Ojibwe history and its long encounter with the transposed Europe of Germans, French and Swedes from the nineteenth-century and before down the decades into the latest century underpins one strand in the fiction. The geographies of the Dakotas and Minnesota with their woodlands and lakes, reservation housing, allotment and scratch farmlands, churches, bingo halls, burial grounds, and townships like Argus and Williston or cities like Fargo, Bismarck, Sturgis and Minneapolis, underpins another. Clan and territory so overlap in the asymmetrical lives of families like the Kashpaws, Lamartines, Morrisseys, Lazarres, Pillagers, Nanapushes and Adares. They touch, move on, negotiate gyrations of desire and discontent, intermarry and feud, and overlap Catholic and Chippewa belief, a huge latticed narrative gallery of calendar and location.

This fiercely intimate world of kinship, fond or just as often embattled and volatile, has its early marker in *The Beet Queen*. Celestine James, a member of the Kapshaw family, watches with her new-born baby a small white spider busy about its labors. "A web was forming, a complicated house" (176). The web-house image holds to one degree or another across all Erdrich's novels. Her storytelling, in this respect, forgoes easeful geometry in favor of spinnerets, doublings-back, unexpected spokes or folds. Dark comedy can enter. Chance adds to the mix. Dream and ghost or religious visions, even on occasion seeming magic, claim place. The upshot is indeed complication, cat's cradle, not to mention hoop, circle or rope-thread in Erdrich's own other expressions of geometry. Whichever best serves, the upshot has been fiction of unmistakable command.

***

The Turtle Mountain Band of Chippewa, the years 1953–4, Federal Termination Bills (HCT 108 among them) with their aim at removing tribal sovereignty, give constituent bearings to *The Night Watchman*. Actual history may well lie embedded in the plot, the threat of loss of land and self-governance previously federally guaranteed. But the novel refashions events in a way that moves the terrain into copiously imagined narrative. However consequential to the Chippewa reservation the issue of termination, and with it congressional malfeasance, Erdrich is clearly out to avoid any slide into documentary. Similarly that requires no turn towards solemnity or grievance. The novel to this end acts in keeping with observations like "most everything was funnier in Chippewa" (26) and "There were no swear words in Chippewa but lots of words for sex" (313). The consequence is to invest a swathe of politics, Turtle Mountain to Washington,

D.C., and a factory scenario of female bench-labor that turns out jewel bearings for military ordnance and Bulova watches, with in-close human idiosyncrasy.

The central players assume due nuance. Thomas Wazhashk, the generous-hearted night watchman of the title at the Turtle Mountain Jewel Bearing Plant and tribal Chairman, acts true to his Chippewa earthdiver name of muskrat as he rallies the community against federal termination of tribal land ("Thomas was of the after-the-buffalo-who-are-we new generation" 88). Patrice (or Pixie) Paranteau serves as co-traveler ("The nickname Pixie had stuck to her since childhood, because of her upturned eyes" 11), feisty nineteen-year old plant-worker, like Thomas a Chippewa speaker, making do but not much more from her scant income, and bound into the quest for her sister Vera lost in drugs and prostitution Minneapolis. Around their inter-generational overlap Thomas, literally ghost-haunted by the death his boyhood friend Roderick from medical neglect in a BIA school, and Patrice with her reservation young savvy, Erdrich builds her latest web or house of mixed Chippewa and white origins, locally residential yet hinged by political circumstance to the nation's legislative capital.

Erdrich's feat is again not just to introduce but sustain close weavings of web and house throughout, family, voice, passion, memory, languages. Thomas holds sway as cautious activist yet also dreamer-soliloquist. The novel designates him in the largest sense "the watcher," for all his flurry and paperwork in the combat against termination also contemplative at his work of the night-sky, warned by a visiting owl, son to his father Biboon who gives tribal past to the present politics, and eventual sufferer of a stroke. His long marriage to Rose bespeaks in-the-grain love, she not only his carer but that of mothering nurse to damaged reservation children. Patrice must negotiate her passage into sexual womanhood through suitors like the boxer Wood Mountain, actual name Everett Blue, for whom she is "Hell on wheels sharp" (179) and who will end up in marriage to Vera and step-fatherhood to her child. He so out-bids, albeit at one remove from Patrice, the local math teacher and boxing coach Lloyd Barnes who has endlessly and cannily been rebuffed by Patrice. Her skimped journey to Minneapolis, employment in a men's nightclub bar as rubber-suited blue water-ox swimming in a giant tank as the show-time attraction, searcher and eventual rescuer of Vera's baby (*gwiiwizens*), and return to aiding Thomas and his committee, amounts to intricate rite-of-passage.

Their developments, as the novel unwinds them, are eventful with just the right degree of journey and maze. They also position the politics of resistance within an engagingly context of foible and quirk. Any amount of insider characterization enters. Patrice's workmates at Jewel, Doris, Valentine and Betty, supply their chorus of sisterhood, love-gossip, culinary and beading know-how, and organizational groundwork in the fight to prevent termination. Chippewa elders and contemporaries speak their piece, whether Patrice's mother Zhaanat ("Old-time Indian," "raised by parents speaking only Chippewa" 24), Thomas's wife Rose with her often devastating homespun insights, her own mother Noko, the Wazhashk offspring Sharlo and Wade, or Juggie Blue, Wood Mountain's tough, cigarette-smoking and greatly spirited mother. The Wobleszyniski family, of likely Polish or Ukrainian origins, whose first generation finessed their way into owning Chippewa land, has a latest incarnation in Joe Wobble, Wood Mountain's nemesis in the boxing ring. The novel plays this mix of populations with shrewd controlling hand, linkages that build inexorably into the one compendium.

Erdrich also brings in a pair of young Mormons on missionary duty, Elnath and Vernon, torn in almost comic angst between spirit and flesh. Their theology Thomas finds humorless compared with the "supernatural figure Nanabohzo" and his-her creation story and trickster feats. He reads the Book of Mormon with its light-over-dark Lamanites as providing "an excuse to get rid of Indians" (321). In Millie Cloud ("irritable and forceful" 233), the only Chippewa member of the band with college training, Thomas and the others have their library researcher and scribe. She brings city-to-reservation legal eye to the fight against Senator Arthur V. Watkins and his ilk in their determination to dispossess the tribe of its protected land. Barnes, mathematics teacher as well as boxing coach with supreme unconscious irony thinks this process the making of the Chippewa into "regular Americans" (182).

That Erdrich in her Afterword steps out of the novel into real-time family history, and the role of her grandfather Aunishenaubay, Patrick Gourneau, in contesting tribal termination (as she witnesses 113 nations suffered termination but not the Chippewa), is less a case of life imitating art than flat-out generational reality. Yet beyond the personal antecedent her retrospect goes further. It highlights how definitively *The Night Watchman* creates widths and depths of storying to emplace all remembrance of actual original event. As much as the novel draws upon its rich trough of Chippewa political experience, and the activism involved, it points up Erdrich's creation of narrative holding-pattern, web or house as her writer's adroit patterning of the history involved.

***

To revert to Erdrich's inaugural fiction, her novels and story-cycles, is to discern how the patterning begins early. As typical a moment as any in *The Beet Queen* occurs when Russell Kashpaw, Chippewa from North Dakota and Korean war veteran, is honored by his state as its "most decorated hero." In fact Russell has been shot to pieces, become an alcoholic, and needs a wheelchair after suffering a stroke. As the celebrants mill about he sees himself as though in a Chippewa death vision:

> This was the road that old-time Chippewas talked about, the four-day road, the road of death. He'd just started out.
>
> I'm dead now, he thought with calm wonder.
>
> At first he was sorry that it had happened in public, instead of some private place. Then he was glad, and he was also glad to see that he hadn't lost his sense of humor even now. It struck him as so funny that the town he'd lived in and the members of the American Legion were solemnly saluting a dead Indian, that he started to shake with laughter. (300)

A number of Erdrich hallmarks come into play. Chippewa history is to be identified as a mix of defeat and victory. The "four-day road" serves as pointer to death and to its spiritual meaning within Chippewa-Ojibwe cosmology. Is there not, too, the smack at the pernicious frontierism of "The only good Indian is a dead Indian"? The irony which can envisage the transformation of Russell from "dead" Indian into all-American "live" patriot carries sting and rebuke. Russell's musings, moreover, give off just the right laconicism, tough, rueful, yet free of self-pity. He will also make other appearances in the subsequent fiction, among them a cameo appearance as wheelchair tattooist in *The Bingo Palace* (1994). In building this, and the rest of her Chippewa-Objibwe reservation world, Erdrich rarely misses a step. Lives, families and histories inter-circle one into the other, and yet, at the same time, recognize missed or near-missed connection like the history behind their making.

Told across a forty-year span, 1932–1972, and through linking soliloquies, *The Beet Queen* opens with Mary and Karl Adare, eleven and fourteen respectively in 1932, who arrive illicitly by boxcar in Argus, North Dakota, to claim kin with Fritzie and Pete, their aunt and uncle and the owners of Kozka's Meats. Their mother, Adelaide, recently widowed and crazy for romance, has dumped not only them but a new-born baby brother to fly south from Minnesota to Florida with The Great Omar, a none-too-successful aviator stuntman. It is a first of many separations, lives whose connection lies in the paradox of their apparent disconnection.

At Argus, the two Adare children themselves part company. Karl, alarmed by a fierce dog, jumps back on the train only to find himself in the amorous clinch of a hobo who rejoices in the name of Giles Saint Ambrose. Despite believing he has found love, Karl plunges out of the train, only to break both his legs and be nursed back to health by the journeying Fleur Pillager, Chippewa medicine woman. Subsequently raised in a Catholic orphanage, he then takes to the road as a salesman of farm and household gadgetry, still to find connection, love, nexus. Mary, meantime, goes about the web of her life in shared disjunctive manner. Her girlhood she spends in fierce tension with her disturbed, glamour-struck cousin Sita, in childhood the human center of what Argus dubs a religious miracle yet also a spinsterish Old Maid and purveyor of beef and pork who takes over the meat business. Her life, too, has become oddity yet still implicated in the whole.

The lives of the two Adares, albeit important, far from preside as the only filaments in the web or house. Clementine James, part-Indian and Mary's life-long friend, allows Karl to father a child on her, whom Mary virtually adopts and promptly names Dot. But Dot's actual given name is Wallacene. This links to Wallace Keff, Dot's self-appointed guardian and the bachelor President of the Argus Chamber of Commerce. Wallace has been the man responsible for introducing sugar beet into the region as a sure-fire cash crop. His life, in turn, circles into that of Karl Adare. For he lives with a lonely secret. The only experience which in any way transforms an otherwise stale round of Babbittry is his darkly comic sexual encounter with Mary's driven but seductive brother. Clementine, too, contributes her brother to the ongoing web, namely Russell Kashpaw, the Korean war veteran more dead than alive. He, if no one else, can recognize breakage as well as ligature inside Chippewa-Ojibwe country.

It is to Dot, however, that the novel finally reverts, with further linking turns into the lives of Adelaide, Sita, the lost Adare who surfaces as Father Miller, a Catholic priest, and others in the Kashpaw and related dynasties. As Wallace Keff intends it Dot will be the Queen in Argus's Sugar Beet Festival. But, again, the web oscillates unexpectedly. She sees that things have been rigged in her favor, gives way to a fury of her own, and like her grandmother Adelaide before her, takes to the skies. That is, she soars off with the local sky-writing pilot only to wheel back to earth when the main events of the festival are over, a last ironic "Indian" shake of the web indeed.

At first sight *The Beet Queen* suggests something less than Native-centered narrative, which is not to say the Kashpaws and their kin do not make frequent appearances. But the novel's "Indianness" lies as much in its oblique style of narrative as any given explicit "Indian" theme. If web or house are to be thought "Indian," then the story doubles back and forth on itself as if to turn both inside out. This is a tale that borders on magic, magic history, perhaps, as much as magic realism. Put otherwise *The Beet Queen* manages to chronicle the oddity of lives connected in discontinuity into its own kind of continuity.

Both *Love Medicine* (1984), fourteen pieces to which four more were added in a New and Expanded Version in 1993, and *Tracks* (1988) with its historical epochs, share the same organizational impetus. "The World's Greatest Fishermen," told in four parts in *Love Medicine*, sets the dynastic web in motion with its account of June Kashpaw who walks to death in night-time snows and Chinook wind outside of Williston, North Dakota ("oil boomtown") after bar-drinking and a casual sexual encounter with Andy, a "mud engineer." Her demise, that of a woman lost to her own best promise, a female Jesus-figure, and its aftermath for her divorced husband Gordie, her niece Albertine Johnson, her mother Zelda, her Grandmother Kashpaw and Great-uncle Eli, her cousin Nector, and the family adoptee Lipsha Morrissey, supplies a kind of prophetic template for the lives still to be unfolded.

The stories, in turn, deal with the tensions between a French-exported Catholicism and Chippewa belief ("Saint Marie" and "Flesh and Blood"); the unexpected, comic turns of tribal conjure as against Catholic observance in affairs of the heart ("Love Medicine"); the role of drink and alcoholism in Chippewa history ("Crown of Thorns"); sexual permutations within an extended family regime ("Lulu's Boys"); Vietnam and the return of the damaged Henry Lamartine ("The Red Convertible"); and actual tribal reality in an era of mythified or cartoon Indians ("The Plunge of the Brave"). As serious in implication as these themes evidently are, Erdrich true to form keeps them free of solemnity or sentimentalism. Narrators, accordingly, can settle old scores, adjust the record as fits, complain or justify, only to have correctives supplied by others in the web or house. Erdrich's deftness, throughout, is to make the one story precisely imply connection into all the others.

Tracks steps back into increments of time running from Winter 1912 to Spring 1924, nine stories given over to the double-jeopardy suffered by the Chippewa from a disease like pneumonia and the loss of tribal lands to outside speculators. Two voices preside, those of old Nanapush, Chippewa tribal Chairman, and of Pauline Lamartine, would-be Catholic martyr, who despite her every effort to break free of her Chippewa allegiances finds herself hexed and drawn back into her Indian heritage. A third, and crucial, human point of reference is given in the person of Fleur Pillager. Varyingly she is thought witch, lover and loved one, and at one point Erdrich calls her in Anishinaabe a *mide* or visionary. To her daughter, Lulu Pillager, she offers special testimony, the wisdom of self-acceptance against odds and the hostility of her detractors. In her voices and those of Nanapush and Pauline, Chippewa culture as site past and present, once more takes on live continuity, the refusal, however humanly vexed, of closure.

Nanapush, for his part, speaks out of the past ("I guided the last buffalo hunt. I saw the last bear shot" 2). His is the witness to government treaty, allotment, the creation of tribal police, and above all to the disease in which "Our tribe unraveled like a coarse rope" (2). He knows, too, that "Nanapush is a name that loses power every time that it is written and stored in a government file" (32). Yet he is also "oldtime Anishinabe warrior" (116), guardian of tribal memory, good medicine, a repository of hunting and preservation skills.

Pauline's furious attempts to divest herself of her Indian identity ("Pauline schemed to gain attention by telling odd tales that created damage" 39) thus makes a necessary ironic point of contrast. She engages in the most baroque Catholicism, would-be martyr and saint, tries a bevy of men, and hovers between sanity and unhingement. Between Nanapush and Pauline, and in each alternating act of story, they tell the larger, and even more important story of how, against history, the Chippewas in all their breakage have managed by near-miracle to endure.

Like its predecessor *Tracks* does not always afford too easy or immediate access, but it continues to exhibit Erdrich's control of interstitial narrative. The history which gives rise to each voice may well deal in bitterest loss but not at the expense of self-pity. Nowhere does this show more affectingly than in the account given by Pauline Lamartine of a prophetic early moment in the life of Nanapush. The memory is tragic yet salutary, a warning and yet a celebration:

> As a young man, he had guided a buffalo expedition for whites. He said the animals understood what was happening, how they were dwindling. He said that when the smoke cleared and hulks lay scattered everywhere, a day's worth of shooting for only the tongues and hides, the beasts that survived grew strange and unusual. They lost their minds. They bucked, screamed and stamped, tossed the carcasses and grazed on flesh. They tried their best to cripple one another, to fall or die. They tried suicide. They tried to do away with their young. They knew they were going, saw their end. He said while the whites all slept through the terrible night he kept watch, that the groaning never stopped, that the plains below him was alive, a sea turned against itself, and when the thunder came, then and only then, did the madness cease. He saw their spirits slip between the lightning (139-40).

This is Chippewa legacy shadowed by colonial death and yet kept in being by will, ingenuity, stratagems necessary to survive. Tragedies of displacement, each outbreak of disease, remain inerasable. But they are shown so as not to crowd out each redeeming human nexus be it ceremony, spirituality, marriage, children, even cunning or the unpredictable pratfalls of desire. The stories in *Tracks*, however discrete in their own right and as the title implies, thereby thread into the altogether larger narrative web or house. In shared virtuosity with her other storytelling they signal a writer who writes with an instinct for human particularity, that or Nanapush, Pauline, Fleur or Lulu, but equally renders them for their lived-out and interactive footholds in the larger community timeline of the Chippewa.

The Bingo Palace (1994) summons familiar dynastic names. Three especially preside. Lipsha Morrissey, returnee from Fargo to the reservation at the command of his formidable grandmother Lulu Lamartine ("My summons by Grandma Lulu" 14) seeks better identity than his usual lackadaisical but keenly self-aware self. He will come alive, find his centering, through burning love for Shawnee Ray Toose, beauteous young mother of her baby Redman. "This beautiful sickness of the heart" (154) he calls it. Lyman Lamartine, Lipsha's half cousin and half-uncle, father of Shawnee Ray's child, and his fellow love-swain for Shawnee, features as the prosperous but himself gambling-addicted intriguer for land and profit under the ironic moniker "Bingo Chief" (116). Zelda Kashaw, mother to Albertine whose insouciance she seeks to replace by virtually adopting Shawnee and child and finagling the young mother's marriage with Lipsha, will eventually re-meet in the wake of a heart-attack of her first and long-ago lover Xavier Toose, Shawnee's uncle. She describes him as "the lookingest man around here… but he wasn't the man I was saving myself to marry. That special man has to be white" 46).

Fleur Pillager, *bruja*-medicine woman and great-grandmother to Lipsha and to whom he goes for a love-medicine, serves as ancestral presence, her footsteps playing into each of the present-time lives ("She's a Pillager, the adopted daughter of Old Man Nanapush, this healing doctor witch" 126). Lipsha's deceased mother June Morrissey enters as ghost-presence to aid his bingo playing and wins and to haunt Lipsha's father, Gerry Nanapush, in a final – and fantastical – snowbound car flight into death as he continues his escape from jail. Shawnee will herself escape to college with money given her by Lipsha, in one sense an unwebbing though not without its irremovable threads to the mix of family dynasties in the reservation.

Another inspired inflection of the Chippewa web/house, the novel with its always wider contributing cast again offers Erdrich at versatile stretch. The patterning again works subtly, elastically. Themes of contrary love create one kind of weave. "Love wrecks things" says Lipsha's conspiratorial Aunt Zelda (48). Lipsha himself confides "I go looking for a home to rest in Shawnee's heart"

(157). Lyman laments "Shawnee Ray, she's in my head every minute, and I know she's not the same about me" (168). Zelda, once Shawnee has left and with men like Nector Kashpaw and Xavier Toose in mind, vows "She would never make herself subject to love, never would be overtaken" (244). Themes of inheritance and land make another main weave. Lyman's plot to acquire Fleur's ancestral holding for an extravagant casino near Matchimanito Lake flounders. He has cheated Lipsha, bankrupted himself by gambling, and lost Shawnee, reversals themselves a pattern. Lipsha recognizes the implications for the Chippewa. "*This aint real estate*" (218) echoes through his mind, with the rider "Everybody knows bingo money is not based on solid ground" (221).

Erdrich inlays any number of purposive signals. At the outset it is said of Lulu "We could pull any string from Lulu, anyway, it would all come out the same degree of tangle" (5). Albertine, Zelda's daughter, on a brief return home from medical studies sees in the imbroglio around her mother, Shawnee and Redman, "patterns developing in the air…Twine pulled, relaxed….telling shapes" (210). Gerry Nanapush, in his would-be flight with Lipsha to the Canadian border in the wake of a crashed flight and the two dead marshals, ponders yet another pattern:

> He knew from sitting in the still eye of chance that fate was not random. Chance was full of runs and soft noise, pardons and betrayals and double-backs. Chance was patterns of a stranger complexity that we could name, but predictable. There was no such thing as a complete lack of order, only a design so vast it seemed repetitive up close, that is, until you sat doing nothing for so long that your brain ached and, one day, just maybe, you caught a wider glimpse. (226)

Much as these latter thoughts speak to Gerry and Lipsha, both complicatedly as fugitive to themselves as the law, they equally carry a reflexive loading for the novel at large. Double-backs, design, ordered disorder, constitute the very workings of *The Bingo Palace*, once again the mainstays of Erdrich's customary flair.

***

The Bingo Palace has long been held to complete a tetralogy of the so-called Love Medicine series of Chippewa criss-crossed lives. They, also, offer shared Chippewa story-threads into the immediate novels that follow. *The Last Report on the Miracles at Little No Horse* (2001) gives striking voice to Chippewa and Christian religious conversion and its implications for gender with a take on the nature of sainthood in a Native setting. *Tales of Burning Love* (2003) explores a live paradigm of different Chippewa wifedoms to the maverick white contractor

Jack Mauser. *Four Souls* (2004) might be almost Elizabethan revenge drama in Little No Horse dress, Fleur Pillager's resolve to have come-uppance for theft of her dynastic land. *The Painted Drum* (2005) connects the Eastern Seaboard of New Hampshire to the Dakotas through a timeline of the passed-down ceremonial hide emblem of the title. Belief, marriage, revenge, legacy all hold place as key themes. Equally, however, Erdrich creates linkages of manner, narration itself as again her own kind of prevailing intricacy.

The novels known as the Justice trilogy form another and greatly indicative follow-on grouping. *The Plague of Doves* (2008) historicizes the dynastic consequence of an unjust 1890s white township execution of three tribal witnesses to murder. *The Round House* (2012) creates in its teenage protagonist Joe Coutts, son of a tribal judge, the would-be revenger for the white-on-Indian rape of his mother. *LaRose* (2016) portrays the impact of a Chippewa couple's adoption of a white boy whose father has killed their son in a hunting accident, a fine-spun take on tribal retributive justice. Each story Erdrich discloses as though a personal court of human rights yet, also and again, as its own kind of overlapping story-web or house.

The range of Erdrich's yet other novels work in shared manner. *The Crown of Columbus* (2003), co-authored with Michael Dorris, works as a novel of doubles, whether the Columbus of his lost Log as against standard "discovery" icon or the love pairing of Vivian Two Star and Roger Williams as modern Dartmouth College researchers. *The Antelope Wife* (2008), with its Rozin-Richard-Frank triangle and the tragic death of the child daughter, Deanna, is played out against the memory of prior Native miscued relationships. *The Master Butchers Singing Club* (2003) draws on Erdrich's paternal heritage, post World War 1 Germany to Argus, Minnesota as a tangled dynasty set against two kinds of old world respectively Native and European. *Shadow Tag* (2010), its footfalls much thought close to her relationship with Michael Dorris, turns to a "modern" marriage, that of Irene and Gil, diarist and painter, and the un-entangling bruise they inflict one on the other. *Future Home of the Living God* (2017), told in the voice of Cedar Hawk Songmaker, enters futurist-speculative territory. An American genealogical dystopia of government regulation especially inimical to Native women it depicts Cedar's uncertain refuge from a Minneapolis detention center in the Chippewa reservation. Understandably comparisons have arisen with Margaret Attwood's *The Handmaid's Tale* (1985). In whatever degree Erdrich has won literary pre-eminence, leading Native American storyteller, leading American storyteller, it derives as much from her crafted patterning as vision.

In the closing chapter of *The Beet Queen*, Dot, renamed from the erstwhile Wallacette Darlene Adare, plots revenge on finding her queenship crown to have been rigged. It causes her to think of family ancestry ("There is a thread beginning with my grandmother Adelaide and traveling though my father and arriving at me" 335). Towards the end of *The Night Watchman* Thomas Wazhashk, recovering from his stroke, dwells upon selective words, shifts back into the Chippewa language, thinks of family birthdays, and draws earthdiver-muskrats in the "circle of light" (377). In the two cases these motifs conjure a breadth of historic family and community resonance. At the same time they do duty for how they give cues to Louise Erdrich's fiction, thread or circle, web or house, and how in conjunction with virtuoso curls of style these work to her storytelling's every imaginative advantage.

Notes

1 Louise Erdrich, *Books & Islands in Ojibwe Country*, Washington, DC: National Geographic, 2003, 23.
2 *The Sentence* was still to be issued at the time of writing this chapter.
3 Faulkner's kingdom he literally maps in *Absalom Absalom!*.
4 Philip Roth, Cover endorsement.

Works Cited

Attwood, Margaret, *The Handmaid's Tale*, Toronto: McClelland and Stewart, Boston: Houghton, Harcourt, 1985.
Erdrich, Louise, *The Sentence*, New York: HarperCollins, 2021.
_____, *The Night Watchman*, New York: HarperCollins, 2020.
_____, *The Future Home of the Living God*, New York: HarperCollins, 2017.
_____, *LaRose*, New York: HarperCollins, 2016.
_____, *The Round House*, New York: HarperCollins, 2012.
_____, *Shadow Tag*, New York: HarperCollins, 2010.
_____, *The Red Convertible: Selected and New Stories 1978-2009*, New York: HarperCollins, 2009.
_____, *The Plague of Doves*, New York: HarperCollins, 2008.
_____, *The Painted Drum*, New York: HarperCollins, 2005.
_____, *Four Souls*, New York: HarperCollins, 2004.
_____, *The Master Butcher's Singing Club*, New York: HarperCollins, 2003.
_____, *The Last Report on the Miracle at Little No Horse*, New York: HarperCollins, 2001.
_____, *The Antelope Wife*, New York: Harper Collins, 1998, 2012.

______, *The Bingo Palace*, New York: HarperCollins, 1994.
______, *Tale of Burning Love*, New York: Harper Collins, 1993.
______, *Love Medicine*, New York: Henry Holt, 1984; expanded versions, 1993, 2003.
______, *Baptism of Desire*, New York: HarperCollins, 1989.
______, *Tracks*, New York: HarperCollins, 1988.
______, *The Beet Queen*, New York: Henry Holt, 1986.
______, *Jacklight*, New York: Henry Holt, 1984.
Faulkner, William, *Absalom, Absalom!* New York: Random House, 1936.

6

Cross-Worlds: The Sight and Sound of James Welch

If we raced a century over hills
that ended years before, people couldn't
say our run was simply poverty or promise for a better end.
We ended sometime
back in recollections of glory, myths,
that meant the hunters meant a lot
to starving wives and bad painters.

James Welch, "Blackfeet, Blood and Piegan Hunters"[1]

Remember when you were here…
You told us in a glance
the moving days are best, when sounds strike
the inner ear from places only the hawk
can name and some wild damned Indian,
eyes full of rainbows and fast jacks, *Achukma!*

Jim Barnes, "Postcard to James Welch in Missoula"[2]

Given interests that alight on patterns of Native self-dislocation with occasional if provisional hard-won recovery, James Welch would not readily be awarded a rosette for writing good-cheer fiction. But he would amply invite one for skills of narration, the command of story rhythm and exactness of detail, the interior mapping of his main players. The five novels, *Winter in the Blood* (1974), *The Death of Jim Loney* (1979), *Fools Crow* (1986), *The Indian Lawyer* (1990) and *The Heartsong of Charging Elk* (2000), each in how they draw on Blackfeet/Gros Ventre, Oglala Sioux, Crow (ancestral antagonists to the Blackfeet), Navajo, or other tribal legacy, and as mainly carried in figures of mixed-blood descent, leave no doubt of adroit orchestration in bridging detail into form.[3] For whether situated in time-now, or time-was, Welch's narratives endow their flow of plotline with a hugely distinguishing power of lens. This quality of particularization in eye and ear invites best recognition, not the only but a presiding hallmark.

Locale can be township Harlem and the cities of Bozeman, Billings or Helena, or the Big Sky Montana of Little Rockies, Mission Canyon, Snake Butte and Milk River, not to say in *The Heartsong of Charging Elk* the Marseille of *le midi*. More circumstantially it can be on or off reservation housing, bar or prairie, football field or basketball court, state penitentiary or the European sites of the Buffalo Bill Wild West Show. Eye and ear in each assume character virtually in their own imaginative right as his poem "Blackfeet, Blood and Piegan Hunters" bears witness in kind with virtually every other contribution to Welch's only verse collection *Riding the Earthboy 40* (1970). Jim Barnes's "Postcard" catches at that same exactitude (a marker, too, of Barnes's own poetry) in phrasings like "eyes full of rainbows" and "inner ear" and with the indicative irony that such also might belong to "some wild damned Indian."

***

If Momaday's *House Made of Dawn* bespeaks landmark, it would be far from injustice to think James Welch's own first novel, *Winter in the Blood*, belongs also at the headwaters of modern Native fiction. These notably, from the 1970s, look to the lyric "homing-in" of Lesley Marmon Silko's *Ceremony* (1977) and the surreal peregrination of Gerald Vizenor's *Darkness in Saint Louis Bearheart* (1978).[4] In Welch's case here was a novel, a novella, born of Montana Blackfeet intimacy, that offers a virtuoso portrait of split and dislocation. But for all that it points to the losses, and for sure the pratfalls, of its un-named narrator and the historic fractures of his family, it also positions them in relation to eventual yet un-pietistic re-sighting and re-hearing of tribal remembrance. The upshot is beautifully styled dark-comic parable.

Mid-way the bemused narrator makes the near classic observation "Again I felt that helplessness of being in a world of stalking white men" (120). It confirms all the novel's subtlety of tone, the modern role-reversal of an uncertain heir to Northern Plains hunter himself hunted. As serious as is the vision of the one contemporary Native life, it also holds itself up as comedy of errors. Self-drift, drinking, absurd chance encounter, dream and fantasy, accusing shafts of memory, all shape his life story. To this end Welch develops a first-person voice full of quizzicality, at odds with itself, with family, and assuredly with the white world. From his return home past the borrow-pit, with its implication of earth lost or evacuated, to his mother, Teresa First Raise, and her new husband Lame Bull, and through to the epiphanous recognition of the blind Yellow Calf as his true Blackfeet grandfather as against "the half-breed Doagie" (159), and the funny-serious burial of his grandmother, the narrator inhabits each of several worlds each off-tilt. In none does he prevail, whatever the degree of understanding he reaches at the novel's conclusion.

The one evokes literal Dodson, Montana, its township bars and commerce, along with his mother's Blackfeet/Gros Ventre Reservation valley holding of hay, alfalfa and fishing country. Another, more internal, bears "the presence of ghosts" (159), the haunting line of dynasty which includes the snowdrift drunken death of First Raise, his father, and of Mose, the fourteen-year old brother mangled and then killed in a cattle round-up whom the narrator might once have saved. Yet another summons his Cree woman, who he thinks to marry, who un-manningly steals his gun and razor, and then who haunts him through the memory of her teeth made green by drinking *crème de menthe.* Nature itself can seem to collude. Yellow Calf calls it "cockeyed." Meadowlarks sing in mock-chorus. Pheasants gabble. Magpies as tricksters argue. A hawk shot by the narrator in childhood is remembered only for its unmoving tongue. His long-time horse "Bird" dies pulled down by mud. The fish have disappeared from the river despite the efforts of white agri-scientists at repopulation. Displacement holds sway as the narrator recognizes in the words "I was as distant from myself as a hawk from the moon" (2).

The story of Amos, the pet duck who survives as its siblings drown, offers the analogy of another family given over to self-drowning. The episode shadows forward to the early tribal widowhood and abandonment of his grandmother; his mother's marriage to First Raise as drinker and who could make white men laugh, yet also a handyman, and who was found dead-frozen in the borrow-pit with his arm pointing homeward; and the narrator's always accusing culpability in the accident and death of Mose. An Eliotic wasteland note recurs, Montana if once a Native ecology then also now dry season. It has become rainless, a place for grail and fisher-king.

Each encounter for the narrator adds to the displacement. Who, exactly, is the aeroplane man from Malta in Phillips County, Montana, clad in white hunter garb, carrying a teddy bear and five boxes of chocolate-covered cherries, and who hires him to get to Canada before his arrest by "the two suits" as a possible FBI fugitive? His own mother's letter to the Harlem priest, with whom she drinks but who refuses Native parishioners burial in tribal ground, he finds himself, almost unself-comprehendingly, moved to destroy. His overnight encounter with the barfly Malvina, one in a line of several women, edges into fantasy, rough yet maudlin and even comic sex, with its bedroom gallery of the woman's photographs. All of these conflate in his hangover reveries, episodes of dream picaresque. The hitchhike back home, in which he gets a lift with a family of Hutterites, exposes him both to a father who asks if "Indians" eat river turtles, having his picture taken like some curio, and a daughter the very instance of anaemia, a sickly whiteness.

Only in his understanding of the example of Yellow Calf, and the love and succour he once gave to the grandmother and to Teresa as the child he fathers with her, does the narrator begin to glimpse a way to confront the unbalance of his life. His bad leg, dating back to Mose's death, has localized the larger malaise, life lived at a limp. But Yellow Calf's revelation, and the linkage it supplies into a better order of Native being, together with the grandmother's burial, becomes a process of rebirth. For even as he wears his father's patched-up suit, Teresa dons red lipstick, coat, high heels and a black cupcake hat, Lame Bull makes a preposterous funeral speech, and the coffin fails to wedge evenly in the ground, rain has at last fallen again. The old lady's pouch, and with it her arrowhead, he himself returns to the earth. Absurdity, comic-absurdly as befits, has in whatever small degree begun to dissolve.

As for the first time, and true to his age of thirty-two against the endless taunts of being called a boy, the narrator finds adulthood in a historic continuity of name, family, tribe, land, and call to health. He makes a self-promise to have his leg fixed and, a vintage touch of Welch irony, even marriage to his Cree. The signs of dislocation remain, nowhere more so than in the inspired motley and rhetoric at the grandmother's funeral. But they do so also in relation to the signs of resuscitation, life however oddly quilted over death. Which is to suggest that the contrary condition of things persists, without some final, transcendent-spiritual redemption or homing-in but rather a kind of working contingency. *Winter in the Blood* so fuses carnival into seriousness, the narrator's life as Native *comédie humaine*, a jugglery while always underwritten by sober enough reality. Welch creates the novel's cross-worlds with nothing if not a poet's sureness of monitoring eye and ear.

***

The Death of Jim Loney offers a protagonist's life from the outset even less likely to resolve into recovery. Welch's circumstantial touch, again, is assured. The narrative of a Montana mixed-blood, displaced in life as environs at the edge of both Belknap Reservation and Harlem township, is given not just with flair but beckoning exactitude. Loney, the name also a byname, who authors his own literal death as against his death-in-life in the shoot-out at tribal-heritaged Mission Canyon, finally gives his face to the spirals of inefficacy however brought on by both family circumstance and his own unresisting complicity. The abandonment with his sister by his Gros Ventre mother, Electra Calf Looking, and white drifter-barfly father, Ike Loney, could have edged into stereotypical mixed-blood blight. His "white" love affair could have given way to formula, easy transgression. Even the intended or accidental rifle killing of his onetime Native classmate carries risks of acceding to melodrama. In the event Welch writes subtler pathology, self-complexities, the torque of wasteland within Loney carefully situated from the latticed history of its making.

The narrative staging, more aptly the ligatures, in how Loney's life unfolds, again take on especial calls to sight and ear. An opening tableau, a "smoky night," has him exchanging with a local farmer about the township football game amid mud, the pounding of rain, and a crucially mistaken play at one with his own erroneous spectator life, and then to follow his arising need to "go downtown for a drink" (3). Night-times have him dreaming of "a large bird and dark" (20), the visionary avatar for his absentee parentage – his mother especially. He sees in mind his father as "a weeping man" (23) and the silhouette of a Native woman, his own or another mother, who has lost her son (34). His dog Swipsey freezes into silence in the ice and has to be dug out. These each supply markers, Jim Loney caught at his own psychological edge as much as at the edges of Harlem.

They also extend into Loney's prime relationships. With Rhea Davis, the beauteous Texas belle who has fled her millionaire family to teach on the reservation, he meets both love and yet resists her call to escape to the city. She concedes that initially he signified fantasy for her, a version of dark Indian warrior manhood. But she also learns better, seeks to take on marriage with him, even though her plan to have them move *à deux* to ocean-costal Seattle where Loney once served in the military increasingly meets his inevitable delay and resistance. With Kate, the sister who has climbed through professional qualification into a role as successful bureaucrat in Indian Education and seeks to take him back with her to Washington DC, the same reluctance holds. How to extricate himself from Rhea's fond illusion that "he was lucky to have two sets of ancestors" and which stirs his contemplative riposte that "He had no family and he wasn't Indian or white" (102). How, as Welch positions him reflexively to free himself of a self whose internal lock has resisted undoing and only a particular kind of "Indian" death will end?

Both the two relationships, and Loney's haunting by a quotation from the Book of Isaiah of the need for the spiritual in human affairs, take their course inside the novel's measure of sight-and-sound corridor. The way-stations are of several kinds accompanied by dips into the "controlled oblivion" (59) he seeks from his drinking. He remembers basketball hoops with Brother Gerard at one of the mission schools, his love of the adoptive aunt "Sandra" (his father's ex-lover) and touch of her hair, his exchange with and final imagined message to the boy

Amos After Buffalo from Mission Canyon to which he himself will eventually flee, and the different exchanges in Kenny Hart's and the other township bars. The sibling image the novel attributes to Loney and his sister as "two half-breed kids caught in the slack water of a minor river" (90) precisely situates each.

In this respect the denouement especially adds particularity. Invited to go deer-shooting with Myron Pretty Weasel, one–time fellow basketball player but also un-liked friend and in contrast to himself the son of a successful Native rancher, their venture becomes both actual and yet phantasmagoric, the shooting of real bullets an act as near out-of-body ancestral ritual. Interpretation has rightly seized upon Loney's confusion as to whether he thinks, in the heat of moment, he is shooting a patrolling bear ("the image spooked him" 129). Pretty Weasel dazzles him in the half-light, modern sports-hunter and yet in ursine form sacred totem. Loney shoots both and, implicitly his own might-have-been incarnation, his own better anima. "I killed a man" (145) he tells Ike, the trailer-resident father he now reaches for and who will give him $60 and a Remington pump gun. Their final meeting enacts starkest father-son sight and sound to be followed by Loney's trashing of the trailer as tell-tale sign that he is indeed the killer of Pretty Weasel.

In his suicidal flight Jim Loney seeks tribal ground "on the reservation" (160). The flight again implies ritual, the remembrance of Amos After Buffalo, the Native calendar as against Thanksgiving, and of his lost mother now a nurse in New Mexico. Pursuit by the township's law officer Painter Barthelme, and the reservation police Quinton Doore and Lefthand, transitions into yet further ritual. Is he simply criminal fugitive or the far deeper death-shadow which, paradoxically, has given the only substance to his life and finally transformed him into death-facing Gros Ventre brave? As he falls and spins he sees "the beating wings of a dark bird as it climbed to a distant place" (179) even as Welch makes audible the slug from Doore that kills him (Painter witnesses "the blast besides him" fired by Doore 178). *The Death of Jim Loney* so closes through the yet one more indicative play of eye and ear in the narrowing vortex of Loney's life. In so doing it gives Welch's novel its own perfect compositional sense of ending.

***

With *Fools Crow* (1986) Welch develops the almost unique re-picturing of tribal Montana in the late 1860s. He himself has been insistent, however, upon how from the start his interest was in infinitely more than spectatorship or even topography. His resolve lay in articulating a tribally centered dimension of clan rite of passage, belief system, language, word and naming, in all the lived and filled human detail of historic Blackfeet culture. This sought-for reality he indicates in interview:

> My main point in writing this book is to present the Blackfeet way of life – daily life, hunting, raiding, ceremonies, mores, belief, preparing hides and food – before the whites made real inroads into their culture. The Indian had a different reality and I try to present that.[5]

Centered on the life of Fools Crow, originally White Man's Dog, and whose change of name marks his coming-of-age as warrior and medicine man, the novel from the outset takes great care to set up a meticulous Native-animist geography. The opening chapter sets terms of reference, atlas-specific while at the same time a poetry. The Montana Rockies become "the Backbone of the World," the moon "Night Red Light," the sun "Sun Chief," winter "the Cold-Maker," death "Shadow Land," and the ancestral Blackfeet deities "the Above Ones." Shadow nomenclature as may be when given in English transliteration each, even so, points to a Blackfeet sense of cosmos and nature-cycle born of its own precisely ordering and cultural semantics.

For this is Blackfeet life alive in circumstance, the three bands of the Pikuni, Kainah and Siksika, and their subdivisions into warrior societies, as well as Fools Crow's family descended from Rides at the Door, his father, mother, and his wife Red Paint and child. Welch attentively delineates a working round of hunt, raid, sweat lodge, courtship, migrations between summer and winter camps, intimacy with Nature and its animals, birds and sounds, diplomacy with other Blackfeet and, unsentimentally, tribal rivalries and different acts of human pettiness and crime. Time joins seamlessly to place, belief to practice, Blackfeet cosmology to Blackfeet everyday existence. Louis Owens has persuasive grounds for terming the novel "an act of cultural recovery."[6] *Napikwans*, white men, operate at a distance, as though situated at the spatial-temporal periphery. Which is not to underestimate the trauma for the tribe of the Baker/Marias River Massacre of 1870, in which 173 Pikunis, mostly women and children, were killed by the military under Major Eugene M. Baker in revenge for the murder of the rancher Malcolm Clarke by the Piegan warrior Owl Child and comrades (Clarke had earlier humiliated Owl Child in a horse dispute). Nor is to downplay the devastating impact of different waves of white-imported smallpox. Both are given place in Welch's novel, but as incidents, however important, within yet others. The effect is to pre-empt the usual emphasis of frontier, farm settlement, and the cavalry, with a tribal perspective, a step aside from the "winning" of the west.

Rather, tribal memory presides. Fools Crow, for instance, remembers:

> the stories told by his grandfather of the origins of the constellations. He had been young then and it all seemed simple. There were only the people, the stars, and the blackhorns. (93)

Whatever the self-estimate of settlers in their covered wagons, or the cavalry in their forts, as white people they are initially thought of in trickster terms and humor:

> At first we thought these Napikwans were animals and incapable of reproducing with human beings. (66)

Blackfeet history, in general, Welch conveys as tough if savvy tribal order, humanly contradictory, and increasingly vulnerable to encroaching white America. Welch, to his credit, eschews any hint of sentimentality. If the Pikunis hold to a warrior etiquette they also have renegades capable of destructive, indeed murderous, action, as in the case of Owl Child and his followers. The situation becomes one of Pikuni continuity yet possible rupture, history as know-how, survival, a way of being, and yet history as also the threat of diminution and erasure. It is a dynamic shrewdly perceived in the observation of the historically actual mixed-blood scout Joe Kipp:

> These people have not changed, thought Kipp, but the world they live in has. You could look at it one of two ways: either their world was shrinking or that other world, the one the white man brought with him, is expanding. (252)

Fools Crow's pilgrimage to Feather Woman as shaman, and as led in imagination by the spirit Nitsokou, becomes a search for the understanding of Blackfeet destiny. He is shown a scroll, a parchment of signs and predictions, which serves as prophecy:

> Fools Crow thought of the final design on the yellow skin in Feather Woman's Lodge. He saw the Napikwan children playing and laughing in a world that they possessed. And he saw the Pikuni children, quiet and huddled together, alone and foreign in their own country. (386)

In this "final design" past and future join to set inheritance against dispossession. Eye and ear again give Welch his point of arrival, the sighting of Pikuni children "foreign in their own country," the sound of Napikwan children "laughing in a world that they possessed" (386). This closing configuration as to the Blackfeet people in time and place is historic, chastening. It also again reminds of Welch's power to have his fiction "see" and "hear" lived history, the mosaic seen in its particularity while as the same time affiliated into the larger whole.

***

The Indian Lawyer offers a different bead on Native fortune. Time and place are modern, explicitly dated as 1988–1989 and the Reagan-Bush presidencies, Native life ostensibly framed as middle-class success – and yet not – in the person of Sylvester Yellow Calf. Stanford-educated and rising attorney in Buster Harrington's upmarket Helena law-firm as may be, he has been born poor and raised on the Blackfeet Reservation by grandparents as fond substitutes for the mother and father who abandoned him. Reversals bad and good follow him. The onetime basketball supremo who thinks to take on a political career he makes a critical wrong step. The Indian who is established city lawyer in the Montana state capital in time becomes the *pro bono* lawyer for water and land rights on behalf of the Sioux of Standing Rock in the Dakotas. The novel catches the ambiguity to a fault.

Welch keeps the narration to an almost a step-for-step Montana thriller format, the one contra-flow elided into the other. That holds whether for Yellow Calf's knowing "performance" of Native identity, Democratic Party state politics, the dance of parole board and parolee, and even the back and forth of the several love affairs. Mixed-blood heritage comes into view, necessarily, but equally so does both reservation and white ethnicity. *The Indian Lawyer* tells a Mountain West novel of both Blackfeet-Crow legacy and white class-strata, each in their paradoxical counter-reflection.

Landscape takes on implication, whether Prickly Pear Valley "dark with a summer storm" (39) or, for Yellow Calf, "the country was not empty, but remote and secluded, even intimate if you were alone" (158) and so lived in by hawk, antelope, or rattlesnake. City and social-circuit comes fully coded (the Harrington mansion "built during the 1880s and '90s in Helena by lumber barons, mining kings, prosperous stockmen and merchants" 40–1). The reservation at Browning's Moccasin Flat signifies "bald poverty" (104), yet under the guardianship of Yellow Calf's grandmother Mary Crow the location of the ancestral family warrior pouch (162) which he will profess to not understanding, then forget, and then later re-find and carry with him beyond Helena. The penitentiary of grey squared cell and un-windowed detention (17) with its deadly regimes of drug, bribery and rape, plays against the "the clean Victorian office" (75) of Yellow Calf. It would be hard to doubt this role of contextualizing location, the novel's geometry as backdrop to Yellow Calf's negotiation of the life's hand given him and then taken.

The plotline works the framing correspondences with aplomb. The double-track of Jack Harwood, educated convict serving his time at the Deer Park penitentiary for armed bank-robbery and of Yellow Calf as Montana Board of Pardons member, links through Harwood's wife Patti Ann who the convict inveigles into a seduction scam as would-be leverage against Yellow Calf. But just as Harwood has been knifed in the prison by the "Indians" who regulate drug and other illicit cellblock traffic ("The trouble was, the Indians thought he still had the money" 133), Yellow Calf and Patti Ann will be pursued under threat of violence by Harwood's paroled white-trash henchmen. Woody Peters and his lover-sidekick Bobby Fitzgerald so become turncoats who see the chance to make off with the heist they think hidden and still available from the original Harwood robbery. That the money has in fact paid for Patti Ann's hysterectomy adds the twist of another kind of knife, an end to any might-be imagined parent and child family future the border-pathological but highly intelligent Harwood anticipates on his long ahead release. The wife as agent-to-be, against plan, falls in love with Yellow Calf. Likewise Yellow Calf will use his lawyer savvy as to probation and prisoner-remand, and his visit to the roadhouse Shanty Bar where he scouts them out, to outmanoeuvre Peters and Fitzgerald. The doors revolve. Welch styles the story as zig-zag, ends against the middle.

The paradoxes accumulate. Shirt-and-tie smart, be-suited, Yellow Calf the might-be congressman for the Democratic Party is also heir to the great-grandfather pictured in deerskin legging. He can be neither fully the lawyer as "new warrior" his lover Shelley suggests and which, for his own part, he fancies himself in line with the once only-Indian on the basketball team. Nor can be fully the lawyer on equal working status with the white world which had allowed him professional entrance. The love affair with Patti Ann that begins when he is a member of the parole will lead to his demission. His announcement of a run for Congress is made at school where he once played Father Christmas, pastiche deepened by the unspeaking of tribal leaders. When a pupil offers him a plywood pipe of peace, it mocks his own Indian-ness, marks the contrast with his grandfather's medicine pouch, and shows up his un-disconnect from actual Native legacy.

Each of the women in his life similarly seeks negotiation of gains and deficits, notably Patti Ann who fantasizes and then both loves and loses Yellow Calf. His grandmother, Little Bird Walking Woman, maintains Blackfeet legacy for him albeit a flapper in her 1920s young womanhood and with a husband who has foresworn all tribal accoutrement as what he designates hocus-pocus in favor of a job in industry. Shelley, Senator's daughter, divorcee and mother of two, contrasts with Patti Ann and her miscarriages, two women who never "see" or "hear" him. Lena Old Horn, Yellow Calf's onetime school counselor, is drawn to him romantically even as she stays in a relationship with Stanley Weintraub, the teacher of English, whose nose he will break on court for how he embodies a whiteness he both seeks and resists. No one relationship in which Yellow Calf is pivotal takes full hold, the un-balance rather than balance of life forces caught winningly by Welch.

Two images especially linger and connect. Yellow Calf remembers seeing a raggedy Indian boy child "playing marbles all by himself" (59) and in which "I saw myself" (59). The closing vignette, playing hoops alone under wind and sleet on a night-time basketball court in Browning and having given up the prospect of a federal congressional career, returns to the same motif – "He was going one on one against the only man who ever beat him" (349). *The Indian Lawyer* has not always won plaudits, whether from Native literary-nationalist critics who persist in thinking it too readily a portrait of the white man's assimilated Indian or from "mainstream" critics who think the plot altogether over-determined. Both do disservice. Welch, rather, develops a novel that subtly sees and hears, and indeed grounds, contrariety, the "Native" success and yet not of Sylvester Yellow Calf caught between the lawyer who is Indian and the Indian who is lawyer.

***

The Heartsong of Charging Elk opens with an explicit act of sight and sound, that of the title character in his eleven year old boyhood participating in the surrender of the Oglala Lakota in 1890 at the Red Cloud Agency in Pine Ridge, Nebraska. Tribes-people led by Crazy Horse and met by Red Cloud ("great war chief...Now he was a reservation Indian" 2) belong in the boy's memory of both the inerasably seen and heard. His is the poignant remembrance of the so-called "Battle," actually massacre, of Wounded Knee. Despite defeat he watches leaders resplendent in full tribal dress and sings with the captive Sioux as they give ancestral chant ("The whole valley was alive with the peace song" 4). The soldiery, the *wasichus* or white people, may surround them, or herd their tribal horses, or fly the cavalry's "white and blue flag" (4). But despite poverty, their bedraggled line, even the tears of Charging Elk's mother, the Sioux look to headdress dignity and proclaim necessary songs of life and survivance. Welch's Prologue provides an unerring eye-and-ear frame for the life-portrait to follow.

For ahead will lie the compendious unfolding of Charging Elk's career, the one transition implicated in the other, Great Plains America into European

France, youth into near middle-age, with the Atlantic passage brought about by his part in the touring spectacle of Buffalo Bill Cody's Wild West Circus. Spoken Lakota, in all its brilliance of idiom and immense cosmography, co-exists for him with eventual French (and Langue d'Oc) under the respective linguistic as well as political mantra of *liberté, fraternité, egalité*. The novel so folds fact-fiction history several ways at once. Sioux history moves from inside to outside, an instance of the Red Atlantic as Jace Weaver has called it.[7] The clash of tribal and settler cross-worlds finds its ironic simulation in Winning of the West circus spectacle. Charging Elk's life, its contra-dance, Welch creates to act in all these respects as embodiment, an intermediation.

The novel, in kind with its predecessors, draws from a huge weave of event, each again persuasively grounded by eye and ear. Across the sixteen years from arrival in France in 1893, and from his lonesome awakening in a Marseille hospital after a horse-fall in the arena through to his cross-cultural marriage and impending parenthood with the farmer's daughter Nathalie Gazier, he lives a life at once memory and almost Gulliver-like encounter. How, as though reverse explorer, to "read," to "hear," and indeed to understand, the discordance of two kinds of Old World? That is no less compounded in the cultural double-take of Cody's circus in which "the young Indians enjoyed the spectacle of themselves reflected in the astonished eyes of the French people" (22).

The world of the Sioux bespeaks *Wakan Tanka* or the Great Mystery, *Nagi* or spirit, liberty in the Oglala Plains, Pine Ridge, and the Dakota territories and badlands of *Paha Sapa*. Charging Elk lives amid buffalo and seasons, his parents Shrub and Double Back Woman, the energy and tease of Lakota society, the Winter Count, his animal helper, and the young man companionship of his *kola* or bosom companion Strikes Plenty and "their wanderings in Paha Sapa" (23). That of France means in all senses other language, variously Catholic Nativity and western clock, *la famille* and *le raison*, table manners and *brasserie*, guillotine and cheese. His employments have him at different times portside fish-worker for the René Soulas family, soap factory laborer, prison gardener, and small-farm laborer at the Gazier fruit and vegetable holding. Other contradiction exerts hold. He retains belief that "the real world" (252) lies in the Sioux after-life as against the present French "dream" with its white jibes at his dark skin, its imprisonment for market theft of bread and subsequently for murder with to follow abrupt "political" release and award of French citizenry. He will be obliged to decipher, always through his own indigenous lexicon, a civilization as much other-world as that met by the French trappers and gold miners who first entered Sioux lands.

Marseille, "a large city and it smelled of the sea" is "noisy with carts and wagons" (40) as against "the wide open country of the Lakotas" (104). The Eiffel Tower, in Charging Elk's sighting, resembles a "naked iron tree" (40). Marseille's harbor arouses similar imagery ("Not even in Paha Sapa had he seen such a strange forest" 62). Caught out by vagabondage and petty theft in France and his "kaleidoscopic images of loneliness and despair" (195), he learns for the first time the inside of a cell as against the outside land-space of his home Plains. He can become the *cause célèbre* of the journalist Martin St-Cyr after killing Chef Breteuil for bordello homosexual drugging and molestation. His subsequent sentence to imprisonment in *La Tombe* can shadow both the Zola of "J'Accuse" and L'Affaire Drefus and Hugo's Jean Valjean in *Les Misérables.* But his thoughts can also summon dream, whether of Black Elk (on whom the novel is loosely based) and Crazy Horse, the Ghost Dance, the Federal Government ban of the Lakota tongue, the emergent reservations, and the dip in Native populations. He can even witness Buffalo Bill as fading impresario, himself the passing parade, as against his own revivication. To this end each stage in Charging Elk's story exhibits Welch's characteristic specificity of grip.

For these cross-worlds, their cultural mirrors, the novel keeps in precise imaginative alignment through to the close. Above all, the exilic chronicle as Welch offers it will cause Charging Elk to steer his way through lattices of stereotype, whether Vanishing Indian ("Even the sacred Paha Sapa had been taken from the people" 195), savagism ("a whooping, naked savage who scared the children half to death" 328), or the exotic ("everyone is different from me in your country" 395). None of which, even as he remembers Lakota legacy in his affecting speech to the court ("he realized that he did not have the French words to explain about evil. It could only be explained in the Lakota tongue" 338), is to deny friendship with the Soulas, sex with his prostitute Marie, or love with Nathalie. But at the core, body and spirit, eye and ear, his rite of passage as told by Welch in *The Heartsong of Charging Elk* involves learning the contrast between the plenitude of his Lakota identity and what exactly has come to be signified by the word *indien.*

***

"I always had a sense of economy from my poetry background" runs an observation in one of Welch's early interviews.[8] It speaks appositely to the styling of the novels that he had then so far written while presaging those to follow. In this respect, and though rarely claimed for a full postmodern, he has his roster of comparable claims. These lie in his story-line sight and sound, the working density in his depictions of cross-worlds, be it dislocation in *Winter in the Blood* and *The Death of Jim Loney,* tribal dynamics in *Fools Crow,* American Dream in

The Indian Lawyer, or the nineteenth-century transatlantic in the *Heartsong of Charging Elk*. The upshot on Welch's part deserves to be thought as commanding as it has been rare.

Notes

1 James Welch, "Blackfeet, Blood and Piegan Hunters," *Riding the Earthboy 40*, New York. World, 1971. Reprinted Lewiston, ID: Confluence Press, 1990, 32.
2 Jim Barnes, "Postcard to James Welch in Missoula," *The Sawdust War*, Urbana and Chicago: University of Illinois Press, 1992, 56.
3 Page references to *Winter in the Blood, The Death of Jim Loney*, and *Fools Crow* are to the Penguin editions.
4 "Homing in" has become standard formulation for the returned Native isolate. See William Bevis, "Native American novels: Homing in," Brian Swann and Arnold Krupat, eds., *Recovering the Word: Essays in Native American Literature*, Berkeley: University of California Press, 1987, 580–620.
5 Cited in Ron McFarland, ed., *James Welch*, Lewiston, ID: Confluence Press Inc., 1986, 161.
6 Louis Owens, *Other Destinies: Understanding The American Indian Novel*, Norman: University of Oklahoma Press, 1982, 128.
7 Jace Weaver, *The Red Atlantic: Indigenes and the Making of the Modern World, 1000-1927*, Columbia: University of South Carolina Press, 2014.
8 Ron McFarland and M.K. Browning, "An Interview with James Welch," in February 1984, Ron McFarland, ed., *James Welch*, Lewiston: Confluence Press, Inc., 1986, 18.

Works Cited

Barnes, Jim, *The Sawdust War*, Urbana and Chicago: University of Illinois Press, 1992.
Momaday, N. Scott, *House Made of Dawn*, New York: Harper & Row, 1968.
Silko. Leslie Marmon, *Ceremony*, New York: Viking Press, 1977.
Vizenor, Gerald, *Darkness in Saint Louis Bearheart*, Minneapolis: Truck Press, 1968. Revised and reprinted as *Bearheart: The Heirship Chronicles*, Minneapolis: University of Minnesota Press, 1990.
Welch, James, *The Heartsong of Charging Elk*, New York: Doubleday, 2000.
_____, *The Indian Lawyer*, New York: W.W Norton, 1990.
_____, *Fools Crow*, New York: Viking, 1986. Reprinted New York: Penguin Books, 1987a.
_____, *The Death of Jim Loney*, New York: Harper & Row, 1979. Reprinted New York: Penguin Books, 1987b.

_____, *Winter in the Blood*, New York: Harper & Row, 1974. Reprinted New York: Penguin Books, 1986.

_____, *Riding the Earth Boy 40*, New York: World, 1971.

7

Storier: Postindian Trajectory in the Novels of Gerald Vizenor

I am a storier, and my stories enfold the creation of a voice, a time, and a place.

Postindian Conversations (1999)[1]

The *indian* is the invention, and *indian* cultures are simulations, that is the ethnographic construction of a model that replaces the real in most academic references. Natives are the real, the ironies of the real, and an unnameable sense of presence, but simulations are the absence, and so the *indian* is an absence, not a presence…The postindian is after the simulation…The postindian stands for an active, ironic resistance to dominance, and the good energy of native survivance.

Postindian Conversations (1999)[2]

I would rather be an exotic menu by my words than a mundane storier.

Father Meme (2008)[3]

Storier. Postindian. *indian* (lower-case and italicized). These and associated Gerald Vizenor usages, typically *storier, survivance, fugitive pose, transmotion,* or *shadow distance,* might seem a long way from the received vocabulary to do with Native America. Yet few writers have been more resolute, or ebulliently ironic, in seeking not only to dismantle stereotype – Vanishing American to Hollywood Indian, Longfellow's Hiawatha to radio and TV's Tonto – but to seek new language, new imagery, for the un-stereotypic pluralisms of Native identity. Born of mixed White Earth Chippewa-Ojibwe (Anishinaabe) and white Scandinavian legacy, city-fostered in Minneapolis, an army enlistee based in Japan, one-time staff writer on the *Minneapolis Tribune*, and holder of professorships at Bemidji, Minnesota, Oklahoma, New Mexico, and the University of California at both Berkeley and Santa Cruz, he himself as much as most embodies that plurality. That he bears an anglicized French Canadian name likely assumed by a forbear for trading purposes adds its own flourish. The verve, not to say abundance, of his writings, has justly if sometimes contentiously put him at the forefront of contemporary Native authorship.

Postindian. Postmodern. The one abets and fuses with the other, writing provocatively, and often startlingly, attuned to moving-on from, or at the very least through and around, *indians.* Postindian, for Vizenor, its sources coevally drawn from Derridean and other modern cultural theory, has been a *mot clef* as developed in the proliferation of discursive writing from *Crossbloods: Bone Courts, Bingo, and Other Reports* (1990) through to *Native Provenance: The Betrayal of Native Creativity* (2019). These each carry his insistence on Natives wrested free of any one defining Euro-American gaze as "Indian" and the language of naming that has gone with it. To that end he has taken on not only the spectrum of custodial stereotype but Natives themselves (for him often in university Ethnic Studies departments) where they have colluded with or at least played into popular formula.

Under this dispensation he has gone on pointing out the process whereby Native peoples throughout the Americas were "othered" well before the Columbian landfall in the Caribbean. Was not the very appearance of "discovered" Native peoples made over into caricature, noble or demonic savagism, to be further perpetuated by missionary religion and anthropology not to say whole swathes of visual and literary imagery? How best to re-affirm Native America's own terms of life, no supposed one pan-Indian story but a massive and evolving cultural diversity of history, tribe, custom, shamanism, language, humor, art, locale, ethnic mix and identity, and dare it be said, individuality?

To this end Vizenor has invented a stirring company of trickster mixedbloods, wily, sometimes wild, lustful, often enough shape-shifters, and pledged always to upsetting the cultural fixed seams and binaries by which Natives have been defined. Each of his successive novels and story-collections positively abounds in these rare incarnations. They include the savvy trans-America pilgrim Proude Cedarfair in *Bearheart*, the text first published as *Darkness of Saint Louis Bearheart* (1978) then *Bearheart: The Heirship Chronicles* (1990); the genially disruptive China-voyager Griever de Hocus in *Griever: An American Monkey King in China* (1986); and the entire multi-named Browne reservation-dynasty (the pseudonymous Almost Browne above all) and their allied tricksters of *The Trickster of Liberty: Tribal Heirs to a Wild Baronage* (1988), *Hotline Healers: An Almost Browne Novel* (1997) and *Chancers* (2001).

Stone Columbus features as Minnesota casino-barge heir to the High Admiral in *The Heirs of Columbus* (1991). Laundry, the lecturer in tribal philosophies, speaks in trickster voice of his encounter with the bear wise-woman

Bagese at Oakland's Lake Merritt in *Dead Voices: Natural Agonies in The New World* (1992). The Chippewa-Ojibwe-Japanese orphan *hafu* Ronin Browne in *Hiroshima Bugi: Atomu 57* (2003) roams the atomic city with a contrary force of will. Vizenor's alter ego, Clement Beaulieu, the name taken from his own family, becomes his persona for different cycles of essays-as-story in *Wordarrows: Indians and Whites in the New Fur Trade* (1978). Beaulieu is used to explore Franklin Avenue, Minneapolis, as "urban reservation," the Bureau of Indian Affairs as the new fur trade, and the imprisoned rapist-murderer Thomas White Hawk as cultural schizophrenic.

Earthdivers: Tribal Narratives on Mixed Descent (1981), its span running from the Sand Creek Massacre of the Cheyenne in 1864 to latter-day Ethnic Studies campus politics, offers a virtual "postindian" manifesto for exploration of the masks and charades implicated in white-Native interface. The mentoring inspiration lies in Naanabozho, the great trickster spirit of the Anishinaabe, whose manifestations blend the antic with the serious, the sly with the heroic. As Vizenor observes in *Summer in The Spring: Ojibwe Lyric Poems and Tribal Stories* (1970, 1981), Naanabozho "disguises himself in many living things to explain and justify through imagination the conflicts of experience in tribal life" (155). Vizenor's tricksters, recognizably contemporary, can be said to give an American update to Chaucer's pilgrims, out-monkey China's own monkey-kings, and by running a blank book business just off the White Earth reservation transpose Berkeley-like library institutional habits. The Columbian legacy they can transpose into a laser show and claim Columbus as both Sephardic-Italian and Mayan mixed-blood returning to Atlantic-Caribbean-American homelands. They can chronicle the murderous replacement of museum tribal bones and skulls with those of academics and anthropologists. They can shout in outrage at the U.S. of the *Enola Gay* and "Little Boy" but also the Japan of the Hirohito-Tojo regime, most especially in the name of massacred children whose spirits he regards further affronted in the passive banality of Hiroshima's Peace Museum.

Landfill Meditation: Crossblood Stories (1991), which features an early appearance of Almost Browne, again plays fast and loose with story-essay boundaries. That applies whether guying Mother Earth sentimentality or AIM pan-nationalist warrior politics as theatre. The trickster-theming of "Almost Browne," as of the piece titled "Ice Tricksters" with its ice-cube sculpture fantasy, and of "The Psychotaxidermist" with its mock-trial format and bear masks, all read in cross-genre mode. Born in a hatchback at the border of White Earth reservation with white Minnesota, neither one hue nor another, Almost himself in his role as entrepreneur of Blank Books wins satiric laurels. In his genealogical mix, and his travels from the Midwest to Berkeley, he teases the very notion of any one fixed "Indian" identity, some pan-tribal aggregate based on Columbus's mistaken map. Native culture, past and ongoing, tribe-specific, languaged on its own terms, remains un-written as it were. The blank books, accordingly, and among other aims, represent Vizenor's uncompromising aim at the vacuity of the cliché Red Indian, each endlessly seductive (not to say financially profitable) Hollywood romance or comic-strip version.

These disruptions, the more soaringly fantastical or baroque the more the point, Vizenor offers in the name of working magic against antagonists who reduce Native life, all life, to the single definition or as Ishmael Reed terms it "uniculturalism." The texts in which Vizenor situates them, thereby, avoid fabulation or playfield for its own sake: rather they almost gymnastically subvert what have long themselves been falsifications. Theatrical, winning, as may be the popular-culture "Indian" of Western dime novel, cinema, comic strip, coins, stamps, or barbershop and tobacco advertising, the impact has been one of holograph or mannequin, a silhouette. For Vizenor these "Indians," or again for him *indians,* amount to "double-others," beguiling but also at times lethal fakery. "My pen was raised to terminal creeds" he writes in "Avengers at Wounded Knee" (235), a chapter in his autobiography *Interior Landscapes: Autobiographical Myths and Metaphors* (1990). It speaks exactly to his resolve upon refusing all unitary definition of Natives and each other human kind.

What image of Natives, for instance, can be said to have prevailed during the so-called "Indian Wars" – the Pequots in pre-Revolutionary New England, the Cherokee Trail of Tears in 1838, the "frontier" Plains tribes of the Sioux, Comanche and Cheyenne, or the Lakota at Wounded Knee in 1890? What image holds for city-raised Natives, male and female, Natives with PhDs, or filmmaker and author Natives? In interview he has even been heard to say "I believe we are all invented as Indians." [4] His fiction, assuredly to his postindian writ, yet also assuredly the name of clearer understanding, seeks to de-invent (and often enough re-invent) the invention.

Vizenor's novels and stories, along with the huge roster of journalism, discursive writing, autobiography, poetry and drama, time and again pitch for better recognition, with new language as need be, not only of Native survival but in his key term of *survivance.* That is, whether on reservation, or in the cities, in the Americas or in the wider globe, Native *survivance* signifies more than just survival but live, enactive, and always creative presence. If, too, that has meant the guying of fantasy *indians* from, say, colonial or screen versions of Pocahontas and Geronimo to out-of-time beads-and-blankets poseur radicals and TV hotline spiritualists, it has in no way meant sidestepping the historic set-backs. Vizenor's writings perfectly well acknowledge, and confront, the broken promises to the tribes, the violent colonial land-thefts and forced removals, the impact of different episodes of disease whether deliberately imposed colonial smallpox and influenza, fetal alcohol syndrome, or on- and off-reservation drug-use and other destructive behavior. At the same time, he would be the last to give concession to victim-mongering, Natives as forever history's losers, and somehow, indeed less than the multidimensional subjects of their own lives.

Vizenor's riposte, in these respects, has been scriptural tricksterism, his often magic-real or baroque roster of novels and story-cycles whose mixed-bloods subvert every would-be essentialist template of the *indian*. This is fiction as serio-comic gaming to embrace plot-lines that circle and reverse-swerve, baroquely named characters, and for sure, his different neologisms. Each text is as likely to cite, or rather refract, a wide eclecticism of sources. That might be indeed Derrida on word-meaning deconstruction or Baudrillard on simulation. Beckett always hovers, the articulacy of silence. Sioux luminaries like Luther Standing Bear are to be invoked on the Carlisle Indian Industrial School and settler arrival. In *Custer Died For Your Sins: An Indian Manifesto* Vine Deloria gives him acknowledged direction on tribal land rights and sovereignty to include the irony of the Native American Citizenship passed in June 1924.

It has often involved Vizenor in taking controversial shies in several directions at once. The arc embraces cinema cliché beginning with D. W. Griffith, Edward Curtis photography, or American Indian Movement leadership like that of Russell Means and Dennis Banks. Vizenor's presence in the Native American renaissance, a label he challenges, has always been his own, the gamester both fierce and gentle, the dialogic inventor of voices and narrative. If he has positively relished reflexivity, Native storytelling as itself story, tricksterism about tricksters, or each reductive travesty of "the Indian" held up to his authorial see-through mirror, this has far from caused him to lose hold of the reality of Native America's sustaining human creativity across hemispheric time and space. To the contrary: it has provided the very rationale for his writing. The trajectory of his novels highlights the point.

***

On initial view *Bearheart*, Vizenor's first novel might distantly summon less Chaucer than Cervantes in its use of the *peregrinus* motif. For the travels in play, from the start, clearly belong to irreality. They involve entering, and traversing, an America as much bereft of spiritual balance as of oil and petroleum energy, at once toxic, cannibal, and literally unlit. Yet for all the dystopian impulse, and as in not only Swift but artwork in the manner of Hieronymus Bosch or George Grosz, Vizenor's own Book of the Grotesque at the same time offers therapy towards better historical grace. If "war words and terminal creeds" (11) serve as his codings for Native life too often told as though in savagist couture and monochrome, then the novel acts as trickster countermand.

The manuscript given by Saint Louis Bearheart to Songidee migwam, AIM radical whose sacred Anishinaabe name she too readily discloses on breaking into the BIA offices, might indeed be a story brought out of hiding. The passage it tells of Proude Cedarfair, fourth of his name, and of his wife, Rosina Parent, from the "sovereign circle" (3) of sacred cedars trees at "migis sandridge" (13) in the Upper Mississippi (or as cited from Anishinaabe the *misibi*) to Chaco Canyon as "vision window" (238) and into the Fourth World, Vizenor pitches as a kind of puppet drama. His "circus pilgrims" (96), each a fantastical mixed-blood whose number includes the seven clown crows and the mongrels Pure Gumption and Private Jones, travel the abandoned interstate highways of America as though across a wasteland of darkest dream. The frequency of violence and death, the extravagant sexuality, have sometimes aroused puritanical complaint. Yet, at the very outset, Vizenor would seem to have issued a kind of Native cum-postmodern authorial health-warning ("The bear is in me now" reads the opening line, vii).

The very names of the pilgrims, and their tics or manners, do reflexive service, starting with Bearheart as woodland tribester yet also ursine spirit-healer, and whose repeated *ha ha ha haah* gives its own ironic acoustic to the novel. Of Rosina, Native woman, the text observes "She did not see herself in the abstract as a series of changing ideologies" (35). Others, usually mixed-blood, assume a shared magical or mongrel physiology, whether Benito Saint Plumero, lover of a green woman statue, and in an old Native piece of bawdy possessed of the endlessly in-service giant penis known as President Jackson, or Pio Wissakodewinni, "parawoman mixedblood mammoth clown," alleged male rapist given female hormones and caught sexually mid-way, or Belladonna Darwin-Winter Catcher, born at Wounded Knee of Lakota father and white mother, and who will die of a poisoned cookie for her narcissistic blather about Mother Earth and related feathers and war paint tribal cliché.

The company extends to Bishop Omax Parasimo, wearer of three metamasks in aiding tribal people to shelter, and who will die of lightning strike; Dr. Wilde Coxwain, dispenser of fake tribal history, and his male lover, Justice Pardone Cozener, lawyer illiterate; Sir Cecil Staples, "monarch of unleaded gasoline" (99), bald, toothless, skin-poisoned custodian of What Cheer Trailer Ruins and the Evil Gambler of Anishinaabe and other tribal myth (a life for five gallons of petrol), and the gargoyle mixed-blood who will die by one of his own killing-devices only when defeated in the game of chance by Proude; Lilith Mae Farrier, abused daughter and mocked one-time teacher, yet loving sexual partner to her twin boxer dogs, who destroys herself by fire having lost to Sir Cecil; and Inawa Biwide, orphan, victim of torture at New Mexico's Palace of Governors, pure spirit in a world of excremental history who will step into the Fourth World with Bearheart.

In their Brobdignagian encounters Vizenor seeks to skewer the legacy of America as Manifest Destiny, its standing as Native mantrap and excessive gasoline and foodways culture. "Interstate" perfectly applies, asphalt routeway yet also the index of a half-human condition. *Bearhear*, appopriately, works as a narrative theatre of episode and mask, the one violent metamorphosis set against another. Often Vizenor accouters them in a rhetoric long identified as his own but which, as ever, works to unfix fixity, the sediments of cooptive past usage: *survivance* as always, *transmotion*, *paramask*, *terminal creed*, *vision bear*, *shaman crow* or *panic hole*. The opening collusion with the federals of Jordan Coward, gin soaked and blustering Chairman of the nearby reservation, to have the Bearheart cedars felled by federal agents serves as perfect image of sell-out, tree-killing petty power as anti-life. It provides a curtain-raiser to the darker, at times near hallucinatory, sequences to follow.

Any number stand out. At the Scapehouse on Callus Road the novel envisages a thirteen-woman poet commune of Weirds and Sensitives, literally poisoned womanhood given to animal-eating, cancer, and group orgy with Bigfoot. At Big Walker the pilgrims barely avoid death as oil-scavenging whites try to seize the silver cabriolet they have been given only to burn to death in the flames. What Cheer yields Sir Cecil, parody aristocrat and bad spirit, to be followed by the novel's most graphic horror, that of the "Hlastic Haces," the Dunfries colony of cripples whose body parts, and faces especially, have been so eaten by cancers as to leave them unable to pronounce "Plastic Faces." When Little Big Mouse, white-woman companion to the giant pilgrim, Sun Bear Sun, seeks to console them with a strip-tease, they lust and masturbate, eventually to cause her death by dismemberment, ruined and parasite ghouls.

At the Bioavaricious Regional Word Hospital language itself comes under imagining as equally cancered, more terminal creed in the form of government or canonical history and never less so than in regard to Native America. At the Witch Hunt Restaurant the target is what Vizenor terms Fast Food Fascism, hanging "witch" women served as edible take-outs. At the city of Orion, by contrast, hospitality is to be exchanged for live spoken story, a suspicion of how, yet again, the fixed written word exerts its own imprisoning. Sun Bear Sun, for example, captured along with the other pilgrims by white authority at the Palace of Governors, is left "answering unanswerable questions" (230). These different close-encounters, and as one after another pilgrims dies or abandons the journey, will lead into Bearheart's own final and transcending bear-entry into the Fourth World.

Postmodern, not to mention postindian, likely only begins to cover the textual gymnastics of *Bearheart*, its command of satiric reversal or grotesquery. Native fiction is often construed as different orders of emergence, vision or homing story.[5] Each indeed plays its part in Vizenor's novel. It is the trickster ethos, however, Native-oral or postmodern-reflexive, if not an interplay of both, which above all gives it storying energy. A Mrs. Grundyism, distractingly, may on occasion have surfaced about maverick violence or offending sex. But the wholly more consequential challenge should not be doubted, tribal history imagined as tribal meta-history, Native America imagined as an awakening from nightmare.

***

Griever, more lightly playful in tone than *Bearheart*, continues the trajectory. Appointed to teach at Tianjin's Zhou Enlai University and accompanied by his savvy rooster companion, Matteo Ricci (named for the Italian Jesuit who brought Christianity to China), Griever de Hocus pledges himself as much to challenge China's party-led and puritanical conformism as America's economic profligacy. The master of antic gesture he liberates nightingales and street-market chickens, becomes a whole serial of Chinese opera figures in paint and costume (the "holosexual clown"), outwits bureaucratic control and censorship of the university curriculum in his role as professor, frees a line of prisoners destined for execution, and gets thrown out of the opening night at Maxim's of Beijing. His pursuit of Hester Hua Duan, beauteous translator, sino-sexual vaudeville figure, does yet more to undermine the established order.

True to mythic-trickster form Griever de Hocus escapes from his trail of reversals and transgressions avianly, by ultralight plane, headed ostensibly for Macao. Flying high, having dived low, and like the story that encloses him, he moves on and out as resistant as always to all closure or final destination. Given a tribal protagonist the virtual twin or cousin of the monkey king himself, Vizenor's China narrative can justifiably be said to subject Ch'-Eng-en's classic *The Journey to the West* to its own inspired, and suitably about-face, re-telling.

***

Vizenor's *The Heirs of Columbus* may not have been the only Native novel to have taken on the Columbus quincentenary of 1992 – *The Crown of Columbus* under the then husband-wife authorship of Louise Erdrich and Michael Dorris and with its New England academic format was another – but it assuredly was the most ingenious. Its trickster version of Columbus as foundational discovery figure, and of his legacy, Vizenor has take narrative shape as a virtual-reality detective quest of sorts. That leads to exhibition of the Genoese as himself a mix of ethnicities and the vie of contradiction, and frequent millennial zaniness.

The novel to this end brings into play a series of sleuths, motley, baroque as ever, the likes of Felipa Flowers, Chaine Riel Doumet and Lappet Tulip Browne, whose task is to track down the mysteries arising out of Columbianism. How, actually, to account for the enslavement of Natives, Spain's expulsion of the Jews, Pocahontas's burial in Gravesend, Kent, or Columbus as template for country and multiple city place-names, Catholic Masonic charity, a lighthouse, and various universities? As the plot weaves from one mystery to another, with insets of a New York trial created to investigate crimes against Native America and whose evidence includes cyber-moccasins, holographic bear sex and sock magic, it becomes clear that Vizenor is once again writing trickster script. Appropriately when Stone Columbus, owner and talk-show of the bingo-barge *Santa María Casino* and yet another member of the world's "mixedblood nation," projects his laser show on to the night sky the figures include Naanabozho, Louis Riel, Crazy Horse, Black Elk and Columbus himself. On offer is metafictive tableau, history, and Native history above all, as a form of sign-writing still far from being anything like finally deciphered.

***

Hiroshima Bugi: it might be thought typical that Vizenor would have one of his mixed-bloods write a chronicle of the world's first atomic-ruin city. Ronin Ainoko Browne, the emblematically named *hafu* offspring of the boogie dance Okichi and her White Earth Anishinaabe lover Orion Browne and one-time Japanese-language translator for General MacArthur known also as Nightbreaker, acts as yet one more trickster emissary to history's tragedy. Ronin's account, in turn, is monitored, and glossed, by Nightbreaker's friend, the Arizona-based author of each sequential "manidoo envoy" (*manidoo* the Anishinaabe for spirit). *Hiroshima Bugi* thereby operates as double-track narrative, two voices given both to measuring the world by atomic calendar (hence the half-title Atomu 57) and to an inspired play of cross-reference between Anishinaabe and Japanese tradition. The latter embraces not only wartime, postwar reconstruction and economic bubble, but cultural abundance to span Ainu, shinto and samurai, kabuki and bunraku, Bashō and Lafcadio Hearne, *Roshomon* and other Toshiro Mifune films by Akira Kurasawa and *Hiroshima Diary* and the novels of Kenzaburo Oe.

The fulcrum of the *Hiroshima Bugi* lies in Ronin's dismay at the Hiroshima Bomb Dome Peace Monument and museum and his cosmic shout against both the collusive antagonism of the Hideki Tojo military-fascist wartime government and the White House-US military process that led to the bombing. He also shouts at greatest pitch at Tokyo's Yasukuni War Shrine (Yasukuni Jinja) for those responsible to seek forgiveness from "the *kami* spirits" of martyred children. He equally indicts the fake post-atomic nuclear peace since Hiroshima, and the death of life it implies, against which his every trickster's sexual-creative energy serves as antidote. Around such Vizenor plies story into story. These include Ronin's relationship with his waitress-lover Miko as they find sexual bliss ironically (and contrarianly) near the Imperial Palace as the very bastion of court formality, or the story of the historical Scots-Chinook sailor Ranald Macdonald as the first-ever westerner to teach English to the Japanese. The novel folds in, and out, of itself as though to emulate a busily peopled and decorated Japanese screen or dwelling (*nihon-ra*). The upshot is a multi-tier narrative of Japan under Native eyes, Japan under its own art's eyes. Postindian? Postmodern? It would be hard to think otherwise.

***

Each of virtually all the fictions in Vizenor's trickster-postindian consortium shares the drive to free Native peoples of imposed monchrome category. *The Trickster of Liberty: Tribal Heirs to Wild Baronage*, fourteen inter-linking tales given over to the Browne dynasty of Shadow Box Browne and Wink Martin, again takes aim at leadership fakery (Coke de Fountain) and all connecting spurious "Indian" pose ("The Last Lecture at the Edge"). In *Dead Voices* Vizenor takes up the footfall of Samuel Beckett, a densely conceived California shaman story dealing in mirror and bear transformation and the ambiguity whereby the printed word of others has as much imprisoned as liberated the understanding of Native lives.

Hotline Healers, further trickster pieces from the White Earth barony, includes Nixon's offer of the vice-presidency to Almost Brown for removal of Castro (the celebrated eighteen-minute lost tape), the ingenious idea of Almost's Blank Book business with its implicit commentary on the writing-up of Native culture and signed Warhol-like and spuriously as if by well-known authors, and yet more New Age and Beauty Pageant "Indians." In *Chancers* the scene returns to the campus, Berkeley to be precise, Native skulls and artefacts made contested ground by two groups, the malign, murderous Solar Dancers and the benign Round Dancers. The fantasia, history seen trans-historically, turns on execution, orgy, and a surreal graduation ceremony involving Pocahontas, Ishi, and the anthropologist Alfred Kroeber.

***

With *Father Meme* (2008) Vizenor takes on priestly sexual abuse of Native altar boys from the reservation, an exquisite, and resolutely unsentimental novella. Indeed it offers a rite of verdict, cleansing, and sacrificial execution. Given the issue of paedophilia Vizenor might have edged into sanctimony, agreed outrage. In fact, in the story of Meme, one Father Conan Whitty, and his co-conspiratorial monk lover, Swayback, in reality Brother Roger Placid Chrisp, their sexual predations upon the boys, Pants, Bush and the narrator himself, and their sumptuously baroque come-uppance, Vizenor weaves a tale true to his past ironic flourish. For this invites being thought his version of *Crime and Punishment*, even *Witness for the Prosecution*, set in the 1950s of Lake Leech and then Namakan and Wiindigoo Lakes, a tale of clerical rape ending in exquisite retribution.

Told in the voice of a Native ex-journalist to a visiting Frenchwoman lawyer over Anishinaabe haute cuisine, with matching quality French wine, at the Mayagi Ashandiwin Restaurant of the Good Cheer Casino, it pitches benign consumption against the memory of its malign counterpart. For Meme and Swayback also act as consumers, but of flesh, boy innocence, and on each occasion be it in vestry or even by church altar as if to summon the larger historic ravage of the Native body through colonial disease, rape, and stolen sovereignty. As the narrator's "ma chère Madame" and other sedulous good-host manners accompany the story, so they highlight the cannibal un-manners of the priestly Jekyll and Hyde pair. Together with dips into Anishinaabe history like the tragic suicide-story of Dane White or shies at AIM luminaries like Dennis Banks and Clyde Bellecourt, the text steers subtly between case-history and carefully paced imaginative narrative.

The key filaments build into gathering rhythm and dénouement. Meme's warning nose-bleeds presage his own ecstatic death by beating. His July 4th sexual groping at Walker by Lake Leech anticipates a whole serial of acts against the boys' bodily independence. The frequent and every-opportunity onanism is unsparing, flesh over spirit, the cleric as neither father nor brother. The trip to the St. Johns Benedictine Abbey, with its high requiems and light-filled architecture and windows, plays against the Lake Namakan trip which Meme and Swayback intend as cover for their all too earthbound lust albeit that the boys trick their tormentors into literally naked and fly-bitten abandonment.

In their altar boy war, however, the trio develop a counter-strategy worthy of the wiliest insurgent. Their Fourteen Torments of Meme, long-range rifle shots not only at him but by implication the Vatican and diocesan authorities who have protected him, transpose the Stations of the Cross into an unforeseen iconography of judicial revenge. As the boys finally lure the naked Meme into his winter fish-house death, he to be sure aroused by the beatings they administer, and with only his red-hair and death's-head teeth grotesquely visible when his pulped body sinks beneath the ice, the story itself buries and cleanses the human stain he has so embodied. This is sacrifice, liberation, Vizenor's novel his own postindian storying of war and peace.

***

Shrouds of White Earth (2010) takes the form of another story-monologue posing as a colloquy. Ostensibly the invitation is that of Douglas Roy Beaulieu, Dogroy, banished from the reservation for his wholly un-literal and extravagantly bold-colored images of sacrificed animals (a series he entitles "Totemic Shrouds") and for Goya-esque portraits of casino and other tribal politicians. The auditor, and implicitly his co-speaker, is none other than a White Earth literary storier with a shared upbringing in early mean-streets and cheap-food Minneapolis. The settings they summon include the Band Box Diner, a major Native gathering-place and eatery, and Hello Dolly's, demolished to make way for public housing. Both serve as touchstones, citied "Indian" world beyond the reservation where stories also have to be remembered and dispensed.[6]

It falls to Dogroy to give notice of the ambition they both share:

> I create traces of totemic creatures, paint visionary characters in magical flight, scenes in the bright colors of survivance, and you create the same scenes by the tease of words and irony. We both have a place in the sun of art and literature, and a place name, but our situations, as artists of irony, are always uncertain with the tradition fascists of the White Earth Nation. (5)

The colloquy between Dogroy and his companion opens into what best, and indeed what worst, "represents" both Anishinaabe and the wider circuits of Native life. The two of them signify visionary storiers, the one a maker of visual art, the other of word. Given the considerable hinterland of playfield in Vizenor's prior fiction, that calls up a round of footfalls, his not un-typical reflexive take on reflexivity.

As Dogroy, in despite of the relevant articles of the White Earth Constitution of which Vizenor was the principal writer, is sent packing by Tradition Fascists as the would-be arbiters of which kind of image passes muster as "Indian," he will summon a dazzling counter-gallery of visual artists to his cause. These painter-magicians, Native and otherwise, cover a widest ambit, be it the Chippewa-Ojibwe George Morrison and David Bradley, the Russian-Jewish Marc Chagall, the German expressionist Otto Dix, the Colombian figure-painter Fernando Botero, or the great Japanese woodblock virtuosi of *shunga* (or erotic art) and *ukiyo-e* (art of the floating world). The attack on Dogroy's satiric shroud-art and cartooning and the killing of his cat Moses, bespeak provincialism, dim-witted revenge. For Vizenor is as much given to waylay narrow reservation-mandated literalism as he is to end kitsch romance-Indian representation. Dogroy so finds his resolve in "a circle of visionary creatures forever in magical flight over the White Earth Nation" (3), "abstract cosmoprimitive art" (17), "imagic liberty" (67), and the pledge to counter "crimes against creatures and native imagination" (150).

The returns are many, a contemporary fable of the fallacy of top-down dogmatic prescriptions of how art, and especially Native art – artifact or word – should or should not operate. Rather the need is for "magical flight," the aesthetic taken from the Chagall of "lumière-liberté." Art, whatever its genre or provenance, for Dogroy as for his literary fellow and co-worker and bibber lies in "visionary creations" (130), its qualities of illumination. The belief he formulates as "My portrayals are sensations not representations" (116) amounts to fighting talk but also offers an adroitly inlaid near-manifesto as to the kind of narrative on offer.

Told in four sequences, *Shrouds of White Earth* affords Vizenor in busiest mode. The foci include species-genocide (Dogroy, even after banishment, continues to create "burial houses for sacrificed and crucified birds and animals" 10), masturbation ("an act of erotic imagination" 28), the status of casinos ("the utmost secular situation" 75), and the vexed issues of authenticity and plagiarism in all Native and indeed other styles of representation. Dogroy deliberately, extravagantly, re-paints canonical paintings, notably Rubens and the Italian classics. He lives with a woman-cat troupe, apostrophizes "creature citizens" (150), and pursues a trajectory that connects White Earth to Paris's Musée du Quai Branley. The true geographical Lake Itasca is linked to the enticingly named Gallery of Irony Dogs.

Louise Erdrich for good reason speaks of Vizenor's verve in terms as shrewd as they are admiring:

> Nobody but Gerald Vizenor could write the words "cosmoprimitive casino series," or "mongrel driving schools," or describe the Band Box Diner with such skewed energy and capture what it means to be an Indian, an Anishinaabe, a human being on and off the White Earth Reservation here in Minnesota. *Shrouds of*

> *White Earth* is another wildly laudable work by our master ironist. A meditation on Native art, Marc Chagall, George Morrison, The Gallery of Irony Dogs, and too much else to mention…I am thankful for Visioner, I mean Vizenor. [7]

Bad faith, corruption of spirit, narrowed down rules-of-the-road art, and be it on the reservation or in the wider world, is simply not to be allowed countenance. Nor is it to allow for dogmatic prescriptions as to Native authenticity, whether of identity or creativity. The ethos at hand is the freedom to imagine Native self and nation, to give history, or place, or identity itself, live and as best suits soaringly baroque and ironic signature. It takes Vizenor's virtuosity, the one composite story told as though an overlap of two voices and in fierce though genial colors of invention to bring home the point with so ready a dispatch.

***

To speak of "late Vizenor" is of course not to offer some species of hopelessly premature obituary or, indeed, literary necromancy. Rather it calls attention to how he continues to yet further hone his long established reflexive repertoire, the feints of voice, the different mirrors and folds of plotline. If the case holds that to an extent every writer creates his or her own genre so, in Vizenor's writing, his storying, that applies with emphasis.

Chair of Tears (2012), twelve story-filaments centered in a Lake Itaska's houseboat Native dynasty and extending to the University of Minnesota's Department of Native American Indian Studies, might almost be thought a moebius strip. Stories loop around, then segue into, each other, full of things recognizably close to actual yet wrapped also in fantastical sheen. An early pointer lies in the observation "Our family was forever bound by teases and stories" (11). Well might the point take on self-referring force given the lineage that descends from Captain Eighty, patriarch of the lake clan and his fifty years younger poker-queen wife Quiver Beaulieu. The plethora of offspring smack of magic genealogy, uncle-aunt branches, and on down to the grandson-narrator and his principal cousins, Dogroy Beaulieu, banished Chagall-ian artist, and Captain Carbon Six Shammer, would-be houseboat helmsman, who will assume center-stage at the university. From the opening page onwards there can be little doubt of further Vizenor storying, further playfield.

Storying is built into the Eighty clan's very nomenclature, a thesaurus of narrative within each invented nickname. True surnames, especially if they involve the federal agent, Sepia Face, never actually receive mention. The ramshackle "nuptial houseboat" (2) sails under the name *The Red Lust.* Captain Eighty and Captain Carbon Six Shammer are named for the elements, respectively 80 the atomic number for Mercury or Hg and Carbon, atomic number 6. The five first offspring, true to Quiver's on-board poker genius, take their names from playing hands, Two Pairs, Straight, Full House for the girls, High Card and Flush for the boys – the latter, the narrator's father, in true Anishinaabe tradition a woodworker. This "marvelous houseboat family" (9), in and of themselves, comes beset with storier and storying.

Quiver has married "a native storier who roamed in the bush, a curious trickster of discrete grace and mercy" (2). His various designations of "storier of survivance" (3), "lusty storier" (9), and "mighty storier" (15) all underline his role as Homeric, preserver and fabler whether of Anishinaabe origin myth or Mississippi headwater monk sex with animals. The generation of mongrels that sail with Eighty each bear suitably baroque story-monikers, respectively Pope Pius, Moby Jean, Monte, Big Wig, Tender, Mustard and Appetizer. One could be forgiven for thinking this an about-face roster from *A Midsummer Night's Dream*. A further colony of dogs, trained by Chance who belongs to the group Women of Creature Arts, function as "irony mongrels, their role to "sense pretense and anxiety" (16). These names also come story-laden as Lévi-Strauss, Turnip, Nixon, and above all Derrida, the "pied noir of the seminars" (20) at the university. The storying takes on characteristic accent, and targeting, in the supposed further training of these dogs:

> Lévi-Strauss and one or two of the other advanced irony mongrels could in most instances sense the distinction between the un-intended irony of Henry Kissinger, Aleksandr Solzhenitsyn, recipients of the Presidential Medal of Freedom, or the *New York Times*, and the notable absence of irony in serious comments by Sigmund Freud, the famous aviator Charles Lindbergh, and Joseph Alois Ratzinger – or Pope Benedict, a citizen of the Vatican. (18)

The appointment of Captain Shammer, sumptuously without academic qualification, appointed by the faux-liberal entrepreneurial Dean Slash and Burn to the Chair of Native American Indian Studies, and mis-identified by some of the grey-dead faculty as Chaplain Shammer, could hardly not lead into comic-serious masquerade. Shammer's ascendancy to the so-called Chair of Tears ("more irony than victimry" 30) with its echo of historic relocation of the tribes, might almost be an update of the Feast of Fools. Certainly Shammer savvily creates a world turned upside down for a faculty that has "deserted stories...disregarded the emotive sentiments of native presence" (24).

Like Melville's shipboard masquerader in *The Confidence-Man* he is given to costume and transformation. He turns up dressed as Custer ("Captain Shammer had arrived by mimicry" 24), wears Native and Hollywood masks among them those of "Jay Silverheels, Sacheen Leatherfeather, Jamake Highwater, and Jimmie Durham" (51), and issues a slew of edicts ("radical schemes and teases, political roundabouts" 33). His conversion of faculty offices into casino stations offers another hall of mirrors ("The Full House Casino slot machines pictured Sitting Bull, Geronimo, White Cloud, Chief Joseph, Little Cloud, and just a faint shroud of Crazy Horse" 47). Little wonder that Shammer is dubbed a "windward storier" (46), a "tricky storier" (68).

Shammer's department reign does not stop there, however. His introduction of the lack-of-irony sniffing mongrel dogs as "shaman healers" to "attend lectures and bark at the absence of irony" (68) does service to undermine cliché, the one or another fixed version of Native life. That includes a Vizenor riff on skin-dunking as a send-up of Native authenticity by skin-hue. He demands confessional Last Lectures, displays holographic laser histories, and establishes Panic Hole radio broadcasts and Denivance Press with its guarantee of instant rejection and publication of signed blank books. Finally, and once again to the point, he tenders out the department at auction ("lock, stock, barrel, skin dunk, casino, and signature blank books" 129) to have it bought by "the Earthdivers, an association of native storiers" (138). Who more apt?

Treaty Shirts (2016) has Vizenor embarking on what can be called Nativefuturism, literary kin of Afrofuturist narrative. Pitched as though written, or rather "spoken," on the literal hundred month and year of his own birth, it apportions its fictional parable into seven choric voices in company with the "storier" Chewy Browne ("a native soprano in her nineties" 7). Each, under nicknaming, and exiled from White Earth for insisting on its liberationist Constitution against a dystopian American-Canada of sectors or *länder*, gives their several ingenious beads on treaty rights and historic tribal sovereignty as though themselves creating "a new literature of survivance" (33). That Vizenor was himself involved in writing the actual White Earth Constitution, ratified in 2009 though entangled in both State and tribal politics, offers the one fictional text its own historical subtext.[8]

The novel opens and closes in the voice of Archive, storier insistent that Native history be remembered whole and in full. His fellow-exiles in their route to Lake of the Woods freedom aboard the *Baron of Petronia* so speak back history and fantasticality. Moby Dick attests to casino sell-out, the government administrator Godtwit Moon, and deformed aquarium display fish. Savage Love descants on exile and its meanings in Native life and literature. Gichi Noodin, Anishinaabe-named, bears witness to treaty and BIA malfeasance as reported on Panic Radio. Hole in the Storm, Native cubist, invokes both poetic and visual out-imagine kitsch. Waasese, "laser holoscene scientist" (10), offers a perspective which can be thought to reflect upon the novel:

> Natives were creative stories, and natives anticipated the turns of postmodern theories, and natives have written and published critical books for more than three centuries. Churches and missions printed the first native books, and some were narratives of godly discovery and conversions, of course, but those stories of monotheistic revivals were never shouted to the same sky or natural motion of the clouds with same spirit as native dream songs, trickster stories, or even the wags of ecstatic shamans. Rightly, the first godly native authors resisted the moronic notions of banishment and the politics of vanished races and victimry. (86)

Together with Justice Molly Crèche, who rules in favor of the rights of murdered animals (among them beavers in the fur trade), this is yet more witness to a lived-in Native "sense of presence" (34). *Treaty Shirts* does service as appropriate narrative theatre.

***

Blue Ravens (2014) opens Vizenor's "historical" trilogy, each of which can be said to insist on visionary powers of creativity at their best when called upon to unsettle, and so outflank or transcend, all static or either-or prescriptions of the human condition. Vizenor's storying, it would be fair to say, was ever so. For as the novel has Aloysius Hudon Beaulieu and Basile Hudon Beaulieu, Native brother-twins (though with a twist) and respectively visual artist and writer, embark upon their rite of passage from White Earth to the Europe of World War I, it unfolds a world and its era at once one of sumptuous artistic break-through and yet brutal historical fracture ("the bloody rage of war" 127). This is to situate the two artist-enlistees, and their Beaulieu-Vizenor dynasty, within a changing but ingeniously linked serial of time and place: Minnesota's turn of the century Chippewa-Ojibwe reservation, wartime gas and trench France as American Expeditionary Forces enter the Great War in 1917–1918, and the Europe of transition from *belle époque* to the 1920s of modernism and Paris. The upshot amounts to hugely ambitious storying, a magic-real tribute to Native presence, in actuality and art, and within a historic trans-Atlantic, or indeed Red Atlantic, spectrum of war and peace.

"Aloysius Hudon Beaulieu created marvelous blue ravens that stormy summer" reads the opening sentence (1). It sets up figuration for the whole novel.

Aloysius will paint huge, magnificent abstract ravens in Chagall-blue across settings both American and European. They are totemic, abstract, as though by this avian fantasticality to give new imagining to nothing less than Native and non-Native world alike. A later age has Christo wrap buildings and cliffs, Banksy exhibit anonymous street graphics, Jean-Michel Basquiat line-draw his pictograms. The Aloysius of Vizenor's text paints his ravens as though, virtually, irreally, they can appear even more transnationally, whether Twin Cities-Saskatchewan Soo Line rail carriage or Seine River bridge, whether Minneapolis's Orpheum Theatre or the Marne and Vesle battlefields. Only in part will they transfer from outside world to inside gallery.

These birds, along with the stories composed by Basile, act as art hieroglyphs fully in their own right. But they also provide filters through which to understand life-affirming liberty, and virtuosity, even as until 1924 the U.S. denies citizenship and its rights to Native populations, and Europe becomes killing-field in the contest for the one or another political ascendancy. Their blueness summons a vast expressive hinterland that includes lapis lazuli, woad, indigo dye, religious stained window, Chinese porcelain, Hokusai woodblock, through to the Blue Period and later canvases of Picasso, Matisse, and the recurrent name of Marc Chagall ("Chagall painted blue dreams, lovers, angels, violinists, donkeys, cities, and circus scenes" 2). The achievement, as the novel insists, is exhilarating, to which the novel itself seeks to do justice, the one and the other two kinds of imagist tapestry.

Vizenor pitches his date-for-date novel to work in parallel with the 24-chapter *Odyssey*, with actual citations from Homer's epic. But in having Basile write Aloysius, and their shared odyssean journey, he equally uses his own style of one narrator for two in a manner to recall *Dead Voices*, *Hiroshima Bugi* and the ex-journalist to lawyer tactic of *Father Meme*. The White Earth scenes assemble a vintage cast, beginning with extended family ("great storiers" 12). The father, Honoré Hudon Beaulieu, is both "singer and woodland storier" 5). The mother, Margaret Beaulieu, "remembers the scent and stories of maple syrup" (5). Augustus Hudon Beaulieu, wiseacre and mentor, take his place as "cunning and ambitious uncle " (2). Fellow White Earth denizens, besides assorted other Beaulieu-Vizenors who serve in the military, number the trickster-savvy trader Odysseus Walker, the healer Missabe, the generous John Leecy of the Leecy Hotel, Patch Zhimagaanish the valiant railwayman-trumpeter, Father Aloysius Hermeneutz the Benedictine, and almost inevitably, a round of Vizenor mongrel dogs. Their world, and the international world beyond, is carried in the White

Earth journal, *The Progress*, later *The Tomahawk*, both to be sold at Ogema Station near the reservation but also in Minneapolis and even across the Atlantic.

In France, fact again overlaps with fiction, not unlike E. L. Doctorow's *Ragtime* (1975). Not only do the brothers face combat as painted scouts ("the war was surreal, faces, forests, and enemies" 130), get captured, escape, and learn first-hand the Hindenburg Line and battles like Montbréhain, they remember benign heroines like Frances Gulick, the YMCA nurse and welfare worker, and Anna Coleman Ladd, Massachusetts sculptress and pioneer of prosthetic masks for impaired soldiers. Survivors, *survivancers*, their plunge into Paris as modernist fiefdom after the 1918 Armistice again elides history and art ("Paris meant more to us than a luminous tourist destination...the city had become our vision of art and literature, and a chance of recognition as native artists" 144).

Aloysius can continue to paint his ravens fantastically upon the Place de la Concorde, Notre Dame, Gare de l'Est and the Bastille. His "Thirty Six Views of the Eiffel Tower" will again echo Hokusai. He does so, however, as together with Basile he reads the wholly actual Apollinaire, meets Chagall himself, comes face to face with the likes of Modigliani, the cubist Marie Vassilieff, Blaise Cendrars, James Joyce, Sylvia Beach, Gertrude Stein, and displays with great Jewish gallerists like Nathan Crémieux and Daniel-Henri Kahnweiler. The expatriate years they take in France, the returns and re-returns both to White Earth and Paris, their part in Native and French banquet gatherings (with yet more Vizenor menus) leads on to a surge of new ravens from Aloysius and narratives from Basile. *Blue Ravens* so parables its resistance story against both Native dispossession and European war, to include intimacies in which Aloysius shares his body with Maria – Vizenor's reflexive vision of Native creativity as though both un-diminishing pigments of blue and un-diminishing filters of story.

***

Late to latest "historical" Vizenor shows no dip in appetite. Both *Native Tributes* (2018) and *Satie on the Seine: Letters to the Heirs of the Fur Trade* (2020) give not exactly Native custody but eye to key episodes in the west's twentieth-century's human passage. The former situates Basile Hudon Beaulieu as Anishinaabe participant-witness with his brother Aloysius, artist and glover-puppeteer, in the 1932 Bonus Army protest by World War I veterans at their forgotten-ness by the Hoover and other 1920s interwar presidencies. The latter, also under the pen of Basile and spanning 1932–1945, takes the form of fifty letters that interlace the colonial encounter of European fur-trade and Native populations with the Nazi occupation of Paris and larger Europe.

In both, history panel and epistolary pageant, Vizenor plays his own identifying shards of metafictive invention into a plenitude of bedrock event. In *Native Tributes* General Douglas McArthur, John Dos Passos and New York's Governor Al Smith can make literal but fantasy appearances. In *Satie on the Scene* history has its reality in *La Résistance* and a Nobel laureate-leftist like Romain Rolland but also imagined hand-glove colloquies like one between Hitler and Gertrude Stein. Admirers have readily seized upon this fact-fiction dexterity, the circling tease and viewpoint. The less admiring murmur of too familiar a repertoire of Native feints and routines. Neither, however, fails to recognize Vizenor's bravura.

Notes

1 Gerald Vizenor and A. Robert Lee, *Postindian Conversations,* Lincoln, Nebraska: University of Nebraska, 1999, 61.
2 *Postindian Conversations,* 85.
3 *Father Meme,* Albuquerque: University of New Mexico Press, 2008, 60.
4 Neal Bowers and Charles Silet, "An Interview with Gerald Vizenor," *MELUS,* 8:1, 46.
5 A greatly influential essay in this regard is William Bevis, "Native American Novels: Homing In," in Brian Swann and Arnold Krupat, eds., *Recovering The Word: Essays on Native American Literature,* Berkeley: University of California Press, 1987, 580–620.
6 One of the standard accounts in this respect is to be found in Donald Fixico, *The Urban Experience in America,* Albuquerque: University of New Mexico Press, 2000.
7 Louise Erdrich, Webpage "Birchback Blog," November 17, 2010.
8 See, in this respect, *The White Earth Nation: Ratification of a Native Democratic Constitution,* Lincoln: University of Nebraska Press, 2012.

Works Cited

Deloria, Vine, *Custer Died for Your Sins, An Indian Manifesto,* New York: MacMillan, 1969. 2nd Edition, Norman: University of Oklahoma Press, 1995

Erdrich, Louise, and Dorris, Michael, *The Crown of Columbus,* New York: HarperCollins, 1991.

Vizenor, Gerald, *Satie on the Seine: Letters to the Heirs of the Fur Trade,* Hanover: Wesleyan University Press, 2020.

_____, *Native Provenance: The Betrayal of Native Creativity,* Lincoln: University of Nebraska Press, 2019.

_____, *Native Tributes: Historical Novel,* Hanover: Wesleyan University Press, 2018.

_____, *Treaty Shirts: October 2034 – A Familiar Treatise on the White Earth Nation*, Hanover: Wesleyan University Press, 2016.

_____, *Blue Ravens*, Lincoln: University of Nebraska Press, 2014.

_____, *Shrouds of White Earth*, Albany: State University of New York Press, 2010.

_____, *Native Liberty: Natural Reason and Cultural Survivance*, Lincoln: University of Nebraska Press, 2009a.

_____, ed., *Survivance: Narratives of Native Presence*, Lincoln: University of Nebraska Press, 2009b.

_____, ed., Vizenor, Gerald, *Native Storiers: Five Selections*, Lincoln: University of Nebraska Press, 2009c.

_____, *Father Meme*, Albuquerque: University of New Mexico Press, 2008.

_____, *Hiroshima Bugi: Atomium 57*, Lincoln: University of Nebraska Press, 2003.

_____, *Chancers*, Norman: University of Oklahoma Press, 2001.

_____, *Fugitive Poses: Native Scenes of Absence and Presence*, Lincoln: University of Nebraska Press, 1998.

_____, *Hotline Healers: An Almost Browne Novel*, Hanover: Wesleyan University Press/University of New England Press, 1997.

_____, *Dead Voices: Natural Agonies in the New World*, Norman; University of Oklahoma Press, 1992a.

_____, *Manifest Manners; Postindian Warriors of Survivance*, Hanover: Wesleyan University Press/University of New England Press, 1992b.

_____, *The Heirs of Columbus*, Hanover: Wesleyan University Press/University Press of New England, 1991a.

_____, *Landfill Meditation: Crossblood Stories*, Wesleyan University Press/University Press of New England, 1991b.

_____, *Interior Landscapes: Autobiographical Myths and Metaphors*, Minneapolis: University of Minnesota Press, 1990.

_____, ed., *Narrative Chance: Postmodern Discourse on Native American Indian Literatures*, Albuquerque: University of New Mexico Press, 1989.

_____, *The Trickster of Liberty: Tribal Heirs to a Wild Baronage*, Minneapolis: University of Minnesota Press, 1988.

_____, *Griever: An American Monkey King in China*, Normal: Illinois State University/Fiction Collective, 1986. Reprinted Minneapolis: University of Minnesota Press, 1990.

_____, *Earthdivers: Tribal Narratives on Mixed Descent*, Minneapolis: University of Minnesota Press, 1981.

_____, *Wordarrows: Indians and Whites in the New Fur Trade*, Minneapolis: University of Minnesota, 1978.

_____, *Bearheart*, Minneapolis: Truck Press, 1978. Originally titled *Darkness in Saint Louis Bearheart*. Revised and reprinted as *Bearheart: The Heirship Chronicles*, Minneapolis: The University of Minnesota Press, 1990.

_____, *Summer in the Spring: Ojibwe Lyric Poems and Tribal Stories*, 1970. Reprinted Minneapolis: Nodin Press, 1981. Revised: *Summer in the Spring: Anishinaabe Lyric Poems and Stories*, Norman: University of Oklahoma Press, 1993.

Vizenor, Gerald, and Lee, A. Robert, *Postindian Conversations*, Lincoln: University of Nebraska Press, 1999.

8

Fiction Off and On Center: Sherman Alexie

Native American. There's an oxymoron for you.

"Dear John Wayne," *The Toughest Indian in the World* (2000)[1]

You throw in a couple of birds and four directions and corn pollen and it's Native American literature, when it has nothing to do with the day-to-day lives of Indians.

Sherman Alexie, Interview, *The Atlantic* (2003)[2]

Sherman Alexie's repertoire of novel, short story, poetry, essay and film script, together with the plenitude of print and live and web interviews, has long put him in the reputational spotlight. In line with the widespread enthusiasm from the reviews he typically gathered points as Bill Clinton's preferred reading. Alexie, it would be fair to observe, has run close to being Native America's literary *Wunderkind*. Early verse and story collections like *The Business of Fancydancing* (1992) and *Old Shirts and New Skins* (1993) were quick to win him admiring readerships. His Young Adult and children's fiction was both popular if at times edged in controversy about sex or violence, whether *The Absolutely True Story of a Part-Time Indian* (2007, and revisions) with its vision of Native transition from reservation to city, *Thunder Boy Jr.* (2016), with its vexed but ultimately healing father-son portrait, or *Flight* (2007), whose Native adolescent protagonist Zits moves from fostering into a fantastical parade of historical and family identities. But it has been the writing pitched for an adult readership where the hallmarks have most gained traction.

For Alexie has justifiably been thought to have acted on Emily Dickinson's "tell it slant." While the axiom does not cover all bases it gives gloss both to the story-work of *The Lone Ranger and Tonto Fistfight in Heaven* (1993), *The Toughest Indian in the World* (2000), *Ten Little Indians* (2003) and *War Dances* (2009) and to the novels *Reservation Blues* (1995) and *Indian Killer* (1996). The Spokane Indian Reservation life-theatre they offer, and that set in kindred venues, has about it both familiarity and yet de-familiarization, variously funny-wry, sardonic, on occasion violent, as if always to insist that virtually all usual versions of "the Indian" have to be unsettled in the interests of altogether necessary greater nuance.

For the 2020s, however, shadow threatens Alexie. There hover charges against him of sexual harassment and abuse. These have led to cancel-culture retaliation, whether speaking engagements or journals that will not accept analysis of his writing. In this light, and despite praise for its achievement, misgivings have also arisen for the text-and-image memoir of *You Don't Have to Say You Love Me* (2017). Centered in the complexity of his troubled yet greatly creative mother Lilliane and her alcoholic spouse, his own childhood hydrocephalus, the only-Indian-in-the-class schooling in Reardon, Washington, and his bow into full-score authorship, this may be life-writing of rare virtuosity. But it has become clouded by the gender and power issues that attach to his name.

***

How, then, best to read his writings, still the exhalations of an exceptional talent or tainted goods on account of the writer's in-life deficits? Time, even the courts, will have to judge his standing as both public and private celebrity, just as they did in the cases of, say, Ezra Pound or Louis-Ferdinand Céline for their politics or Nabokov for the Lolita-syndrome. For present purposes the emphasis falls on the agility of styling in Alexie's fiction, the command of turn of voice in making the seeming off-center into center across the roster through to the fiction republished in *Blasphemy: New and Selected Stories* (2021) and to the novels.

Spokane and other reservation life provides evident context but Alexie's storytelling avails itself of idiosyncratic filters that take it well beyond, or outside, any suggestion of the reportorial. His fiction, rather, and in kind with his poetry, makes for tactically disjunctive versions of the everyday reservation or of Seattle. Friendships take their shadow from remembered disquiet as much as bonding. Parenting goes both right and wrong, mother or father absenteeism yet a grandmother's love, the wanton father yet dying of cancer, or two brother-uncles fighting in sweat and drink yet full of sibling devotion. Broken relationships so mirror the frequent broken cars or make-do HUD housing both within and beyond the Spokane/Wellpinit Indian Reservation. Nor is it lost that whites also live within or at least close to reservation land and township.

Basketball or salmon both recur as lodestones, literal to the reservation but also memorial traces that transit into speech as metaphor or figuring. Crazy

Horse, ponies, the defeat of Custer, likewise supply footfalls, "real" history yet also vernacular slipknots. Foodways range from remembered healthful wild rice, herbs, or berries, to fry-bread and Trading Store and commodity high-sugared junk food with diabetes always a threat. Alcohol, to challenge stereotype, often makes its appearance in the person of recovering, if not recovered, alcoholics alongside the drunks. Diet coke can feature as much as bar-fly and six-pack drinking. Alexie's portraits of Native-white encounter especially come in at an angle, be it hate, love, language, sexuality, each light and dark-matter comedy of error. His mixed-bloods, male, female, bisexual, gay, and of different ages, thereby give witness as much to the revolving helixes of gender as to the turnings of ethnicity.

Above all the focus turns upon the paradoxes inherent in "being Indian," each interior selfhood, each life amid family and compeers, each strength or reversal of inter-friendship from childhood onwards, and each knowing double performance of "Indians" for non-Indians. Little wonder, given his takes on these center and off-center shadings, that Alexie makes a tease of the oxymoron within "Native American." That means a full regard for his deployments of cross-view, his use of angled incongruity to the point at times of the near-magical.

***

Few first novels, Native-written or otherwise, to this end have more made their bow with irony as punchily innovative, and yet serious, as Alexie's *Reservation Blues* (1995). "Thomas Builds-The-Fire's stories climbed into your clothes like sand, and gave you itches that could not be scratched" (15) reads one cue. "I'm a recovering Catholic" (146) or "Nobody ever notices the sober Indians" (151) give others. The touch is playful, full of well-targeted satiric tease, yet perfectly alive to defeat, even pathos.

The novel's Spokane Coeur d'Alene reservation world has its share of HUD sub-standard housing, basketball, alcohol babies, competing churches, and tribal infighting. But it serves also as a place of living myth, dream memories, jumps in time, benign fakers like "the end of the world...crazy old Indian man" known as "the-man-who-was-probably-Lakota" (11), or an overseeing musical shaman like Big Mom of nearby Wellpinit Mountain. As in his subsequent fictions, full-length or short, Alexie shows himself always the storyteller resourcefully quick on his feet, precisely the fancy dancer in the titling *The Business of Fancydancing: Stories and Poems*.

From the magical arrival at the reservation crossroads of Robert Johnson, legendary Mississippi bluesman with his guitar music born of his compact the devil, the latter white and known as "The Gentleman," through to the rise of Coyote

Springs as a "warrior band" (77) – albeit a Rock band, the novel pursues an odyssey across an America of "Indians" real and imagined. Thomas, "the misfit storyteller of the Spokane tribe" (5), serves throughout as part good-fellow, part savant and visionary. With Victor Joseph, drinker and bully yet who inherits the guitar and indeed plays like the devil, Junior Polatkin, his binge partner and uncertain drummer, and the two Flatfoot Tribe sisters, Chess and Checkers Warm Water, who sing back-up, together at first with the blonde "New Age princesses" in turquoise strings and beads, Betty and Veronica, he seeks to make music, "reservation blues," as a stay against confusion, his own act of resistance.

The results lead into cavalcade, picaresque, from Spokane Indian Reservation to Arlee, Montana as the first of a slew of tavern and other gigs, and from a disastrous visit to a New York recording studio to an eventual journey in Thomas's iconic blue van to Seattle. Each episode en route does bittersweet, and often bitingly funny, service. Johnson's guitar early speaks in its own voice ("The blues always makes us remember" 22). CIA and FBI agents disguise themselves as Indians "but didn't fool anybody because they danced like shit" (34). Father Arnold hovers deliciously between spirit and flesh, between his mission to the Spokane and his passion for Checkers. Thomas's journal lists entries for the different incarnations of Coyote. Mean-spirited reviews of the group appear in the tribal press (83), often at the behest of the Tribal Chairman, David Walks Along, whose muscled convict-nephew, Michael White Hawk, exudes threat. A remembered half-fantasy basketball game between Samuel, Thomas's drunkard father, and the cops, becomes a replay of past "Indian wars."

Each fade and dissolve happens at high pace, a fiction of itself fast-moving fictions. Alexie especially shows his paces when Cavalry Records, under the commercial management of latter-day intertextual "generalship" like that of Phil Sheridan and George Wright, and they, in turn, under a boss named Mr. Armstrong, offers the group a studio try-out ("Indians are big these days" 224). History, kind of, replays itself, Little Bighorn shadowed in a recording company. The group, Victor Joseph at least, becomes "too violent" and trashes the studio. Betty and Veronica, stage Indians to a fault, become the acceptable purveyors of tribal music.

In turn Big Mom comes to think "Indian men have started to believe their own publicity and run around acting like the Indians in the movies" (208). Victor trades in Junior to the Devil even as Robert Johnson receives a cedar flute from Big Mom, a life for a death. As he drives out of the reservation, with Chess and Checkers, Thomas finds songs for all the warrior horse spirits of "Indians" dead and alive (306). The note is fond, restorative, the visionary and half-magical epilogue to all the mediating ironies of *Reservation Blues*. Alexie has often enough expressed the wish to see Native writing move on from Momaday and the domain of the established Native American Renaissance names. Respect, but not filo-piety, obviously applies. The singularity of his own imaginative pathway could not be in doubt.

***

Alexie's first story-collection, *The Lone Ranger and Tonto Fistfight in Heaven* (1993), shares the honors as to early invention. The title hints of the traffic ahead. How to un-figure the larger cultural equation behind Tonto as buckskin retainer and monosyllabic sideman to the white but masked ex-Texas Ranger? How to un-figure how, and where, Native American life can at one and the same time turn against its own best interests? Alexie, from the outset, has had little truck with either cooptive stereotype or with avoidance of self-imposed damage in reservation communities. The latter has not always won him Native community plaudits.

"Every Little Hurricane," the collection's opening story, typically takes up the implications. When the main figure, the boy Victor, hears from his basement room both torrential rain and the HUD drunken house party above, he also hears the splatter of more endemic division. An earlier observation gives the guiding note in the observation "There was so much that Victor feared, so much his intensive imagination created" (7). The weather, its "thermals and undercurrents" (7), and the alcoholic love-hate fight between uncles and stupor of his parents, have become the weather of Native history itself. The house in disarray, he lays himself down between his passed-out mother and father, reservation life as one of "survivors" even despite "losses" and "random debris and broken furniture" (11). The wording, laconic, poignant, reads indicatively, Alexie's contra-flow in which love can be absolutely real yet also muted, conditional, an island amid the fracture.

This play of angle runs through each accompanying story, the subtly editorial voice positioned within the very story being told. "Imagining the Reservation" gives an especial instance, a singular imagist sequence in which reservation setback or indigence becomes transformed through creativity of mind and art. The prescriptions almost deliberately disconcert or upend, from "Imagine Crazy Horse invented the atom bomb in 1876 and detonated it over Washington D.C." (149) to "Imagine a drum which wraps itself around your heart. Imagine a story that puts wood in the fireplace" (153). The last paragraph, reflexively, offers the touchstone in the observation "Imagination is the politics of dreams" (152).

Therein, for the storyteller, lies riposte to working graveyard hours at a Seattle 7-11 with a hold-up thrown in, reservation life designated "unsinging," and a diet typified by commodity beef. Rather memory of family food-colored potatoes or "imagined oranges" redeem the quotidian. Despite the national celebration of July 4th, or the "Indian boy who blew his fingers off when an M80 exploded in his hand," there arises the call to "a new language when the language of the enemy keeps our dismembered tongues tied to his belt" (152). The latter signals the "new life" granted by Native self-imagining. Alexie carefully cross-hatches Native loss with escape into redemptive imagination be it story, humor, irony, acts of craft, skill at hoops or creative acts of kindness. The direction of travel is indicated in Victor's "All I know is that I count coyotes to help me sleep" (152).

Disjuncture in life is one thing. But it also gets put to use as creative idiom throughout the stories in *The Lone Ranger and Tonto Fistfight in Heaven*. "Crazy Horse Dreams," with its powwow setting, has Victor trying to cope with a woman who during their tryst in her Winnebago motor-home entertains the sexual fantasy of him as Crazy Horse. When he tells her of Plains Indian women who rode horse eighteen hours a day and could shoot consecutive arrows, their exchange (Alexie acknowledges the old joke) is vintage:

> "Just my luck," she said, "An educated Indian."
> "Yeah," he said, "Reservation University." (42)

That he ends up wishing he *were* Crazy Horse, Little Big Horn warrior or latter-day sexual warrior, conveys a just right ironic implication.

"Indian Education" unfolds as the First to Twelfth Grade diary of a reservation boy's life full of creativity lived within a circuit of HUD, welfare, basketball, and posed classroom photographs. This is story as ingenious paradigm, the "schooling" of Indian personality. In "Jesus Christ's Half-Brother Is Alive and Well on The Spokane Indian Reservation" he plays solo basketball watched by the baby James whom he has rescued from fire and whose parents have died of their burns. He reports "I play and play until the music of my shoes against every pavement sounds like every drum" (115). Acerbity underwrites the congeniality. Alexie's ability to have his speaker's words, oblique, cryptic, en-seam the human turns of reservation culture or history has been a major identifying strength.

Two frequently anthologized stories show Alexie taking similar aim. "This is What It Means to Say Phoenix," the film adaptation as *Smoke Signals* using Alexie's own screenplay, has the near indigent Victor flying to Arizona to deal with the father long absconded but now dead of heart-failure. He has Thomas

Builds-the-Fire for company, the unstoppable storyteller who he once drunkenly bullied yet who has offered him financial help. "I'm half magician on my mother's side and half clown on my father's" (66) Thomas tells an Olympic gymnast they meet on the plane. Having collected the father's ashes, driven his truck back to Spokane, Victor and he ponder their friendship and Thomas's belief that "Mine are stories which can change or not the world" (72). "Crazy storyteller" (74) he may be but Thomas, as Alexie behind him, layers stories of Native life to redeem those of death. The ingenuity at work, Thomas as Alexie's surrogate voice, points to restorative magic, the one storytelling for another.

"The Approximate Size of My Favorite Tumor" turns another death story into one of life. The marriage of Jimmy One Horse or Many Horse and Norma, precarious at best, has to contend with Jimmy's humor even as he is diagnosed with terminal cancer. Alexie invests their relationship, their Edward Albee-like playacting as though they might be fond suburban spouses and which extends to visitations in the hospital, with graveyard dark wit. Norma's frustration at Jimmy's un-seriousness in the face of the tumor, and her leaving him only to return from another liaison because the new lover was "so fucking serious about everything" (170), gives a familiar about-face. She has returned, she insists, because dying has to be done "the right way" (170). She also inserts her one great alimentary prowess into the soberness of death in another Alexie laconicism that "making fry bread and helping people die are the last two things Indians are good at" (170). Once again the reverse angle is requisite.

Wit, in this context, serves as necessary ingredient throughout. "*Indians make the best cowboys*" (18) opines the voice of "A Drug Called Tradition." "I was born a goofy reservation mixed drink" (27) says the narrator of "Because My Father Always Said He Was The Only Indian Who Saw Jimi Hendrix Play 'The Star-Spangled Banner' at Woodstock" of his conception to a whiskey-father and vodka-mother. Victor, Spokane Reservation regular, is pictured in "All I Wanted To Do Was Dance" wanting "to drink so much his blood could make the entire tribe numb" (90). Selective novels from Alexie's subsequent chronology confirms no let-up in situating off-centeredness at the center.

***

Indian Killer (1996), a novel which enacts how cliché (savagism, scalping, silent killer) might steal its march on reality. Are the Seattle killings "Indian" or faux-Indian, those of a tribal murderer or imitation "Indian" killer? Whether or not John Smith, adoptee as newborn by white-suburban Daniel and Olivia Smith from a fourteen-year old reservation girl, is indeed not the eventual Seattle killer then who is? The novel, to this end, and a part of the storm it caused, pursues an uncompromising double-take: Indian Killer/Killer of Indians.

This ambiguous two-way reflection runs through the narrative for Alexie is about mysteries within mysteries, starting with Smith's very naming not only for the Elizabethan ship-captain colonialist of Jamestown but the conjunction of the two most common names in English. The emergent mystery will be one of history itself: the Indian in modernity, the Indian of street and casino, the Indian taught in classrooms, the Indian among other Indians, the Indian as heir to a genocide. Smith's enigmatic "silent" personality, locked inside his twenty-seven-year old and more than six-foot frame, carries a representative storehouse of memory.

He dreams in nightmare of himself as the abducted Native child ripped from his mother's breast amid bullets in a helicopter military raid. Internally he faces growing awareness of his deculturization as "white" Indian though brown, the arena of private school, affluent suburb, move into the city away from his infertile and liberal-adoptive white parents, and name-calling as "Chief" by white passers-by and fellow-workers. He variously fantasizes a happy reservation life, one of enough food, books, grass-dancing, the storyteller in which "Shakespeare was an Indian woman" (62), even himself pregnant. Fissure pursues him, whether "he looked like some cinematic warrior" (32) or "He knew if he were a real Indian, he could have called the wind" (36).

The retreats into silence ("John never danced. He barely talked" 296) bespeak a pathology of stillness with its arising if incompletely understood compulsion for redress ("John needed to kill a white man" 37). His final Seattle skyscraper jump, having worked in Mohawk-style as steelworker, implies far more than his own death-plunge. He literally embodies downward flight from centuries of white-settler enclosure. In other words Alexie points in his figure of John Smith to not just any one killing, and in Smith's own case self-killing, but to all the generic forms of "Indian killing" whether literal or subliminal. That holds through lost sovereignty, mortality rates, illness, unemployment, drugs, city homelessness, and the cumulative human cost to spirit as much as body. Too readily, also, the loss lies in un-recognition of Native creativity, life and arts.

The murders, knifings, scalp removal, trademark owl feathers, are accompanied by entrance into the killer's psyche, his relish, his sense of pure efficacy. He remains, appropriately, un-named. The suspects for the sequence of murders and the chilling highjack of the child Mark Jones amount to virtuoso portraiture on Alexie's part. Father Duncan, the Indian Jesuit who befriends John, like some messianic prophet or fantasma disappears into the desert. To John's question, "Was Jesus an Indian?" his reply makes cryptic reading "He should have been" (24).

Marie Polatkin, student activist, sandwich-supplier to the homeless, calls time on Clarence Mather, white anthropology professor of "Native Studies" who thinks *The Education of Little Tree* authentic Cherokee authorship and steals recordings of community elders telling tribe-only stories. Authentic street expertise, much as Marie herself has been given a hard time on the reservation as mixed-blood, confronts fake expertise (Mather thinks Indian-killing a by-product of capitalism). Can she be the killer? Can it be her cousin, Reggie Polatkin, one-time tutee of Mather but up for race-war? Can it be Aaron Rogers, the white nationalist whose brother David has been found butchered (in the event by two white men for his casino winnings)? Or is the main contender Jack Wilson, ex-cop, Indian wannabe whom Marie thinks a vulture, and popular crime novelist and inventor of Aristotle Little Hawk ("the very last Shilshomish Indian, who was a practicing medicine man and private detective in Seattle" (181)?

Across each echoes the hugely popular shock-jock reactionary voice of Truck Shulz, Limbaugh-clone, his ready media diet of accusation and "Indian" conspiracy-theory. The Indian Killings, as they pass into Shulz's everyday parlance and beyond, could not more be one thing and many. To that end Alexie closes his novel with the chapter "A Creation Story." "The killer" has become iconographic, death-singer, bearer of scalps, ghost dancer through time ("The killer knows this dance is over five hundred years old" (432). He/she is also masked, a revenant created precisely by history's Indian-killing ("With this mask, with this mystery, the killer can dance for ever" 433). The novel's careful alternations, the revolving entrances and exits, allows Alexie to shadow with rare bravura the larger indigenous and other killings implicated in the history – the histories – of America. The novel, in all these respects, is not for well-meaning gesture resolution, forgiveness and move-on.

***

The story-collections that have since accrued through to *Blasphemy: New and Selected Stories* (2012), whether reservation or the city with the rez an ever-present but receding horizon, show no lessening in play of angle. *The Toughest Indian in the World* shows Alexie almost classically about his off-center paces in a story like "Dear John Wayne." Told as though a taped interview in 2052 at the St. Takawitha Retirement Home in Spokane, the interviewee, Etta Joseph, "one hundred and eighteen years old" and "last of the Spokane Indians" (190), revamps her love-affair with Wayne or Marion Morrison as she knew him under his true name. The other opening name, for Saint Takeri Tawkawitha, Mohawk-Algonquin convert eventually canonized in 2001, bears its own ironic implication. The affair has begun against the Monument Valley backdrop and been consummated on a Pendlelton "Indian" blanket as Wayne is playing Ethan Edwards in John Ford's *The Searchers* of 1956, the whitest of white guardian homesteaders.

The configuration scores to a fault. Hollywood Wayne vies with vulnerable Iowa-born Marion. Beauteous screen Native woman archetype yields to actual Native woman and, in future-present time, to Etta as Indian elder now about her prayers. On screen stalks off-screen. Wayne/Marion's cancer-doomed ghostly last call to Etta both echoes the affair's end ("my family needs me…They need me to be John Wayne" 205) and subverts the myth of cinema's greatest cowboy hero and the "Indians" who play his supporting cast. "Was the story true or false?" ponders Spencer Cox, the interviewer (208). Well may he ask, aware or not of the implicit larger question, that of real over invented Indians, real over invented white men.

Other fantasy, though none of it untied to recognizable actuality, likewise marks out this collection. "South by Southwest" has the white man, Seymour, who wants to enter history as the "Gentleman Bandit" and dollar-thief at the International House of Pancakes, pair with a "salmon-tribe fat Indian" (59). He sees himself also as "The Man Who Was Looking for Love" (59), Alexie's take on male tenderness beyond sex. The story parodies Sundance Kid outlaw mystique, men without women in Hemingway's phrase fashioned into a story-ode to compassionate better maleness. "The Sin Eaters" trades in sumptuous dream-gothic, a "blood parade" (90) as the narrator Jonah calls it. The story acts as gathering cauchemar of Native abduction, imprisonment, surgical assault and sexual spectacle eventually housed in a Piranesi-like fortress. Uncompromisingly it gives vision to Native history as dystopia, time past and beyond as grotesque, monumental blood-letting. It is another occasion when Alexie takes few prisoners, his angling once more resourcefully off-centered.

***

The collections *Ten Little Indians* and *War Dances* act in concert with the impetus to come at storytelling through oblique lens. Their focus, however, turns far more than previously on figures situated at the interface of Native and white America, a kind of negotiated dual cultural citizenship in an America neither all victimizer nor all victim. The bandwidth so widens in sight and sound.

In "The Search Engine," which opens *Ten Little Indians*, this hybridity is made highly particular, the "vision quest" as she calls it of the Spokane literary sophomore Corliss Joseph ("a middle-class Indian, she seemed destined for a minimum-wage life" 5). The object of her search, Harlan Atwater, 1970s Spokane poet of *In the Reservation of My Mind,* has long passed into anonymity. Mocked by family members for her bookishness, the call to poetry, even as she is drawn cross-culturally and in shared part to the writing of Hopkins, Dickinson and Auden as of Ortiz, Harjo, Silko and Adrian C. Louis, Corliss recognizes deficits as a well as ties that lie within Spokane life. She guards herself against too ready an Indian or white affiliation, preferring access and space for both.

Harlan, adopted and raised by white parents, bequeaths a row of masks. Biologically Spokane, he has lived out the paradox of being both actual Indian yet the necessity to play pretend Indian in adulthood and poetry. One-time professor he becomes the panhandler. The early poet his work gets squandered after a book-signing amid drinking Indians. Corliss's suspicion that he be a trickster ("an illiterate heroin addict with a gift for the gab" 32) adds to the possible masking. In tracking him down in Seattle, she sees increasingly how identity, Indian identity especially, is always multiple, eclectic, and especially in a hybrid nation like America. It underlines for her the fault-line in all cultural binaries.

Her arising observation speaks across ethnic borders, the love she harbors for the best of Spokane legacy of which her "bipolar storyteller" mother (18) is the custodian and yet the fact that Indians "are every bit as relentlessly boring, selfish, and smelly as [white folks] are" (11). Just as she acknowledges that beyond tribe, clan and public and private names "everything else she knows about Indians was ambiguous and transitory" (52), so, too, she acknowledges that whiteness likewise comes in its own diverse hues and packages:

> It was easy to hate white vanity and white rage and white ignorance, but what about white compassion and white genius and white poetry? (14)

To its imaginative advantage Alexie leaves his story at a suitable crossroad. In giving Harlan's book to the nearby bookstore she does so with "its front cover facing outward" (52). The one yet another kind of "Indian" text stands equal in availability with all of America's other texts. Harlan has exited without disclosing his "real name" (52). No one "Indian" author, no one "Indian" authorship, holds. This story, true to pattern, again fuses and un-fuses center and off-center, Alexie's continuing forte.

War Dances, each contribution prefaced by a situating short verse, oblique as usual, extends the contrarian dance. To this end "Breaking and Entering," another opening story, situates Indianness as part of but actually incidental to the more generic city story of teenage burglary and house-owner fatal response. But however much the break-in of Native-born George Wilson's home by black

Elder Briggs sounds like life imitating cliché, the one more "ethnic" city crime, it equally possesses a flourish of fuller imagining and markers to do with racial profile and fear, manhood and marriage.

Wilson, resident of Twenty-seventh Avenue in Central Seattle, a working film editor used to cutting and splicing ("I am paid to make connections" 10), and whose latest project is a sex film, finds himself drawn into an event that might have stepped from screen to reality. Armed with his ten-year old son's Little League small but metal baseball head-strikes he kills Elder as intruder. The call to 911, the revelation that the sixteen-year old has been a good student, the emergence of his extended black family, and the verdict of Elder's mother ("He's just another black boy killed by a white man" 13) lead into a wider slant on how the event is indeed to be "edited."

Ethnicities, white, black, and in Wilson's case Native, jostle in perception, one "cut" for another. Credentials enter. Wilson may be "an enrolled member of the Spokane Tribe of Indians" but, pale of skin, "I don't look Indian, or at least not typically Indian" (13). Other detail requires that he mention part-white grandparents, having married a white woman (currently away in Chicago with their son) and in a nimble much-to-purpose image "at my palest" having "just spent months nested in a dark editing room" (13–14). A white Indian, un-intending killer, property-owner, guilty liberal, he steers clear in a final scene of jaywalking black men. Has time been called on his own era of ethnic fellow good feeling? What relevance being "Indian" here? How, for him in company with the story's reader, to "edit" these events? The issue of whose true reel is playing underwrites the one break-in.

Alexie's conjunction of angle in this story confirms no drop in his ability to align sign against signal. As in the general thread of his fiction the centers and borders of his imagined Native world fall always under lowered ironic eye and tilt. Obliquity but not obscurantism, continues to rule. The body of his work in this regard, its turns of off-center gradient as they shape story and novel, remains wholly particular, a rare invitation.

Notes

1 "Dear John Wayne," *The Toughest Indian in the World*, New York: Atlantic Monthly, 2000, 189–208.

2 "Interview on line," *The Atlantic*, 2003.

Works Cited

Alexie, Sherman, *You Don't Have to Say You Love Me*, New York: Little Brown, 2017.

______, *Thunder Boy*, New York: Little, Brown, 2016.

______, *Blasphemy: New and Selected Stories*, New York: Grove Press, 2012.

______, *The Absolutely True Diary of a Part-Time Indian*, New York: Little, Brown, 2009a.

______, *War Dances*, New York: Grove Press, 2009b.

______, *The Absolutely True Story of a Part-time Indian*, New York: Little, Brown, 2007a.

______, *Flight*, New York: Black Cat, 2007b.

______, *The Lone Ranger and Tonto Fistfight in Heaven*, New York: Grove Press, 2005.

______, *Ten Little Indians*, New York: Grove Press, 2003.

______, *The Toughest Indian in the World*, New York: Atlantic Monthly, 2000.

______, *Indian Killer*, New York: Warner, 1996.

______, *Reservation Blues*, New York: Atlantic Monthly Press, 1995.

______, *Old Shirts and New Skins*, Los Angeles: UCLA American Studies Center, 1993.

______, *The Business of Fancydancing: Studies and Poems*, Brooklyn, New York: Hanging Loose Press, 1992.

9

Memory Theatre: The Fictions of Louis Owens

I felt almost dizzy with the reality of memory. Old memories had become both more real and changed in the same moment.

Louis Owens "Finding Gene" (1999)[1]

I grew up being told I was part Cherokee, part Choctaw, part Irish, part Cajun, perhaps Welsh, too. What that meant, I came to know somehow, was that people before me, who in generational history had birthed me, had been both wanderers from far places and dreamers and warriors and storytellers in this place called America.

Louis Owens, "Shared Blood," *Mixedblood Messages*

(1998)[2]

Mississippi is in many ways a kind of phantasmagoria in my memory, a fantastic wealth of images and impressions.

Louis Owens, "Outside Shadow" (2004)[3]

It takes no undue familiarity with the authorship of Louis Owens, both his fiction and the formidable roster of discursive and cultural analysis, to recognize that issues of "the reality of memory" hold a center place. Any number of skeins come into play, existential and tribal, geographic and sexual, familial and oneiric, not to mention the ongoing play of memory within spoken story and humor taken from a spectrum of Cherokee, Choctaw, Navajo-Chinle, Apache and other Native traditions. These traditions Owens has made a point of incorporating, and subtly repositioning, across much of his fiction. Nor has memory as a working concern gone unattended in critical interpretation of his work. Far from it. Precisely because it holds so determining a place across all his output, it can easily withstand more attention.[4]

Memory, almost of necessity, underwrites Owens's great central concern with mixed-blood identity. It does, too, his other pre-eminent themes, whether each egregious cultural appropriation of "the Indian" or the "sacred geography" of land and natural environment as he calls it in *Mixedblood Messages* and which embraces the Mississippi Delta's Yazoo River, the desert Southwest of Arizona and New Mexico, coastal and campus California, and the Pacific Northwest of Washington Cascades peaks and Glacier Park Wilderness.[5] For in remembering "generational history," with "phantasmagorical" Mississippi but one specific memorial time-and-place among many, Owens bequeaths a passkey, a working routeway, into the texturing of his fiction.

In *The Art of Memory* (1966), her celebrated and greatly erudite taxonomy, Frances Yates addresses the role of the mnemonic in a line of visual and written image spanning classical Greek to the European Renaissance. This, aptly, has come to be known as "memory theatre." Allowing that the John Steinbeck of his early scholarship was a begetting influence more than, say, William Faulkner and Yoknapatawpha, the designation applies in greatest degree to the fiction of Louis Owens. Each of the five novels, all with threads that interconnect and aided no doubt in part by having written within a closely compressed time-span, makes its claim in this respect.

Wolfsong (1991) shadows the iconic 1876–1877 flight of the Nez Percé's Chief Joseph, the one contemporary Pacific northwestern native life remembered through reference-back to the other. *The Sharpest Sight* (1992) references US military conflict and trauma down a corridor of time from the so-called Indian Wars remembered in allusion to Vietnam. *Bone Game* (1994) creates mutually reflective memorial layers given over to Santa Cruz as at once the site of serial murders of young women in the 1970s and the cruelties bequeathed from Spanish mission colonization in the seventeenth-century. To these events Mississippi-Choctaw elders bring ancestral tribal healing in the face of Evil Gambler sorcery. *Nightland* (1996) embeds a modern drug-money thriller inside far older New Mexico plies of territory and dynasty. And *Dark River* (1999), with its fictive Black Mountain Apache modern reservation-setting in eastern Arizona, opens into Owens's *tour d'horizon* of Native multiplicity of identity and how the tribes and white-settler America have been historically if long uneasily interwoven from progeny to land use and access. Remembrance, in all these respects, presses hard, a signature Owens feature full of his characteristic invention.[6]

***

"A hundred years ago I would have known who I was" (*Wolfsong*, 197). So thinks Tom Joseph, full-blood "Stehemish" returnee from university in Santa Barbara, California, to the aptly named Cascades valley township of Forks for his uncle Jim Joseph's funeral.[7] The eventfulness of the novel's time-present could hardly be in doubt. Logging and its crews give context, a narrative gallery of voices arising out of work habits, grit, and always risk and injury. An ancient Indian man fires at bulldozers, dump-trucks and Caterpillar tractors as they clear forest land. Not only will there be Jim Joseph's heart-attack forest death and funeral but also that of Sara Joseph, Tom's mother. A blighted love with Karen, the girl left behind, undergoes tugs and eventual final separation. Unhidden logger hostility to Tom's "injun" identity leads into various bar fights and shootings involving the local J. D. Hill family and its employees and the son Buddy with whom Karen, pregnant by him, will live in a make-do marriage. The novel's denouement looks to the dynamiting of Honeycutt Copper's ten-thousand-gallon water tank and an escape-flight and pursuit across wilderness mountain and ice into high wolf country.

At every turn the depictions of a meticulously observed animate Nature, be it cedar branch ravens or glistening Lake Image steelhead trout, memory shapes and weighs. Owens suffuses his plot-line with the recall of time-and-place "past" percolated down but kept wholly and enactively alive inside the present. This emphasis comes into play right from the start of *Wolfsong.* Jim Joseph, as he battles the company machines, summons the memory of having been required to master English at government school at the cost of tribal language ("sewing in different tongues while the children slept" 5). The process of one tongue silencing the other, literal colonization of tribal voice by English or another European language, offers a locutionary trope shared with Momaday's *House Made of Dawn* and Silko's *Ceremony.*

A rich memorial irony lies within the attitude towards Jim of the white logger Dinker – "Thinks he owns the whole goddamned woods cause he's a injun" (8). Amel Barstow, who has given Tom a lift in his long-distance truck back to Forks, gives his remembrance of Jim Joseph as "I knew him since I came back here in the thirties. There was more of your people back then" (19). John Hanson, a Korean War veteran known as Mad John, brings the presence of an American Asian war to that of settler and tribal skirmishes fought in the regional west and northwest. On his return Tom tries to summon the tribal names for peaks like Whitehorse, Skullcap, Dujack and others. Central is Glacier Peak in its white naming but for Tom to be remembered as Dakobed or "mother mountain" (91), a "Stehemish" designation that speaks memorially to Native belief in the bond of Native inhabitant and topography.[8]

Memory's tracks and footfalls persist throughout the further body of the text. Tom is said "to imagine what it would've been like to be a real Indian, before the whites came and began to cut the trees" (37). Land and ancestry stir him to remind his drink-inclined brother Jimmy of their uncle's insistence ("This used to be Stehemish land" 120). Active memory, however, belongs not only to Tom and his uncle. Abe Masingale, retired logger, taunts his fellow drinkers with the remembrance of "when there wasn't no roads in these mountains" (186). The ranger Martin Grider ("I patrol this area" 160) recognizes the clash of J. D. Hill, Honeycut copper magnate ("we're going to modernize" 200) with right preservation of the terrain. Deep mining means injudicious tree-felling. Sierra Club environmental hobbyists hover to well-meant but little effect.

A lesser writer might have tilted towards nostalgia, tribal time past as time simply mourned or sentimentalized. Owens clearly has learned his lesson from novels like James Welch's *Fools Crow* (1986) or Gerald Vizenor's much vaunted "survivance." [9] The past, and especially the "Stehemish" Native past, operates throughout the novel as always its own species of present, at once un-ended and kinetic. That is not to disallow how memory has slipped. Owens has Aaron Medicine, who conducts Tom's sweat lodge ritual say "One time I had this famous Indian poet out here who's always writing about Raven…and found out that he didn't know the difference between a raven and a crow. So many of our people only know the cities now" (193).

As Tom's eye and other senses situate him within the peak and thunderhead cloud vistas of the Cascades, or as he listens when hiking trail or with his logging crew to the many languages of coyote, deer, and notably wolf, as of owl, raven, crow, hawk, buzzard or peregrine, and even more as he hears the voice and re-sees the silhouetted visions of Jim Joseph, so memory in the novel comes over as a wholly dynamic staple within his time-present.

Other kinds of memory loop into actual history or prior literary texts. The Everett Massacre of 1916 involving the IWW/Wobblies in their fight for jobs and conditions and the ensuing clashes with law-enforcement vigilantes, is recalled at one point. Owens adverts, intertextually, to *Moby-Dick* both as a source of epic and in the story of Mad John to a distant echo of the swiveled prophet Elijah whom Ishmael meets at the dockside. But the presiding memory-textures reside in the interaction of Tom with "Stehemish" country as geo-history, a natural cosmos of growth and cycle. Seeking to find his life-direction he draws both from the memorial legacy passed down from his uncle and his own seasoned and hands-on close encounter with Nature's rhythms from within the valley and northward into Canada.

In his final lone flight, Krag rifle in hand and with J. D. having been killed in the water-tank explosion, and friend and foe from Forks in pursuit against a sky of scintillant and inspirational blue, Tom posits the predatory greed of Honeycutt, J. D. Hill and their like, in terms of one of the great tribal-memorial mythologies. "Old Man Coyote, he remembered, had once devoured himself in a fit of greed" (231). Owens may well have written an early species of thriller, his own beginning *noir* as a form of narrative that takes on yet more emphasis in the novels to follow. *Wolfsong*, however, also insists upon the issue of earth as itself memory, a self-renewing and self-remembering storehouse of life. In this, as Tom recognizes, it serves as a call to passed-down tribal best practice in respect of habitation, hunting, seasonal passage, animal and bird presence, and cedar and all other forest growth.

None of which is to say that Owens does not have his novel recognize that the tribes, those especially that have been dispersed or attenuated, have themselves often defaulted on that ordinance. Jim Joseph, after all, is a loner, the sole bearer of not just tribal memory but life-practice. His nephew re-embodies him, the fugitive enduring wolf and his song as against mining "development" and literally lost ground. At the same time there is no sentimental illusion of latter-day Stehemish, or any other tribe, as ever the perfect eco-warriors. But the novel throughout, and in the trajectory and mythical wolf reincarnation of Tom Joseph, points both Native and non-Native peoples to the earth's own cycles of memory as means to restorative health of land and inhabitant.

***

Memory, to be sure, is but one lens through which to read Owens's fiction. As in *Wolfsong*, his ensuing *The Sharpest Sight* yields a full repertoire of action, from post-traumatic breakdown to parallel murders, with sexual intrigue and violence in the Californian town of Amarga connected to swamp Mississippi-Choctaw ghosts and spiritual medicine. Each takes its course against the memorial eddies of the literal but also emblematic Salinas and Yazoo rivers. Yet these dynamics, Attis McCurtain's death through to his brother Cole's return of his bones to their Choctaw ancestral homeland, involve a complex filtering of remembrance. However much the novel offers a mystery of sorts, meticulously suspenseful in its unraveling, Owens infuses the process with shelves, or perhaps more aptly sieves, of competing remembrance. The upshot is narrative that richly, almost reflexively, and for all that it won a *roman noir* prize in France, resists any assumed single literary genre.

Memory in *The Sharpest Sight* contributes not just to one but several interstices that are made to overlap even as they each follow their course. The very title gives a pointer, a phrase taken from the Great Awakening vision of death's arrival from unseen quarters in Jonathan Edwards's "Sinners in the Hands of an Angry God." The Greek myth of Diana and Attis, the one of goddess, the other of priesthood, ritual slaying, and retribution, is remembered in both the character naming (Nemi to add to the others) and sacrificial lake and woods location.[10] Owens's use of other canonical reference, a roster that includes *Hamlet*'s prince, Faulkner's Chief Doom, Edward Lear's playful nonsense animals, along with Tennyson and the Matthew Arnold of "Dover Beach," is put under the construing of the Choctaw elders Uncle Luther Cole and Onatima Blue Wood. Citation is also given from the Bible's Psalm 23. These exert a double effect. They open America's cultural narrative to non Euro-American scrutiny and insist upon full recognition, and so remembrance, of wholly co-existent, and in terms of spoken word far antecedent, Native voice and story.

The novel, it would not be unfair to observe, turns and turns again on memory as continuum, the way story or "pattern" (6) as Uncle Luther calls it is ever caught up in the process of creating (and re-creating) its own remembrance. Attis will kill Jenna Nemi and be killed in turn by her sister Diana. Cole will be sought by the FBI as the Vietnam draft evader only to become the peacetime warrior who will find and return his brother's bones for Choctaw burial in Mississippi. Hoey McCurtain, their father, will aver "I guess I don't know how to be Indian anymore" (56) yet remember that his son Attis's body will need to be found and the bones interred before "balance" can be re-established. He will also remember Andrew Jackson and the Choctaw leader Pushmataha for their role in the War of 1812 and the subsequent government betrayal of the Choctaw people. It will fall to Cole and his father to steer a path out of the murders, those of Jenna, Attis, and the psychopathic tavern owner and rapist Jessard Deal, and negotiate the final settling of Attis's unquiet spirit. In Choctaw cosmology outside (*shilup*) and inside (*shilombish*) shadow are to be reconciled and *nalusachito*, the soul-eater, withstood.

Owens, for sure, may not be writing Proust, but he displays a rare talent for using memorialization as an axial dimension of *The Sharpest Sight.* The process of remembering holds for each other major presence in the novel. Mundo Morales, Amarga township deputy, Attis's closest friend and co-veteran of Vietnam, will remember the original royal Spanish grant to his family dynasty yet also remember the passage of time and *mestizaje* that makes him into a present-day Chicano. He will also remember the Mekong jungle, the use of Native and South Vietnamese/AVRN soldiers as point, and the hospitalization of Attis as a PTSD sufferer and who has killed Jenna with a knife-stab through the heart. In this, and his search for Attis's river-born body after his escape from the hospital through the machinations of Diana and the gullible but bribed "sympathetic-to-Indians" intern, he will be aided, and guided, by the memorial voice of his ghost grandfather

Antonio Morales ("Somehow it all seemed related, tangled up together like a ball of used baling wire" 196).

Memory, however different its course, likewise stalks each of the other main players implicated in Attis's death. Most notably that centers on Diana Nemi in her remembered jealousy of the lovemaking of Jenna and Attis, her own retributive sexual seduction of Attis, and her inerasable rape by Jessard Deal. Lee Scott, the laconic FBI agent with his recall of Vietnam as True Grit and A-Team bravura, reveals himself to be as full of faux sympathy for Native Americans as he is of racism towards Mekong villagers. Bucky Travis, damaged adolescent, remembers his grandmother by grotesquely disinterring her corpse and installing it in his car under the label "Just Buried." In each case memory harbors death, the darkness of a broken psyche. The Mondragon sisters in Amarga's faded hotel, communicants with ghosts, supply visions of remembered Mexican and Native dynasty and place. Theirs is memorial haunt, a California of spirits, specters, and liminal and unfinished history. None of which is to say that all memory in the novel is to be thought finally agreed upon: the story's "ending" wryly comments upon the competing official against the McCurtain remembrance of events.

No figures more carry, and at the same time more create, memory than Luther and Onatima. Their longtime love, ongoing sexual byplay and bawdy, maverick trickster and medicine woman couture, discussion of the books passed from the college-educated Onatima to the Mississippi swamp-savvy Luther (he saves the befuddled agents Harwood and Hicks), and their necessary inwardness with a Choctaw sense of the world's balance to include traditional good and bad spirits, all braid memory into what the novel offers as current time. Luther remembers his role in raising Hoey, and Attis and Cole. Onatima remembers her out-of-joint marriages. Jointly they engage in a running memorial colloquy as to how Choctaw legacy can understand and help expiate the malevolence that has so fatally held away. Owens takes care not to engage in undiluted filiopiety.

However much grounded in passed-down tribal sources theirs is also a pragmatics, some made up as it goes along, but tradition or improvisation or a mix of both always a way to position and then address the setbacks encircling Attis and the others. Luther may well remember his bemusement at white Pentecostalism's promise of graves opening on judgment day or how to read the presence of horned owl or panther. But he shows yet fuller reserves of memory in his response to reading H. B. Cushman's *History of the Choctaw, Chickasaw and Natchez Indians*, the 1899 volume given to him by Onatima. Its Noble Savage ethos, ready heroization of warriors and beauteous Choctaw women, causes him to remember not only how Onatima was beaten by her husband Old Man Blue

Wood but also the figure of Queequeg in *Moby-Dick*. In both cases, husband and wife un-pairing, and Ishmael's en-coffined loss of his alter-self, Luther recognizes a fundamental disruption of life balance – subtleties and remediation well beyond Cushman's account.

His tribally inflected commentary again turns upon which memory is to hold sway: "we got to be aware of the stories they're making about us, and the way they change the stories we already know" (91). As Attis's sacred cedar-box of bones is duly carried back to Mississippi, and in the knowledge passed on to Cole, it is that kind of memory ("the stories we already know") that clearly most matters. For if it offers a pathway into Choctaw-centered re-harmonization in the wake of all the human fractures explored in *The Sharpest Sight*, it also carries major implications for worlds both imagined and actual far beyond.

***

When, in *Bone Game*, the only two Native faculty at the University of California Santa Cruz get their chance to fully introduce themselves their exchange carries a number of implications. Ostensibly it is identification even as it hints of mock politesse. Alex Yazzie, transvestite Navajo warrior and clown, doubles as assistant professor of anthropology. Cole McCurtain, twenty years older than he was in *The Sharpest Eye*, divorcee from his lawyer wife Mara, father to college-aged Abby, Choctaw legatee, holds tenure as full professor of Native literature. Above all their encounter is memorial, a reminder of Native past-into-present:

> "Alex Yazzie. Salt Clan, Born-for-Water. Chinle" …
> "Cole McCurtain. Choctaw-Cherokee-Irish-Cajun, Mississippi and Oklahoma by way of New Mexico and California." (26)

Their shared story has little choice but to deploy memory. Two epochs are to be seen in parallel and if not exact then approximate mirrors. The killing of the cruel mission priest, Padre Andrés Quintana, by the Ohlone tribal figure of Venancio Asisara in 1812 in revenge for Spanish colonial and sexual cruelty, finds reiteration in the murders and dismemberment of young student women in the California of 1983. By design the novel has the one remembrance live hauntingly inside the other, Cole's disturbed and greatly memorial Evil Gambler dream-visions and the memory-in-the-making of each contemporary Santa Cruz homicide.

Bone Game undoubtedly reflects Owens's interest in the thriller-mystery format, the alternations of delay and suspense. How to think otherwise given the serial "butcher murders" (132)? Other components would not be hard to list.

Cole fires his rifle at what might be a real or imagined harlequin gambler-ghost. A warning prayer stick with human flesh attached appears in front of his house. The abduction by traffickers of the Navajo woman Katherine Begay which Hoey McCurtain and Uncle Luther forestall bespeaks ill-spirit beyond California. The later endangerments to Alex and Abby, the one to be almost fatally shot and the other under the threat of rape, requires and eventually receives solution. Cole may have returned the bones of his murdered brother Attis to Mississippi. But he still sees him in imagination. Even the dog-poisoning of the exquisitely named Custer implies riddle, a conundrum.

The novel also deals in what Alex calls "ghost sickness" (96). This takes form both in Cole's visionary dream memories of the vengeful black and white painted specter of Venancio and the nightmare-into-reality of the two live killers Paul Kantner, deranged Vietnam Special Forces veteran, and Robert Malin, Cole's graduate assistant and at once "dark haunted self" (16) and, as Cole dubs him, "white Indian" (206). Robert's obsessive immersion into tribal lore, his too ready acceptance of *Black Elk Speaks* as finessed by John Neihardt into romantic victim-hero, and his self-appointed, not to say murderous "Native" role in acting to regulate the world's "balance," especially adds to the malignity signaled in his name. Kantner, killer pathology personified, fatally believes his grasp of reality more secure than that of the "Elfland" student cultists with their woodland Tolkienism and circle sex-parties. It makes sense, in these interconnecting lights, for Owens to re-introduce the Mississippi medicine elders Uncle Luther and Onatima. Their shared memories, and wit, give a necessary touchstone for how best to comprehend, and then counter, the "witchery" bequeathed by Venancio (however understandable his revenge upon the priest – the phrase *Eran muy crueles* is repeated through to the novel's last sentence) and coexistently at work in contemporary Santa Cruz.

The opening epigraphs to *Bone Game* signify the colonizer's memory, the view of Quintana and his fellow Franciscans that the Native populations amount to children (*neófitos*) and savages (*bestes*). Venancio, ghost-spirit, acts as counter-memory, one of Ohlone Bear ritual and shamanism from within a culture fully centered in its own universe of belief and non-calendar time. Alex Yazzi's field-dressing of a handsomely antlered buck on the Santa Cruz campus even as he is cross-dressed in skirt and running shoes may well deliver a comic taunt at the assumed couture of white and Native worlds. But it also brings into view a memorial Navajo sacred clown, and with it the practice of the deer dance and antler ceremony, gut arrow strings and blood smears, even as Alex acknowledges that he has also put in mock-memorial touches for his white-liberal campus watchers. None of which, despite his good disposition, saves him from death.

These patterns of memory not only coalesce but also contend. Robert will recall hearing that the Santa Cruz campus has been built "right on an Ohlone burial site" (42) with all the un-respect that this action implies. Alex will speak of his baroque Hollywood script that envisages digging up the Winthrops's Old North Church in Boston "where they buried all those Puritans" (180). He imagines the graves yielding "artifacts, buttons—whalebones corsets, dildos, things we can sell to collectors" with bones and skeletons "on display" (181). The one kind of memory, or rather non-memory, is parodied in the other. Owens has them serve as opposing markers, conveniently forgotten Native life and death as against celebrated memorialization of New England's City Upon a Hill mythos so coined by Winthrop in 1630. Together they offer manifestations of the ways America has selectively embedded its history.

As they pass through the "Indian Country...of Navajo and Pueblo and Hopi land" (88), Luther reminds Hoey that this topography will equally be remembered for Los Alamos and the A-Bomb, the Albuquerque nuclear site at Sandia, missile testing at White Sands, and uranium mining at Laguna. Robert Jim, too, the Navajo elder hitching his way home, gives his emphasis to the memory inherent in the land, its role as life-source as against life-destruction. Which memory, runs the implication, should most prevail? Onatima is in no doubt – "They would imprison us in their vision and stories…We have to have our own stories" (140). Such can be said to hold for the text's larger purposes and for the memory of what has been signified in Cole's matching double-history of Venancio and of Kantner and Malin. Long after any one event of plot the McCurtain dynastic remembrance, guided by Luther and Onatima and with trickster aid and abetment from Alex, becomes nothing less than the novel's own remembrance of itself.

***

"We're out here chasing deer and a suitcase full of money falls out of the sky" (59). Billy Keene's remark to Will Striker, Cherokee mixed-blood best friends as both struggle to extract a living from their near bankrupt and drought-parched small ranches in New Mexico, gives a taste of the laconic wit that underpins *Nightland*.[11] The million dollar cache of drug money that up-ends their two lives leads into a zigzag of event. Revenge killings enter. Helicopter chases and shoot-outs feature. An extravagantly beauteous Mescalero Apache femme fatale who holds a Berkeley PhD with a thesis of Indian sovereignty makes her bow. A disquisition on queer cowboy networks has its own page. Newspaper sex ads get invoked. Ghost conversations between a Cherokee elder and a Pueblo dead smuggler thrown out of the delivery plane take place. The dried and then replenished water well in which loot has been hidden becomes yet another memory.

The "corpse money" (6, 187) changes hands, bullets fly, bodies accumulate, and buzzards avian and human, mythic and actual, hover. The narrative's menu hardly lacks for action or variety. The windings of this fourth novel, indeed, might invite comparison, however unexpected, with the magical opening sky-fall in Salman Rushdie's *The Satanic Verses* (1988) or with Chester Himes's use of the emblematic cotton bale in his crime-thriller *Cotton Comes to Harlem* (1965). Geoffrey Gray's *Skyjack: The Hunt for D.B. Cooper* (2012), with its account of the still unsolved $200,000 historic ransom and parachute escape into the Pacific Northwest, offers yet another bearing. Each of these texts, allowing for their own singular plot-lines, throws light on Owens's play of memory in *Nightland.*

The conjoined lives of Will and Billy give the novel its main thrust. But they have much company. Black-humor exchanges between the dead-alive revenant Arturo Cruz with Grandpa Siquani Kaneequayokee (a name meaning suckling pig), and during which they play spectral chess recur. Siquani takes a Land Cruiser driving lesson from a ghost instructor. Together they carry for burial Arturo's decapitated body in a wheelbarrow, fine grotesquerie.

The episode also reads as though memorial revenge. For Arturo's uncle, the meticulous *narcotraficante* Paco Ortega, runs his drug operation less for dollars than to counter-infect a white Euro-America whose historic will to genocide he locates in Lord Jeffery Amherst's use (proven or not) of smallpox-infected blankets against Pontiac's Ottawa people during the Seven Years War (1754–1753). One era's blight for the other, heroin, cocaine and other modern narcotics ("the white powder that made its way northward" 143) for the virus that decimated the tribes, has been Ortega's credo. To Duane Scales, his eloquently foul-mouthed hit man who paradoxically cares about the environment with a passion, he so confides "I'm giving those blankets back" (171).

Ortega's view pulls no punches in its interface of remembrance and time-present. Speaking earlier to Duane he delivers the following memory: "I know about history…For example, I know that right over there in Acoma...the Spanish cut off the right foot of every adult male and made slaves of the women and children" (163). Linking this to the Amherst episode his conclusions are summary, an uncompromising accusation: "They killed ninety percent of the Indian people who lived on this continent…Today they use alcohol and toxic waste instead of blankets" (163).

The entire drug operation that leads to Arturo's juniper tree impalement and embroils Will and Billy from their initial deer-poaching and a seeming spirit-deer in the Cibola National Forest to their respective come-uppance through the calculated wiles of (Dr.) Odessa Whitehawk, the novel has derive from this ladder of historical memory. Odessa, who late in the story asserts she has "a PhD in genocide" (209) throws her own dark light on Ortega, her one-time lover before Billy, and his role in the memorial process: "Paco was an idealist, his only flaw besides me" (193).

Other memory, for sure, comes into play. Paradoxically one key seam of memory has to do with forgetting. Billy early avers that "I can't remember all that stuff" (8) in relation to Siquani's Cherokee world-view, a heritage to be set against the Very Large Array whose radio telegraph dishes (looking like white faces) map another cosmos as does Albuquerque's Atomic Energy Museum. Siquani will tell Arturo that "So much has been forgot...Cherokee people don't remember…" (132), a prophecy of why Billy's severance from his inherited but always adaptive community culture will lead to his death. As a Cherokee elder, quirky, wry, visionary, Siquani embodies memory as guideline into present and future and in the face of Billy's irreverence that it signifies only "Cherokee hocus-pocus" (109).

In him remembrance lives loud and clear. He makes recall of the Cherokee genesis story of Kanati the hunter and Selu Corn Woman. He takes his shy at the Bering Strait version of Native origins and "Indian" identity by blood quantum. He calls up the bone dance and ceremonially purifies himself in the nearby lake. History is remembered in his allusions to the Trail of Tears and the role of Oklahoma in Native and white-settler history (to which Billy's family photographs of Cherokee-white marriage will also apply). Owens, above all, has Siquani think of the precept passed down from his ancestors "You got to remember everything they said" (157).

Mouse Meléndez, the burly and contradictorily blue-eyed Chicano heir to the original Spanish land grantees, remembers history his own way but under the rubric "This was all Indian land" (89). His utterance is exact. The Will/Billy story of miraculous dollars and violent redress, worn-down ranch holdings and the fractured loves of Will with his lawyer ex-wife Jace and Billy with Odessa, play out exactly within this memory of past-into-present. Odessa, too, for all that she is to be associated with witchery, deadly modern *brujería*, is to be heard thinking:

> The past was a white man's illusion, the future a white man's dream. Stories were what Indians had, and the story was born anew with every telling. What mattered was the telling, and every story could be changed, had to be. It depended upon who did the telling. (144)

This stream of thought hangs utterly upon memory. It re-emphasizes how and why the remembrance of stories and their storytelling lie at the heart not only of the plurality of "Indian" history but of wider America. Owens's *Nightland* gives every grounds of having transposed the ongoing memorial contraries and overlaps into his own winning feat of narrative.

***

Dark River, Owens's last novel and a kind of summa well beyond the fact of his own ill-fated early demise in 2002, deploys memory in ways that increasingly reverberate beyond the considerable story-line.[12] Jake Nashoba, psychically troubled Vietnam ex-Special Forces, affiliated with the Apache fictional Black Mountain community in eastern Arizona and employed as tribal game warden in the Dark River valley, thinks back to his Choctaw grandmother's warning about the horned owl as harbinger of likely threat: "*Ishkitini*, he thought, remembering, as he did every time, his grandmother's stories and hardening himself against them" (49). This is also the Jake, two decades into living as an outsider in the Black Mountain reservation, who "grew up remembering ever more vaguely that he was half something called Choctaw" (109).

Both the owl warning and mixed-blood heritage lie steeped in remembrance. That becomes the more so when having been hunted and shot by Captain Steve Stroud, Vietnam fellow veteran and the former officer become entrepreneur behind "the war game business" (165), he enters into his protracted death-dream with its vision of restored "full" identity ("Jake lay within the tangle of roots and considered his death" 259). Memory, likewise, underwrites his life hitherto. It comes into play as he negotiates the elk-poaching scam of the corrupt chairman Xavier Two Bears and Sheriff Sam Baca, a fake vision quest business, a lethal militia group pledged to the "New World Order" while offering wilderness experiences for suburban eco-clients, and the risk to the albeit wilderness savvy granddaughter-by-marriage Alison.

Jacob Nashoba so embodies memory both positive and otherwise. If he can dimly think back to the Luther figure of his Choctaw origins he also remembers Choctaw tribal division and mean-spiritedness. On return from overseas combat, and through his Apache wife Tali's help, that has led him to Black Mountain where he remains joined yet un-joined. Black Mountain gives him the provisional succor of home, family and offspring, whether Tali herself and her children by previous marriages or Alison. Even so, and in the continuing spirit of contradiction, "after twenty years he had remained a stranger" (50). In Jessie James, his semi-adoptee with the bank-robber name, he fails to check the failure of remembrance behind the younger man's Vision Quest Enterprises whose wolf costume fake-memorializes spiritual ceremony. That in a perfect ironic reversal Jessie is accidentally shot and becomes a ghost speaker for the French vision hunter and martial arts expert Sandrine Le Bris supplies the latest remembrance for Jake.

The memory wheel turns again in the shared debilitating remembrance of "the hopeless glory of Vietnam" (120) and not only in the persons of Stroud, Lee Jensen, and their fellow American combatants but in Phuong Nguyen, the tough, now middle-aged one time ARVN ranger with his comfortable golf and real estate life. Both Stroud and Jensen are given to sardonic oratory, half as though Nietzsche, half as though Chaplin's Great Dictator. Their clients, among them a dentist and an insurance salesman, are clad in "surplus camouflage uniforms" (148), contrived memory hunter-soldiers, each an uncertain blend of wannabe Indian, Cooper's Chingachgook and Stallone's Rambo. Jake's own actual past soldiery, however, has brought on the fractures of PTSD violence despite his lone comfort in the skills of valley trail and season, river and animal life. Not only has Vietnam in its way led to the break-up of his marriage, but also it is given haunting return from the Mekong in the person of Stroud and even more of the pathological Jensen as Evil Gambler. That Jake himself will garner the nickname of Lone Ranger adds tellingly to these memorial spirals. The bullets to ensue, whether fired by intent at the hands of the militia or accidentally by their signed-on client (and Owens is a longtime adept in the ways of gun culture), imply the perfect correlative for the cross-fire within Jake's memory-damaged psyche.

Around Jake each Black Mountain elder brings a distinctive corridor of further memory to bear. Shorty Luke, story thief and "a walking history book" (48), remembers with no inconsiderable reflexive wit his life as Hollywood Indian along with "Italian" imitators like Iron Eyes Cody – the Sicilian-heritaged and the tearful "Keep America Beautiful" icon rowing his canoe through city detritus. Domingo Perez, like Shorty an "only surviving twin" in a joke kept in play throughout the novel, and bayoneted in the stomach during the Japanese occupation of the Philippines, brings to bear also the memory of hobo-boxcar life in the wake of World War II. Owens keeps him compassionately human, if quirky, as when with shampoo borrowed from Tali he washes and hair-dries his dead cat.

Avrum Goldberg, Jewish anthropologist who bids to out-Indian his Apache hosts in breechcloth, leggings, and moccasins, his *wikiup*, and devotion to ceremony and deer and berry cuisine, will find memory no final protection against the militia gunshot that kills him. His proposal that Black Mountain become a "traditional tribe again" (71), a riposte to the commerce of nearby casino and white deer-trophy hunting, may be memorial but it is memory as static, locked in past time or even worse nostalgia and not without its eye to tourist commercial returns. In Mrs. Edwards, Native but named for her absconding evangelist husband but also for Connecticut's eighteenth century Congregationalist Jonathan Edwards, the tribe has its matrilineal reservation story-holder. She holds sway as at once Grandmother and guardian of how to use memory protectively, as in her nursing watch over the invalided Domingo and over Alison, but without whose traditional but adaptive medicine the trickster Jessie will go to his death.

Memorial plenty again aids and abets. The electronic sign in Jake's office of a white man paddling lake waters in his canoe, first static and then repaired into motion, cannot but memorialize colonial and so-called westering possession. Jacob, after a nighttime visit by Tali, ponders whether "the whole idea of the Indian was an invention" (92) and that "maybe anthropologists were the real Indians" (92), Owens's succinct shy at the history of simulated "Indian" identity and whether sourced in Baudrillard or Gerald Vizenor. But as the plot unravels, the deceits and killings, and as Jensen and Alison and the remaining cast give their competing versions of what might be the "conclusion," Owens takes his novel into self-reflexive waters. Exchanges ask how Jake Nashoba's story will most pass into remembrance. Will it be Bad Guys triumphant, Good Guys triumphant? What role ghost chorus? Has Indian warriordom passed from men to women? Has tribal land and sovereignty been irrevocably won or lost or even both? The term "mystery" applies as much as anywhere in that kind of challenge to the reader's own reaches of memory.

Owens's fiction has not quelled disquiet at a certain airlessness, the occasional tendency towards disquisition. At the same time his gains have rarely been in doubt. It would be remiss to underestimate the wide historical excavation and insider allusion to tribal custom, the hugely informed observer eye for animal, bird, landscape and climate. Nor should his shafts of tease be overlooked whether at the expense of Tony Hillerman or Russell Means. Given these contributing features, memory itself could never be all in the Owens literary narrative. But its filaments and textures in *Dark River* especially cannot be missed, always a coeval and ever insistent process.

Certainly memory can be seen as working to beneficial effect in the voices of Luther, Onatima or Siquani. But Owens also uses it to show undercurrents, notably in the gallery of Diana Nemi, Venancio Asisara, Paul Kanter, Robert Malin, Odessa Whitehawk or Lee Jensen. Jake Nashoba, on being rescued in Albuquerque from drunken collapse by Tali, herself remembering life as a stripper, gives yet another bead when he acknowledges the costs of self-endangering "memory gaps" (34).

***

In *Other Destinies* Owens observes of James Welch's *Winter in the Blood* (1974), with its parable of displacement set within Montana's Fort Belnap Reservation, that in essence it enacts a "re-remembering," "fragments of the past" made into "a significant whole." He might well have been pointing towards the imaginative configuration of his own novels.[13] The analogy with Welch is perhaps not wholly exact but assuredly it suggests a near neighborhood. Memory theatre, to re-invoke Frances Yates, works in similar vein, a notation of how the different narratives of remembrance bridge into the yet larger vision of Owens's fiction.

Notes

1 Louis Owens, "Finding Gene," *I Hear the Train: Reflections, Inventions, Refractions*, Norman: University of Oklahoma Press, 2001, 14. Essay originally published in *Weber Studies*, Fall, 1999.

2 Louis Owens, "Shared Blood," *Mixed Messages: Literature, Film, Family, Place*, Norman: University of Oklahoma Press, 1998, 192.

3 A. Robert Lee, "Outside Shadow: A Conversation with Louis Owens," in Jacquelyn Kilpatrick, ed., *Louis Owens: Literary Reflections on His Life and Work*, Norman: University of Oklahoma Press, 2004, 32.

4 Early and greatly perceptive recognition of this dimension of Owens's writing is to be found in Chris LaLonde, *Grave Concerns, Trickster Turns: The Novels of Louis Owens*, Norman: University of Oklahoma Press, 2002. For an enlightening comparative sight-line, see Kimberley M. Blaeser, "Vizenor and the Power of Transitive Memories," in Birgit Däwes and Alexandra Hauke, eds., *Native American Survivance, Memory, and Futurity*, New York and London: Routledge, 2017, 75–89.

5 "Blood Trails," *Mixedblood Messages*, 150. In *Wolfsong* Owens has Tom Joseph cite his uncle and observe to his brother "This used to be Stehemish Indian land. He said that country was sacred up there" 120.

6 Owens gives his own summary of the first four novels in "Motions of Fire and Form," *Mixedblood Messages*, 181–2.

7 In "Motions of Fire and Storm," *Mixedblood Messages*, 160, Owens refers to the region's originary Salishan culture. "Stehemish" is the novel's fictionalization of that people.

8 See, in this regard, "Mapping, Naming, and the Power of Words," in *Mixedblood Messages*, 211.

9 Survivance has now become almost required usage in discussion of Native culture and writing. See, especially, Gerald Vizenor, ed., *Survivance: Narratives of Native Presence*, Lincoln: University of Nebraska Press, 2008.

10 Both LaLonde in *Grave Concerns, Trickster Turns* (2002) and Linda Lizut Helstern in *Louis Owens*, Boise: Boise State University Press (2005) give useful summaries of the Diana myth. See also, as vintage scholarship, James Frazier,"The King of the Woods," *The Golden Bough: A Study in Comparative Religion*, 2 Vols, 1890.

11 Page references are to *Nightland*, Red River Books edition, Norman: University of Oklahoma Press, 2001, updated from 1996.

12 In this regard Susan Bernardin writes "Considered by Owens to be his 'summa,' *Dark River* ultimately provides a metacommentary on ongoing debates about the status, role, and future of American Indian-authored fiction." See "Moving in Place: Dark River and the 'New' Indian Novel," in Jacqueline Fitzpatrick, ed., *Louis Owens: Literary Reflections on His Life and Work*, Norman: University of Oklahoma Press, 2006, 104–5.

13 Louis Owens, *Other Destinies: Understanding the American Indian Novel*, Norman: University of Oklahoma Press, 1992, 147.

Works Cited

Black Elk, *Black Elk Speaks*, with John Niehardt, New York: William Morrow and Company, 1932.

Gray, Geoffrey, *Skyjack: The Hunt for D.B. Cooper*, New York: Penguin Random House, 2012.

Himes, Chester, *Cotton Comes to Harlem*, New York: Putnam, 1965.

Lee, A. Robert, "Outside Shadow: A Conversation with Louis Owens," in Jacqueline Kilpatrick, ed., *Louis Owens: Literary Reflections on His Life and Work*, Norman: University of Oklahoma Press, 2004.

Momaday, N. Scott, *House Made of Dawn*, New York: Harper and Row, 1968.

Owens, Louis, *I Hear the Train: Reflections, Inventions, Refractions*, Norman: University of Oklahoma Press, 2001.

______, *Dark River*, Norman; University of Oklahoma Press, 1999.

______, *Mixedblood Messages: Literature, Film, Family, Place*, Norman: University of Oklahoma Press, 1998.

______, *Nightland*, New York: Dutton, 1996; Norman: University of Oklahoma Press, Red River Books, 2001.

______, *Bone Game*, Norman: University of Oklahoma Press, 1994.

______, *Other Destinies: Understanding the American Indian Novel*, Norman: University of Oklahoma Press, 1992a.

______, *The Sharpest Sight*, Norman: University of Oklahoma Press, 1992b.

______, *Wolfsong*, Albuquerque: West End Press, 1991, Norman: University of Oklahoma Press, 1994.

Rushdie, Salman, *The Satanic Verses*, London: Vintage Books, 1968.

Silko, Leslie Marmon, *Ceremony*, New York: Penguin, 1977.

Vizenor, Gerald and A. Robert Lee, *Postindian Conversations*, Lincoln: University of Nebraska Press, 1999.

Welch, James, *Winter in the Blood*, New York: Harper and Row, 1974.
Yates, Frances, *The Art of Memory*, London: Routledge and Kegan Paul, 1966.

10 Changing Points of Compass: The Novel 1990s-2020s

It is by now well established that N. Scott Momaday's *House Made of Dawn* (1968) won more than a Pulitzer Prize. It won the way for a re-awakening of American Indian literature, particularly the novel.

Robert Franklin Gish, *Beyond Bounds: Cross-Cultural Essays on Anglo, American Indian, & Chicano Literature* (1996)[1]

Any legitimate map of the modern Native/First Nations novel would be hard put not to emphasize plurality of signature. That holds beyond the acknowledged names, Momaday or Silko, Erdrich or Alexie, Welch or Vizenor, into diversities of vision, new circuits. The authorship taken up in this chapter, ten novels in all, gives confirmation, a flow, or if not a flow a cohabitation, of different narratives and sightings. Approximately they group one alongside the other as comprising the sequence indicated in the Introduction, namely as varieties of "history" (Linda Hogan, Betty Louise Bell, Margaret Verble), neo-realism (Thomas King, Tommy Orange), the interwoven narrative of a single-generation of Native women (Linda LeGarde Grover), city and seaboard village coming of age (Erika T. Wurth, Eden Robinson), a one variety of the postmodern (Stephen Graham Jones), and ventures into the antic-speculative (D.L. Birchfield). Other titles, other might-be categories, could readily contend, but this one selection bids to give flavor, an indicative compass.

***

In her poem "Neighbors" Linda Hogan has a run of lines which do good service as a prologue to her novel *Mean Spirit* (1990):

> In this country, men have weapons
> they use against themselves
> and others. It is the dying
> watching death. Light a candle.[2]

The story on offer, turn-of-the-century Osage dynasty caught out by historic Oklahoma land politics, uses the recurrent image of oil as the earth's seeping blood. Densely and adroitly webbed throughout, told at gathering pace, and given a large cast of players from oil-scatters to Hill Indians, and from the sinister fixer John Hale to the legendary coyote ghost John Stink, it secures its own "Indian" mystery-story out of a true American conspiracy itself still fully to be given light or, indeed, resolution.

Beginning with the unsolved murder in 1922 of beautiful, oil-rich Grace Blanket, Osage full blood, then the adoption of her daughter Nola by Belle and Moses Greycloud and their extended family, and moving from the invented Oklahoma town of Watona to Washington DC from where the Lakota-born agent, Stace Red Hawk, takes up the detection, Hogan creates a tale grounded in history but transposed into its own encompassing corners and entanglements. At one level this is Warren Harding's America as land-grab, predatory, anything-goes Gatsbyism, with the Osage, like other Native peoples pre-1924 in law non-citizenry whose lands become fenced in, and out, as much by statute and picket as by each installment in the "ring of murders" (242). *Mean Spirit*, however, in no way cedes to victim history, for another level operates in the form of Grace's Osage life-legacy as carried forward by the Greyclouds and Nola.

It is first to be met with in the surreal, near oneiric, "silent bedchamber" opening scene, indoor beds placed outdoors to deal with the nights of an Oklahoma summer. The linkages to the novel's other Native lore are many. The sacred fire is maintained by the water-diviner Michael Horse whose almanac, *The Book of Horse*, he shows only to Stace. Sorrow Cave, the many-chambered sacred Osage refuge, has its resident bats and memorial pictographic wall drawings. The Hill Indian watcher-runners keep guard over Nola. The stallion, Red Shirt, is both sought and respected by Horse. Belle's bees attack and kill the ill-intending Sheriff Gold ("Bees were like Indians, Belle thought to herself, with a circular dance, working together for the survival of the next generations" 312).

None of these, for sure, stops the murders of Grace, or a community which includes Benoit, John Thomas, Walker, the Indian deputy Willis, and others. Nor does it wholly explain the role of Hale, or the lawyer Forrest whose son, Will, marries Nola, or the photographer John Tate who finally kills his own wife Ruth, twin-sister of Moses Greycloud, or even the deathly black Buick which delivers the killers. For the conspiracy, from the fictional Watona to Osage murders elsewhere in America, and even as far away as England, Hogan tells as an always elusive thread, and whose origins lie as much in the federal Government as in local Oklahoma white greed and connivance.

Hogan is equally careful not to make all whites into villainy, as Hale's one-time mistress, China, and the departing physician, Dr. Black, give witness. Native life equally has its push-and-pull divides, as in the case of the grandson, Ben Greystone, or Belle's daughter, or the fate of the mixed-blood preacher Joe Billy and his wife as they work their way out of Baptist Christianity back towards Native belief. Stace, modern law-agent, learns his own meaning as a Sioux. But it is the resilience of the Osage themselves, most of all the Hill Osage, and their own protective commitment to sovereign culture and place that offers a counter-resource to the dire workings of the oil conspiracy to hand. Hogan in no way veers towards sentimentality. The novel ends, toughly, with the land indeed lost and scarred by rigs and boreholes and the Greyclouds themselves in flight. Hogan's novel can in this respect be thought a species of palimpsest, a Native version of history written over, or at the interstices of, Oklahoma as Indian Country. *Mean Spirit* gives notice of a mystery whose true meanings, its feints and shadows, even for Hogan still await their solution.

Betty Louise Bell's *Faces in the Moon* (1994) also pursues past into present history. Her narrator Lucie Evers, college teacher in California, recent divorcee from a Jewish husband, and like Bell herself a Cherokee mixed-blood daughter, returns to Oklahoma to witness the dying of her long put-upon yet wayward mother Gracie. Lucie summons the Evers lineage as through "women's voices" and from across a "kitchen table" (4), a family she has grown up as passed-around "Indian child" and as the grown woman who "every year [becomes] more Indian" (33). Her homecoming stirs "thick memory" (33), a litany of anti-romance:

> Dust, outlaws, pretty black-eyed women raising children alone, chopping their way through cotton, good ol' boys and no-good men. Full-blooded grandmothers, mixedblood renegades and lost generations, whirling across the earth in forty-nine Chevys, drunk on homemade beer, and aged by years of craving under the hot Oklahoma sun. (5)

The voices that speak to this memory play one into the other, witness and accusation, comfort and recrimination. They each, in turn, however particular, even idiosyncratic, have their origins in the spiral begun from Cherokee displacement.

Gracie Evers, never much above poverty, defiantly yet pathetically goes on repeating her credo as one of "Don't mess with Indian women," to be emulated, always, by her sister Auney's' "Naw, I sure wouldn't wanna do that." In her drift from man to man, drinking, newspaper cuttings and second-hand clothing, Gracie becomes the perfect gatherer-up of white America's trifles. From the Depression onwards, and in an Oklahoma whose shack lies in the shadow of historic Fort Sill, hers has been a world of margins, loss more than gain. Her sister, baptized Rozella but known as Auney, plays Gracie's companion colloquist, also a "lost generation" daughter of Hellen Evers, the grandmother who at her death "told my mother, then nine years old, would always be watching her from the moon" (56). Auney, equally, lives a life of make-do, aping white appearance to the point where she peroxides her hair to calamitous result, a woman always voluble yet as un-centered as her sibling.

From a generation before them stands the redoubtable Great Aunt Lizzie Sixkiller Evers, full-blood keeper of Cherokee wisdom, austere Christian, TB sufferer, and a farmwoman and purveyor of family chronicle who, for a while, raises Lucie. In her Lucie finds a more complete voice of the history which has made her the child dreamer who once shouted "'I am Quanah Parker!'" (73) in identification with the great Kwahadi Comanche leader of the South Plains, eventual cattle rancher, and mover in the use of peyote out of which would arise the Native American Church. Lizzie acts as a means for Lucie to go back in memory to the Trail of Tears, to imagine the first Dawes Act tribal enrollment interview of the Georgia-born Robert H. Evers, to call up the Dust Bowl's impact on tribal life, and to situate the Evers line in the larger history of Cherokee names and places.

Accordingly Lucie writes not the romance of her own child notebooks and which she finds among her mother's belongings, but the contradictions of hope and poverty in her long, winding family-tribal ancestry. Asked "What's it like being an Indian?" (59), her reply carries a perfect impatience with stereotype:

> I wish I had Indian stories, crazy and romantic vignettes … Anything to make myself equal to their romance. Instead I can offer only a picture of Momma's rented house, a tiny flat two-bedroom shack in a run-down part of town. (59)

Years later, seeking out the Dawes Commission's Cherokee Rolls, an encounter with a supercilious white male librarian at the Oklahoma Historical Society brings on the riposte "I am your worst nightmare: I am an Indian with a pen" (192). Two kinds of implication ally. The one reflects Lucie's will to word. The other underscores the history within and behind that word. Bell has both engage, and appeal, throughout *Faces in the Moon*.

In *Cherokee America* (2019) Margaret Verble aims for the big sweep, a historical fiction set in 1875 Oklahoma "Indian Territory" and told through the dynastic lives of the Singers, Corderys and Bushyheads. Check Singer, actual given name ironically "Cherokee America," holds center-place in the novel, matriarch (of her own five sons and extended family), co-owner of the thriving potato farm in the Bottoms, and then widow of her Yankee-merchant husband Andrew Singer. Herself a complex mix of white and Native lineage ("She was mostly white, but from a large, influential Cherokee family" 29) she is to be heard explaining to her second offspring Hugh:

> Our lives are shaped by our history ... We're all family. All connected. And the elders don't leave us just because they've died. They're still with us, guiding us in what we do. You are a Cherokee. You'll never be alone. (246)

Be it legacy, styles of Native, white and black housekeeping, murder, pistols, gold-hunt, detection, admixtures of tall tale and ghosts, robbery and water-witching, brothel and other sex, and albeit at risk of edging towards the schematic, Verble could not be accused of failing to deliver the wide screen.

With the Cherokee Nation as matrix the novel deploys frequent alternations and fades, at once adventurely, cross-ethnic, and unforgetful of relevant history. Andrew Jackson and the Trail of Tears give reference. The Civil War in which Cherokees fought for both sides offers complicating dimensions. Postbellum Federal-Cherokee tension as to land and jurisdiction plays into the story as do issues of tribal membership. White and Cherokee slaveholding casts its shadow with recognition of intra-tribal splits especially after the past generation's Chief Doublehead and his land finagling. But this is history more backdrop than not, though seasoned in snippets of Cherokee custom and language.

For the main propulsion lies in plotline as it works through the three sequences of intrigue and lattice. "The Coming of the Owl," with the night-bird harbinger of Andrew's Singer's dying, hinges into the wider Cherokee parameter of neighbors like Sanders and Nannie Corderey and their clan and Dennis and Alabama Busheyhead (Dennis the National Treasurer of the Cherokee Nation).

In the onward passage through "The Search for Gold," part reward and punishment thriller, and "Justice" as the tension between Cherokee and Federal legal authority, the tempo accelerates.

Crow Colbert is shot at the bawdyhouse, as is the sex worker Claudette, which will implicate Hugh Singer. Jenny Corderey, child daughter of the Cordereys, goes missing to be found injured down a well which may or may not lead to hidden gold. Connell Singer will try to meet his sexual heat in pursuit of Florence Taylor. Turtle Smith, aging fullblood well-witcher, is hacked to death by the white pair Sam Garrett and Jake Perkins in search of his divining stick which will set in motion a community pursuit. Puny and Ezell Tower, free blacks from Ohio working for the Singers, find themselves steering back into love after Puny has fathered a child on the girl Lizzie. Sheriff Bell Rogers will finesse the Federal marshals Rusk and Bowden as they seek to take over the Turtle Smith search and thereby win control over Cherokee sovereignty. Verble displays a ready verve, Native "history" told under epic popular guise.

***

"I was used to conversations with Harlen that didn't make much sense and didn't seem to go anywhere" (169). The quizzical note, realism with a twist, acts invitingly. The speaker in Thomas King's *Medicine River* (1990), Will Sampson, son of Rose Horse Captive and an absentee, long-dead white father who worked in rodeo, makes any number of attempts to pin down his friend and *alter ego* Harlen Bigbear. For Harlen it is, community fixer, benign trickster, tribal good spirit, who has brought Will back from Toronto to the Medicine River of Canadian prairie and the Rockies. There he has shrewdly finagled him into setting up his photography business (wonderfully against stereotype given the view of "Indians" as spooked at the thought of their spirit being stolen by the camera), made him play basketball for the Medicine River Friendship Center team, and sought to get him married to Louise Heavyman, single mother of South Wing, herself teasingly named not for some Indian Princess but after the hospital ward where she was born.

Harlen, in fact, serves as an apt figuration of modern Native life, a fixer and mender of lives (some of them in his basketball team like Floyd and Elwood). Yet King makes him no cartoon Noble Indian, all spirituality and oneness with Nature. Harlen Bigbear falls ill with flu, loves endless tattle and gossip, and typically misreads maps, even getting lost, of all places, at the Little Bighorn. Unlike, too, some latterday Chingachgook or Hiawatha, and having had Will buy, and help repair, an old canoe in a yard sale, he manages to crash it in the whitewater of the upper Medicine River. He is said, contemporarily, to like "basketball …

cars … golf" (201). For all his savvy, he can also find himself treading lightly round Bertha Morley's scheme, as he mistakenly believes it, to marry him after she has advertised herself in "The Calgary Centre for the Development of Human Potential" as "a Blood Indian woman in good health …. I like to go fishing and hunting, and I play bingo every Thursday" (178). King's touch is light, his verve comic-real as much as serious.

Will Sampson becomes the recorder, and quite literal image-maker, of Harlen's Medicine River, a *Winesburg, Ohio* George Willard figure, who also frequently brings into play the memory of his own boyhood as non-status Indian with his brother James and hard-pressed mother. The family thus has both tribe and city in their make-up, an Indianness both of the Rockies and Calgary, both the Reserve and tough, economically stringent urban life. Each photographic image Will processes in his studio, and its neo-realist writing-up as story, helps fill out his own circle as much as the reader's.

This holds for his close encounters with not only Harlen and Louise, but the bingo antagonists Big John Yellow Rabbit and Eddie Weaselhead, the "marriage doctor" Martha Oldcrow, January Pretty Weasel as abused tribal wife, Harlen's storyteller brother, Joe Bigbear, the tribal elder Lionel James, and the self-divided AIM *aficionado* David Plume. Each builds into a live Medicine River, "Indians now" as it were. Even Will's sense of place changes and grows, Medicine River if a modern Canada, and within it a modern Alberta, of TV, fast food, pick-up trucks, federal and provincial government and the RCMP (or Mounties), then also, an older tribal world of Chief Mountain and Ninastiko with its ceremonies, trickster myths and play.

King's achievement is to write neither nostalgia nor case-study. *Medicine River*, rather, carries its stories as the oral lightly assumed in the written. Motifs old and new so blend. The "leather rattle made of willow and deer hide," for instance, which Will receives from Martha Oldcrow, serves as a Native form of the musical top he buys for South Wing and which, in parallel, makes "a sweet, humming sound, the pitch changing as it [spins] in its perfect circle" (260-1). As Will's insights deepen into Harlen's obliquities, not to say into Medicine River itself, and his own rite-of-passage, so the novel shows a tribal past making its own kind of way into the present.

At one point, even so, Joe Bigbear looks back on his world trips pondering how the world prefers its "Indian stories" rooted in "olden days'" version:

> But those people in Germany and Japan and France and Ottawa want to hear about how Indians used to be. I got some real good stories, funny ones, about

> how things are now, but those people say, no, tell us about the olden days. So I do. (173)

The point perfectly reflects on *Medicine River*'s own workings, a world of present over past, live substance over dead shadow.

For his part, Will thinks of the air flights in which he has fantasized for fellow passengers the father who indeed was the itinerant, drink-addled "rodeo cowboy" (80), and whose letters he once read to his mother's anger and upset. He makes him into a "senior engineer with Petro-Canada" (78), pilot, career diplomat, and perhaps most to the point given Will's own vocation, photographer (80). It throws a fitting cast on the novel at large, *Medicine River*'s sense of Native legacy as inerasably historic, actual, even as has become encased in invention.

Three decades on the compass needle of neo-realism takes another turn. Gertrude Stein's "There is no there, there" in *Everybody's Autobiography* (1937) has long had legendary purchase. But it readily gets forgotten that the "there" in question was Oakland, precisely the working locale for Tommy Orange's *There There* (2018). Twelve principal characters, forty of so chapter episodes, a prologue on the historical gothic of Native decapitation and dismemberment from colony to frontier, an essay-interlude on the powwow as tribal gathering, and a gathering story-line of intended Indian-on-Indian robbery of prize-money at the Great Oakland Powwow, in all contribute to a fierce literary bow. Virtuosity presses from the start, a crafted story-theatre of the post-reservation city, the "real" of Urban Indian life written told with genuine feats of style.

"We've been defined by everyone else" (7) reads the prologue. Orange covers the tracks. TV's "Indian head" test card yields to the early chamber of horrors that saw the beheading of Metacomet/King Philip and Bay Colony habitants kicking severed Native heads for sport. The traveling show of the bottled head from the real life figure behind John Rollins's Murieta is matched by subsequent displays of Sand Creek body parts. The Cheyenne "rolling head" myth moves on to Iron Eyes Cody as faux-Indian and Chief Broom as living façade in *One Flew Over the Cuckoo's Nest*. Once so framed the novel is then able to turn fully, at times graphically, to a galaxy of Urban Indians ("We ride buses, trains. and cars across, over, and under concrete plains" 11) and a plot about literal plot at the powwow to be held at the AFL's Oakland Raiders coliseum. "Prologue," thereby, takes on double loading. As much as it gives textual entry into the novel it also situates its reader inside the historical currents that have led to Oakland as modern Native city.

The lives of the dozen-fold cast of *There There*, for the most part Cheyenne-descended, Orange weaves one into the other in an intricacy of inter-generational kinship and breakage. Tony Loneman, the novel's opening voice, Fetal Alcohol Syndrome-slowed (referred to as "the drome") conspiratorially finds himself pulled into carrying bullets for the robbery. Dene Oxendene, tagger (as "Lens"), plans a documentary of life-stories and photography on Oakland as Native dispensation albeit that he observes "Sometimes not having a story *is* the story" (148). Opal Viola Victoria Bear Shield and sister Jacquie, raised by activist but neglectful parents first at the Alcatraz Occupation and then in family dispersal that involves Jacquie's daughter Blue, learns from her own mother killed by cancer the truth of the saying "the world was made of stories" (57). Edwin Black, obese, ever constipated, an internet addict, tries to negotiate mixed ancestry ("For me to say I'm Native seems wrong" 71). Jacquie's adoption of Orvil Red Feather as his grandmother (actually great-aunt) and Orvil's own role as brother to Loother and Lony become major family pivots in the story. He inherits Opal's denial ("Opal had been openly against any of them doing anything Indian" 118) yet acts on his intention as dance competitor at the powwow in full though ill-fitting regalia. He so plays Indian playing Indian yet in the costume of actual historic Indians, the one "fit" inside the other. Orange works the Urban Indian identity-changes with adroit touch.

The two groupings, the committee for the powwow of Dene, Edwin, Blue and others, and the would-be robbers, the homeboys Octavio Gomez, Calvin Johnson, Charles and Carlos, and with Tony in tow, share Oakland idiom. Their dynasties both join and fracture. The surrounds are all city, the noise, fast food, beers, tags, cars, heroin, weed and other drugs, and to eventual fatal effect, Oakland Powwow gunfire to which Tony's dying to birdsong gives lyric contrast. The Interlude offers a guiding comment:

> The tragedy of it all will be unspeakable, the fact that we've been fighting for decades to be recognized as a present-tense people, modern and relevant, alive, only to die in the grass wearing feathers. (141)

Given the powwow, and the last-episode killings in a heist gone catastrophically wrong, Orange's authorial comment brings to bear the "real" of Native memory even as it dramatizes precisely the "real" of the novel's Native present. It helps in construing authorship of genuinely rare aplomb.

***

A novel of three Chippewa-Ojibwe women tied into a single generation spanning the 1970s to 2020, *The Road Back to Sweetgrass* (2014) by Linda LeGarde Grover (Bois Forte Anishinaabe) gives fresh impulsion to modern relationship on and off reservation. The invented Mozhay Point Reservation, Minnesota, historic and yet busily inhabited by the present, provides the setting for the rest of the trilogy which includes the story-collection *The Dance Boots* (2010) and the ensuing novel *In the Night of Memory* (2019) with its account of the fostering and tribal return of two Chippewa girls. Often as LeGarde Grover has invited comparison with Louise Erdrich, she maintains her own clear and particular life-narratives in *The Road Back to Sweetgrass*, those of Margie Robineau (to become Margaret Mary Washington), Dale Ann Dionne and Theresa Rooney as they move out of and then back into Mozhay Point.

These narratives, or one enclosing narrative, the novel delivers to careful antiphonal effect. They first draw upon a force of context. The italicized prologue discloses symbolic heredity in the burial of an umbilical cord, sewn in a deerskin bag and wrapped in sweetgrass ("*The Odissimmaa Bag*" 1-2). It serves as the token of birth into place, earth, Muskrat clan, the very odor of creation. In the figure of Zho (Joseph) Washington, benign elder, whose son Michael will capture Margie's girl-time love but who will marry Theresa, the muskrat-clan history has its chronicler. Himself renamed Washington by the *zhaagdashig*, the white Mission School authorities, from the Anishinaabe genealogical muskrat name Wazhushk, he will act as official but in fact surrogate "husband" to Margie, and "father" to Crystal, her child by the handsome powwow dancer and ricer Michael. He it is who explains the role of the muskrat as earthdiver and savior, the courageous, determined animal avatar.

Allotment and post-allotment La Force/Miskwaa divisions of land, the shadow of termination politics, the novel shows to impose their residues of time and ownership. The seasonal acts of "ricing," the collection and storage (and sale) of wild rice, further locates community threads of identity. LeGarde Grover also reveals, and puts to iconographic use the culinary secrets of good frybread of which Margie becomes a doyenne ("Margie's frybread was so light it all but rose from the plate" 5), alimentation also to include maple sugaring and cooking rabbit (an inspired chapter on "The Art of Dressing a Rabbit"). These, along with plentiful insertion of Anishinaabe phrase and tease, interact as necessary working textures.

To follow the lives of the women is to move through increments of time. Margie will evolve from youngster to restaurant counter-hand to motherhood to Chi-Waabik Casino management and wife, yet not quite wife, with the elderly

Zho. She will assume wisewoman status, inward, often lyric, and in the face of her own "ghosting" by Michael ("Here is part of Margie's secret: Unrequited love" 11). Dale Ann, counter-worker yet bright in the classroom, enters the Federal Relocation Program for Indian women, moves to Duluth to become a Long Distance Operator ("an example for other young people at Mozhay Point" she is told by the administrator Mr Gunderson, 55) and where she is patronized by affluent white college roommates. She will move back to Mozhay and marriage with the prosperous and eventual tribal Chairman Jack Minogeeszhik. Theresa, Margie's early friend, will be the one who marries Michael, mother to his children and their family line, an affluent matron in the reservation. These women's histories, at Mozhay Point or in cities like Minneapolis and Duluth, LeGarde Grover keeps well out of range from stereotype. The portraiture is savvy, keen, persuasively grounded.

***

Crazy Horse's Girlfriend (2014), the debut novel of Erika T. Wurth (Apache-Chickasaw-Cherokee), while ostensibly the coming of age of the Native city girl Margaritte, could as easily be thought a portrait of having come of age. Pitched in first-person sixteen-year old's High School idiom with due sex and punk metal music reference, it tells essentially a den narrative, young peer lives of mainly mixed and fostered Native lineage (Jake, Julia, Treena, the older ex-rez Lakota couple Megan and Will, he a heavy drinker) under just-about-managing duress in the township of Idaho Springs close to Denver. Daughter to a work-weary mother abused by her whiskey-violent husband Doug, sister to child twins Mary and Carrie, dealer in weed with her Cheyenne cousin Jake which involves her in a knife episode and he is sent to juvie (juvenile hall), Margaritte edges along an uncertain path into pending adulthood. That she becomes pregnant after a casual sex encounter adds its part even as she starts an intimacy with her non-Indian affluent beau and coke-user Mike Walker. The risk might have been familiar, even formula, life-passage. Wurth, however, shows herself well able to invest the narrative with fresh bite, sharpness of dialogue.

"I was feeling good," Magaritte confides as she parties with Mike, "the booze and weed beginning to dance through my blood in a violent ballet" (81). A phrase like "violent ballet" holds for the larger reach of the novel. Her inebriated father will crash the car with injury to her mother Christine and herself. She will withhold word from Mike that the pregnancy is not of his doing. He in turn betrays her with Julia and is beaten by Jake who is given probation and community service for assault. "Nothing was OK" (180) becomes the mantra for Margaritte, a state of play, however, that will see her refuse an abortion and give birth to a daughter. A final confessional letter from Mike, in rehab in California, leaves her positioned once more mid-way.

Silhouetted against this life-round, Walmart, pizza cuisine, Stephen King reading, TV soaps, beer and drugs, the novel posits a counter-frame. Crazy Horse's name and Pine Ridge are summoned. Will remembers sundance ritual and grass dancers. There is purchase of Navajo earrings, Native hip-hop music, and Denver's Indian center. Obliquely, but insistently, they lie each at the edges of her coming of age, affecting silhouettes from histories beyond the city. *Crazy Horse's Girlfriend* remains a first novel, with occasional flatnesses, dips. Yet it also lowers an affecting gaze on citied Native young womanhood and its rites of passage, Wurth's cautionary tale.

To embark on Eden Robinson's *Monkey Beach* (2000) is to head north of Vancouver into the First Nations ocean-shore community of Kitamaat, Haisla country. The portrait of Lisamarie Michelle Hill, a growing-up told in different time folds of infancy, childhood, vexed adolescence, and young womanhood edged in drink and drugs, it turns on how she seeks balance, a tribal understanding, of the loss at sea of her loved roguish AIM-veteran uncle Mick Hill and, subsequently aboard the *Queen of the Night* of her swim-obsessed younger brother Jim and their kinsman Josh. Robinson writes a full round of Haisla family, modern parenting faced with offspring High School and other scrapes, ancient custom in the person of the grandmother Ma-ma-oo. The novel is strong enough to negotiate various kinds of balancing act.

Fishery as a tradition of tides, seiners and gillnetters plays against fishery as workplace village Alcan factory. Home life, the close domestic round of cousins, aunts, uncles, schoolmates, is set against Kitamaat's greater circle of geographies, Prince Rupert, Namu (a name meaning whirlwind), Clio Bay, Canoe Mountain, Blind Pass, Kitlope River, and the location which will feature as final emblem, Monkey Beach. Much as Lisa's evolution carries modern trappings, boys, hair, early sex, partying, it also carries the signs of her Haisla inheritance. These embrace the Haisla language itself, death-heralding crows, the shapeshifter raven Weegit, tree-spirits, ghosts, the "little man" who haunts her in dream, and always the sasquatch or bigfoot which in Haisla becomes B'gwus. For all the fast food binges, Mick's repeated gifts of ice cream especially, there is equal attention to oolichan, sockeye, crab meat, sights of orca, seal, otter and whale, and Ma-ma-oo's Haisla-named medicines, shoots, and crabapple and other berrying (*qºalh'm*, *oxasuli*, *pipxs'm*, *c´ixºa* and more). The feat is to keep these aspects wholly in imaginative play.

Above all the ocean itself assumes double-identity. On the one hand it gives respite ("There is nothing like being on the ocean to clear the head" 138). On the other, and as the novel opens, "my brother is lost" (5). It also provides the setting for the novel's ending-twist. That Jim kills Josh from aboard the *Queen of the Night* on learning that the latter fathered a child with Jim's beauteous love-interest "Karoake" which she aborted, and then, the would-be Olympic swimmer, drowns or at least disappears, implies both truth and myth. Lisa, whom Ma-ma-oo thinks possessed of other-world gifts yet whose life has edged towards this world's waste, finally dreams her visionary healing return to Monkey Beach where she once sojourned with Jim. Coming of age in Robinson's fashioning has signified the immediate call of body but also of ancestral spirit, the copious twine of two-kinds-in-one ongoing First Nations existence.

***

"The truth is never in the facts" observes Stephen Graham Jones in his Author's Note (215) to *Ledfeather* (2008). Certainly his own prolific output, the dozen-plus novels and over a hundred stories (in the journals and web as well as dark-gothic collections like *Bleed into Me* 2005, and *The Ones That Got Away* 2010) from a writer barely fifty, has acted on that cue. It has held, too, whether he has been writing crypto-westerns saturated in pop culture (his first novel *The Fast Red Road: A Plainsong*, 2000), fiction-histories (*Ledfeather* or *Growing Up Dead in Texas* 2011), crime noir that edges towards Science Fiction (*All The Beautiful Sinners* 2003, or *The Bird is Gone: A Manifesto* 2003), Tex-Mex border absurdist-supernatural (*It Came from Del Rio* 2010), or slasher comedy-horror (*Zombie Bake-Off* 2012 or *The Last Final Girl* 2012). Truth he indeed takes to operate less through fact than competing skeins, time-folds and overlaps of voice, each the indicators of postmodern sway.

Jones not been shy in having his fictions signal their own processes of formation. *Demon Theory* (2006), Halloween spook-story, is told in the format of a film treatment. Director markings, and over 400 footnotes, cannily underwrite the one storytelling locked inside the other. *The Long Trial of Nolan Dugatti* (2008) edges towards Kafka in the shape of a narrator left in sole charge of customer relations for a long redundant video-game company and whose father's near-absurdist suicide notes cannily inscribe their lost-and-found relationship. The telling might almost be that of a narrator haunted by his own voice, a contender in the metafictional stakes.

"I remember you" (9) reads an opening epigraph in *Ledfeather*. Un-glossed, stark almost, and printed as though from an ancient typewriter (the text later implies it was written on a "caligraph") it might be the very prompt to enquiry into historical detection. For the novel quickly whirls into complication and alternating shifts of time. Two Blackfeet suicidal boy figures, Doby Saxon and Lead Feather, and two tribal eras, those of contemporary Browning-Glacier Blackfeet reservation and the Starvation Winter 1880s, parallel each other even as they thread with increasing luminosity into the one continuum. A host of contemporary narrators speak, from on and off reservation, township and school-goers, and in the figure of Francis Dalimpere, Federal Indian Agent sent to the Blackfeet in 1883, the novel has one of history's ghosts and one guilt-stricken at Federal insouciance and the 600 winter deaths from hunger of the tribes-people. His ever more haunted letter-writings to Claire, his actual but ever more fantasized wife in the East, will pass down time as though messages in a bottle, a capsule to have the Blackfeet past reverberate into the Blackfeet present.

To enter *Ledfeather* is first to hear the voices that give witness to Doby Saxon, Blackfeet-Yellowtail-Piegan intending self-killer as he stands before highway headlights "waiting for another car to come kill him" (45). Son of Malory Sainte as protective but in-and-out of jail mother and Earl Two Jobs (born Piney Saxon) as drifter and elk poacher, snow-frozen, bloodied, displaced, he is ushered like a phantom into the East Glacier convenience store ("This was the Blackfeet Reservation on a Saturday night in late November" 14). Each witness to Doby – the caring white woman store assistant and her Blackfeet co-worker Junior, the hospital nurse, the tourist wife out to buy curios and who witnesses the casino fracas, and the High School circle among whom Doby has been basketball player and oddity – all underline a figure caught short by history. How to account for this rush to self-harm, this descent into self-loss? How to account for the clutch of papers he carries? As the novel unfolds the patterns of causation grow clearer, a formidable Blackfeet tableau of antecedent bearings to include not only 1883-4 but the brute Marias (or Baker) massacre of 1870 to which James Welch turns with vivid assurance in *Fools Crow*.

"Like them I am starving" (47). Francis Dalimpere's almost first words set the measure, as does his judgment that "the situation is unsalvageable" (49). He calls to mind the white-hunter killing of the buffalo and the Blackfeet dependence on Federal rations in their reduced homeland. Most, however, is his near-surreal account of the twelve-year-old boy, Lead Feather (so-spelled) hurling black stones into the sky in hopes that one will descend and kill him. The one that nearly does, gashing his ear, becomes a virtual stigmata for the agent "in my position as ambassador of the American government" (62), the live embodiment of his anguished call to redemption ("If I can just save one, Claire …." 65). The horror of Blackfeet hunger and eradication presses ever more into him to the point of phantasmagoria ("In the midst of it, I do not even recognize myself" 79). To Claire he writes "you are my confessor" (147).

His bid to discern Blackfeet meaning is mediated through the silent-sharer figure of the tribesman Yellow Tail (however much he is reported as saying) who, in tacit accusation, bears his own memory of a wife killed alongside all the other Blackfeet at Marias. He offers Elk fables and reveals that he fed his tribe even though it cost the lives of two white trappers. Dalimpere speaks fur-trader French to him and thinks he is entrusting his letters to Claire. His condition becomes one of transfiguration, the would-be metamorphosis of himself against all spiritual or corporeal appearance into "Indian," and none other than a Blackfeet. Given the spectacle of suffering amid what, at one point, he thinks a Montana Eden, he has reason to observe that "Hell for a white man would simply be to be forced to live as one of his subjects" (155). The colonial prism so reverses, subject into object, the hegemonic into the other.

The "gauntlet of the staring dead" (104) possesses Dalimpere (graphically when yet another starving Piegan youth makes it his task to keep the eyes of these dead in guardianship of their spirit). His senses are ravaged by the burial area of the Sandhills, in the one perspective hundreds of Blackfeet ghosts rising, or in another, the gas of decomposing Blackfeet bodies. The cruel farce of spoilt Federal rations ("the quarterly stipend" 161), the mockery of a Thanksgiving meal with Sheffield, in charge of the visiting soldiery, Collins, his predecessor as Agent, and Marsh the translator, and the contaminating soldier rape of a Blackfeet woman which causes the tribe to forego the remaining provisions, add to the dereliction in which he is embroiled. He, too, moves outside of himself into the third person, notably in imagining the consequence of his well intended but wholly imperfect effort to feed the tribe:

> The next time the soldiers came up now, they would be leaving with the Agent in chains. Not for killing the six hundred Piegan … but for slaughtering the twenty-four government cows. For it was an action that would become legend … (185)

The implications work severally. What moral scale is to be understood? How does a single legalism, the killing of the cattle, stack up against tribal genocide, "the encampment of the dead" (104)?

The only redemption for Dalimpere, however small in scale as he recognizes given the enormity of the enclosing death, lies in saving Lead Feather to whom he feeds the chewed tongue of the cattle, whom he nurses, and in the wake of whose slow recovery (not unlike Brian Moore's Jesuit, Father Laforgue, from the Huron in *Black Robe*) he can exit into the snows to disappear from history and text. It is this story, or rather the story of the Blackfeet that has become his, that will pass to Doby in the form of the letters ("this sheaf of antique papers" 180), another Blackfeet both harmed and self-harming. The Agent's trauma both shadows, and highlights, the trauma within the history which connects the Starvation winter to Doby's contemporary reservation:

> The word coursed through the Indian Agent, finally came to rest at the back of his throat, like a word he could swallow down if only his eyes would close tight enough. (98)

The imagery speaks with eloquence, un-sayable Blackfeet death, the choke of American "Indian" history carried from past to present.

As Lead Feather heads incrementally towards recovery, Doby ("bleeding again" yet seated in a last car scene) holds the hand of a possible lover mimetically called Claire from another reservation. The saga to which Dalimpere has given epistolary form, obliquely, and with a fine sense of proportion on Jones's part, looks to find its final destination, its trans-historical addressee. The one event elides into the other. Images transpose and pair. No single narrative authority has sway. Witness is both past and wholly present-time. Interior self-speech runs alongside community dialogue. A shelf of gain, a saving, against loss is offered. The upshot is a Book of the Dead but also a Book of Life. Jones's novel, polyvocal, heteroglossic, and positioned to move in both parallels and diagonals down corridors of event, memory, language itself – English, French, Blackfeet. It carries the insignia of the postmodern while remaining at once history, or a version of it, and in William Styron's astute phrase from his Author's Note to *Confessions of Nat Turner* (1967) "a meditation on history."

***

In both *The Oklahoma Basic Intelligence Test: New and Collected Elementary, Epistolary, Autobiographical, and Oratorical Choctologies* (1997) and *How Choctaws Invented Civilization and Why Choctaws Will Conquer the World* (2007) D. L. Birchfield puts tribal history into speculative, and greatly ingenious, format. Both give diligent panorama to Choctaw and related indigenous culture, whole bedrocks of community practice, timeline and geography. But they also carry strings of playfulness, teasing inventions of approach or layout ("Choctology 101" or "Slouching Towards Hillerman"). Much, too, as the contributing chapters confirm an alert eye to scholarship, be it Oklahoma as vintage Indian (and Okie) Country, the role of Andrew Jackson, the frontier, the prairies, oil, Route 66, or

Texas and its Rangers, each with bibliography, there is no lack of recognition of how tribal culture has ancestrally dealt with inheritance ("Indians know that stories are more reliable guides to a people and their past than works of history"). That again exhibits itself in *Black Silk Handkerchief* (2006), the first of his antic Hom-Astubby Chocktaw lawyer mysteries ("Hom Astubby viewed himself as a victim of luck" 6). Without being unduly hoist by category, *Field of Honor* (2004), his principal novel, clearly belongs in the same imaginative arena.

"Have You Heard About America?" (19) an early riff in *The Oklahoma Basic Intelligence Test*, gives a guide to Birchfield's style:

> They want to be your friends 1
> They want to build a wagon road
> through where you live 2
>
> Then they want you to move 3
>
> Then they want you to build a railroad
> through where they moved you to 4
> Then they want to move in with you 5
> Then they want you to keep quiet
> and stay out of their way
> while they tell the world
> that ever since then
> your nation has been past tense
>
> 1. Treaty With The Choctaw, 1786
> 2. Treaty With The Choctaw, 1801
> 3. Treaty With The Choctaw, 1830
> 4. Treaty With The Choctaw And Chickasaw, 1866
> 5. Oklahoma Statehood, 1907

The "test" stands well enough in its own right. But each footnote to the seeming conversational snippets ("They want …") wryly points up shaping truths-to-history. Choctaw encounters with white America are to be understood as a chronology of fake friendship, land-grab, removal, and would-be imposed vanishment.

The inventory provides a near perfect point of entry into *Field of Honor* whose satiric war-and-peace fabling, and serio-comic display, invites comparison with *Slaughterhouse 5*, *Catch-22* or *Little Big Man*. For however much a vision of the historical-colonial chain from Indian Removal to LBJ and Vietnam, the techniques in play unmistakably belong to the metafiction. Ironic alternation of realm come into play. Teasing version of history include Christianity, American

Independence (that of a people referred to throughout as German Europeans or in Choctaw *Na Hollo*), the Civil War, Mississippi, and Oklahoma itself. Indians, the Choctaw but also the Natchez, in their below-ground regime have become counter-Indians.

For under Birchfield's authorial purview the text turns on its own axis. The process begins as Lance Corporal Patrick Pushmataha McDaniel, US Marine Corps, mixed-blood Choctaw, panics in Vietnam, gets confused in the jungle (an "Indian" cliché turned on its head), is thought captured, and finds his way back to the States to await capture in McGee Valley, southeast Oklahoma. Over a lost decade (it is 1976 yet he supposes the Vietnam war won in weeks with the military engaged to hold down student riots), and as he goes rogue, he takes on the paradoxical role of Marine renegade who uses training in jungle-camouflage, traps, tree-dormitories, and the burglary of military hardware, to await seizure and sentence by his admired fellow Marines for desertion. In his own fantasy "the most dreaded deserter in the history of the Marine Corps" (33), he hopes his honor-code capture will confirm the Corps's "few good men" legend. On being captured, in fact, it leads to his mistakenly being thought a Vietnam hero for having escaped Viet Cong clutches, promotion to Major, and the award of huge back-pay. This zigzag, and the Catch-22 runs of plotline in which it is embedded, indicates the board-game befitting Birchfield's well-known chess prowess.

Events are made to turn ever more counter. McDaniel is said to suffer Stockholm Cowardice Syndrome Dysfunction, finds himself accidental sports-hero witness to a vast underground Choctaw world technically advanced and which occasionally sends its people to infiltrate the above ground world, and becomes embroiled in a Pentagon conspiracy headed by the unhinged Colonel Fay to discover the location of lost oil-reserve sites started in the 1920s under Coolidge. Vietnam, it turns out, was simply a ruse to keep attention focused elsewhere. Another of American fiction's truants, when finally, and once again, McDaniel is obliged to light out, it is less for Huck's territories ahead than for those immediately to hand, or in the novel's Oklahoma figuring of locale, those immediately underfoot. For in Choctaw terms, as the text discreetly indicates, he embodies the folk-mythical *chukfi* or rabbit of the *Okla Hannali*, one of the tribal branches, trickster yet also the tricked.

Field of Honor, throughout, gives full rein to this counterfactual play. The valley terrain vaunts names like Bugaboo and Wildcat Canyon, Crooked Creek and Chimney Ridge. McDaniel's identity contradictions become a serial: deserter-hero, Corporal-Major, and once he has fled down through the cave labyrinth into the Choctaw underground, a Lighthorseman superhero of the Ishtaboli stickball game yet also widely thought a retard (not to mention drugged hospital patient for having run into the wall while scoring the goal that makes him a celebrity). Above ground, Fay's Black Berets use a fake company as mask yet, in Sergeant Kelley, they themselves have been infiltrated by the actual Kelley, Captain in the Choctaw and Ishtaboli ranks. Geological and other survey maps have been changed by Fay and his cohorts to mislead enquirers. Beneath ground Birchfield has McDaniel, mentored by the boy Little Ejay, learn tribal alter-history, sovereignty discourse, the whir of an advanced technological civilization, in all the Choctaws as might-have-been. Just as it satirizes life above ground, the text also takes any number of genial shies at tribal life – a leadership system that apes university promotion and tenure systems, reverse Choctaw erotica and courtship (in the person of the beauteous Elena), or even comparative spelling and numbers in English and Choctaw (itself broken into Missionary and Standard Choctaw replete with Laurence Sterne-style diagrams) with a riff on the use of colons and semi-colons.

The account McDaniel gives Fay on his return to the surface again shadows the deflections of the text in its own right:

> "Sir," McDaniel said, "I got a little bit sidetracked because I thought I'd stumbled into a secret subterranean civilization of Indians, and they got me hooked on some kind of dope that wrung me out pretty good. I mean, it almost caused me to get married. They're right below us, Sir. A huge underground city. Lordy mercy, they've got subways and trains and theatres and schools and hospitals and women like you wouldn't believe. And their religion is ball play …." (220-1)

In having McDaniel pretend to think the underground Choctaw both fantasy and "part of the celebration for the two-hundredth anniversary of the Marine Corps" (221), Birchfield engages in a closing narrative maneuver. Historic roles have reversed, and reversed again, and his novel adjusts its own speculative workings to suit.

***

These diversities of vision, as of narrative kind and form, leave little to doubt that no ready holding pattern applies. The widening of Native/First Nations authorship has become a simply indisputable truth. The benefits are manifold: re-visioning of history, shifts in idiom, ingenuity. Hogan to Birchfield, Bell to Jones, the notion of paradigm dissolves. New voice enters and holds. Readerships, likewise, find themselves enjoined to discard easy expectation of any one composite entity designated "The Indian Novel."

Notes

1 Robert Franklin Gish, *Beyond Bounds: Cross-Cultural Essays on Anglo, American Indian, & Chicano Literature*, Albuquerque: University of New Mexico Press, 1996, 54.
2 Linda Hogan, *Savings*, Minneapolis: Coffee House Press, 1988, 65.

Works Cited

Bell, Betty Louise, *Face in the Moon*, Norman: University of Oklahoma Press, 1994.
Berger, Thomas, *Little Big Man*, New York: Dial Press, 1964.
Birchfield, D. H., *How Choctaws Invented Civilization and Why Choctaws Will Conquer the World*, Albuquerque: University of New Mexico Press, 2007.
_____, *Black Silk Handkerchief: A Hom-Astubby Mystery*, Norman: University of Oklahoma Press, 2006.
_____, *Field of Honor*, Norman: University of Oklahoma Press, 2004.
_____, *The Oklahoma Basic Intelligence Test: New and Collected Elementary, Epistolatory, Autobiographical, and Oratorical Choctologies*, Greenfield Center, New York: Greenfield Review Press, 1998.
Grover, Linda LeGarde, *In the Night of Memory*, Minneapolis: University of Minnesota Press, 2019.
_____, *The Road Back to Sweetgrass*, Minneapolis: University of Minnesota Press, 2014.
_____, *The Dance Boots*, Athens: University of Georgia Press, 2010.
Heller, Joseph, *Catch-22*, New York: Simon and Schuster, 1961.
Hogan, Linda, *Mean Spirit*, New York: Athenaeum, 1990.
_____, *Savings*, Minneapolis: Coffee House Press, 1988.
Jones, Stephen Graham, *The Last Final Girl*, Portland: Lazy Fascist Press, 2012.
_____, *Zombie Bake-Off*, Portland: Lazy Fascist Press, 2012.
_____, *Growing Up Dead in Texas*, Douglas, Isle of Man: MP Publishing, 2011.
_____, *The Ones That Got Away*, Gaithersburg, MD: Prime Books, 2010.
_____, *It Came from Del Rio*, Lyons, Colorado: Trapdoor Books, 2010.
_____, *Ledfeather*, Tuscaloosa: Fiction Collective 2/University of Alabama Press, 2008.
_____, *The Long Trial of Nolan Dugatti*, Portland: Chiasmus Press, 2008.
_____, *Demon Theory: A Work of Fiction*, San Francisco: Mac/Adam Cage, 2006.
_____, *Bleed into Me: A Book of Stories*, Lincoln: University of Nebraska Press, 2005.
_____, *The Bird Is Gone: A Manifesto*, Normal, IL: Fiction Collective 2, 2003.
_____, *All the Beautiful Sinners*, New York: Rugged Land, 2003.
_____, *The Fast Red Road*, Normal, IL: Fiction Collective 2, 2000.
Kesey, Ken, *One Flew Over the Cuckoo's Nest*, New York: Viking, 1962.
King, Thomas, *Medicine River*, Markham, Ontario, New York: Viking, 1990.
Orange, Tommy, *There There*, New York: Alfred A. Knopf, 2018.
Styron, William, *The Confessions of Nat Turner*, New York: Random House, 1967.

Verble, Margaret, *Cherokee America*, Boston: Houghton Mifflin Harcourt, 2019.
Vonnegut, Kurt, *Slaughterhouse 5*, New York: Delacorte Press, 1969.
Welch, James, *Fools Crow*, New York: Viking, 1986.
Wurth, Erika T., *Crazy Horse's Girlfriend*, Chicago: Curbside Splendor Publishing, 2014.

Part III

Short Story

11

Story Panorama: Anthology, Author Collection

I will tell you something about stories ...
They aren't just entertainment,
Don't be fooled.
They are all we have, you see,
all we have to fight off
illness and death.
You don't have anything
if you don't have the stories.

Leslie Marmon Silko, *Ceremony* (1977)[1]

Do you ever wonder how it is we imagine the world in the way we do, how it is we imagine ourselves, if not through our stories?

Thomas King, *The Truth About Stories: A Native Narrative* (2003)[2]

Story, storytelling, as in all indigenous tradition, lies at the very core of Native American expressive culture. From the outset this has meant the spoken word, a vast, enactive thesaurus of legend, storying, ceremony and song in a plurality of historic languages. They each bear tiers of memory, the one or another prism into habitations of time and land. Whether Kiowa creation myth, Navajo coyote and other trickster fable, Hopi tales of clan and adventure, Chippewa-Ojibwe woodland narrative, Sioux accounts of horse and buffalo, Pueblo and Cherokee fables of childhood and witchery, or Cree versions of cosmology, their passage into story has always allowed for improvisation, spontaneity in styles of delivery.

That holds, equally, for each other tribal-oral portrait of community, love, war, craft, medicine, latterly even city life, and always comic mishap and tease. It is a legacy, of which a compendious and hugely indicative collection like *American Indian Myths and Legends* (1985), under the editorship of Richard Erdoes and Alfonso Ortiz, provides the necessary hinterland to Native *written* authorship. That the Native short story, reservation or beyond-reservation based, has also assumed modern focus, is equally beyond doubt.

To speak of Native story publication as a force in its own right is also to situate it within the spectrum of the Native novel and poetry, along with Native autobiography, drama, and the plethora of evidentiary and discursive writing. As in all the writings of Native America and First Nations Canada, this authorship crosses borders. The epigraphs taken from Leslie Marmon Silko and Thomas King give witness. Since Momaday's *House Made of Dawn*, his virtuoso homing novel, it may well be that longer narrative fiction has tended to win the limelight. But that in no way diminishes short story achievement, be it as earlier tier, one-off author collection, or edited anthology.

***

Where the novel looks to John Rollins Ridge's *The Life and Times of Joaquín Murieta* (1854) as inaugural text, so the short story has its working first benchmarks. Zitkala-Ša, Yankton Sioux activist, Carlisle Indian School teacher, violinist, opera-writer, contributor to *Atlantic Monthly* and *Harper's*, and also known under her English-language name of Gertrude Simmons Bonnin, gives one kind of pointer. Her political writings may well have had the stronger impact but both *Old Indian Legends* (1901), pitched mainly for children, and *American Indian Stories* (1921), with their mix of autobiography, essay and fiction and reflection of the intricacies of Sioux legacy and costs of assimilation, show a ready enough virtuosity. Charles Eastman, the Santee Sioux physician who attended at Wounded Knee in 1890 and whose *Indian Boyhood* (1902) won a considerable readership, gives markers of another kind. Following his interpretations of tribal culture and his animal and war stories, first published in *Harper's* and other leading magazines, he successively collected in *Red Hunters and Animal People* (1904), *Old Indian Days* (1907) and *Smoky Day's Wigwam Evenings: Indian Tales Retold* (1910). Companion strings of other early story equally invite full note.

Alexander Posey's *Fus Fixico Letters*, the work of an Oklahoma Muscogee Creek satirist with a shrewd eye to federal and tribal politics and published in his Eufaula newspaper *Indian Journal* in the 1900s, offers a case in point. Behind the ostensible epistolary form lies a fund of canny story-creation and character. E. Pauline Johnson's *Legends of Vancouver* (1911), *The Shaggannapi* (1913) and *The Moccasin Maker* (1913) as the posthumously collected stories of a celebrity Six Nations Canadian Mohawk poet and touring actress, take on a mix of Native terrains. Whatever the occasional dips of style they encompass an ambitiously bicoastal span of Iroquois to Squamish history.

Mourning Dove's *Coyote Stories* (1933) transcribes grandmother-told tribal legend into on-the-page story. John Milton Oskison begins his career with the religious-themed and titled story "Only The Master Shall Praise." D'Arcy

McNickle, albeit best known for *The Surrounded*, bequeaths the western-frontier and international stories posthumously collected in *The Hawk is Hungry* (1992). John Joseph Mathews, whose *The Osages: Children of the Middle Waters* (1961) offers a trove of documentary tribal custom and timeline deftly sourced from the talk-stories of his own Osage origins.

Each of these earlier names differs as much in their story-styling as in cultural ancestry. They also, several times over, confirm that Native authors fall under no absolute obligation to write only Native-themed work. Undoubtedly the roster of written Native short story has moved into fuller come-uppance under the pen of moderns and contemporaries in the wake of Momaday. But these first strata were, and remain, necessary landmarks.

***

Collections, the modern non-Native story-cycle in particular, vaunt well enough known mainstream-canonical titles, whether James Joyce's *Dubliners* with its vernacular city world of Ireland or Sherwood Anderson's *Winesburg, Ohio* with its portrait of American small-town claustrophobia. But Native authorship quite also has its ranking contributions to the genre. The names accorded their own chapters in this book give proof positive, flare, variety of perspective. They embrace Erdrich's *Love Medicine* (1984), Gerald Vizenor's *Landfill Meditation* (1991), Diane Glancy's *Firesticks* (1993), Sherman Alexie's *The Lone Ranger and Tonto Fistfight in Heaven* (1993) and Stephen Graham Jones's *Bleed into Me* (2005). Other established authorship, however, has far from gone missing.

Simon Ortiz brings the seasoned poet's ear of *Woven Stone* (1992) and *Out There Somewhere* (2002) to his *Men on the Moon: Collected Short Stories* (1999). This easefully told mix of life-stories range through the title-story's ironic contemplation of an age of astronauts for reservation culture ("Men on the Moon"), Pueblo upbringing and family life ("What Indians Do"), Idaho migrant labor ("Woman Singing"), Vietnam and a lost son ("To Change Life in a Good Way"), and West Coast hippie-wannabes ("The San Francisco Indians").

Elizabeth Cook-Lynn, the tenacious founder-editor of *Wicazo Sa Review* and novelist of *Aurelia: A Creek Crow Trilogy* (1999), writes *The Power of Horses and Other Stories* (1990). Her portraiture affords Upper Plains reservation life, whether family dysfunction ("Last Days of a Squaw Man"), sad-comic missionary blunder ("A Visit from Reverend Tileston"), or grand-maternal love of dynasty and earth ("Mahpiyato").

Maurice Kenny's *Tortured Skins and Other Short Fiction* (2000) proffers assured styling to Haudenosaunee Mohawk legacy as well as other tribal history. His stories display a nuanced exploration of white ethnocidal policy ("Black

Kettle: Fear and Rescue" and "Forked Tongues" in the case of the southern Cheyenne), give voice to shape-shifter myth ("Bacon" and "Blue Jacket"), and delve into human and wildlife eco-kinship ("One More"). His forte is to situate tribal realms of past inside the present, Haudenosaunee/Iroquois practice and craft as it throws illumination upon too often insouciant modernity.

Joseph Bruchac (Abenaki), longtime all-rounder as poet, musician, anthologist, founder of the Greenfield Review Press and Center, and storyteller of both adult and children's fiction, also mines a range of U.S.-Canada lore, rarely with livelier returns than in *Turtle Meat and Other Stories* (1992). Whether a laconic piece like the title-story with its clash of generations in which Homer and Amalia, themselves old and turtle-like, persist in ancestral ways as against their would-be contemporary daughter, or "The Fox Den" with its portrait of the Abenaki as tribal fox-people both hunters and hunted, the collection displays a shrewd insider touch for tribal ways of continuance and knowing.

Ralph Salisbury, whose autobiography *So Far, So Good* (2013) notably traces his mixed-blood Cherokee-Shawnee poet's life, a "medicine path" as he calls it, from impoverished Depression-era farm Iowa to World War II, Korea, and Pacific Northwest academia, has long shown his hand as a short story talent with issues of masculinity, rite of passage, and war as keystone themes. His likely best-known volume, *The Indian Who Bombed Berlin and Other Stories* (2009), offers the poetically fine-threaded drama of a Native boy's coming of age ("Bathsheba's Bath, Bull Durham, and a Bottle of Old Grandad"), Native sexual stereotype and actuality set in a world of European diplomacy ("The New World Invades the Old"), and the epiphanic war encounter at the heart of the title story ("The Indian Who Bombed Berlin").

Anna Lee Walters (Pawnee and Otoe-Missouria) creates a delicate octet of stories in *The Sun Is Not Merciful* (1985), winningly her clear-eyed story of alcoholic damage in "The Warriors," careful parsing of a reservation girl's molestation and relationship to her mother in "The Apparitions," and updated telling of a celebrated Native rebirth myth in "The Resurrection of John Stink." Michael Dorris (Modoc) writes with great exactness albeit at the risk of a certain dryness in the fourteen stories of *Working Men* (1993), whether the burial of a drowned child by a pond-designer obsessed with precise measurement and his wife in "The Benchmark" or the re-plaiting of an Alaskan tribal folktale of marital betrayal and spirit-wife as told to an all too unwitting anthropologist in "Shining Agate."

Anita Endrezze (Yaqui), justly recognized for her poetry and artwork, turns to a range of world folk-myth in *Butterfly Moon* (2012), the spectrum ranging from sixteen-century Yaqui evisceration ("White Butterflies") through to contemporary shapeshifters ("The Vampire and the Moth Woman"). In Adrian C. Louis (Paiute), and his collection *Wild Indians & Other Creatures* (1996), Native short fiction has a battler, coyote and raven stories given sardonic hard edge both for themselves and as they play into and upset actual lives, be they Sioux marriage, veteran but also gay Gulf War soldiery, affectingly a Downs child, or even white enquirers after the supposed truth of the 1970 western *A Man Called Horse* with its Sioux capture and English aristocrat warrior.

***

Canadian First Nations author collections, of which Thomas King's *All My Relations: An Anthology of Contemporary Canadian Native Fiction* (1990) gives an important selection, has been its own force. Basil Johnston (Chippewa-Ojibwe), voluminous author and an Anishinaabe as well as English speaker, offers Runyonesque drollery in *Ojibway Tales: Moose Meat and Wild Rice* (1978), whether "Yellow Cloud's Battle with the Spirits" in which the trickster-demon Windigo gets conflated with a local white preacher's car headlights or a lake-fishing pastiche at the expense of the Department of Indian Affairs like "A Sign of the Times."

Beth Brant, First Nations sovereignty and gender activist, gives voice to a range of woman-focused Native experience in *Food and Spirits: Stories* (1991), variously "This is History" with its gynocentric turtle-creation mythology and "Wild Turkeys" as the story-memoir of long ago abusive relationship. E. Donald Two-Rivers (Chippewa-Ojibwe), Ontario-born but long resident in Chicago and an established playwright, creates a tough gallery of Native city-lives in *Survivor's Medicine* (1998), typically crime and its aftermath as in "Joe Walks-Bear Comes Home" or broken minds as in "Smoking Gun Syndrome." It would be remiss not to invoke, besides their novels, the story contributions of Ruby Slipperjack, Peter Blue Cloud (Mohawk), Jeannette Armstrong (Okanagan) or and Joan Crate (Cree),

In this respect, Joseph Boyden (Métis), novelist of the *Three Day Road* (2005) with its account of the wounds and then healing of two Canadian-Cree soldiers in World War I, covers a wide range in his debut collection *Born with a Tooth* (2001). Centered in a northern Ontario reserve and given over to accounts of youth damage ("Gasoline"), intoxicants ("Painted Tongue"), even a punk band ("You Don't Want to Know What Jenny Two Bears Did"), it closes with a subtly orchestrated and reflexive story-quartet in which contesting viewpoints seek to understand the suicide of the tribal student Linda Cheechoo.

***

To opt for any one selection of story taken from well-known anthologies might well give hostage to fortune, especially given the formidable range of theme and operative design. Perhaps appropriately one can open with Scott Momaday's "She is Beautiful in Her Whole Being" (*Talking Leaves*), inset within *The Ancient Child* and engagingly textured in bear, pollen and star myth. This love-story of Set and Grey conjures a far older story from behind its apparent contemporaneity, the damaged Kiowa man who finds redemption in his Navajo lover recently returned from an America outside the world of her mother's *Diné-Lukachukai* people in Arizona. Grey's ancestry of Navajo custom and language, as much as her beauty, and its renewal of Set's spirit as much as body through the shared life in their hogan and their subsequent vision ceremony of joining, bespeaks the continuity of what the story designates "tradition out of time" (207). Legend so elides into life, spirit into body.

That does so also in short fiction like "Bone Girl" (*Earth Song, Sky Spirit*) by Joseph Bruchac with its respect for "Indian ghost" meaning, and "This is a Story" (*All My Relations*) by the Okanagan Jeannette C. Armstrong with its Coyote/Kyoti folklore narrative of Canadian ancestral salmon-run as against the latter-day river of dam and oil slick. A yet more specific sense of place presses in "Fear and Recourse" (*Earth Song, Sky Spirit*) by Maurice Kenny of the events leading to the 1868 bluecoat cavalry attack on Black Kettle and his southern Cheyenne at Washita, Oklahoma. Beginning from the perspective of Black Kettle's daughter, Monahsetah, the story offers a line of remembrance into Comanche near-evisceration. The effect is one of story-theatre to include tribal divisions over whether to attack or make peace with settler whites, the memory of the Sand Creek Massacre of the Cheyenne in 1864, actual citings from military figures like Generals Sherman and Sheridan, and the invocation of the Washita River encampment before the murderous attack under the command of George Custer. It interlaces Black Kettle's peace overtures with extracts from white soldier war letters and diaries. The Plains are invoked as one-time buffalo plenty but now turned famine and bitter winter privation by destructive white hunting. Kenny keeps the connecting layers of his story tight, above all their implication of place as repository of tribal memory.

Other locale enters the story spectrum in a variety of ways. In "From Aboard the Night Train" (*Earth Song, Sky Spirit*) Kimberly Blaeser has her Chippewa-Ojibwe narrator rail-travel back to her reservation township first home. The rail journey, Wisconsin to Minnesota, yields memories of seeing a Fourth of July celebration, a summer stay in France's Haute-Savoie, and nightmares of being at risk in some violent major city. Both on arrival, and on her return trip home, an

Our Town reservation panorama of twenty years previous comes into view: main street and store, eatery and hotel, even a funeral parlor. But the presiding change is the casino, "Las Vegas-style gambling" in its gains-and-losses significance for the Native community. That leads on to thoughts of other transformation, noise over quiet, satellite TV where once there was the parlor and veranda. A closing metaphor summons the TV report of a returning Russian cosmonaut, knees uncertain, after a sixteen-month stay in space. This Native home, one among many, has likewise become shifting ground, for good or not as subject to the folds of change as any other America.

In "Snatched Away" (*Talking Leaves*) Mary TallMountain (Koyukon Athabascan), justly acclaimed for her poem "There is No Word for Goodbye," develops an intricate memory-fiction set upon the sub-Arctic Yukon river and close to the bankside towns of Nulato and Kaltag. The Yukon, varyingly calm but also given to "fierce, frowning mood," at once Native and non-Native habitation, and a place of death and yet sustaining salmon run, mirrors the community life evolved on and about its presence. The figure of the fisherman Clem Stone, the loss of his Athabaskan wife Mary Joe to tuberculosis, the adoption of their children, and death of his brother-in-law in a river drowning, fuses literal into a metaphoric time and tide story. In TallMountain's contemplative fabling and as Clem steers his way one more time along the river, the memory of all he has learned from the community plays into his present life ("Indian. Indianness. The words floated through his thoughts" 266).

Native family, and within it childhood, necessarily finds an array of voice of which Ruth Slipperjack (Ontario Fort Hope Chippewa-Ojibwe) gives a rich vignette in "Coal Oil, Crayons and Schoolbooks" (*All My Relations*). Its unnamed narrator tells a working-day, bacon and coffee breakfast in a reserve cabin home, cold weather, outhouse, morning trout-catch, sibling play and scurry, schoolroom, clothesline, forgotten key, and the presence of a kindly elder called Medicine Man. The account exudes warmest intimacy, a First Nations everyday communal round.

For Greg Sarris, of Miwok-Pomo background, in "Slaughterhouse" (*Earth Song, Sky Spirit*) the focus is more one of disconnection, that of an ethnically mixed California boy-adolescent set within seedy, run-down "in-town-reservation-living." Frankie's peer status in his Santa Rosa Avenue gang, his disjunctive home of drink-addled father, disheveled Aunt Julia and other relatives, the would-be sexual pursuit of Caroline, and his adventuring into a local barn made over into a brothel, all ply into dark portraiture. The image of family here is one of uncertain Native circuit, lives close to broken wheel.

Rayna Green (Cherokee) in "High Cotton" (*That's What She Said*) uses as target a whiskey-drinker husband, Will, bamboozled in his DTs into thinking his church-woman wife in her flannel gown the down-from-heaven figure of Jesus calling him to sobriety. Told as though feisty kitchen-talk by a Tahlequah, Oklahoma Cherokee grandmother to her young kinswoman Ramona, it runs full of cryptic aside, off the cuff comedy. Infinitely to the point the narrator, long seasoned in marriage ways, terms the happenings (and by implication the story-telling) "snakebite medicine."

Linda Hogan offers another kind of woman-centered story in "Aunt Moon's Young Man" (*Talking Leaves*), that which circles around Bess Evening, Chickasaw spinster medicine-woman whose affair with Isaac, a younger full-blood Native man, puts her wartime Pickens, Oklahoma small town neighborhood into a frenzy of church and street gossip. The girl-narrator, Sis, her own family "mixed like Heinz 57," gives the story just the right measure. Bess's role as *curandera*, mentor, lover of Isaac who beats the men-folk at poker, for the woman who sends her on her way to college life with gifts of herb and feather, she becomes the "small beautiful woman in my eye."

An equally agile irony plays into "Moccasins Don't Have High Heels" (*American Indian Literature*) by the Choctaw fiction writer and playwright LeAnne Howe. Told as breezy vernacular, swearing included, it gives a brief first-person diary of a Native woman who in the wake of market greed and crash disgustedly bows out of her office bond-trading job ("I was getting rid of my high heels and putting on my moccasins"). The itinerary that follows involves acerbic swipes at more "Indian" stereotypes, and at Reagan-era predations on the environment, Wild West hoopla, and archeology's digging up native bones. No more "Indians" as margin, periphery, shadow, runs the story's staccato ending.

Thomas King's "The One About Coyote Going West" (*All My Relations*) uses the archetypal trickster figure to deliver a savvy, colloquial story "all about who found us Indians" (68). European discovery history, be it by Norsemen, Columbus or Jacques Cartier, attracts his different parodic hits. Coyote's own "discovery" story leads into a duck-clan rite of passage, curious fowl having grown impatient with his trickster's digressions and mistakes who turn themselves into Indians. The upshot is genial creation-myth, edged in fun, about-turn, quirk, even excremental smell, short storytelling as altogether larger story.

***

Anthologies have played every part in making known the Native/First Nations authorship on offer. General anthologies from Erdoes-Ortiz (1985) to Velie (1979, 1991) give situating tribal-cultural and literary context. Story compilations, King

(1990), Lesley (1991), Trafzer (1992), Blaisdell (2014), all serve to emphasize the sense of gathering literary volume. In Green (1984), Allen (1989), and Wong (2008), Native womanist voice has its deserved representation as it does, symptomatically, in the multi-genre *Reinventing the Enemy's Language: Contemporary Native Women's Writings of North America* (1997).

Ongoing collections suggest not only panorama but force of ambition. For the Native and First Nations short story lays equal claim to presence alongside novel and poetry. Given in brief survey or otherwise there can be no doubt of efficacy, narrative to locate both inner identity and locale, reservation or city, the one world of home yet journey, and the world of nation and transnation. As genre, theirs, too, necessarily, memorably, give literary inscription to the enlarging multiple kinds of Native and First Nations human map.

Notes

1 Lesley Marmon Silko, "Ceremony." Preface to *Ceremony.*
2 Thomas King, *The Truth about Stories*, 95.

Works Cited

Alexie, Sherman, *The Lone Ranger and Tonto Fist Fight in Heaven*, New York: Atlantic Monthly Press, 1993.

Allen, Paula Gunn, ed., *Spider Woman's Granddaughters: Traditional Tales and Contemporary Writing by Native American Women*, Boston: Beacon Press, 1989.

Blaisdell, Bob, ed., *Great Short Stories by Contemporary Native American Writers*, Mineola: Dover Publications, 2014.

Boyden, Joseph, *Three Day Road*, Toronto: Penguin, 2005.

_____, *Born with a Tooth*, Toronto: Cormorant Books, 2001.

Brant, Beth, *Food and Spirits: Stories*, Ithaca: Firebrand, 1991.

Bruchac, Joseph, *Turtle Meat and Other Stories*, Duluth: Holy Cow! Press, 1992.

Cook-Lynn, Elizabeth, *Aurelia: A Crow Creek Trilogy*, Niwot: University Press of Colorado, 1999.

_____, *The Power of Horses and Other Stories*, New York: Arcade, 1990.

Dorris, Michael, *Working Men: Stories*, New York: Henry Holt, 1993.

Dove, Mourning (Hum-Ishu-Ma, Christal Quintasket), *Coyote Stories*, Caldwell, Idaho: Caxton Press, 1933. Reprinted Lincoln: University of Nebraska Press, 1990.

_____, *Cogewea, the Half-Blood: Given Through Sho-Powtan: A Depiction of the Great Montana Cattle Range*, Boston: Four Seas, 1927. Reprinted Lincoln: University of Nebraska Press, 1990.

Eastman, Charles, *Smoky Day's Wigwam Evenings: Indian Tales Retold*, Boston: Little, Brown and Company, 1910.

______, *Old Indian Days*, New York: McClure, 1907.

______, *Red Hunters and Animal People*, New York: Harper & Brothers, 1904.

______, *Indian Boyhood*, New York: McClure, 1902.

Endrezze, Anita, *Butterfly Moon: Short Stories*, Tucson: University of Arizona Press, 2102.

Erdoes, Richard, and Ortiz, Alfonso, eds., *American Indian Myths and Legends*, New York: Pantheon, 1985.

Erdrich, Louise, *The Red Convertible: Selected and New Stories 1978-2009*, New York: HarperCollins, 2009.

______, *Love Medicine*, New York: Henry Holt, 1986; expanded version, 1993.

Fisher, Dexter, ed., *American Indian Stories*, Lincoln: University of Nebraska Press, 1985.

Glancy, Diane, *Firesticks*, Norman: University of Oklahoma Press, 1993.

Green, Rayna, ed., *That's What She Said: Contemporary Poetry and Fiction by Native American Women*, Bloomington: Indiana University Press, 1984.

Harjo, Joy, and Bird, Gloria, eds., *Reinventing the Enemy's Language: Contemporary Native Women's Writing of North America*, New York: W.W. Norton, 1997.

Johnson, Basil, *Ojibway Tales: Moose Meat and Wild Rice*, Toronto: McClelland & Stewart, 1978.

Johnson, E. Pauline, *Legends of Vancouver*, Vancouver: G.S. Forsyth, 1911.

______, *The Moccasin Maker*, 1913. Reprinted Tucson: The University of Arizona Press, 1987.

______, *The Shagganappi*, Toronto: Briggs, 1913.

Jones, Stephen Graham, *Bleed into Me: A Book of Stories*, Lincoln: University of Nebraska Press, 2005.

Kenny, Maurice, *Tortured Skins and Other Short Fiction*, East Lancing: Michigan State University Press, 2000.

King, Thomas, *A Short History of Indians in Canada*, New York: HarperCollins, 2005.

______,*The Truth About Stories: A Native Narrative*, Minneapolis: University of Minnesota Press, 2003.

______, *A Good Story That One: Stories*, Toronto: HarperPerennial, 1993.

______,*All My Relations: An Anthology of Contemporary Canadian Native Fiction*, Toronto: McClelland & Stewart, 1990. Reprinted Norman: University of Oklahoma Press, 1992.

Lesley, Craig, ed., *Talking Leaves: Contemporary Native American Short Stories*, New York: Dell-Laurel, 1991.

Louis, Adrian C., *Wild Indians and Other Creatures*, Reno: University of Nevada Press, 1996.

Mathews, John Joseph, *The Osages: Children of the Middle Waters*, Norman: University of Oklahoma Press, 1961.

McNickle, D'Arcy, *The Hawk Is Hungry*, ed., Birgit Hans, Tucson: The University of Arizona Press, 1992.

______, *The Surrounded*, New York: Dodd, Mead, 1936.

Momaday, N. Scott, *The Ancient Child*, New York: Doubleday, 1989.

______, *House Made of Dawn*, New York: Harper & Row, 1968.

Ortiz, Simon, *Out There Somewhere*, Tucson: University of Arizona Press, 2002.

______, *Men on the Moon: Collected Stories*, Tucson: University of Arizona Press, 1999.

______, *Woven Stone*, Tucson: University of Arizona Press, 1992.

Oskison, John, *Brothers Three*, New York: Macmillan, 1935.

Posey, Alexander, *The Fus Fixico Letters*, ed., Daniel F. Littlefield, Lincoln: University of Nebraska Press, 1993.

Ridge, John Rollin (Yellow Bird), *the Life and Adventures of Joaquín Murieta, The Celebrated California Bandit*, 1854. Reprinted Norman: The University of Oklahoma Press, 1977.

Salisbury, Ralph, *The Indian Who Bombed Berlin and Other Stories*, East Lansing: Michigan State University Press, 2009.

Silko, Leslie Marmon, *Ceremony*, New York: Viking Press, 1972.

Trafzer, Clifford E., ed., *Earth Song, Sky Spirit: Short Stories of the Contemporary Native American Experience*, New York: Doubleday-Anchor, 1992.

Two Rivers, E. Donald, *Survivor's Medicine: Short Stories*, Norman: University of Oklahoma Press, 1998.

Velie, Alan R. ed., *American Indian Literature: An Anthology*, Revised Edition, Norman: University of Oklahoma, 1979, 1991.

Vizenor, Gerald, *Landfill Meditation: Crossblood Stories*, Middletown: Wesleyan University Press/University Press of New England, 1991.

_____, *Griever: An American Monkey King in China*, Normal: Illinois State University/Fiction Collective, 1986. Reprinted Minneapolis: University of Minnesota Press, 1990.

Walters, Anna Lee, *The Sun Is Not Merciful*, Ithaca: Firebrand Books, 1985.

Wong, Hertha D. Sweet, Muller, Lauren Stewart, and Magdaleno, Janet Sequoya, eds., *Reckonings: Contemporary Short Fiction by Native American Women*, New York: Oxford University Press, 2008.

_____, *Old Indian Legends*, Boston: Ginn, 1901. Reprinted Lincoln: University of Nebraska Press, 2001.

Zitkala-Šá/Zitkala-sha/Red Bird (Gertrude Simmons Bonnin), *American Indian Stories*, Washington: Hayworth, 1921. Reprinted Lincoln: University of Nebraska Press, 1985.

12

Whole Parts: Scripting Diane Glancy's Short Fiction

When I read a story
I want to know who the story is happening to
And where I am.
I want to see the setting.
I want to hear the voice of the narrator.
And I want to hear real people talking words I recognize
As real words.
I want to connect with immediacy with what's happening.
I don't want to have to stop and ask what's going on here.
"A Short Story Is Something Happening,"

The West Pole (1997)[1]

I like experimental writing. A mix of several things together. Fragmented. *Choppied.* I like to make up words to fit the broken disenfranchisement I feel.
"She-ro-ism"

The Cold-and-Hunger Dance (1998)[2]

Diane Glancy runs little risk of being accused of literary skimping. Across a profusion of literary forms, poetry, stories and novellas, longer fiction, chapbooks, plays, anthologies, screenplays, creative non-fiction, she has maintained a simply resolute, almost heady, output. This expanse of forty or more titles has made the focus of her interests well enough known, whether mixed-blood Cherokee and white Arkansas family legacy, Bible Christianity, wife-mother-divorcee gendering, the road and family geography of Oklahoma, Kansas, Missouri and other west-of-the-Mississippi (to include the Minnesota of Macalester College where she held her long-time teaching post), or, reflexively, authorship and the role of writer-professor.

Her productivity has far from slowed through to verse collections like *The Book of Bearings* (2019) with its perspective on "the Magnetic North" and Inuit and Cherokee life, and *Mary, Queen of Bees* (2017), her documentary fiction of Mary Wesley the sister of Methodism's founder John Wesley. That includes her ongoing shorter story-telling. Not only has there been an abundance but the command of small-scale exactitude has from the outset carried larger freight and implication. The upshot gives good reason to be thought Glancy's own style of imagism, a flair for economy, concentration of phrase.

"What is life like for you? That's what you should begin writing about" (90). So, in the title essay of *Claiming Breath* (1992), runs in summary Glancy's presiding credo. Certainly all four of her story-collections, *Trigger Dance* (1990), *Firesticks* (1993), *Monkey Secret* (1995) and *The Voice That Was in Travel* (1999), leave no doubt of her eye for the corners and often awkward contingencies of life. Her in-small narratives of Cherokee grandmothers, born-again lovers of Jesus, Oklahoma small-town and country wives and husbands (often ex's), truckers and seamstresses, not to mention waitresses – especially the figure of Turle Heppner in her six part novella-cum-title-story "Firesticks" – and writer-travels to Europe and Australia, all bespeak typifying difference, to include their different wells of human loneliness.

At the same time it is to recognize how Glancy's stories give a sense of context to her people, the working tread of both Native and white township and rural history. Such can be, in fact usually is, quotidian enough, whether the marriage or liaison worn over time, house-tending, women-prepared meals, the passing sexual encounter, church, or driving the interstates. In addition there can be little mistaking a ready grasp of topography, be it indeed township and hard-scrub Oklahoma or like regional settings whose span runs from border Texas to farm Arkansas to citied Minnesota.

The Native footfalls, of necessity, abound, whether Great Spirit allusion and dream or the ancestral Native markings within North American place-names. Sweat-lodge and fry-bread, pow-wow and horse culture, shawl-fringe and feathers, all itemize in the stories as gathering iconography, just as they do in her poetry and other writing. In the case of the Cherokee, especially, Glancy deploys slivers of speech, remembered sayings, community reference to "little people" as well as Christian conversion, along with presiding historical landmarks like Sequoyah's syllabary of 1823 and the Trail of Tears from Georgia to Oklahoma in 1838. Each helps anchor, and texture, the lives in view.

"Writing," Glancy also asserts in *Claiming Breath*, "is the hammer & chisel that breaks down the established way of thinking. A concrete event, then an abstraction. An image then a thought" (23). She even speaks of using herself "as a found object" (23). The emphasis upon hammer and chisel, the transformation of event or image into larger resonance, gives a vital and not to say typically aphoristic sense of direction. In *The Voice That Was in Travel*, her Preface speaks directly to her short fiction – "The stories migrate between connectives and *disconnectives.* Sometimes with disrupted syntax...Sentences sometimes shortened to a few words. Sometimes without a verb. Sometimes run on" (vii). The aim, as it were, is to find styling, a right particularity of narrative, for the discontinuity as much as continuity in experience. Her story lay-outs with their often distinctive paragraphing and line-breaks, contrarieties of wordplay and syntax, even varieties of typography, and the recurring Cherokee usages alongside English, thereby go well beyond mere display. As Glancy's own compositional observations indicate they aim to encipher the storytelling's very meaning.

Typical stories in the four collections begin with a show of declaration, stagings as it were, even capitalizations – "BILL NAVAT WOKE THAT SATURDAY WITH THE DREAM OF APPLES" ("The Orchard," *Trigger Dance* 83); "We weren't allowed to have accidents" ("A Family To Which Nothing Happened," *Firesticks* 31); "Rain blew through the screen" ("Lead Horse," *Monkey Secret* 3); or "Carleen was on the road all the time" ("Road," *The Voice That Was Travel* 21). These launchings might seem to invite over-abbreviation, the passing episode. Yet however "fragmented" their telling, or in Glancy's neologisms "choppied" and given to "disconnectives," her stories do no such thing. Decisively they take possession of the materials in play. Whichever the scale, from vignette to novella, sketch to colloquy, the upshot rarely fails to convey its own fullness, the sense of a completed whole. This quality of scripting, scriptedness, invites its own deserved recognition. For at best, and that is far from infrequently, Glancy's storytelling can approach the luminous.

***

In the preface to *Trigger Dance*, the dozen or so pieces which make up her first medley, Glancy summons the Oklahoma "where I first heard/the voices of my heritage" (n.p.). The power of locale is palpable, Oklahoma as not only geography but time, memory, story, each past-into-present intersection of Native and white. Nor, in her phrase from *Claiming Breath*, can there be doubt of storytelling in which "connectives and disconnectives" come into play. From the outset her mixed-blood histories, wry, circumstantial, and however given over to dealing in fissure, set-back, small triumph, or odd forms of savvy, have always been formatted to match.

The lives in view invariably throw up more consequential freight than initial appearance, stories with their own double-ply. "Anaadarko Powwow," its dancers Kiowa, Caddo, Creek, Chickasaw, Cheyenne, Ponca, Pawnee, Osage and Cherokee, ward off the live but also dead "hopelessness" (9) of other young Native men in the arena-ground by keeping "the old language" alive and staying "in tune with the dead" (10). "A Sense of Continuity and Presence," with its matriarchal Elma, silhouettes her "sermon" on family, however vexed or even broken its disposition in her own case, against the larger family memory of the 17,000 Cherokees "who crossed half of this continent on foot in the dead of winter and survived to build their lives again" (43).

Similar doubling occurs in "The Voluble Rap," in which the harassed mother-of-two caught out by a violent absconding husband, bills and loneliness, finds herself uttering the ironic threat "I'm going to believe in GOD!" (6). In "Keyo," the story of a dyslexic Native boy caught out by words (19-21), and "In This Mission School" (89-92) where Dubbue dreams of broken parents and religion, the schoolhouse serves as forum for things un-learned in equal part with those learned. "Broken Spell" (27-33), set in the Northeastern Oklahoma Cherokee County Shelter and under sweltering June heat, portrays a bodily aging Anna America dreaming Native-avian dreams of leaving the earth. ("One day soon she would walk the sky" 33). "Holation" (67-77) uses the backcountry cabin of the "Indian hermit" Joseph Stink, likely kin to John Stink of Osage and Kiowa legend and also used by Linda Hogan in *Mean Spirit*, as the setting for an interview he gives as once word-experienced journalist and traveler yet in his present the searcher and user of every-day-a-new-word.

This framing of the duly particular and the wider schema can be historical. The Trail of Tears references are but one instance. Religion can be Cherokee fire-creation myth under their tribal nomenclature of Keetowah, or synchronistic as in the invocations of the co-presence of the Great Spirit and the Christian godhead for all that, as a committed Bible Christian, Glancy believes Native belief-systems to be "incomplete."

A story like "Aunt Parnetta's Electric Blisters" (11-18), with its title-phrase jugglery, especially brings home the point, the very compound of the one and yet larger story and told with an ease that belies whatever deliberation lies behind its composition. To this end the title has its follow-on in the various imagistic riffs on a broken-down refrigerator owned by the old-married Cherokee pair Aunt Parnetta and her husband Filo. The twenty-year old fridge, which ironically has packed up in the summer after "walking" through the winter and spring, for Aunt Parnetta is animate, a live being. Filo, in frustration, even shoots it ("... a man had to take revenge. Had to stand against civilization" 11-12). Parnetta thinks of it a kind of white coffin which might have had the decency to last until the next winter when they could set the milk outside in the frost. Their trip to Muskogee to buy a replacement brings them into contact with the salesman they dub "The Yellow Hair Custer." Their uncertainty as to the purchase Parnetta vernacularly likens to surrender ("Izend thad the way id always iz?" 13). Filo dresses in war feathers, stomps, "whoops and wars" (13) in an effort to revive the old machine – to no avail ("Not with a bullet hole in it" says Parnetta cryptically, 13).

The new refrigerator ("gleaming white inside" 14) falls under similar auspices, the perfect receptacle for all the milk, butter, frozen waffles and orange juice Parnetta buys in the Tahlequah grocery store. But it also hums, disturbing her sleep, "a giant hog in the kitchen. Rutting and snorting all night" (14). Even when Filo covers it with both geese quilt and Indian blanket it continues to disturb her. She associates it with a long-ago winter trip to Minnesota, petitions the Great Spirit for relief, and joins its whiteness to the white America about her ("she was a stranger in this world. An Indian in a white man's land" 17). Suddenly, however, she begins to realize that, in her own being, she could be thought to resemble the refrigerator ("she was always moaning like the fridge" 18). Are not its electric coils, its "electric blisters," just like "Keotowah fire," "the warmth of the Great Spirit" (18). The imaging works perfectly to advantage, to narrative good purpose.

The refrigerator's inside heat so becomes the very analogy for her having been touched by Great Spirit as life-force, its "holy bonfire" (18). Parnetta has grasped a way to incorporate the noise and irritation of white-consumer civilization into ancestral Cherokee world-view. The equation saves her, recognition through the fridge of "the purification of the Great Spirit" burning within "each hard, old pinecone heart" (18). Keetowah fire, the gift of the Great Spirit, gives warmth, electricity, amid "ice rivers" and "glaciers" (18), heat inside cold, life inside death. So, too, it does to Parnetta. The narrative tease of kitchen refrigerator and creation myth, metaphor as reality and vice versa, make for a characteristic show of craft, Glancy's shaping resources of word and story-art. The story leaves no doubt. This is double-speak, "Indian" domestic half-comedy under infinitely larger tribal-historical shadow.

"Trigger Dance," as title-story, again works to a similar compositional double-track, a one burnt-down house that leads into contemplation of the world's fiery creation and likely de-creation. Told as though spoken story it centers on the "far thinking" (97) of Roan, Cheyenne country husband, father, sweat lodge maker, preacher, amid his property "just south of Lawton, Oklahoma" (94). As he speaks of life and death to the spirits, as his wife quilts her scraps of cloth, and as his sons tussle, his own father, Grandpa, living with his sister Weazel, announces his resolve to be cremated as though to fall in with the way of the world ("I look around & see cremation. That's what I want done with my body" 105). Roan's son Kolar marries and find creative sexual happiness in his new wife while

Roan's wife, quilt-maker, sees in Grandpa's wish the very pairing of "Creation & Cremation." In the event Grandpa gets himself burned into ashes inside his own house ("It's what he wanted" says Weazel, 129). Creation-Cremation: the angle is odd, sardonic, a species of chiliasm Cheyenne-style, or in other words, vintage Glancy.

For a kind of theological gothic holds throughout the story. The world of Great Spirit genesis has also become a world edging towards fire-born destruction. In the light of Grandpa's self-cremation Roan, shaman-chorus, calls up a sense of Native spiritual design beyond the family's life as make-do, merest trigger-dance:

> I hear the voices of our people struggling in their daily lives – some of them falling, some rising – bless them, Great Spirit. I hear some of them stepping out of their own visions into Chief Christ's. I see the decisions being made. Otherwise it's a trigger dance we're doing. (135)

His own vision, and Weazel's, as they watch Oklahoma's "red autumn" (137) of sun, rocks, sumac, leaves and prairie is of first and last things. In Roan, Glancy has her aptest persona, Native story-giver as Native visionary yet speaking in just the right slicks of Oklahoma drawl.

***

All three of Glancy's ensuing story-volumes show her taking different pathways in the storytelling transmutation of parts-into-wholes. *Firesticks* steers more towards cycle-strategy. The six-part title-story, "Firesticks," acts as a spine, a coordinating story-line. *Connectives and disconnectives*: Glancy's pair-phrase bestows an almost literal construing to the collection. The portrait of Turle, forty-something and seen-it-all or seen-most-of–it diner waitress in Guthrie, Oklahoma, her taking up with the truck-driving and migrant worker Navorn, their trip to Frederick to see her ailing father (his death to follow), and their eventual uncertain resolve for a road life together, is told as a gapped sequence within and between the collection's other stories. Further, each of the six parts works not to the one time-scale but to one in which later can precede earlier events.

The ostensible life-round looks to Turle's work-shifts at the diner, the road, and also to lineage (hers part Cherokee, his one of what Turle calls his "Wisconsin dude" ancestry 30). It includes the sexual heat and successive if awkward bed-nights together. But, as customary in Glancy's stories, another hovers, more imbued and composite. That lies just behind the hash and fast food, the prairie and tollbooths, even Turle's ongoing dialogues with Navorn. For as she negotiates a provisional intimacy with Navorn, her dreams begin to soar ("I dreamed again of wild horses and a herd of buffalo" 92).

Navorn's windshield wipers on his truck transmute into Native hunting tools ("Arrows flew" 93). The horses, buffalo, along with turtles, serve Turle in her sleep as "a vision of what our lives had been" (93). Places like the Barbed Wire Diner, or the several Flea Markets and antique stores with their Native trinkets, build into a kind of wrap or circle. Names take on imagist weight. Keetowah and Kiowa summon tribal pasts-into-present. Oklahoma has its Indian-named towns, notably Chickasha, which Turle and Navorn approach en route to Texas at the story's close ("We're almost to Chickasha. Do you want a hamburger?" 132). Navorn lists Wisconsin tribal towns like Oconto, Okemah, Wetumka and Wewoka. To these are to be added Mount Scott where Turle's father wishes to be buried, the Wichita Mountains, Altus Air Base, the Black Hills, and an every-town street address like North Twelfth. Each of these bespeaks wholly actual yet figural cartography, the literal map yet also the story's poetry of time and place.

For in Glancy's scripting this is Native and Native-white history as both memorial and still-live, always huge, threaded, and subject to every manner of human overlap. In family terms it means the summoning of Turle's "Indian grandmother" (39), and "my Cherokee great-grandfather" (40) of nearby Hulbert, Oklahoma ("something that I'm not sure of passed between us" 40), and equally of her white family from grandfather to ex-husband. If one axis lies in her present-day waitressing at the diner, life before and with Navorn, the other lies in her ever augmenting consciousness of Native presence. Towards the close, and as she rides with Navorn, she thinks "Strange warriors. In dreams I hear your talk" (132). Glancy has Turle personify both connectives and disconnectives, differing but allied laws of motion.

"A Family To Which Nothing Happened" (31-5) catches to perfection a girlhood sense of the small-town quotidian as cheat, stasis. The story's opening litany works as though double digit book-keeping, the happening and the not-happening:

> We weren't allowed to have accidents. Things only happened to others. A neighbor four houses down the street was run over by his truck. The brake gave way just as he walked in front of it and left paralyzed from the waist down. Across the street a boy with rheumatic fever sat on his porch for what seemed our whole childhood. Several houses up from him a man left his wife and two children. In those days when the wife didn't work it was like clamping off their air. (31)

The everydayness of these events, in one measure near banality, is accorded just the right inflation when filtered through the girl's consciousness. The neighbor's paralysis, the boy's rheumatic fever, the husband's desertion: each might remind of Sherwood Anderson's Winesburg, the scale of small as large. The fact that this is a "middle-of-the-road" (32) family set down in "middle of America" (32) Kansas, Missouri, carries its own irony. Middle has become un-middle, normal un-normal, and from the story's girlhood vantage-point and with parodic vengeance, the mean-average the un-average.

Momentum builds, though, in a typical Glancy paradox, it is momentum which emphasizes un-momentum. When, with her friend, Linda Elson, the narrator visits the paralyzed neighbor, Mr. Scofield, and he thinks to make sexual contact with Linda, no abuse actually happens. When the narrator's mother gets involved in an odd break with Linda's mother it is left unexplained, a mystery. The family house may be situated in a dangerous climate-zone but it exists as though islanded, caught in stillness. "War tornado famine blizzard earthquake sucked the world but never at our house or yard" (32) runs the unpunctuated catalog. Polio comes to Kansas City but not to the narrator or her brother. Even the things that "nearly happened" (33) keep their distance. A bombing during a strike remains the periphery. The disappearance from their street of a woman and her two children occurs without explanation. Other happenings might be almost non-happenings, the stockyard butchering for beef, the Scofields' daily round in their house, or even the heart-attack of Linda's father.

With her own father's change of stockyard job the family drives off for Indianapolis ("I sat in the backseat thinking maybe there was an exit...a move to someplace where finally we would be worthy of something happening to us" 35). Is there not also a touch of Bartlebyism, not to mention Beckett in the story, the near-absurdist child sense of life as part not whole yet at the very same time told, again paradoxically, as the achieved whole of its seeming discordant parts?

A similar force of design holds for "Stamp Dance" (69-77), another child's-eye story, that of the mixed-blood boy Mack's absorption into philately as a figurative route into avian-global travel. His Uncle Al, working in the town's Post Office, serves as guide, or more to the point latter-day scout. Mack himself is a food-stamp child, his father at one time overseas in Vietnam in the military and then "lost in action" (72) in the cities, and who has to ask who Marianne Moore might be and why she has her own celebratory stamp. Al can tease him, but Mack becomes the inveterate collector, a haunter of the Post Office. When his friend Billy is cruelly smacked by his father, Mack's response draws into itself his passion ("They should cover Billy's father with stamps and send him somewhere" 73).

A whole lexis seizes the boy, franking, glue, perforation, stamps bearing animals, ships, trains and planes. But, in line with the wordplay of the title and its implication of powwow or dance ceremony, Glancy also develops a gathering Native dimension into the story. At the outset the sight of Buffalo stamps causes Mack to reveal himself dimly aware of, but also uncomprehending of, hunter ancestors. As he then surveys the Post Office display-case of stamps he sees that there are also "even Indians. Or their war bonnets at least" (75). He writes a school-time essay on "My Stamp Collection," as though viscerally writing his will-to-journey, real-life and in imagination. He is dazzled at stamps in sheet form, their quantity and cost, yet manages to ask for the one individual stamp with "the feathered war bonnet" (76). In his dreams these same stamps become "white, creamy birds," ascending geese, all caught up in stamp-flight bound and destined in a loaded phrase for "long migrations" (77). He, himself, has become the stamp-poet, his own Native-born boy version of Marianne Moore. In which respect there can be no mistaking the good working order, the pattern and integration, of the story's imagism.

Each story within the main story can turn on boyhood avian fantasy as in "The First Indian Pilot" or take the form of a girl's cryptic diary like "A Family to Which Nothing Happened" in which accidents, death, tornado, sexual harassment of her friend Linda Elson, all bypass the township banality which is her own life. "A Phenomenon of Light" links the spiritual elation of the narrator's seeing the beauteous reflection of Mount St. Helens in Spirit Lake with the flatness, and craters, in her own life. A vignette like "Proverb, American" playfully teases the genesis and then the need to organize words each "running loose" as if they were lexical free spirits (134). It makes for an oblique but elucidatory comment on how *Firesticks* seeks to arc its own various word-stories into the one parabola.

Few stories perhaps serve as well as "Jack Wilson or Wovoka and Christ My Lord," Cast in a speaking voice no doubt biographically close to Glancy's own, it takes off from the visit of a Native male poet to the narrator's Minnesota student literature class. As she watches him vaunt his post-alcoholic kitsch warriordom and show himself clearly on the sexual make, the narrator's thoughts begin to construct the various paradoxes in play for a contemporary mixed-blood woman like herself.

A sense of discretion is registered at the outset in pondering her white and red history ("I shouldn't really be talking about it but it's hard to be quiet" 11). School is recalled for how she was nick-named Pecan-Face. She thinks of "Indians" as she herself has known them, each of them under nicknames of "High Hooters," "Rooty Fluters" and "Ghosters" (12), more seeking "good times" than any vaunted "care for the land" (12). She further weighs into "Indian" showcase posturing, be it as macho chasers-away of the white man, callers-back of the buffalo, supposed honorers of the ancestors, or tough-guy handlers of firewater. In other words this is a voice unwilling to speak required piety or simply stay quiet. At once wary, un-collusive, and if both white and red it pledges itself to take charge of the contributing seams ("The fact that I had opinions that mattered took me from Oklahoma to Minnesota to realize" 11).

She takes umbrage at the visiting speaker's victim-pose yet his "superior-ass stance in front of everyone" (12), and at his assumption of her "invisibility" (13) even though she was the one to invite him. She notes his eying of a girl in the class and his "tough-guy learned responses" (13), invoking her own contrasting and less theatrical role of "school-teacher, provider, minority, and everything nobody else wanted to be" (14). At the same time her choice of expression shadows, and even teases, her own life ("An Indian because I wasn't white. An Indian because I could synthesize the fragments and live with hurt … Yipes" 14). Acknowledging her "grumpiness" (14) she nevertheless insists on real over fake presence, in her case, crucially, her odd-silent turning to Christ amid the animal hallelujahs of fellow born-agains ("I went to the altar without making a sound when everyone else was howling Jesus like the baboon in the zoo at Tulsa" 14).

Her speculations extend. She summons the historic memory of Wovoka, Northern Paiute shaman and Ghost Dance prophet, and as Jack Wilson the step-son of a white Christian rancher. She ponders styles of intercourse, sexual and spiritual, in Heaven; take a shy at "Indian intellectuals" who write "surreal coyote tales" (15); recall a further dubious visiting speaker on "Indian spirituality" (16); think ruefully upon her divorce from her white husband; and even questions the supposed sway for good or otherwise of Coyote. Her last imagining is of a full-metal Indian on easy-rider cycle, black hair "streaming like crows" (17), and who would never get through security check at an airport. These she frames in her mind by the remembrance of seeing from her own taxi-ing on the runway another plane "in the air ahead of us like a cross with its arms outstretched" (17). Mixed-blood identity, classroom, kitsch Indians, her marriage and children, the bruised feeling of having been undervalued, and the found symbolism of the Christian cross in a plane taking to the air, coalesce in the one telling.

"Jack Wilson or Wovoka and Christ My Lord" co-ordinates each of these seeming contrarieties, the story as the negotiated sum of discrepant parts. The narrator's one account embraces the several, whether of those who most proclaim "Indian" identity or of her own ambiguity of "Indian" status. "Native American heritage is something I don't like to get into" (11) reads the story's opening line.

By its close, and under Glancy's orchestration, the encompassing fuller irony of that statement has become engagingly clear.

***

Monkey Secret, the three stories and the title-novella, exhibits nearly all Glancy's customary and best weights and measures. Each works as memory-narrative, careful imagist riff or cycle. "Lead Horse" (3-14), the portrait of the aging Nattie as in company with her man Joes she entertains her mixed-blood and not a little oddly comported and dysfunctional family after their arrival aboard a twenty-year old Plymouth in a violent prairie storm, evolves into her own uniquely presiding spiritual vision. Just as Nattie has played lead horse for the family (if uncertainly given that she has managed to drive both her husband and daughter away) right through to this celebration of Cousin Wilhelmina's fiftieth birthday, so the storm – its tremor, sounds, energy, force – becomes the inspirational lead horse in her mind. She sees it as though from "the spirit world," the "LEAD HORSE OF LEAD HORSES" (13). Nattie's story is that of belief, image as world, but in scripting meticulously precise on Glancy's part.

In "At the Altar of American Indian Architecture" (15-23) the Cherokee narrator, Fletch, driving with his new girlfriend Liss to her borrowed cabin in the Ozarks, and with his own two daughters by different mothers in the back seat, seeks language to make "the multiple parts" (23) of his life cohere. But it is language also teased by the figure of a miniature Jesus on the dashboard in which INRI is confused with HENRY, word and faith dangled before him as though the "architecture" for a life since Cherokee "removal" of its own parts rather than wholes. Fletch's story is framed by that of the story around him, one of double-language, Cherokee and English (not to say Latin), history, religion. This is the story's own implied "story," and told ironically, elusively, beyond Fletch's own first-person and insisted-upon telling.

"Minimal Indian" (23-34), in which James and Crowbar visit James's "bible-brained" (26) and "back-hill Cherokee" (27) sister Renah in Red Star, Arkansas, sets their wholly earth-bound interests (having Renah cook for them and Crowbar's wryly inventoried salvage business "Trucks and Stuff") against her vision of God. The three of them crash into a farmer's truck full of chickens and, dazed, swept up, she sees Deity, God the Father and Son, Heaven itself and the angels, in the wizened face of an old man. This is another story given to the larger whole of its all too immediate run of detail. Renah insists on Christmas flowers at the snow-covered graves of her dead parents. The well-named Starbrite singing group is to be heard in chorus. Cherokee Oklahoma becomes a "magical kingdom of animal transformations and mutations of borders ... and a Christian God ... Who could come for them anytime" (31).

"Minimal Indian" might hint of Flannery O'Connor. But "Monkey Secret," the collection's longest story with its valley Arkansas girl-into-womanhood portrait of Jean Pierce, more suggests Eudora Welty's *Delta Wedding* or Carson McCullers's *The Heart is a Lonely Hunter*. The story's two epigraphs, from the *Book of Genesis* ("In the beginning God created the heaven and the earth" 35) and the *Popol Vuh* ("So this is why monkeys looks like people; they are a sign of a previous human work" 35), imply a world both God-given and simian, celestial and terrestrial. So it proves. For Jean's rite of passage under the auspices of the Pierce dynasties – her two uncles Bently and Stanley and their families and her father Harrison who still prays at the grave of his first wife and their child also lost at birth – bears on her awakening to love with her cousin Cedric, her Christian conviction, and finally her turn to art.

The ambit of Haran, Arkansas, Kingdom Road, summer lake cabins at Bull Shoals, acts as a magic farmland locale of kin and seasons, creeks and dogwood, yet also tough heaven-and-hell Bible country. In one after another panel of lyrically intense recollections of "family" are to be found what Jean herself acknowledges as "sketches of the artist as a woman" (111). The panorama is one of kinetic moments not only of dynasty but of Jean's inner creative consciousness as she seeks word, a narrative language, for self and circuit. Long story or novella, "Monkey Secret" has to be one of Glancy's most affecting story compositions, full of rippled happening, circles of image, and told at evenly judged pace.

The allusions are highly concentrated. As child the mixed-blood Jean early has visions of "the ancestors" (35) and hears in her mother's Native-inflected stories "snaps of electricity on a cold night" (35). Her father's pig-stabbing makes her think of "*jelly rollers*" (38), Jesus-blood. Her will-to-write begins early ("I hungered for words, the way Harrison hungered for his first wife" 40). Her ownership of a wooden box carved in pomegranate design and of a stuffed toy owl accorded the saint-name of Nicodemus and given her by Cedric might be writer's tool-kit and fetish. The weathered lake boat, *The Commodore*, becomes both plaything and a kind of dream-vehicle to reveal Cedric's secret cove. Cedric himself, TB-threatened and who will break with Pierce religious belief, serves as Jean's lover-prince and yet eventual betrayer when he returns from the University of Missouri a married man.

Cruelties intrude. The cousins slit the tongues of crows to find out why they sing with the result of a small-time avian bloodbath. Jean's mother chastises her when she spills the communion cup and fixates on the wine-as-blood ("It was

Jesus everywhere" 67). The retarded son of the hired wife and husband helpers hangs his dog. Sister Whatley, quilt-maker, spinster, exhibits one-phrase eccentricity ("Glory to God" she repeats). The Reverend Stonesifer, stern Bible literalist, presides over a congregation urged unrelentingly, bible-threateningly, to total repentance and rejection of Satan's writ. His sermon ("Reverend Stonesifer was going at a pitch" 86) literally appears to summon a storm even as it envisages the world as monkey-regime redeemed only by hill-Protestantism's belief in an uncompromising Christ. Black snakes can be seen to exist even within the Pierce bucolic order.

These, all, Jean inherits, and makes subject to her own custodial voice, her own flights of image begun in her early-written poems. Words for her, she confides to Cedric on one of their early perambulations, are "little sparks of light," "little energy fields" (84). She even tells him she wants to be "a visionary" (84). In Cedric's dying, and having come to know her history's minuses as well as pluses, she wants no other choice in womanhood than to have this ambition find its pre-ordained confessional expression. Glancy gives "Monkey Story" its perfect reflexive turn, her story in all its burgeoning intimacy none other than the self-same story Jean Pierce has been born to tell.

***

The Voice That Was in Travel gives grounds to be thought Glancy's most collagist story-gathering. The twenty pieces she gives over, variously, to European and Australian travel, barrio marriage, Native girl-murder told as though tribal-oral narrative, casino gaming, seamstressing, and parades both Cherokee-ancestral and Oklahoma-modern. At first reading the stories appear even more stubby, spiked, angular, than previously, yet still always complete in themselves.

In "Reaching For Air" (3-7) the jet-lagged author-traveler, newly arrived in Hanover and self-consciously the American among Europeans in a breakfast-room of German food and words, takes stock:

> You're a middle-aged, mixblood woman alone in a foreign country on a U.S. Information Service tour … it turns out the fractures of your heritage, your mess and the struggle to get through it, made stories you travel to read. There is even a fullness, a volume, you feel sometimes in the difficulties of your life. Even when it frightens you. (4).

For Glancy, as for her narrator, the observation could not be more to the immediate point, life as fracture yet fullness, story as part yet whole. Each other story, in differing degree, bears witness.

"Reaching For Air" itself opens with a catalog-in-small of "foreign country" (3) items. These include different breakfast habits, the Gideon Bible in German, the phone-book's non-English names, tourist animal-dolls, museums and train and bus stations. All are to be compared with "the foreign country of your head … the real and facsimile you have in your head" (6). Glancy, however, pitches this one overseas "travel" for how it liaises with others, whether indeed abroad ("There's a limitless amount of things you can do in a foreign country to prove you're an American" 3), or at home and overworked in her university duties ("You have an academic position. You're on tenure track" 7), or religious ("Sometimes you see right through the waters to the amplitude of heaven" 7).

Likewise the story "Crossing The Specific," with its opening of "Australia's upside down" (35) links the Ayers Rock visit of its main character, Pruny, into walk-about dream, her own Aboriginal dot-art. In likening the rock to a "loaf of bread" (38) and the Rock visit to the Stations of the Cross, the story renders the one act of tourism – and with it Pruny's provincialism of spirit – into Aboriginal-shadowing "dream-flight" (40). Specifics again enlarge into larger perspective.

The process holds elsewhere. "In The Burrito" (41-2) the brief portrait of Layla, a *barrio* or as she miscalls it *burrito* companion-wife to Saldo, looks to her life as an odd aggregation. Its "traffic," among the plenty, embraces "boyfriends and lovers, husbands and former husbands, children and stepchildren, wrong turnings." Mealtimes of *chorizo con huevos* and *mole* join the list. A remembered episode has her saving an old woman fallen in the snow (42). "Clutter," however, Layla's uncertain sum of particulars, co-exists for her with "lives inside" (42). In "Sumac," set out in slash-divided typography and in both lower-case and italics, Glancy attempts a lover's murder-story told as though recitation. The fracturing brute arrow-death, and the girl-victim's blood imaged as sumac, becomes Native spoken ballad, another style of story-whole made over from story-parts.

"The Great House" (53-63), its scenario that of reservation casino and Black Jack, Poker, Keno and Slots, transforms for its initially ear-muffed player, into the phantasmagoric replay of Aztec games played with severed heads. Her mind soars back into Plumed Serpent blood cruelty, the deadliness of the ancient game-cult mimicked in "Indian gaming. Reservation gambling" (62). "A Woman Who Sewed For Me a Dress That Sleeves Didn't Fit" (79-82) edges its narrator's dress-making, from school to adulthood, into a vision of sewing Jesus's Lamb of God coat. Her Singer Sewing Machine, in accord, takes hold as an agency of spirit as much as clothing. It gives hope for her uneven life, the "machine that heals as it sews" (82).

"America's First Parade" (89-114), situated in Tahlequah, Oklahoma, links a Cherokee café-owner mother's inept truck-driving to "the forced march of our people Cherokee people from the southeast" (91). Her belief in spirits holding sway over the truck's engine (she calls it her "spirit truck" 99), the postcards that arrive from her ex-husband with their different recipes, her consultation of the Bible in Cherokee, her powwow dancing, her having her café painted with the name *Redlands*, even her jealousy at her son's dalliance with Janet Gillette, re-enforces her conviction that amid all the varying "parade" of her times she has somehow managed to become a warrior-woman. She has heard the ancestors. The truck's accelerations and lurches and the changes-of-menu she reads on her former spouse's cards give the metaphors of one kind of "parade" – to which she herself links parades of family, health inspectors, earth and planets, migrations, trees, "failures and setbacks," in all "parades across time" (113). She manages to see them gathering into the one greater parade. The process she terms "Survival. Or struggle for survival. Or retrieval ... depending where you were in the parade" (116). As so often, in her momentum and design, Glancy scripts her telling to match. This story, one more in her consortium of stories other-way told, yields the greater whole.

Notes

1 *The West Pole*, Minneapolis: The University of Minnesota Press, 1997, 75.
2 *The Cold-and-Hunger Dance*, Lincoln: University of Nebraska Press, 1998, 96-7.

Works Cited

Andrews, Jennifer, "A Conversation with Diane Glancy," *American Indian Quarterly*, 26, 2002. 645-59.

Glancy, Diane, *The Book of Bearings*, Eugene: Wipf and Stock Publishers, 2019.

_____, *Mary, Queen of Bees*, Eugene: Wipf and Stock Publishers, 2017.

_____, *The Voice That Was in Travel: Stories*, Norman: University of Oklahoma Press, 1999.

_____, *The Cold-and-Hunger Dance*, Lincoln, Nebraska: University of Nebraska Press, 1998.

_____, *The West Pole*, Minneapolis: University of Minnesota Press, 1997.

_____, *Monkey Secret*, Evanston, Illinois: TriQuarterly Books, Northwestern University Press, 1995.

_____, *Firesticks*, Norman: University of Oklahoma Press, 1993.

_____, *Claiming Breath*, Lincoln: University of Nebraska Press, 1992.

_____, *Trigger Dance*, Normal, IL: Fiction Collective Two, Illinois State University, 1990.

Hogan, Linda, *Mean Spirit,* New York: Atheneum, 1990.
McCullers, Carson, *The Heart Is a Lonely Hunter*, Boston: Houghton, 1940.
Welty, Eudora, *Delta Wedding*, New York: Harcourt, 1946.

13

Dark Illumination: The Noir Story Collections of Stephen Graham Jones

What in me is dark
Illumine …

John Milton, *Paradise Lost*[1]

Turn up the lights – I don't want to go home in the dark.

O. Henry (last words)[2]

"I should mention that I'm Indian, except everybody's always doing that for me"

Stephen Graham Jones, "Rocket Man"[3]

Fiercely *noir*, or, perhaps more aptly, *neo-noir*. Fiercely prolific. Could anything less be said of Stephen Graham Jones? Now fifty years of age, he could even so be awarded his stripes as a ready American *Wunderkind* on the basis of the truly compendious roster of more than a hundred short stories, twenty or so novels (with others announced), and array of discursive and digital works and interviews. Nor, notwithstanding the west Texas upbringing, would any profile of his work leave unmentioned his Blackfeet ancestry, rarely given more abiding measure than in his Indian Country hallucinatory picaresque *The Fast Red Road: A Plainsong* (2000) and Montana parallel-time novel *Ledfeather* (2008). Add in his infinitely savvy reworking of Western to horror, cyberparable to werewolf and vampire lore, and one encounters a writer of rare pliability.[4]

Yet even as this fierce output has been drawn to familiar popular-culture literary neighborhoods, Jones has created his own working terms and conditions, his own dark pathways into illumination. In centering attention on the story-collections *Bleed into Me* (2005), *The Ones That Got Away* (2010), *States of Grace* (2013) and *Zombie Sharks with Metal Teeth* (2013) – which is not to ignore the novellas that make up *Three Miles Past* (2013) or the collection *After The People Lights Have Gone Off* (2014) – the aim is to underscore not only Jones's powers of vision but also of his styles of story-fashioning. Assuredly, *noir* has been his plenty, in which he is boldly inventive, full unexpected turn. It has, however, been a genre buttressed by his adept, if at time oblique, tactics of disclosure, his plotlines as torque, and his whole skeins of ingenuity of image.

Whether in the Blackfeet life-stories of *Bleed Into Me*, the haunts and shape-shifting that run through *The Ones That Got Away*, the diary-entry "flash fiction" of *States of Grace*, or the rips of experimentalism in *Zombie Sharks with Metal Teeth*, his shorter, like his longer, work has done enough to situate him alongside a wide range of kindred authorship. His *Indian* narratives, Native lives full of singularity albeit lived at the fault-line and recounted always at an angle, invites comparison with the reflexive fabling of Gerald Vizenor, Sherman Alexie, or D.L. Birchfield. The fantasy and dark-matter fiction of *The Ones That Got Away*, for which *Strange Stories: Amazing Facts* first published by *Reader's Digest* in 1975 served as his youth-time bible, puts him closer to H.P. Lovecraft, Cornell Woolrich, Shirley Jackson, and the author he greatly admires, Stephen King. The short short stories of *States of Grace* offer a yet different, if still connecting, bead, episodic prose haiku as it were, the one moment caught ad held from within a given life's upbringing and relationships. *Zombie Sharks with Metal Teeth* hints of William Burroughs and Kathy Acker, chartings of mad scientists, aliens, the end of days, and apocalypse now, the living dead, and, not least, the figure of Rod Serling. Whether in actual or shadow worlds, there can be no doubt that Jones's forays into the ways of darkness visible call upon a unique kind of lens.

***

Invited to contribute to Gerald Vizenor's *Native Storier* series, published by the University of Nebraska Press, Jones came through with *Bleed into Me*, sixteen or so story-vignettes of mixed-blood life in which the angle is indeed oblique, the tangent all.[5] It would be hard to think otherwise, given how the collection is book-ended by two Native threads, sardonic takes on Native fortunes in the wake of America's Manifest Destiny westering. The Prologue puts the Discovery Myth under Native auspices as though it were remembered child trauma:

> Columbus landed in the second grade for me, and my teacher made me swallow the names of the boats one by one until in the bathtub of my summer vacation I opened my mouth and they came back out –Niña, Pinta, Santa María – and bobbed on the surface of the water like toys. I clapped my hand over my mouth once, Indian style, then looked up, for my mother, so she could pull the plug, stop all this, but when I opened my mouth again it was just blood and blood and blood. (7)

This is legacy given in counter-version, the Columbus landfall a pathway into slaughter, the would-be evisceration of the tribes. The paragraph approaches imagist cameo. Swallowed names. A summer vacation bathtub. The psychosomatic iterations of blood in the mouth. Pulling the plug on Discovery history. Each nudges, and plays associatively, the one into another. Jones's symptomatic route-signs can be said to have come into play, with the register of voice pitched at the darker edge and with, as always, the bold contraflow of metaphor. This style makes a perfect entry into the rest of the collection, a contemporary Native landscape caught off tilt.

The epilogue, in the voice of a student sent to Indian School, serves to give more framing. Allusion to standard textbook learning and boyhood pranks yields to remembrance of tribe, trickster, buffalo blood clot and other birth myths, human flint sculpture, horses, foodways of duck and berry, and even of one-time tribal resort to mobility by foot only. Beyond the school's standard academic syllabus the boy so summons quite another:

> The way it really was that they kidnapped us from our reservations and cut our hair off and burned it and cut our tongues out and used them for bait and called our parents savages and then scraped the religion off their walls and chewed it up and spit it into our mouths and told us it was enough, that we didn't need anything else. (143)

The litany does honor to genealogy, the narrator or one of his companion boarders for a moment metamorphosed into a latter-day buffalo brave.

To step into "Halloween," the first story proper in the sequence of *Bleed into Me*, is to be sharply reminded of time-now, with a controlling Native trailer-family father who lives out parody rituals of pipe smoking (with its ceremonial hint) only on July Fourth and beer drinking only on New Year's Day. Each emphasis contributes to a portrait of fracture. He terrorizes his wife, not least with the threat of a bullet from one of his guns ricocheting into the butane tank outside their trailer. He would have his three child sons head towards manhood by following him into all-too-early beer drinking, along with cigarette smoking, shooting at cans, and "training us even then to be little versions of himself" (2). Cryptic to a fault, the story figures him as "a man of observances," yet who "wore his monster mask every day of the year" (3). At the same time, it also figures the storyteller, now himself an adult, as becoming his own kind of mask-wearer (in kind with his bothers respectively six, nine and twelve). He, no less than his father, has begun the process of acquiring the mask of stranger to and for himself.

This parent-offspring axis, mainly sons and fathers, holds across a number of key stories, with each, again, told in a register always slightly disjunct or slant. The effect is one of unsettling the easy version, simple cause and effect. Few invite more deciphering in this respect than the title story "Bleed into Me" (99-109), set in Martin County, Florida, in which the funeral of a compulsive thief devolves into the surviving brother's memory of his family's overall dislocation. Alternating between first and third person, the story depicts the narrator moving from a scene of funeral to one of life, albeit near-absurdist life. The sight of his casketed brother "waxy and fixed" spans back to the brother's thieving and desperations and forward to their father's phantasmagoria that he might have "saved" the dead elder son by having him, as the story puts it, bleed into himself (99). The story leaves no doubt of real hurt, close-felt love yet damage. But its telling keeps just the right authorial distance, a triumph of encryption.

Uncenteredness, as in many of Sherman Alexie's stories, becomes center as the increments of event plait into a single pattern. A hearse waits. A fish lure is found snared in the funeral-hall pillar. A glove compartment posthumously yields photographs of the two brothers as children. The dead brother thieves from his own home: steak knives, plates, a typewriter, his mother's rosewood desk. A school parking-lot fight cracks open his skull, the blood spilling over his younger sibling. The mother edges towards her own unhinging as she tracks down the stolen family goods in local pawnshops, hides in the garden to try to catch her son in his raids in the family home, thinks she might again breast-feed him, and speaks his name hauntingly to herself. The father deposits his son's Moon Boots on the grave as memorial, drifts through a corridor of jobs – from customer service to video-game employee, parachute packer to a roofer who falls through the ceiling – and even tries to become a cemetery worker, to somehow resurrect his son. Mosaic, bricolage, uncentering: the upshot is a family at odds with both world and self.

A last turn of the loop has the narrator son, himself having done jail time, suggesting his father could qualify as a comedian. "The world was a funny place" the father thinks (108). Well he might, given the near irreality of a passing windowless car with a desk (the mother's?) strapped to its roof, two shadow arms trying to keep it from falling. That the father ends up an animal handler, guiltily tearful, aging, and given to thinking himself afoot in a street he imagines to be full of mocking laughter as he carries his bloodied dead son, joins with his life's fantasy zoo. In turn, his comfort when he feels chimpanzee hands around his neck, as if mementos of dependent offspring, connects to the "blood" elder son he might have saved. Comparison of "Bleed into Me" with James Welch's *Winter in the Blood* would be far from out of place, two serious yet unmistakably antic fables of Native life in which the self has become entrapped against itself.

Each of the collection's stories, both those explicit and those tacit in Native allusion, works in similarly abbreviated manner. "Venison" (5-10), its viewpoint that of the boy Sid, runs close to comedy, a flourish of incongruence among its features: the illegal shooting of a park deer, a father-and-uncle card game, a wrecker-driver's wife about to give birth, trucks and troopers, and a water melon used to ward off flies from purloined meat. "Captivity Narrative 109" (11-19) upends the old-time formula, a *Driving While Indian* episode in the life of Aiche ("like the letter" 11), who picks up two white children after they mistakenly identify his red truck for that of their uncle. Throughout their "captivity," with Aiche's own likely to follow, Jones slyly mimics the captivity narratives that came before him. The boy, influenced by his Manimal toys, asks if Aiche is going to transpose into a wolf. Aiche himself, an unwitting mixed-blood Blackfeet in overalls, calls to mind a long-ago scout on the lookout for cavalry.

"Discovering America" (139-42), ostensibly the serial annotations of a Native playwright, or so he seems, writing *The Time That Indian Started Killing Everybody*, does a further about-face take on Columbianism. Patterned to the refrain "Because I'm an Indian in …" (139 passim), the story's serial encounters across different American geographies skewers commodity *indianness*. Medicine pouches have become Tallahassee, Florida, consumer fashion. Animal spirits serve as student fad in Little Rock, Arkansas. An Odessa, Texas, oil worker asks if *indians* continue being run over as Montana road sport. A Clovis, New Mexico, warehouseman slams the narrator's face near where a feather has been added to smiley-face in the narrator's locker. A field crew in Carlsbad, New Mexico, suppose that the narrator is savvy about animal tracks, call him "Chief" (141), and ask about his latest scalping, while a Carlsbad clerk with an eye to Southwest heat implies he will know about rain dances. Encrusted cliché repeats itself, the persistent unhistoricization of Native history. Jones again fashions the one ostensible story-line elliptically, not to say reflexively, to tell the other, and with persuasive touch.

The same kind of purposive, and greatly agile, interlayering of theme and allusion runs throughout *Bleed into Me.* Two pieces especially represent this further. In "Bile" (39-50), its centerpiece the depiction of a dying father hospitalized with cirrhosis and in need of what is whispered might be a "*liver messiah*" (40), circles out to what paternity and alcohol have come to signify for this one Native family and indeed Native life beyond. Who would be best to supply an organ transplant, *indian* or white, and how long will the replacement organ last? As the portrait of an "old Indian guy, short hair, bad skin, one milky eye" (39), the story delineates sundry related family issues, the father's transient hotel existence, a ward nurse's drinking party, hidden gambling chips, and the purchase of more beer. The story's web is one of disconnects, sober and drinking *indians*, connection and drift, and the scant comfort that is available. "Carbon" (111-21), as though semi-hallucination, summons a Native girl-boy drifter pair ("We lie. We steal. We cheat" 120), both of them emaciated, caught in a knot of heroin and substance use, participants in a maybe-intended mutual suicide from garage car fumes, with hospital treatment for the young woman, Casey. One of his more sobering parables, "Carbon" yields its meanings fully in kind with the collection's obliquity. These are Native lives clearly possessed of their own vitality, their own figurings, and dreams. Yet, as Jones renders them, they are also lives conducted at near-ground zero, just above the dividing line of death.

***

Embarkation into the pieces that make up *The Ones That Got Away* carries the reader into somewhat different terrain. The *noir* at hand lies closer to the twilight zone, although Jones rarely does less than cannily maneuver around even a hint of formula shock-horror. To highlight any one story in the collection, be it about werewolves, enghosting, cannibalism, murder, or vampirism, is also to underscore the variety on offer. Inside-out history, the ironic reversal, and, as often as not, an overlap of one time-scale with another, all assume their individual styling. Yet however separate the stories's filterings, they nonetheless share the embracing arc of light shone into shadow.

If linkage were to be made with *Bleed into Me*, it is likely the title-story (201-8) of *The Ones That Got Away*, a would-be kidnapping turned macabre. There is more than a hint of farce in its account of the teenage pair, the narrator and his friend, Tim, whose debt to their twenty-something drug supplier, Mark, is to be repaid by helping to terrorize a family in payment for a prior debt of Mark's own. An escape van, pizza-delivery routine, duct tape, ski-mask disguise, error as to the right address, not to mention an intake of drugs, all hint at life imitating pantomime. The stage props pale in comparison, however, to Tim's beheading with a "glinting" machete by the father whose family they have contracted to abduct; the man's boy-son Nicholas witnesses the beheading (208). The story, moving ahead in time, deftly turns the wheel. Nicholas himself will transition from damaged child to juvenile delinquent to dealer. The narrator will be haunted by guilt at fleeing the scene, end his own drug-taking, endure self-hate and sleeplessness – and get married, becoming the straight family man. Yet he will also turn sick at the remembered pizza smell and wonder whether there was a purpose to this small-town crime and punishment saga. Whatever its formal closure, story and theme, "The Ones That Got Away" shrewdly and contrarily (as hinted at in its titling), reminds of un-endings: the footfalls of time-past, the hints of being memorially haunted into the future.

"Wolf Island" (105-15) gives a perhaps more indicative pointer to the collection in the round, a werewolf tale under guise of being an island marooning story. Its meticulous account of Rupert, man-wolf who has savaged passengers on the boat that went down; his two legged to four legged transformations; his consumption of the marooned Emma; and his eventual comeuppance by the dolphins he befriends (whose offspring he eats but who entice an orca to destroy him) works towards a justice-served twist. Lycanthrope, even as he changes forms, falls to killer whale in a revenge led by dolphins. These are settings, and events, that do not exactly come from the usual werewolf playbook. Land predator is made sea prey – a credit to invention.

The portrait of young-boy's bed-wetting fear of the dark, or an authentic childhood ghost haunting, or both? "Till The Morning Comes" (23-33) engagingly offers overlaps, one pathology wrapped in the other. The story keeps its focus tightly wound, a one-family saga of the narrator aged twelve in the story; his younger brother Nicholas, "who my dad called Señor Accidento" (23); the night-shift father himself; the mother; and her brother Uncle Jamieson, ex-military and now ambulance-driver who keeps band posters tricked out with skeletons on show in his room. Jamieson's medical horror stories, in particular that of a crashed VW bus in which music plays spectrally from the other side of death, give context to the story. The disappearance of Nicholas, the father's accusing assault of Jamieson that puts him in a coma, and the ghostly nighttime doorway return of Nicholas in the uncle's arms (ending the narrator's bedwetting) steer between the maybe illusory, the maybe real. The family will later fissure, with Nicholas attempting suicide multiple times and the father absconding. The narrator will burn the skeleton posters even as a childhood red toy car keeps turning up as if to remind him that key memories can never disappear. His child-into-adult memory of Jamieson's liminal appearance supplies the one image of safety in a life clearly riven with unsafety. A story's end, once again for Jones, is shown to run at odds with any supposed life-episode ending, the past always lodged in place with the capacity to disrupt in the present.

"Teeth" (118-44), for which Jones acknowledges a debt both to Stephen King's story of self-cannibalization, "Survivor Type," and Raymond Carver's meditation on kinds of blindness in "Cathedral," gives a truly dark-side turn to cops-and-crime detection.[6] Laconic and Bogeyish, its case of Martin Roche as pursued by Detective Krupier edges towards *Doppelgänger* fare. Fingers found in a park, lung blood, a limbless but live body, a detached arm that can draw, together with police files, bars and snitches, all fuse into the one and continuing tale. Krupier, retiree, widower, fond grandfather, and himself suffering from the invasion of cancer, sees himself in Roche's ingestion of his own body parts. The regurgitated owl-pellets that give the story its point of departure anticipate both Roche's self-consumption and the detective's cancer: the criminal "mystery" to be unraveled that of the body as it becomes, by cellular break-down, itself also antibody.

Murder under two construings lies at the heart of "Captain's Lament" (167-73). One version belongs to Quincy Mueller, known as Muley, the hospitalized and hook-for-arm mariner co-opted into the jilted nurse Margaret's knifing and then hanging of her former lover, William Jackson. The other lies in the newspaper account of the mariner as an escaped mental patient who, having severed his own arm with a glass bottle to escape, ropes Jackson from a tree branch, killing him. Echoes of Melville's *Billy Budd*, whether a calculation on Jones's part or not, reverberate, the one death encased in myth or at least distorted or covered-up in newspaper reports. The account is offered as though its events took place twenty-years ago, the one-time mental patient drawn back to ocean salt and spray and either truly suborned by his nurse for his knowledge of knots or engaging in a fantasy to cover his hospital escape. Either way, and in naming his subsequent ships *Margo* and changing his own name, Muley, in reference both to his life on land and at sea, assumes a voice akin to that of the biblical Job whom Melville quotes at the end of *Moby-Dick* –"And I only am escaped to tell thee."[7] The story thereby issues its own meticulous challenge of possibilities: participant witness statement or the voice of delusion, a recitation of fact or a vernacular seagoer's knowing yarn.

For "Monsters" (91-104) Jones avails himself of vampire fare, though as always pitched at unexpected angle. A twelve-year old boy's summer stay with his grandparents, his fond half-romance with the girl Elaine, his responsibilities of garden-watering and taking care of the neighbor's dog Matey, and his boardwalk saunters, add up to an opening scenario as benign as could be wished. But when Matey, who is revealed to have been trained as a cadaver dog, bites a bloodless leather-clad vampire as the vampire passes among the holiday-makers, and the narrator, under dire threat, is inveigled into helping in the throat-slash feeding on Elaine, things come wholly about, a loop into the sinister. Whether Matey has been taken over by the vampire, or the vampire has killed Elaine and the dog is responsible, or the narrator himself has been vampirized, regardless, the nightmare lives on in the boy's psyche. That his mother later suggests he might like a dog for himself adds a darkest sweet-sour addendum. "I've already got a dog" he responds, "His name is Matey. He lives in my head. Maybe we'll come and see you one of these days" (104). The one tale circles into the other. Shadow once more gets extracted from light. Memory again becomes haunt. In transposing a first love and animal pet story into one of the undead, blood, and predation, especially as accoutered in a setting of neighborhood ordinariness, Jones again shows his paces in the different possible directions of *noir.*

The collection's other stories also, and equally, share the interplay of illumination and dark, and just as important, a similar styling. Whether "Father, Son, Holy Rabbit" (15-22), with its snow time tale of lost-in-the-woods animal-helper survival; "So Perfect" (43-65), with its schoolgirl take on disembowelment and beauty-myth; or "Crawlspace" (209-38), with its blue-collar husband's scare at believing his TV has telepathic powers and ghost twins, the narration – the play of doubles and contrasts, the deliberate shifts of rhythm – are very exactly tailored into narrative. The *noir* in question gains confirming resonance, evidentiary weight, and, often enough just the right ambiguity, in the disclosing voice. In this respect, where *The Ones That Got Away* offers highly various galleries of disequilibrium and vacillations of shade lit as though only for the moment, it does so in idiom sure of step and wholly requisite.

***

Suitably published in pocketbook size, *States of Grace* has the feel of a small scale memorial life-album, with remembered intimacies, quirks, corners. One quickly reaches for terms to suit. It could pass as a Book of Days, vignette, memoir (especially of twelve year old and other early adolescent rites of passage), story chapbook, almost but not quite a cycle in the manner of Sherwood Anderson's *Winesburg, Ohio* or Tomás Rivera's *... y no se lo tragó la tierra/ And the Earth Did Not Devour Him*. At the same time, and however closely local – Texas, for the most part – this is also the quotidian seen under distancing lens, be it of youth or adulthood. As in all his fiction, Jones keeps the angle slant, given to careful indirection or the side-on view.

The *noir* in this collection may not be as graphic as in the other collections, but it is unmistakably present, one of life met in not-too-readily-explained tranches. The forty story panels emerge seamed in quizzicality, an arcade of things known close at hand yet, for those involved, never finally sieved. In appearance, they suggest one-offs, snapshots or footage, whether the small fare of growing up, school time, and family or neighborhood and marriage. But this emphasis on the local and quotidian also serves to deceive. Whatever the fragmentary appearance, each story amounts to rounded-out storytelling; each plays across or into the unfolding whole. In keeping these dimensions tactically in balance, *States of Grace* gives pitch-perfect magnification to its scenes of provincial life.

"In the beginning" (2), aptly the opening cameo, offers guidance, at once a marker for the stories to follow and enactment in its own imaginative right:

> Ask and you shall receive, she said to me in the back seat of my Dodge Rambler, parked at the end of the old airstrip we all knew about, my tires pulled right up to the edge of the crumbling asphalt, then leaned over the front seat just far enough to tune Tulsa in on the radio, just far enough that I could see the fig leaf tattooed into the base of her back, and then I drew her down to me and we closed our eyes to the cattle nosing our windows, waiting to be named, and it was good. (2)

The backseat of the Dodge Rambler – and now lovemaking, eyes closed – affords one kind of note. The cryptic bible echoes of *Genesis,* twice-over, the title and "it was good"; Adam and Eve footfall; allusion to "ask and you shall receive" from *Matthew* 7:7, and even the fig-leaf tattoo, add another. Each detail is enclosed circumstantially within sight and sound of airstrip, asphalt, Tulsa radio, and cows. The whole, insistent and not a little lyric in detail, plaits into personally held memory, almost ritual. The process is symptomatic of *States of Grace* and its capsules of both moment and permanence.

Story upon story works likewise. Those whose donnée is childhood or youth assume an especial force, time past, certainly, yet far from time actually lost. "The Complete Absence of Cats is Another Definition of Silence" (7-8) works exactly in this way with its remembrance of a tornado during "my fourteenth year" (7), the topsy-turvy impact of Mrs. Zimmer's upturned station wagon, a church's broken window, lifted-up store shelves yet with no eggs broken, a red straw lodged in a telegraph pole, the dispersal of wigless manikin heads around the countryside – some of them nosed by the Great Dane Rudolph – and, above all, the missing cats. The narrator, battered like his father by the tornado gusts, is also caught smoking, his boyhood transgression given momentary let-off in the words "I'll pretend I didn't see that" (8). This disjuncture of parts, tornado and house scatter, uncollected plastic scalps, fatherly reprimand, cat silence and smoke exhalation, presses into geometry, disjuncture as its own memorial pattern.

The collection, in fact, is very much a serial portrait of generations. Youthfare recurs, from "The Talk" (11-14) – with its closely observed Friday-night hot tub conversation between a clearly uneasy father and his fifteen-year old daughter, a gossip-heavy conversation about cheerleading and phones – to "Doors &

Passageways" (49), a boy's glimpse into father-mother mutual warring and which fuses into his enduring sense of childhood alienation. "Fabergé" (18-20), for the most part an unpunctuated interior monologue, offers a boy's rumination on what it means to have his mother discover his soft-porn magazine with its centerfold image of female flesh and a small diving airplane. "Matinée: A Love Affair" (35-7) deals in the lure of movies, centering on a trio of child friendship for whom the screen becomes refuge, shadow life, eating place, playground; they come to think of themselves as kin to the crows who peck at the kernels behind the theatre.

"The Family That Reads Together" (94-5) could not be further from round-the-hearth domestic Victoriana. Its account of a brother and sister's overnight prank of re-shelving their father's collection of six thousand books, their spines in rather than out, segues into a fantasy of their parent's bibliocentric "living in the walls" (95). In the story's figuring, fact having elided into metaphor, the father has closed the book on his offspring, opting, as the title hints, for the private rather than the shared page. The *noir* at issue thereby becomes that which exists within the family, the longtime walls and gaps within its parent-offspring relationships.

The stories in which styles of adulthood are the focus likewise give off their own dark ambiance. "Modern Love" (4-6), a collage of six numbered paragraphs, offers semi-irreal pictures of life at maturity in which the quotidian turns inside out and back on itself. The span runs from remembrance of a son's breathing, heard on the baby monitor, and later his arm being dotted with ball-point markings in imitation of his kindergarten teacher's heroin tracks, to a husband's unspoken but inwardly conjured-up love for his wife as they watch a TV commercial, which might have come straight from a Dalí canvas. "Cops & Robbers" (33-4), in which a longtime marriage is imagined as detective-and-culprit thriller, has a couple entering a wholly new mystery plot as they head into retirement alongside each other. "Abducted" (62-5) does a wry comic take on fading sexual prowess in the person of Donald, Dr. Collins's medical patient, who masks his prostate and erectile difficulties in classic deferral references to ever-more-infrequent UFO visitations. "The Bridge" (78-81), its scenario one of office and lunchtime bungee jumping, deals in a couple's own kind of plummeting relationship, their own chance-taking or lack of it. Jones works these, and the volume's other miniature stories, with just the right astringent dispatch, adult times seen from the corner of the eye, and darkly, as always.

***

To step into *Zombie Sharks with Metal Teeth* is to be met with Jones in hyper-outré mode, a near extravagance of invention. The title story (121-34) carries much of the collection's flavor, with its research bio-science lab into "applied telekinesis" as theatre of dark. Jones keeps from dipping into mere weird-fiction or brilliant-but-mad-scientist formula in several ways at once. He gives a genuinely speculative edge to the story's chill experimental details of wired mice, dolphin heads, severed and electronically controlled brains, biohazard disposal, and, indeed, eventual metal-teethed shark. The play of time shifting and the story's account of camera and video use likewise work to good purpose, the one clock and its tank and cage lab happenings visually monitored from the vantage-point of an hour's lapse in time. The narrator, for his part, takes on a compassionate participant-observer role, agent and victim of the scientist Ronald's post-Frankenstein forays into life creation and alteration. This kind of configuration – jigsaw *noir*, the real as virtual – could easily risk obfuscation, the reader's full grasp. But the positive returns, as "Zombie Sharks with Metal Teeth" underscores in plenty, are not to be denied.

"The thing about using space lobsters as storage devices for people's minds is that it wasn't an entirely known process" (58). Off-beat, even startling, the voice in play in "The Sea of Intranquility" (51-64) offers another instance of Jones's capacity for baroque fantasticality. Its story of Rock Turner, a future-dwelling private investigator sent to the moon to trace a lost spouse whose consciousness has been warehoused (just one of many) in the lunar lake's giant lobsters, can be said to mask quite another. How, in an era after earth invasion, is it possible to take up the challenge of out-deathing death? Jones's inventiveness equally lies in fusing tough guy thriller-noir with science fiction, would-be insurance scam with alien encounter. The picturing of mind disinterred from body, not to mention being put into crustacean storage, gives fresh impetus to far older explorations in the possibility of immortality. Or as Turner, with a playful Jones behind him, confides "Dead and Loving It" (64).

If these compositions give a benchmark for the collection, for its dark side and idiom, others add their respective weights. "Nearer to Thee" (39-46) folds the dance band on the *Titanic* into a small-town August "Founders' Day" (39), with thirty-one-year-old oddball and quiz virtuoso Dexter (in attendance with his mother) coming to realize that the world is at its end. His identification of the town's scratch orchestra with the names of those aboard the Atlantic liner sunk in 1912, and the heading of an iceberg meteorite from the frozen space of the Kuiper Belt toward "a fateful interaction with Earth" (45), transform what has begun as local celebration into apocalypse. The trademark song based on the "unsinkable" survivor Molly Brown gives added ironic indication, as does the sight of an old man re-arranging his lawn chair as if it were one of the *Titanic*'s deckchairs. "This is how it ends" (39) reads the opening sentence, perhaps a T.S. Eliot echo: "This is how it ends" (46) reads the last. The story imagines the arrival, or threat, of a new dateline – one to be remembered in some future galactic quiz archive – with no small degree of ingenuity.

The further stories in the menu hardly deny themselves. "The Age of Hasty Retreats" (7-11), with its after-the-plague landscape and survival strategies of fighting the consequent zombies by distracting them with the flesh of live cats and dogs, edges close enough to parody. But it also tells the story of a son with a broken leg who sacrifices himself for his father in the face of a zombie attack ("it would be a travesty for me not to stand, run, keep living. For him, always for him" 11). The story's double helix is typical, the one tale humanizing the other. "Old Meat" (35-8), related by a long-married husband in the form of a "Dear Abby" letter, again treads a fine line between plausibility and spoof. Will he survive their nights in bed, his skin ever thinner, given that his wife shape-shifts in sleep into a werewolf? What advice – "please share this with your readers" – what best confidence can be shown "in hope of morning" if the choice is love or suicide (38)? Tease has long played its part in Jones's darkness. "Because My Therapist Asked Me to Tell a Story Using Hamsters" (145-7), part rodent sex story and part send-up pet story, operates in similar vein. The faux Disney or Beatrix Potter nomenclature – Father and Mommy Hamster – and the lustful father's mistake in thinking a dummy wife-hamster his true object of desire, all conducted within cage and wheel, give their own darkening to a seeming children's animal fable. Innocence of surface hides a wholly darker hue and implication.

Sports serves as axis in "Rocket Man" (135-44), in the form of high school baseball played with a zombie left fielder. The narrator, hoping to catch the eye of the local belle Amber Watson, tries to show off by having the ball land, and stick, in the molten face of the dead Michael T. He fails. The resulting squelch belongs to the world of the bitten and unbitten, of life after plague in which zombie-ism is part of the assumed order of things. The story poses as a memory being told from atop the diamond's emblematic rocket, school-time nostalgia for home run, girl, and peer status – a memory that grimly, and as always, darkly does an about-face. A recognizable version of homage underwrites "Submitted for Your Approval" (107-14). In centering on Rod Serling, begetter not only of *The Twilight Zone* but the earlier *Night Gallery* for TV and subsequent *The Zero Hour* for radio, Jones allies himself with a fellow traveler across alternative or out-of-body domains. The story has Serling "watching himself on television and watching himself watching himself on television" (107). His obsessing over the episode, "*1492*," with its speculative meeting of Vikings and Indians, and his Kafkaesque sense of himself as extending double both point to the writer of *The Twilight Zone* as being reflexively and even self-scaringly a real-unreal figure in one of his own dark scripts. A Native emphasis so fuses with vintage *noir*, the two memorably melded one into the other, the perfect syncretic marker for Jones as a writer elusive of any one fixed category.

***

Stephen Graham Jones remains an author about whom opinion has yet to settle. The sheer quantity of story-making can daunt, with whole loops and arcades of behind-the-mirror mystery. There will forever be those to whom popular genre remains surface, diversion more than depth. But none of this fully recognizes the virtuosity of. Jones's writings. He works his literary métier with rare eye and ear, Indian/Native to mystery/horror, and often with the shrewdest overlapping of both. Darkness illumined goes some distance towards recognizing his achievement, and rarely more so than in the contours, the chosen detail, of his story collections.

Notes

1 John Milton, *Paradise Lost*, Book 1, 16, 1667.
2 O. Henry, Reported last words at his death in June 1910.
3 Stephen Graham Jones, "Rocket Man," *Zombie Sharks with Metal Teeth*, Portland: Lazy Fascist Press, 2013, 135.
4 This span I have annotated in "Native Postmodern? Remediating History in the Fiction of Stephen Graham Jones and D.L. Birchfield," in Cathy Covell Waegner, ed., *Mediating Indianness*, East Lansing: Michigan State University Press, 2015, 78–9.
5 The title story "Bleed into Me" is included in Gerald Vizenor, ed., *Native Storiers: Five Selections*, Lincoln: University of Nebraska Press, 2009.
6 Jones acknowledges both of these influences in his "Story Notes" to *The Ones That Got Away*, 245.
7 Herman Melville, *Moby-Dick*, Evanston and Chicago: Northwestern University Press and The Newberry Library, 1988. 573.

Works Cited

Anderson, Sherwood, *Winesburg. Ohio*, 119. Reprinted New York: W.W. Norton, 1996.

Jones, Stephen Graham, "Letter to a Just-Starting-Out Indian Writer – And Maybe to Myself," in Billy J. Stratton, ed., *The Fiction of Stephen Graham Jones: A Critical Companion*, Albuquerque: University of New Mexico Press, 2017.

_____, *After The People Lights Have Gone Off*, Chicago: Dark House Press, 2014.

_____, *States of Grace*, Denver: SpringGun Press, 2014.

_____, *Three Miles Past*, Smyrna: Nightscape Press, 2013.

_____, *The Last Final Girl*, Portland: Lazy Fascist Press, 2012.

_____, *Zombie Bake-Off*, Portland: Lazy Fascist Press, 2012.

_____, *Growing Up Dead in Texas*, Douglas, Isle of Man: MP Publishing, 2011.

_____, *The Ones That Got Away*, Gaithersburg, MD: Prime Books, 2010.

_____, *It Came from Del Rio*, Lyons, CO: Trapdoor Books, 2010.

_____, *Ledfeather*, Tuscaloosa: Fiction Collective 2/University of Alabama Press, 2008.

_____, *The Long Trial of Nolan Dugatti*, Portland: Chiasmus Press, 2008.

_____, *Demon Theory: A Work of Fiction*, San Francisco: Mac/Adam Cage, 2006.

_____, *Bleed into Me: A Book of Stories*, Lincoln: University of Nebraska Press, 2005.

_____, *The Bird Is Gone: A Manifesto*, Normal, IL: Fiction Collective 2, 2003.

_____, *All The Beautiful Sinners*, New York: Rugged Land, 2003.

_____, *The Fast Red Road*, Normal, IL: Fiction Collective 2, 2000.

Melville, Herman, *Moby-Dick* (1851), Evanston and Chicago: Northwestern University Press and The Newberry Library, 1988.

_____, *The Confidence-Man: His Masquerade*, New York: Dix &Edwards, 1857. Reprinted, ed., Hershel Parker, New York: Norton, 1971.

_____, *Billy Budd.Sailor (An Inside Narrative)*, eds., Harrison Hayford and Merton M. Sealts, Chicago and London: The University of Chicago Press, 1962.

Rivera, Tomás, *".... y no se lo tragó la tierra"/And the Earth Did Not Part*, Berkeley: Quinto Sol Publications, 1971.

Vizenor, Gerald, ed., *Native Storiers; Five Selections*, Lincoln University of Nebraska Press, 2009.

Part IV

Poetry

14

Poetry Remembrance: Joy Harjo, Wendy Rose, Diane Glancy, Luci Tapahonso, Kimberly Blaeser

Remember you are all people and all people
are you.
Remember you are this universe and this universe is you.
Remember all is in motion, is growing, is you.
Remember language comes from this.
Remember the dance language is, that life is.
Remember.

Joy Harjo, "Remember"[1]

With electric everything and my computer whirring
I *work* my way through memories and philosophies.

Kimberly Blaeser, "Dictionary for a New Century"[2]

These headpieces from Joy Harjo and Kimberly Blaeser as to the force of memory in their verse, and by implication in that of fellow Native poets, give indicative witness. How, in the one reach, to find ongoing measure for the remembrance of passed-down custom, belief-system and language, the one and the many tribal legacies? How, in the other, to create the personal signature, the pull of individual identity, relationship, gender? The challenge across the board has been to make memory itself memorable, a reflexive mirror.

Styles in this respect have taken on every form, free verse or prose poem, epic or sonnet, and whether belonging to the themed collection, the miscellany, or the chapbook. In "A Share of the Stair (or As I Talk I'm Becoming What I Say)" Diane Glancy offers well-taken touchstones:

Memory is a moraine. A little clutter of stones the glacier left
when it retreated …

> You see memories are shape-changers moving among us. So we
> create what we remember.[3]

Moraine, retreating glacier, memory as shape-changer, and the rubric of "we create what we remember" all do pertinent good service.[4] For Luci Tapahonso, writing in "All the Colors of Sunset," memory serves as indispensable oxygen, breath, the very nerve-system of her Navajo heritage:

> I understand now that all life has ceremonies connected with it, and for us, without our memory, our old people, and our children, we would be like lost people in the world we live in, as well as in the worlds in which our loved ones are waiting.[5]

Both Glancy and Tapahonso offer lanterns, remembrance as moving part, remembrance as itself ceremony. Taken with Joy Harjo's injunction always to remember the dance of language and Kimberley Blaeser's particularization of memory of poetic archive, these are bearings to savor. For their begetters they feed into literary repertoires of longstanding, be it prose, drama, performance, and in Harjo's case, music. In settling upon a single volume by each, however, the bid is to seize upon close register, poetries speaking from and to memory in unique delivery.

***

The appointment of Joy Harjo in 2019 (through to 2020) as Poet Laureate of the United States, the first-ever Native author to hold the post, carries wide implication. It pays necessary tribute to the Muscogee Nation writer whose bow with *The Last Song* (1975) extends across a dozen-plus verse collections, through among others to *The Woman Who Fell from the Sky* (2001), *How We Became Human: New and Selected Poems 1975-2001* (2002) and *An American Sunrise* (2019), along with *Crazy Brave: A Memoir* (2012). Other writings accompany, the work for children, screenplays, anthology work, photography, and the song compositions and alto-sax playing with her groups *Poetic Justice* and *Arrow Dynamics.* Harjo has from the outset been a hugely intimate voice while at the same time always contemplative of her own Creek and other tribal-historical memory.

She Had Some Horses exhibits this double-hinge with indicative flair.[6] The collection's title sequence does necessary service (63-9). Horses in this verse quintet take on pattern standing, a huge ligatured animal imagery of life-spirit. The opening line, "She had some horses" (Section I, 63) leads into remembrance of the material world ("sand," "maps drawn of blood," "skins of ocean water," "blue air sky," "splintered red cliff"). The horses become figurations of human feeling ("who laughed too much," "who licked razor blades"). They carry cycles of birth and growth, sun and moon, bodies and souls. They summon "Creek Stomp Dance songs," the cruel spit at "male queens," and both liars and truth-tellers. They serve, above all, as holders of secrets, whisperers, participating attendants on both destruction and resurrection and companions through nights with their mix of lovers and haters ("They were the same horses"). The imaging could not be more apt for forces to be recalled as having shaped and held domain within the speaker's life.

Each subsequent panel in the sequence fills out the memory-line. "Two Horses" (II) summons a Sangre de Cristo Mountain sunrise in Rocky Mountain Colorado as expressive also of a lover's self-awakening ("My heart is taken by you/ and these mornings since I am a horse running towards/a cracked sky where there are countless dawns breaking simultaneously"). "Drowning Horses" (III) speaks in the voice of a phone colloquist with her suicidal drinker friend or relative in whom she sees herself as also "a running horse." "Ice Horses" (IV) bespeaks residual memories of broken intimacy, the fire and ice hooves of bloodied spirit as well as body ("They are the ones who love you/They are the horses that have held you/ so close you have become a part of them").

"Explosion" (V) looks to a highway quake "near Okemah, Oklahoma" (68) as signage of the planet's larger riposte against its abuse ("But maybe the explosion was horses,/bursting out of the crazy earth"). There is anticipation of rebirth in wet fields, frogs, and a "Creek woman who dances shaking the seeds in her bones." The explosion event extends to "South Dakota, Mexico, Japan and Manila" as though a way to awaken "the horses with their hearts of sleeping volcanoes" and to cleanse the earth of remembered hatreds both ecological and within the hearts of its human dwellers. The sequence carries Harjo's symptomatic strengths, command of image and line, memory to be understood as always kinetic and in process of its own making.

Other poems in the collection further share the flair of this will to memorialization. "New Orleans" (42-4) conjures into being the city streets like Conti, Royale or Decatur, tobacco history, Creek traces, the French Market, tiled Spanish horses, shops with African and Native magic stones, trolley cars on their "silver path" rails, above-ground tombs and "black mammy dolls/holding white babies" (44). Perhaps most of relevance reside "voices buried in the Mississippi mud" and "stories here made of memory" (43). The poem also remembers the conquistador Hernando de Soto, the first European to cross and yet die of fever by the Mississippi ("Maybe his body is what I am looking for as evidence" 44) and magically reincarnated in a Bourbon Street bar "dancing with a woman as gold/as the river bottom" (44) "I have a memory," says the poem near midway, "It swims deep in blood,/a delta in the skin" (42). Each city remembrance of history and place overlays the other, a striking collage precisely of how Native and related memory infuses and so relives itself in the present.

The landscapes of memory extend. "Skeleton of Winter" (30-1) uses the season to think of always ongoing meteorological cycle, be it memorialized in fish skeletons at low tide or prehistoric horse cave engraving. The closing lines give the perfect summary:

> I am memory alive.
>   not just a name
>
> but an intricate part
> of this web of motion,
> meaning earth, sky, stars circling
> my heart
>
>   centrifugal. (31)

"She remembers the future" (46) uses the figure of her volatile friend Noni Daylight to think of life lived at full measure, the "colored horses" of spirit as she calls them by which to remember "that we are alive/we are alive." "What I Should Have Said" (50) looks the other way, the life of a Santa Fe/Albuquerque relationship remembered as though existing at both geographic and emotional distance ("there is no motion/either way"). In the connected poem "Motion" (54) the voice again remembers the fragility of love and with it the poet's mantra "we exist/not in words, but in the motion/set off by them." "September Moon" (60), told as a lover`s phone call between San Francisco Bay and Albuquerque, projects memory-making itself as analogy. The landscape of Sandia Mountain sky, wind, moon and ridge leads into the abiding call of remembering in the phrase "Look/ We are alive" (60).

Harjo's Introduction to *She Had Some Horses* offers her own guidance to how she remembers the horse as image. "A horse can be a streak of sunrise," she testifies, "a body of sand … the imagination of the wind" (x). It can even, reflexively, be a "song … a book of poetry" (x). When asked by Laura Coltelli about memory in an interview for *Winged Words: American Indian Writers Speak* (1992) Harjo speaks of it as "a wealth" at once specific and generic:

> It is Creek, and touched in the larger tribal continental memory and the larger human memory, global. It's not something I consciously chose; I mean, I am not a full-blood, but it was something chose me, that lives in me, and I cannot deny.[7]

"Chosen to remember" might be thought the near perfect credo to accompany entrance into Joy Harjo's both *She Had Some Horses* and her ongoing bodies of poetry.

***

Almost defiant in its titling Wendy Rose's *The Halfbreed Chronicles & Other Poems* (1985) draws upon her mixed Hopi-Miwok and white urban ancestry as a major dynamic. Born Bronwen Elizabeth Edwards to a full Hopi father and part-Miwok mother and raised in San Francisco, identity becomes not just personal but linkage to global *mestizaje*. She has long been a battler in poetry like "For the White Poets who would be Indian" (1980), with its smack at "white shamanism," and "Notes on a Conspiracy" (1993), with its fierce visionary attack on the life-erasing museumization of Native skulls.[8] Her best-known collection, *The Half-Breed Chronicles* especially arises out of keen personal remembrance, a reflection of early AIM activism and her anthropological interests (she holds a doctorate from Berkeley) in the metaphor of bone and body as ways into the understanding of Native history.

Adeptness in free-verse voice, the brace and vigor of her imaging of memory, is to be met in the opening poem "Sipapu" (8-9), named for a Hopi emergence-story:

> Hand by hand
> bone by bone
> dancing on the ladder …
>   we emerge
>   we emerge ….
>
> a sound of birth
>   a whirl of blood
> a spin of song. (8-9)

The bone allusions, with their implication of remembered timeline, give points of bearing for the companion poems to follow – beginnings, presence, the Native ritual of voice.

Another kind of memory is to be heard in "To the Hopi in Richmond (Santa Fe Village on San Francisco Bay)" 10). The geography is modern, one of city indigence ("My people in boxcars," "your roof full of holes"). But the poem also gives remembrance of better spirit ("So remember the sun … rain on the mesas"), of restoration amid setback, and of repair for the broken house. "What My Father Said" (19) offers homage to "remembered stone," "adobe," " grass," and "summer rain" as against "the asphalt" and " black shadowed" structures of the inhospitable city. Generosity according to custom beckons, health from remembrance, food for the hungry, and the grandmother's singing as continuance ("you may hear your clan"). In these and other memories the poet-speaker's father says in behalf of active over costricted breath "live in my tongue/ and forget/your hunger."

"Story Keeper" (27) gives an entire vow to Rose's sense of memory. Native storytelling, "braided in my hair," is to be recovered from the "rock" and "moss" of willed or simply casual forgetting. Against "fossil" loss, Native imagination must keep true to the "new house," "our first/Hopi morning." This memory has been bequeathed by the stories she insists "the spirits" have "trusted us/to remember … right":

> I feel the stories
> rattle under my hand
> like sun-dried
> greasy gambling bones. (27).

Involved is imaginative debt, not always easily retrieved but essential, at once self-need and at the same time duty of care beyond self.

With "Wounded Knee" (28-32) Rose seizes upon iconic history, her personal memorial not just to warrior men but to women ("Jeanette, Jancita, Yellow Thunder, Anna Mae") – their shared burial, ironically, "in a white grave" and without "star quilt" or "song." Once again spirit is invoked, the dance of life over death and to which the poet pays her own arresting obeisance:

> Wounded Knee dies dancing
> and my hand
> forever holds my tongue! (29)

She ponders the temptation to "let it go," and yet not, the utter emplacement within her consciousness of "smoking leaves," "skull of buffalo," "banners of four colors." As though herself on the receiving end of bullets she fantasizes "they shoot at me/at all my relations." Yet rebirth remains, sourced from both past skulls and future children's play, knowledge of the once "frozen" Lakota bodies of the 1890 massacre unfrozen and reseeded "to begin … again."

Memory's variety of manifestations runs through the volume's poetry. In "The Poet Haunted" (41-2) ghosts of every kind assemble, those of the Native past ("these clans … these Chippewas") and those of her own vexed life of pill and bandage ("Ghost of myself fooled … my body, my massacre"). "If I am Too Brown or Too White for You" (52-3) remembers "the crystal arithmetic" and "matrix" of mix as imposed damage against self-whole. Later poems give memorial idiom to disrespected Tasmanian-Aboriginal burial ("Truganinny"), Japanese-American Pacific heritage ("Isamu"), the hand gesture of a zoo-caged gorilla ("Hanabi-ko (Koko)"), government killings of migrants "from the mountains/ of memory" ("The Day They Cleaned Up the Border"), and radiation poisoning at Hiroshima ("Yuriko"). "The Building of the Trophy" (43-6) offers a species of verse curriculum vitae, infancy to thirties womanhood through gains and losses ("Twenty years it took/to ask if it mattered/how dark her skin"). The course of memory Rose delineates as "taking stock," "glue," "ghost books," "uneven pavement," and on a reflexive note that also suggests their sedimentation into the whole of *The Halfbreed Chronicles,* "these words."

***

An observation in *Claiming Breath* (1992), Diane Glancy's "diary of personal matters," give a frame to her poetry. Mindful of her mixed-blood Cherokee and white Arkansas family legacy, and a life of domestic gains and losses, she speaks to how

> Only poetry or a form of new writing captures the thoughts that entomb the mind, the disorder of memory, the un-chronological order. [9]

This might be regarded as Glancy's own version of Ezra Pound's "Make it New," an entrance-point, itself poetically articulated, to *Rooms: New and Selected Poems.* Memory she summons as reflecting the contrarieties within her life. For her that embraces Native-white identity, un-breakable allegiance to Bible Christianity, the memory of daughter-wife-mother gender roles, the circuits of road travel and classroom across Minnesota, Oklahoma, Kansas, and Missouri in her role as English and Creative Writing professor at Macalester College and elsewhere, and always the call to literary word. Each of these facets press into different, though often overlapping, verse remembrance.

"Here I Am Standing Beside Myself" (65), initially published in *Lone Dog's Winter Count* (1991) can act as an axial composition for *Rooms* in this regard, a prose-poem of movingly focused memory images as to background, history, family, and name. Opening with an injunction to search memory ("Just look at the family album"), it speaks immediately of her "white mother" and sisters and her father and brother sporting the skin of sparrow hawks on their heads. The latter detail links to two next observations, suitably accoutered with snippets of Cherokee. The one bears on flight, fugitive migrancy ("My father said his grandfather fled Indian Territory <*kuna'yeli st'di* > [claw-scratch-like] when he'd done something wrong"). The other implies margin ("We were outcasts now as well as Indian. & only part of them. Outcast of outcasts."). But a ripple of counter-memories enters the reckoning. Under the rubrics "It's when I remember ..." and "The feeling we weren't but really were," they lead into what might be thought a Native aide-memoire: cornbread soaked in squirrel-grease, Cherokee hymns, a corn-god Jesus, moon and sun deities, and a raccoon turtle deer nibbling her feet. These all come into the speaker-poet's mind as she curls into herself (legs pulled up, fingers inside out, arms in chest and "my ears & nose into my head"). This is memory as albumed Native absence and presence, two languages, and a self of displaced but restorative connections. It is also a world of remembrance made over into strong poetry.

"Tuning" (31), sonnet-length, and initially published in *The Shadow's Horse* (2003) does allied imaginative duty. The speaker alludes to early "exile" life, tough, economically at the sharp end, one of tract housing and hands-on physical labor. That has meant, for her father, the stockyard and slaughterhouse "yarding" of cows and pigs, and for her mother the move from farm to city. It has meant the family moves (Kansas or Indianapolis), her child's eye view of them above her in flight as she makes houses in the sand, and the haunted feeling that "something terrible" in the past has caused the family to move.[10] This she links to her Native heritage – "My father's Cherokee heritage tucked under/some sort of shame." She ends by calling "to them above me," in their afterlife as in her own plane-flight as it were, to aid not only the will-to-memory but to making coherence of that memory. How, runs the poem's implicit question, and in accord with its title, to "tune" memory towards a decisive understanding of an awkwardly angled past, white-Native and blue-collar, with its tableau of girlhood, flits, animal rendering, abattoir, and Native shadow?

This plait of remembering takes on almost startling force in her six-part "The Stockyard Series: *Remuda*" (33-8), also originally issued in *The Shadow's Horse.*[11] Each part again takes up family memory, her father's Depression-era cattle work in the stockyards, the cattle headed for slaughter, packing house and meat-cars, Indian buffalo, and the *remuda* with its memorial reference to selection of horse and cowboy round-ups. But these remembered scenes she also suffuses with a fervent Christian eschatology, Glancy's remembrance of how the whole slaughterhouse process and its blood for her call up martyrdom, heaven and hell "as if Christ stepped from his cross." This is the Bible-Pentecostal Christ of "creative" remembering amid the world's flesh and offal – "Christ in the convent/sacrificed like cattle," beasts whose voices are "Gregorian chants," a "processional" of "cattle crowned with thorns" and "hogs crucified," and where the long-ago stockyard memorializes not only her deceased father but a "Christ of manure." These flights of image, sacrificial life into death and death into resurrection, make for vistas not un-akin to those of Gerard Manley Hopkins in "The Wreck of the Deutschland" or Flannery O'Connor stories like "Greenleaf" or "A Good Man is Hard to Find." Memory turns visionary, little short of apocalyptic.

Native heritage of necessity enters Glancy's field of memory in *Rooms*. "Portrait of the Artist as Indian" (64), initially in *Lone Dog's Winter Count*, can be thought symptomatic, laconic, iconoclastic. As the titular Native woman of an earlier time field-dresses her buffalo so, reflexively, she can be seen to be field-dressing history. Buffalo hide is carefully severed. "Pouches, vessels, the stomach, liver,/bladder" are extricated. "Meat on sticks" are dried upon a line, and ribs cut. The working gloss points up the poem's iconographical meaning – "She dismantles the carcass/the way old stories are carried in the heart" (64). Entrails washed, hide tanned, a medicine pouch made of ears: the unwasteful Native art of life is so remembered, and transposed, as also the Native life of art.

***

"Prayers and memories protect us" reads Lucy Tapahonso's "A Birthday Poem" (79) in *Blue Horses Rush In* (1997), her verse-and-story collection that follows in kind with the earlier and justly acclaimed *Sáanii Dahataał/The Women Are Singing* (1993). In the limning of her Navajo/Diné world, with its home for her of Shiprock (or *Tsé Bit'a'í*), New Mexico, and where she grew up bilingually in a clan-extended family, Tapahonso could hardly not write from a deep force of memory. Her ambit as poet, even so, has not infrequently extended beyond *Dinetah* (meaning "Navajo Country," as she explains in "In 1864," one of her best-known poems in *Sáanii Dahataał* and which summons the persisting historic memory of the "Long Walk"). "The Pacific Dawn," also from *Sáanii Dahataał* (53-4), speaks of how Hilo's Hawaiian colors, volcanoes and currents "force themselves into my memory."

Memory in *Blue Horses Rush In* (11-13) has a formidable marker in "In Praise of Texas" (11-13). In one sweep it offers a playful litany of the Lone Star State through its airports, the country and western songster George Strait, a fond moment with her husband, and a plane's eye view of "scattered herds of horses." In contrast, it is the remembrance of her *Diné* birthplace and birthright (and in particular of *Hózhó* – the Navajo ethos of balance, harmony) that most draws her interest.

"A Birthday Poem" (79-80) memorializes the meaning of Hózhó yet more emphatically. Opening lines speak of sunrise as "a brilliant song," its "sacred beams" at once "gifts," purveyors of "Hózhó," and a means whereby "Diyin" (holiness – *diyin dine* are Navajo god-presences) is to be recognized. The speaker's prayer goes up for not only Hózhó but for its attainment through "precise prayers/ and stories to ensure balance," together with a tranche of "the humor Diné/elders relish so" and the continuing renewal of "soft hills, plains, and wind." Driving through Kansas she thinks of the Diné Night Ceremony, the Fourth World, and right prayers as bulwarks against succumbing to "foreign ways" and being "overwhelmed" by the world. To which end, always to be remembered, "each morning we pray to restore Hózhó, Hózhó, Hózhó, Hózhó." The poem thereby itself becomes restorative prayer, the remembered figuration of "each morning" birth and re-birth. Memory here is sacral, the Diné spiritual pathway into life's true balance.

That same process, the poem as self-enactive ritual of memory, holds for "Rain in the Desert" (21-2). That "Rain in the desert is overwhelmingly beautiful," as announced in the opening line, is given confirmation in "early morning scents," "city shine," "crisp air," and Apache Country's "White Mountain people drinking coffee and cooking breakfast over an open fire." The Pueblo Grande Museum in Phoenix, and its architectural park, are invoked, the grates and pipes muddy under each downpour and the homeless trying to catch drinking water. But from out of this mix of climate and place the poem moves to remember "the spirits of the Hohokamki," ancestral Sonora Desert and Salt River agricultural people and forerunners to the O'odham.

The poem gives its own memory to ongoing Hohokamki presence ("Do they hover under the city, alongside the sewer lines,/or in the scrappy trees left in the Park of Four Waters?"). Do they not see, it asks, present-day joy in the falling rain, the refreshed air? Did not the Hohokamki, too, set out vessels to catch the rain, drink the water, and use it for crop-raising, cooking and the mud-and-color ceramics and paintwork which bequeaths their creative signature down through the ages? The irony is not lost on Tapahonso of how, under all the architectural apparatus, the canals "which were witnesses/to the ingenuity and success" of the Hohokamki "are now lined with cement."

But it is a legacy given ongoing continuity by the rain-nourished trees close to hand, each a species of natural memory-chamber:

> The old gnarled trees also bear centuries of memories –
>   Of disasters, of celebrations, of transitions of all types. (22)

The poem's closing line of "That the trees and the land survived is a wonder in itself" underlines precisely these "centuries of memories" of the Hohokaki as ancestral culture, their cultivation of earth, creative artifacts and buildings, great systems of irrigation canal, and very emblem in the name Four Waters. The trees, gnarled, time-marked, icons of benign and un-benign transition, give abiding memorial, and wholly in keeping, from within each ongoing cycle of rain-in-the-desert.

***

It could not be more appropriate that Kimberly Blaeser's *Apprenticed to Justice* should open with "Family Tree" (3-4), an "all my relations" poem of mixed-blood genealogical memory. To the one side is the German legacy, the "boxer grandfather," sire of six big-handed, beer-drinking sons and a father given to crooning "*Mona Lisa,//Mona Lisa, men have loved you*," and the never-met grandmother, genetically large of thigh like the speaker, given to a sweet tooth, and begetter of sauerkraut and venison sausage family-recipe. To the other side are the Chippewa-Ojibwe grandmother, midwife, herbalist, mother of twelve with two babies lost to influenza, a son killed in war, and others "limbo Indians turned to alcohol." "My Indian grandpa," squints out from old photographs. Working rocky allotment land gets invoked as does "my first memory at two." Through them is bequeathed the speaker's mother, born "in a reckless moon of miscegenation," lifelong seamstress, pattern-maker of shirt and quilt. This calm documentation, memory in measured rhythm, typifies Blaeser's poetry. Its strengths are untheatrical, those of patiently mediated recall and observation.

The remaining three stanzas of "Family Tree" fill out the family – the two uncles who fled Minnesota's Pipestone Indian boarding school, the aunt who lost fingers working at a laundry press yet mothered four children ("beaded, kneaded, quilted and braided" as the poem evocatively calls it), and the houses and camps full of cousins some on probation, some drunks, other softball players. The latter have all been tender towards the speaker's own suckling children. But remembered beyond these, however intimate, is the great grandfather, the dynastic link to earlier Anishinabeg (Chippewa-Ojibwe) history. In him memory is live presence, a veteran full of honor to his tribal name and centered in an earth of fertile seed and pinecone:

> My great grandfather *Nii-Waan*,
> *Mii-nii-waan-noo-gwosh*, Lover of Natural Things,
> whose Antell heart I am said to bear
> who carried his name with humbleness
> as I try to
> and sometimes with rage

> fire brown eyes sharp as any weapon
> who cupped his hands around fertile seeds
> brown fingers the pinecone
> shelled house of protection. (4)

The language remains exact and yet lyric in its evocation of the great grandfather, Elmer Antell, a man both humble and fierce, eyes as weapons and yet protective. Blaeser's observant working of lineage back to the family's oldest personally known figurehead fills memory with live presence. "Family Tree," its calling-up of warmths and losses, is unmistakably a poet's remembering.

This same deliberation of meticulously styled memory persists throughout *Apprenticed to Justice*. It shapes family portraiture like the prose-poem "Shadow Sisters" (5-10) with its 1951-92 chronology of Anishinaabe women's lives from reservation hard times to casinos and new tribal college students, in all "celebrating 500 years of survival." It marks out "A Boxer Grandfather" (11-12) with Ben Blaeser in his nineties flooring the drunken farmer who insults his daughter at the local pool hall. In return the speaker's mother wryly, fondly, lets him cheat at two-handed solitaire all afternoon. It runs through "Memories of Rock" (34), a day-out in the Boundary Waters Canoe Wilderness (BWCA) with son Gavin pebble-skipping upon Minnesota's Farm Lake and finding "a perfect triangle stone." The stone's "tiny black mystery," sinking from sight, does perfect memorial service for permanence amid "the honeycomb patterns of ripple and reflection." It is a style of memory that appositely holds sway in "Haiku Journey" (48-50), a four-season sequence of remembered 17-syllable landscapes. Spring life and flowers give point of departure ("gathering crows," "may's errant mustard"). Summer vaunts its animals and birds ("turkey vulture," "snowy egret"). Fall yields wind and sky ("empty garbage cans dance," "sky black with migration"). Winter, finally, dispenses the bareness of twig and just a few deer ("lace edges of ice," "words turn with weather"). The gathered outcome is Nature as felt pageant, a kinetic, intimate memory-landscape.

More explicitly Native-themes poems take memory in yet other directions. "Indian in Search of an Entourage" (61) cryptically summons savagist mystique, albeit modern-style ("He was an Indian/blown into town on a white girls dream/wearing destiny like a ten-gallon hat"). Figured throughout as actual and fantasy Indian with Geronimo-length hair – singer, poet, preacher, powwow dancer, politician, Native language speaker, and night dancer – the poem gives recognition even as it gently mocks. Cat's eyes and Jim Thorpe physique, an ability to "sing Indian/dress cowboy/talk justice," he is both reality and image, "mascot" more than team-member and "not-quite new-age, not-quite-for-sale/Indian." Remembered as "small frame," "chiseled cheekbones," he indeed embodies the disaffiliated Native, nether wholly in out of history. The poem's ironies work to advantage, memory as a way into picturing the paradox of the one Indian cajoled or choosing to play the other Indian.

"Goodbye to All That" (66-71), with its Robert Graves title and diptych form, looks to a past and present in White Earth history. In the first part memory travels back to when the Anishnaabeg fought the Dakota Sioux "over whitefish and beaver territory," to "histories of dog-eaters and Chippewa Cows," and to the ensuing European intrusion with its "smallpox survivors" and "French fur traders" (66). Each has a successor population of "trackers and scouts in new bloodless legal battles" (66). Memory, however, is not allowed to be sentimental. How best, asks the second part, and as new remembering, to deal with "the follies of White Earth tribal leaders," a Chair "under the influence of civilization" who drives a pickup down the railroad track, who fails to check and aid "rabid casino bucks," or who does not give actual and political nutrition to the community?

A shared press of history lies behind "Housing Conditions of One Hundred Fifty Chippewa Families" (79-83), an at-length meditation on the 1938 report by Sister M. Inez Hilger as to the resistance of the reservation to moving from "*old ramshackled, tar-paper-covered* homes" into "*those fine new houses/the Indian Bureau built for Indians*" (79-83). The poem ponders how the good Sister's paper tabulations, her Order of St. Benedict "tight-lipped post-allotment spirituality" could ever or even half-way have met the "white clay" and woodland cultural heritage of the Anishinaabeg, the chant and drum of "each Midē wiwin elder" (83). This is to give remembrance to two orders of life, one of ledgers, tabulation, the other in its outward poverty and fracture of inner unbroken tribe.

That same remembered continuity runs through Blaeser's title-poem "Apprenticed to Justice" (104-6), a salute to both the memory of "this history of loss" and at the same time "fertile ground/ from which we will build/ new nations." Each Anishinaabe and White Earth marker, "teeth marks on birch bark," "Medicine voices," "camps," "red nations falling/when they are remembered," and "new nations/upon the ashes of our ancestors," make for a composite call to keeping the past remembered. But that reads also, and in terms full of impetus, as poetry with its own memory of the future. [12]

***

Four individual poems under other authorship offer further corridors so to speak, but also mainstays. For Rayna Green (Cherokee) in "Coosaponakeesa (Mary Mathews Musgrove Bosomworth), Leader of the Creeks, 1700-1783," a poem reprinted in *That's What She Said* (1984), remembrance dwells upon colonial Georgia and its historic Creek and settler interface.[13] Bosomworth as Muscogee translator straddles the two worlds in negotiating away land with the colonist leader James Oglethorpe. The poem has her "all woman/part swamp rat," maybe a sell-out, maybe regretful, but remembered by generations-later "Creek girls of Oklahoma" as how for the present-day to yield nothing ("no deals this time … it's all/or nothing").

Paula Gunn Allen, in "Powwow 79. Durango" (*Shadow Country*, 1982) takes on altogether more modern remembrance, the ambiguity of a powwow somehow both taken from tribal timeline and yet awkwardly at odds with time. [14] For all the six drums, 300 dancers, flag songs, there is also "the opening prayer by some guy/who works for the BIA" and her daughter "stoned,/brown face ashy from the weed." The mix of respect and wryness continues as blue jeans and jackets overlap with beads and "dark braids" and the speaker wonders about herself and daughter being "dressed right." The watchers in the bleachers hear "beating drums" and see "exploding colors," one domain as it were pressing into another.

In "up & out" (*Small Bones, Little Eyes*, 1982) nila northsun (Shoshone-Chippewa), lower-case in name and line in e.e. cummings mode, the memory of living at the margin presses hard ("we total it up for/income tax/hoping to get a little/back").[15] The move into the city has led to gains ("we made more money than/we've ever made before"). Yet that has come at cost ("high rent high food high medical/high entertainment high gas") the implication one of feeling "poorer." How to balance the "cute" lunches, the "quaint" bars" against "gramma's old house" and the reservation? If the latter had "wood stove," "one tv channel," mere pool hall "chips & coke," "government commodities," and poor medical care, there were always "relatives" like the local mechanic. The upshot is tally, gauge, the memory of hating life on the reservation yet coming to the comparative view that "now/it doesn't look so bad."

"Star Quilt," not only the signature but title poem of Roberta Hill Whiteman (Oneida) in *Star Quilt* (1997), remembers one of the great, and beauteous craft icons of Native art. [16] The tradition of quilt embroidery at women's hands carries memory, color, legend as though the endurance of land and sky brought imagistically to cloak the speaker's body at nighttime. "The quilt unfolds against sheets," reads the poem, its "linen threads and patches" at once animate and protective. History lies in its fabric, the remembrance of Oneida relocation from Great Lakes New York to Wisconsin. "Sewn from dawn light by fingers/of flint" the quilt localizes both history and place, an anointment as Whiteman calls it of "grass and twilight air" against "bitter roots." "Star Quilt," art variously "purple, yellow, red like diamond suckers," so bids to serve as a medicine ("It covers my cuts") and another vital Native memento of resistance ("pushing back against the dust").

***

Memory throughout these different authorships inevitably assumes varying direction: idiom, image, different kinds of tribal connected femininity. There can be no doubt, however, of a shared will to remember Native heritage not only for time-past but time-present, the transition into the contemporary and even the future. In Harjo, Rose, Glancy, Tapahonso, and Blaeser, and those who have been their coevals, it has also to be said that the variorum of memory-voices achieves no less than its own claim to memorable register.

Notes

1 Joy Harjo, "Remember," *She Had Some Horses*, New York: Thunder's Mouth's Press, 1983, 40.
2 Kimberly Blaeser, "Dictionary for a New Century," *Apprenticed to Justice*, Cambridge, UK: Salt Publishing, 2007, 84.
3 Diane Glancy, "A Share of the Stair (or As I'm Talking I'm Becoming What I Say)," *Rooms: New and Collected Poems*, Cambridge, UK: Salt Publishing, 2005, 118.
4 In her Preface to *Blue Horses Rush In: Poems and Stories*, Tucson: The University of Arizona Press, 1997, xiii, Luci Tapahonso gives a perfect account of how oral storytelling can work: "Obvious advantages of oral storytelling are the expressions of the teller, the responses of the participants, and the gestures as well as the inflections in the voices. Although many the stories or jokes that can be told can be translated and relayed fairly well in written form, the clears sense of voices and characters is diminished in some ways, so that even though it's obvious when I tell a story that I'm not the protagonist or other person, the reader of the story may interpret it otherwise."
5 Luci Tapahonso, " All the Colors of Sunset," in Joy Harjo and Gloria Bird, eds., *Reinventing the Enemy's Language: Contemporary Native Women's Writings of North America*, New York: W.W. Norton, 1997, 325
6 Joy Harjo, *She Had Some Horses*. All page references are to this first edition.
7 Laura Coltelli, *Winged Words: American Indian Writers Speak*, Lincoln: University of Nebraska Press, 1992, 57.
8 Wendy Rose, "For the White Poets Who Would Be Indian," *Lost Copper*, Banning California: The Malki Museum, 1980, "Notes on a Conspiracy," *Going to War with All My Relations*, Flagstaff: Entrada, 1993.
9 Diane Glancy, *Claiming Breath*, Lincoln: University of Nebraska Press, 1992. Preface.

10 "Here I am Standing Beside Myself," as quoted before, helps explain the point – "My father said his grandfather fled Indian Territory … when he'd done something wrong." *Rooms*, 65

11 "The Stockyard Series: *Remuda*," *Rooms*, 33-8.

12 It is hard not to be conscious of the ongoing roster of this authorship. Names include Tiffany Midge (Hunkpapa Lakota), Susan Power (Dakota-Standing Rock), Ofelia Zepeda (Tohono O'odham), Heid Erdrich (Ojibway/Chippewa Santee Frazier), Carole LaFavor (Anishinaabe), Cinnamon Spear Kills First (Northern Cheyenne), Ernestine Hayes (Tlingit), Janice Gould (Maidu), Gwen Benaway (Chippewa/Métis), Layli Long Soldier (Oglala Lakota), Cedar Sigo (Suquamish) and Elissa Washuta (Cowiltz). Contemporary First Nation authors continue the reckoning in writers like Joanne Arnott (Métis), Tanya Tagaq (Inuk) and Therese Mailhot (Seabird Island).

13 Rayna Green, ed., *That's What She Said: Contemporary Poetry and Fiction by Native American Women*, Bloomington: University of Indiana Press, 1984, 117.

14 Paula Gunn Allen, *Shadow Country*, Los Angeles: American Indian Studies Center, UCLA, 1982,

15 nila northsun, and Jim Sagel, *Small Bones, Little Eyes*, Fallon: Duck Down Press, 1982.

16 Roberta Hill Whiteman, *Star Quilt*, Minneapolis: Holy Cow! Press, 1997.

Works Cited

Allen, Paul Gunn, *Shadow Country*, Los Angeles: American Indian Studies Center, UCLA, 1982.

Blaeser, Kimberly, *Apprenticed to Justice*, Cambridge, UK: Salt Publishing, 2007.

Coltelli, Laura, ed., *American Indians Writers Speak*, Lincoln: University of Nebraska Press, 1992.

Glancy, Diane, *Rooms: New and Collected Poems*, Cambridge, UK: Salt Publishing, 2005.

_____, *The Shadow's Horse*, Tucson: University of Arizona Press, 2003.

_____, *Claiming Breath*, Lincoln: University of Nebraska Press, 1992.

_____, *Lone Dog's Winter Count*, Albuquerque: West End Press, 1991.

Green, Rayna, ed., *That's What She Said: Contemporary Poetry and Fiction by Native American Women*, Bloomington: University of Indiana Press, 1984.

Harjo Joy, *An American Sunrise*, New York: W.W. Norton, 2109.

_____, *Crazy Brave: A Memoir*, New York: W.W. Norton, 2103.

_____, *How We Became Human: New and Selected Poems, 1975-2001*, New York: W.W. Norton, 2002.

_____, *The Woman Who Fell from the Sky*, New York: W.W. Norton, 2000.

_____, *She Had Some Horses*, New York: Thunder's Mouth Press, 1983.

_____, *The Last Song*, Las Cruces: Puerto del Sol, 1975.

Harjo, Joy, and Bird, Gloria, eds., *Re-inventing the Enemy's Language: Contemporary Native Woman's Writings of North America*, New York: W.W. Norton, 1997.

northsun, nila, and Jim Sagel, *Small Bones, Little Eyes*, Fallon: Duck Down Press, 1982.
Rose, Wendy, *The Halfbreed Chronicles & Other Poems*, Los Angeles: West End Press, 1985.
Tapahonso, Lucy, *Blue Horses Rush In: Poems and Stories*, Tucson: University of Arizona Press, 1997.
_____, *Sáanii Dahataal, the Women Are Singing: Poems and Stories*, Tucson: University of Arizona Press, 1993.
Whiteman, Roberta Hill, *Star Quilt*, Minneapolis: Holy Cow! Press, 1997.

15

A Native Sense of Existence: The Poetries of Simon Ortiz, Ray A. Young Bear, Tommy Pico

> I've spent a large part of my lifetime away from Acoma Pueblo –out there somewhere in America – away from the Acoma village area of Deetseyaamah where I grew up. But while I have physically been away from my home area, I have never been away in any absolute way …. Yet at the same time that we are away, we also continue to be absolutely connected socially and culturally to our Native identity. We insist that we as human cultural beings must always have this connection because it is the way we maintain a Native sense of Existence.
>
> Simon Ortiz, Preface, *Out There Somewhere* (2002)[1]

A Native sense of Existence. Whether Acoma Pueblo, or beyond, Simon Ortiz's phrase serves as an accommodating hallmark. Assuredly it holds for his own poetry but also for that of Ray Young Bear (Meskwaki) and Tommy Pico (Kumeyaay), writers for whom like Ortiz the voicing of first-hand specific existence, tribal and beyond-tribe, has been a wholly conscious impulse. Together they come close to forming a lineage, three kinds of Native existence, three poetries. To this end, helpfully, they each have delivered the one or another *ars poetica*.

"Creating Language" in Ortiz's *After and Before the Lightning* (1994) gives emphasis to language, best used, most risked, as much for how it creates the speaker-writer as it is the expressive instrument of that speaker-writer:

> To use a language,
> the speaker has to know
> its real bones, guts, blood,
> spirit, mind, heart.
> He has to know its pain
> and its joy.
> He has to know its creation.

And the only way he can
is to know
he is being created
as he speaks it.
He is a creator then
of that language.[2]

In *Black Eagle Child: The Facepaint Narratives (*1992*)*, Young Bear's autofiction which plays the borders of prose and verse in the persona of Edgar Bearchild, the emphasis falls upon custody of voice:

> For too long we have been misrepresented and culturally maligned by an ungrateful country of Euro-American citizens who have all but burned their own bridges to the past. I will not tolerate such transgressions of my being and character.[3]

In interview Tommy Pico, flâneur-like as to how to recreate voice from the street, from sex and pop music, and from the contrasting worlds of the Kumeyaay Viejas reservation of his California upbringing and the Brooklyn he moved to full time in 2018, the call is one of ventriloquy:

> I can make my voice do pretty much anything, so I try and write to my strengths and affect emotion with my voice. When I write I'm very conscious of how it's going to sound when it comes out of my mouth. I wouldn't write anything that felt disingenuous to say. I've also always been so reverent to people's voices …[4]

Idiom, in all three poets, differs greatly. For Ortiz it means for the most part the open line taken from both Pueblo speech-story and Whitman. Young Bear in *Black Eagle Child* manages a double or fused style of narrative, verse with non-verse, the both elided into affecting prose poetry. Pico in *Feed* (2019) works through verse-like sequences, racks of direct speech to the reader, street and rap colloquialism, asides, seeming fragments, teases, and Kumeyaay usages to food-speak. The respective poetries they offer, and the poetics that they assume for all their difference, share the discernible will to refuse any one expressive paradigm. At the same time they give confirmation of the ever widening range of Native poetry.[5]

***

Few poems by Ortiz better locate the image of maker and text than "A Story of How a Wall Stands" whose phrasing supplies the title for his landmark collection *Woven Stone* (1992). Understandably it has become one of his best-known compositions. That it bespeaks the seeming precariousness of Acoma existence and yet its durability immediately catches the eye:

> At Aacqu, there is a wall almost 400 years old which supports hundreds of tons of dirt and bones – it's a graveyard built on a steep incline – and it looks like it's about to fall down the incline but will not for a very long time. (145)

The note is personal, father-to-son:

> My father, who works with stone,
> says, "That's just the part you see,
> the stones which seem to be
> just packed in on the outside,"
> and with his hands puts the stone and mud
> in place. "Underneath what looks like loose stone,
> there is stone woven together."
> He ties one hand over the other,
> fitting like the bones of his hands
> and fingers. "That's what is
> holding it together." (145)

Insistence on "a certain texture," mud and stone carefully woven by palm or finger "until they become/the wall that stands a long, long time," implicitly summons Acoma genesis, lineage imaged as woven stone from across time by the hands of its makers. But it also implicitly writes in the poet as creative presence, practitioner of an analogous craft, as born out in a succession of collections.

Going For The Rain (1976) yields another time-map, one of Ortiz's travels from Acoma to Albuquerque and life lived under duress and at the existential edge. Train, bus, airport, bar, the Midwest, the South, East and West Coast supply itinerary coordinates in a voice at once accessible, even talkerly, yet shaped by darker shadows of drift and drugs. Dislocation marks the route, especially in "Last Night" (46) whose speaker lacks center or sustaining destination:

> New York City almost got me
> last night at Kennedy Airport.
> So messed up,
> making phone calls to places
> I can't remember.
>
> Just held on tight
> to my bag of poems, my life

fighting off sleep,
the moments that can swallow you
without your knowledge of where
you are disappearing to.

Finally, got a cab,
finally, got to a friend's place.
A phone call to you then,
lay on a carpet,
ate couple of good apples,
drank glass of bourbon,
and it was already morning. (46)

He does, however, manage a phone call to "you":

But, finally, I got to talk to you.
It was good, that part,
and I went to sleep on the floor
beside the phone and two apple cores. (46)

The self-gains, as the talking-voice relates them, are small but important, restorative, intimate, in the wake of feared self-disappearance.

"Spoken narrative" is how Ortiz designates *A Good Journey* (1977), whether Coyote poems ("Dostoevsky Coyote" he calls the trickster at one point), invitation-to-eat poems ("How to make a good chili stew"), or more travel-map poems ("Places We Have Been"). In "Irish Poets on Saturday and an Indian" (113) one especially hears the press of personal life – the talk of poetry, affection for the Blackfeet novelist and poet James Welch, memory of the buffalo, and the slippage within his own and other Native lives:

We bought each others drinks,
talked poetry talked about Welch,
Blackfeet from Montana, good poet,
that Indian chasing lost buffalo
through words, making prayers
in literary journals. Yeah,
strange word, drinking bourbon
and water and then beers. Tony,
one Irish poet, and Sydney,
the other Irish, who laughs deeply
at a name Tony says. Murphy,

Murphy Many Horses, laughing Irish
whiskey Indian, we laugh for the
sound of our laughter.
    And then,
I tell about the yet unseen translation
where Indians have been backed up into
and on long liquor nights, working
in their minds, the anger and madness
will come forth in tongues and fury. (113)

The pitch is rueful, plaintive, full of rage at history but also self-rage.

With *Fight Back: For the Sake of the People, for the Sake of the Land* (1980), true to the spirit of his title, Ortiz gives voice to his eco-politics of homeland and the recovery of community health. These, for the most part, act as story-poems, portraits of lives caught short by mining, corporate finagling, and behind both, the territorial dispossession of the Acoma and the tribes across the Southwest. As he says in "We Have Been Told Many Things but We Know This to be True" (35) – "The land. The people./They are in relation to each other./We are in a family with each other." In "Returning It Back, You Will Go On" (41-2) the indictment is explicit:

Corporate power companies
from the East and from the West
bought the processed uranium
from the corporate oil and mining companies
who minded the land.
That's Indian land …
the jail will not be enough
to hold all the nations of the People,
and they will have risen.
They will have risen. (41-2)

A poem like "Crazy Gook Indians" (13), with its shadowing of the Vietnam War, vividly captures the overlap of both Native and Asian savagist stereotypes.

Danny and Emmett got back from Vietnam
and went to work in the mines.
Danny said, in Section 30
One afternoon, we blasted
and my partner, Emmett, thought

we were back in Vietnam,
back in the tunnels,
after the enemy, you know.
He picked up that drill
like it was an M-60
and tried to defend us against
the shift boss who'd been in the Marines too.
I got Emmett quieted down
and held him in my arms for a while.
The boss just laughed
and later on I heard him laughing
with the superintendent
about the crazy gook Indians
on his shift.
I guess I should have let my partner
defend us against that Marine. (13)

"Crazy gook Indians" in the uranium mines succeed Asian "gooks" in their insurgent tunnels, two warrior populations literally positioned underground yet juxtaposed through Ortiz's evidentiary voice.

from Sand Creek (1981) voices earlier history and the toll to the tribes of Manifest Destiny and the inexorable march of the western frontier. Not one but two war memories again intersect, the 1860s massacre of Cheyenne and Arapaho in tribally-named Kiowa County, southeast Colorado, and again the Vietnam War in the persons of Native ex-combatants recovering at the VFA hospital, Fort Lyons, Colorado, during the 1970s. The Preface leaves no doubt of resolve:

> How to deal with history. That was the question on my mind when I began to write *from Sand Creek*. By *history* I meant the history that included me personally as a Native American, the history that included Native people and culture, the American history that I and other Natives sometimes felt foreign to. (6)

Ortiz so fashions a volume that aligns an American history that includes "me personally as a Native American" and an American history that does not.

"Grief memorizes the grass" reads an opening line. Ortiz precisely, and clinically, first sets out the bloodbath perpetrated on the Southern Cheyenne at Sand Creek on November 19, 1864. The ensuing lines specify the Rev. Colonel John W. Chivington and his well-armed Colorado Volunteers in despite of the flag given in 1863 to the Cheyenne leader Black Kettle by President Lincoln as token of Federal protection. To which is added the rider "By mid-1865, the Cheyenne and Arapaho People had been driven out of Colorado Territory." The poem's remembrance is to see from the vantage-point of subsequent search-and-destroy history, that of Vietnam, and in its wake, Native veteran rehabilitation at Fort Lyons. The damage Ortiz seeks to articulate lies as much of damage to mind and nerve as to body.

Both Sand Creek and Vietnam, the collection underscores, have inflicted grievous damage, peoples of two eras caught in historical wound, the one an America-at-home and the other an America-abroad of military conflict. "Remember My Lai," brought up at the outset, is made to parallel "Remember Sand Creek" two egregious massacres. Both bespeak iconic yet "raw" memory, "red-eyed and urgent." The introduction of the figure of Toby personifies the feeling of self-erasure ("Yes,/he is Indian./ He hides and tends/ the shape of his face"), war-trauma which causes his tongue to be "frozen," "frantic."

The further analogy deploys (and italicizes) that of "Buffalo ghosts," their power and their defeat by white hunting as remembered in tribal history:

> *Buffalo were dark rich clouds moving upon the rolling hills and plains of America. And then the flashing steel came upon bone and flesh.* (20)

Once again past violence haunts, buffalo "dark rich clouds" as against "flashing steel," revered beast as against recreational trophy.

Toby, as inaugural figure, haunts the La Junta Café, is advised by VA doctors "not to worry" though "sick" with evident post-traumatic stress disorder, stares into a window neurasthenically, and in memorial tribal manner "closely tends to his shadow." He serves, symptomatically, as the first among others. W. and Nez are to be heard singing within a Rocky Mountain vista of "Land and sky; flowers and generations." For Ortiz their melody means "summoning eternity" and even though they themselves "did not know how/they were patriots."

Billy, another of their fellow hospitalized, disappears ("Like his words,/ he could be anywhere"), a wounded drifter seeking "shadows" and for whom "Memory was his lost trail." The Polka Dot Kid has ended confused, in a skid-row hotel and not knowing whether he is in Amarillo or Denver. Dusty plays piano before the start of the movies at the VA hospital, his fingers blunt ("Throbbing/ bullets and aches") and for whom "Memory ... rattles in dry cells." Apache, a Korean War veteran, dreams freedom even in his confusion. The "man/who cried for his mother" causes Ortiz's own throat "to constrict." Oklahoma Boy sits slumped ("There is beauty/in his American face,/but the dread implanted/by the explosive/ in Asia denies it," the depression-sufferer whose un-voicing is given dedicated voice by the poet.

History attracts different kinds of remembrance. The silhouette of Sand Creek is replayed in references to World War II, then Korea and Vietnam. White settlement and its intrusions are noted ("Swedes, Germans,/Mennonites, Dutch,/ Irish, escaping Europe"). Depression, alcoholism, and the "persuasion and force" of the hospital persists. At the same time Ortiz does not overlook pointers to better health, better sources of memory. They lie in Sand Creek's "own flowers/and new grass," "the magpie," "corn," "rain," "quilts," and "young blood," and both the legacy of Black Kettle ("He swept his hand/all about them./The vista of the mountains/ was at his shoulder") and the resonating call of Walt Whitman to an America of spiritual health ("Whitman was a poet I loved").

Likewise, and on the one hand, the stigmata wounds not only to tribal body but to tribal land, is to be remembered as plentiful ("*The blood poured into the plains, steaming like breath on winter mornings*"). Hope, on the other hand, lies in cyclical repair ("*The breath rose in clouds and became the rain and replenishment*"). "Spring wind," alongside "flowers" and "new grass" give promise. For all, thereby, that *from Sand Creek* unsparingly memorializes historic Native injury, and its traverse from one American era to another, it also reminds of Ortiz's equally memorial belief in the continuing Native wellsprings of life. *from Sand Creek* remains one of Native poetry's greatly consequential voicings.

In the Preface to *After and Before the Lightning* (1994), with its account of the time he spent among the Lakota under conditions of winter cold and snow, Ortiz writes:

> When the poems came about and I wrote them, I felt like I was putting together a map of where I was in the cosmos. I'm not sure if "map" is the correct term, and I'm not certain if, as a writer and a poet, I was even successful in noting and expressing what I wanted and needed most of all: reassurance that by facing reality – winter and my life – I was doing the right thing. (xiv)

The key lies in the word "map," that of the poet in search not just of self-center but right idiom. Given the dips and breakages in his own life it is perhaps none too surprising that Ortiz opts for a species of absolute self-confrontation. That is, he makes the winter he spends at Rosebud Sioux Indian Reservation, among the Lakota, into a species of existential mirror, the South Dakota prairies as context for thinking through – and transposing into verse – his own meaning and that of the people and land within which he opts to spend his sojourn.

Out There Somewhere (2002), or as Ortiz says "away from Acoma Pueblo – out there somewhere in America," steers between the close-to-hand personal ("Be a good Buddhist in jail" he says in "Chant" 19) and indictment of stereotypes of live Native peoples. "Where are the Indians?" he asks in "Greatest Believers Greatest Disbelievers." Perhaps as great an accusation as any voiced by Ortiz is that which has led to the "invention" of Indians – the transposition of live bodies, live time and space, into some pan-Indian diorama of fantasy mask and figurine. His opening lines in the poem "Even 'The Indians' Believed," makes the point wryly, voice as colloquy:

> Indians were made up?
>
> Yeah.
>
> They became what people in Europe believed them to be?
>
> Indians,
>
> Indians?
>
> Yeah, Indians.
>
> Soon there were Indians all over the place. But mainly in the New World, especially in America! That's where they were seen the most.
> That's where they "belonged." That's where they were most Indian!
>
> Soon even "the Indians" believed they were "Indians."
> Soon even the "Indians" believed they were Indians.
>
> Nonetheless they were people.
> They were hanoh. They were people who were themselves.
> They were people who were their own people. (51)

Reading Ortiz here, as through the considerable roster of his other poetry, is to become aware of his commitment not only to legacy but to the quest for witness voice. The upshot recognizably bears urgency, unyielding in recognition of both tribal and personal fissure even as it honors Native arts of existence over death. "Indians all over the place" fits exactly, Ortiz himself a major contributor to the poet's voicing of past-into-present Native existence.

***

In his poem "the birds are housed in a small glass house" Ray A. Young Bear explicitly calls poetry "the act of remembering."[6] It could hardly better hold for *Black Eagle Child: The Facepaint Narratives* (1992), the writing by which he has become best-known. Closely autobiographical and cast as verse-prose, it works as a cross-over of poem, diary, letter, dream, ceremony, and 1960s-and-after allusion to popular culture and music. That the text rewrites even as it derives from Young Bear's life in, and occasionally beyond, the Meskwaki Tribal Settlement (not reservation) of his own raising in Tama County, Iowa, is unmistakable. But always the effect is of poetry even in the narrative prose, whether Young Bear has Edgar voice the gallery of event within his career, or the literal politics of America, or the Meskwaki language in parallel with English.

Black Eagle Child has every reason to be read as poetry alongside the more formally recognizable verse of *Manifestation Wolverine: The Collected Poetry of Ray Young Bear* (2015) and the collections from which it is drawn like *Winter of the Salamander* (1979) *The Invisible Musician* (1990) and *The Rock Island Hiking Club* (2001). Across the span of November 1965-Winter 1989, the sixteen wry-funny, sometimes angry, memory-panels work as though working circle even as they look to be sequential. In this way, tribal-centered, and always toughly unsentimental, the poetic ledgering rounds into the one expressive whole.

The very conception is usefully signaled half way into the text. In 1975, in his twenties and like his begetter, Edgar applies for a creative writing fellowship from the Athens-based Maecenas Foundation. He sees this as written "sarcastically," a "vindictive application," his poet's revenge on institutions often inimical to Native creativity. How, then, for Edgar as memorialist to fully "speak" Black Eagle Child's settlement life?

The response is to give voice to past but also contemporary ancestry, his wise-traditional grandmother or "Nokomis," his parents Tony and Clotelde Bearchild, his partner/wife Selena Buffalo Husband, his uncle Winston Principal Bear, his different Paintface relatives but cousin Ted Paintface above all, and each different growing-up and adult compeer from Settlement to College and back to Settlement. Other dynasties enter, notably from the Kingfisher, Sturgeon, Hummingbird, Fix-King and Beaver clans. Masquakie and Fire-Keeper/Star-Medicine creation stories and star and ghost mythologies preside even as they vie with missionary but distant "white" Christianity ("To me,/the Spirits were ever-present regardless/of ceremony"). Iowa geography become iconic, whether nearby Why Cheer township, schools, diagonal railway tracks, river-bottoms with their periodic flooding, and in the distance Grinnell and Des Moines. Each holds the equations of his existence.

Above all, the Settlement as existence signifies, its episodes and contradictions ("While we were a 'tribe' in every respect,/it was unconscionable to help another/individual, family, or clan achieve/any degree of success in their public endeavors"). At the same time it looks to the kind of continuity advocated, paradoxically, at Thanksgiving by the ceremony-presiding grandfather of his cousin Ted Paintface ("He concluded/Indians basically had little to be thankful for/on this national holiday, but what was crucial/was continuation of our culture"). Each intimacy of this community existence, its spite or occasional uproariousness, not only fill but give lived variety to the text's speaking memory. That extends into various initials denoting status like EBNO ("Enrolled But In Name Only") or EBMIW ("Enrolled But Mother Is WHITE"). It takes another turn in Henrietta Youthman's language-confusion as to whether or not a white farmer is talking dirty to her. Tribal existence, on this account, comes over as fond but contrarian, even darkly comic.

In the opening sequences *Black Eagle Child* looks to the pluses and minuses of ceremony. The Thanksgiving Party at Weeping Willow Elementary uses improvised gifts of painted eggs and mission surplus. Edgar's recalls his familiarity with drink-to-death friends. In the company of Ted, and Ted's war-hero uncle Clayton Carlson Paintface, there is the hallucinogenic *na qwa o ni* "praying ceremony," otherwise known as Star Medicine yet with a picture of Jesus Christ on the wall. The mix of high solemnity and near-farce continues. Black Eagle "word-songs" accompany Edgar's upset stomach on eating the relevant herbs and need to urinate. "Visions and ghosts," real or imagined, align with motley-dressed tribal celebrants like John Louis and Percy Jim. Ceremony so yields its ironic menu.

Edgar invokes the memory of his three-years-later autobiographical launch into writing, a SciFi fantasy of extra-planetary Scandinavian settlers in the Midwest decried by his writing professor at Luther College. Lost writing notes are involved. A failed first-love with Dolores Fox-King occurs as "Baby Love" by the Supremes plays on the car radio. Other remembrance calls up similar disjuncture. Visiting Ontario tribes-people bear witness to the ancestor-village that simply and mysteriously died. The story is told of Brook Grassleggings who inveigles Junior into a love-tryst only to be revealed as a hermaphrodite. Edgar's time in student and LSD "Jefferson Airplane" mode at Pomona College ("it was an era of war-protest – and drugs") plays against his mother's affecting letters with small amounts of cash enclosed. In Ted Paintface's voice there is recall of California drift and intending return to Black Eagle Child. A despairing white man offers to have himself killed for money. In Carson Two Foot's voice the memory is revived of 1908 allotment practice and meagre government pay-outs. Each is told accoutred in asides, tics and flourish of memory, Edgar in poet's voice as himself source of existential disclosure.

This register continues in Edgar's maybe out-of-body experiences with Selene near his geodesic riverfront home (built courtesy of Maecenas Foundation money). Is it a supernatural light cluster or some random strobe ray? He remembers Yakima Pat "Dirty" Red Hat, revered tribal singer killed in a crash in 1975 as Edgar and friends form the group The Young Lions ("we sang songs of commemoration"). He recalls the vexed Grassleggings dynasty with its hugely overweight, waddling witch-broodmare mother ("Mathylde Hi-na – better known as Patty Jo") who somehow doubles as *curandera* amid her differently fathered hooligan offspring.

He thinks back to his role in the *Black Eagle Child Quarterly* as tribal publication and report of Claude Youthman throwing a cantaloupe in court when arrested for contesting Iowa state's reneging on construction of twenty new Settlement houses. He also remembers publication, with the teacher Lorna Bearcap, of the Weeping Willow Manifesto against petty tribal sleaze-politics. Finally, he has a vision of the haunted alcoholic decline and expiration of Ted Paintface. Each turn of existence, voices within the one voice, Young Bear inscribes with assured flair.

This droll menu, and its filtering into Settlement awareness ("Twenty-four hours after anything occurred, it was recollected"), gives *Black Eagle Child: The Paintface Narratives* a status to relish. "Memory starts under the earth" writes Young Bear in "Emily Dickinson, Bismarck and the Roadrunner's Inquiry"[7] The line connects illuminatingly to *Black Eagle Child*, the Meskwaki vista of, tribe, community and self made over into quite one of the most engaging poetries of a Native sense of Existence.

***

Tommy Pico's *Feed* completes the tetralogy (a term Pico himself guys as top-heavy) begun in *IRL* (2016), *Nature Poem* (2018) and *Junk* (2019), each a folder in the portrait of the artist as gay, indigenous and a reservation-to-city American contemporary. Under the persona of Teebs Pico writes as though entrammeled in different velocities of encounter. They implicate him in the highs and instabilities of homocentric desire, pop-culture from Internet to Beyoncé, classics from Plato to Orwell, politics from historic white-settler predation against the tribes to the warring Middle East of Iraq and Syria, and throughout, New York City as always energy and den. The upshot might have given way to over-hurried diary or annotation. In fact, and in degree, Pico brings all four volumes into a one composite and widely thought exhilarating scroll.

To arrive at *Feed* does not necessarily require readings of its predecessors but, however freestanding, they provide corridors, entry-points. *IRL*, with its online abbreviation for In Real Life, develops a Brooklyn-rooftop view of Teebs's coming-of age, Joycean splices on queerness and body, media news and ads, pop music snippets, US internal colonial history, and lyrically, the memory of Kumeyaay song. *Nature Poem*, again written in short paragraphs of observation and aside, begins in the refutation that Native-heritaged poets must write Nature ("That's not the kind of nature I would write a poem about" 7). How to decipher identity lived fragmentarily under city lights, and in which punk and rock, boyfriends and redress to name-calling ("I'm a weirdo NDN faggot" 2) jostle with remembrance of tribe? *Junk*, pitched in couplets, tackles accumulation, be it consumerism, gay, bi- or other sex, twenty-four-hour news cycle, fast food, therapy, land grab, and each and all surge of "information." Again the detail is vivid, eclectic, dexterous in pacing, Pico's bid for self-center in a culture of seductive peripheries. *Feed*, while it exerts full claim to its own respective auspices, shares a swathe of the components and processes which make up each preceding volume.

The title noun of *Feed* offers Pico's *mot clef*, the challenge to make sense of modernity's ever-accelerating "feeds" and the appetites it arouses or denies. Literal city menus, dishes, eateries, kitchens, sugar rushes, his mother's cooking, stores like Whole Foods, abound in contrast with "the Food Distribution program on Indians Reservations." Headlines spin, whether "MASS GRAVES OF IMMIGRANTS FOUND IN TEXAS" (57), "THIS WHAT A NUCLEAR STRIKE WOULD LOOK LIKE IN THE HEART OF MANHATTAN" (73), or "MUSIC IS MY BOYFRIEND" (78). Time-space and godhead becomes conversation, whether "The Gaia hypothesis," "The Earth Similarity Index" and the exo-planets, or the Black Hole cosmos of Stephen Hawking. Frank O'Hara-style ambles map the street, the traffic, the populous box, of New York as metropole. TV and radio report word of the Proud Boys and the Trump White House's Kellyanne Conway.

A whole paradigm, allied fragments, builds into the one shared unfolding. Within such Teebs as Pico's proxy voice searches for a sense of how best to meet, to nutrify, his own hungers, be it for lovers, an end to loneliness, or the ambiguities of literary fame (risingly so given book successes and tours). Early into the account in this regard, now citied to a fault, he looks back to origins:

> Once, I wrote about being ancestrally from a desert
> that drought made me restless
> searching for a nourishing territory ...(10)

That "searching" summons other vectors. The flowered Meadow Walk, previously the High Line between 23rd and 25th Street, Manhattan, a "feed" of seasonal flowering amid urbanization, provides the backdrop for the break-up of his romance with Leo. Memories crowd in of their road and food trips to Oaxaca and further Mexico. Wilkes, his close woman friend with whom he shares spliffs and exchanges on friendship and death, crosses gender divides. News, to his consternation, drifts in from the rez ("My cousin died today"). Each feed compounds the existence of the other.

American tribal histories add their historical table. "What's this town called?" he asks, giving the rejoinder "I'm not asking you/I'm asking them." His list of "them" is iconographic

> The Ohlone, Costanoan, Muwekma,
> Duwamish, Suqamish, Muckleshoot,
> Shawnee, Lenni-Lenape, Tocobaga, Moscoso,
> Multomah, Anishinaabe, Ojibwa,
> Ottawa, Potawatomi. (61)

Beyond Brooklyn or Chelsea, or the West Coast, these constitute yet another poetry, this one of indigenous name and the vast human worlds within each.

As Pico/Teebs shows his digressive hand, word-play, puns, sex and street usage, or ponders tunes and lyrics for the inner as well as outer ear from nineteen music tracks, "XO" by Beyoncé to "Up the ladder to the Roof" by The Supremes, he persists in pondering which feeds to seize upon and believe. He can even speculate with "Imagine being fed, and feeding./ Imagine getting what you need" (76). The voice of a gay bi-coastal Native writer, heir to both tribal and colonial language, often enough lonely amid human plenty, his query may well run "Shall I be a poem for you?" (10). *Feed* indicates, in its speed and proliferation, a resounding yes.

***

A Native sense of Existence. Poetries. The terms are meant to go beyond simply the one poem or even collection. Rather, be it Ortiz, Young Bear or Pico, they carry the sense of the author who sees his life as in equal part "the poem." That might not be thought unique. Whitman or Ginsberg come to mind. But all three give making poetry of existence a distinctive coloring, their own hugely expressive testimony and stamp.

Notes

1 Simon Ortiz, *Out There Somewhere*, Tucson: University of Arizona Press, 2002, 109-10.

2 Simon Ortiz, *After and Before the Lightning,* Tucson: University of Arizona Press, 1994.
3 Ray Young Bear, *Black Eagle Child: The Facepaint Narratives*, Iowa City: University of Iowa Press, 1992, 139-40.
4 Tommy Pico, *Interview*, with Tara Kenny, On-line, March 27, 2018.
5 Something of this range I have tried to indicate in Chapter 2.
6 Ray Young Bear, "the birds are housed in a small glass house," Unpublished poem. Cited in Robert Franklin Gish, *Beyond Bounds: Cross-Cultural Essays on Anglo, American Indian & Chicano Literature*, Albuquerque: University of New Mexico Press, 1996, 86.
7 Ray Young Bear, "Emily Dickinson, Bismarck and the Roadrunner' Inquiry," in Duane Niatum, ed., *Harper's Anthology of 20th Century Native American Poetry*, San Francisco: HarperCollins Publishers, 1988, 270-5. Republished in *The Invisible Musician*, Minneapolis: Holy Cow! Press, 1990.

Works Cited

Ortiz, Simon, *Out There Somewhere*, Tucson: University of Arizona Press, 2002.
______, *Men on the Moon: Collected Stories*, Tucson: University of Arizona Press, 1999.
Telling and Showing Her: The Earth, the Land, Buffalo: Just Buffalo Center, 1995.
______, *After and Before the Lightning*, Tucson; The University of Arizona Press, 1994.
______, *Woven Stone*, Tucson: University of Arizona Press, 1992.
______, *Fightin': New and Collected Stories*, Tucson: University of Arizona Press, 1983.
______, *From Sand Creek: Rising in This Heart Which Is America*, Tucson: The University of Arizona Press, 1981.
______, *Fight Back: For the Sake of the People. for the Sake of the Land*, Albuquerque: New Mexico Institute for Native Development, 1980.
______, *A Good Journey*, Tucson: University of Arizona Press, 1977.
______, *Going for the Rain*, New York: Harper and Row, 1976.
Pico, Tommy, *Feed*, Portland: Tin House, 2019.
______, *Junk*, Portland: Tin House, 2018.
______, *Nature Poem*, Portland: Tin House, 2017.
______, *IRL*, Minneapolis: Birds, Lic, 2016.
Young Bear, Ray, *Manifestation Wolverine: The Collected Poetry of Ray Young Bear,* Open Road Media, 2015. This collection also includes three previous volumes, *Winter of the Salamander* (1979), *The Invisible Musician* (1990), and *The Rock Island Hiking Club* (2001).
______, *Black Eagle Child: The Facepaint Narratives*, Iowa City: University of Iowa Press, 1992.

16

Oklahoma International: Jim Barnes and the Sites of Imagination

Bones beneath my feet, I make
a song for all of them.
"A Song for All of Them"

A Season of Loss (1985)[1]

In another country, I push
aside the leaves, and my own loss begins

to fade ...
"In Another Country"

The Sawdust War (1992)[2]

Wherever I go, it seems I never get too far away from home
but what I am reminded of it.

On Native Ground: Memoirs and Impressions (1997)[3]

Issish ibakana, a Choctaw phrase Jim Barnes himself glosses as "mixed-blood from Oklahoma" in his fine-grained prose and verse autobiography, *On Native Ground: Memoirs and Impressions*, offers a point of departure (169). For if he has dwelt fondly upon his American family plait of Native, Welsh and English origins, at the same time it has been accompanied by the insistence on not being bound to any single categorization. To his often self-acknowledged consternation this includes Native American Writer. Rather, with Native America but one realm of lineage, Barnes has given his now considerable range of poetry, fiction, life-writing and discursive work to an unfolding variorum of sites both in and beyond America.

These different geographies of his life, moreover, provide a double-seam, physically lived-in sight and sound yet always the figurative landscape of feeling or memory. They begin for Barnes with the Great Southwest, as he calls it, the

Somerfield of his birth in eastern Oklahoma in 1933 and hard-scrub upbringing in LeFlore County's Fourche Maline and Holson Creek. It was there, during a Depression-era and World War II boyhood with parents pressed to find ranch and herding work, and obliged, albeit within a limited perimeter, to move the family from one house to another (he speaks of them as "gray" in *On Native Ground*), that he acquired his poet's abiding sense of the importance of site as at once exterior but intricately, and always, inward. A brief poem like "Surveying near Ellsworth, Kansas" in the collection *La Plata Cantata* (1989) succinctly gives emphasis to the point:

> All that's left is hard,
> the bone-dry creek,
> the knife shade of a single tree,
> the prairie burned brown by a screaming summer sun,
> and a lone marker,
> stone, belonging god-knows-where:
> *scalped 1853.*[4]

Oklahoma's *tierra* of smallholding, farm, pasture, bluff, ridge, pond, tree, river, orchard, wind, bird and animal life, season and skyline, not to mention the small-town life of high street and school, sheriff's office and jail, church and store, and each residual Choctaw burial mound and arrowhead, has long featured for him as a first archive. Of all the sites in Barnes's poetry none matches in weight of association, a timeline of mind as much as place, and whether literal topography, or the layers of Native and settler history, or his own arriving consciousness. Even so he has resisted any temptation to romanticize Oklahoma, however beguiling its Choctaw and Anglo making along with the human *métissage* to which it has given rise. In this respect he invites comparison with a range of contemporary Native authorship taken up with mixed dynasty and the migrations and sitings that has entailed.

Restless, chafed, stir-hungry, in 1951 he would step westward from Summerfield to Eugene, Oregon, where he had family, and to employment in logging through the years 1954-9 in the Cascades and Willamette Valley. The Pacific Northwest's mountain forestry, nature and commerce, and work with chain, rig and team, again has stayed with him, a vital next source of place in his writing. It was in Oregon that the call to writing, long nascent, became yet more emphatic: the emerging first stories and verse, the early imitations of Faulkner and Hemingway. A liberal arts degrees from Oklahoma State in 1964, with a triple major in English, Drama, and French and a double minor in German and Journalism, and then an MA and PhD from the University of Arkansas in 1965 and 1970, with a brief teaching stint at Northeastern Oklahoma State University, led to more than three decades (1970-2003) as Professor of English and Comparative Literature at Truman State University, Kirksville, Missouri, but also of creative writing. Missouri, like Oklahoma, becomes another ambient Mid-west of townships and people, rivers and land. His editorship of the literary and translation journal, *The Chariton Review*, and the long-term outlet it has provided for creative work, would travel with him to Brigham Young University when in 2004 he took up a Distinguished Faculty position.

Beyond America he has made little secret of relishing his stints as overseas author-resident. The trajectory includes successive stays at Lake Como's Bellagio on Rockefeller Foundation Fellowships (1990, 2003), a Senior Fulbright year at the University of Lausanne (1993-4), guest residencies and funding in Munich, (1995) and then Stuttgart (2000), and the two Camargo Fellowships at Cassis within the painterly landscape of Arles and *le midi* in general (1996, 2001). The French capital has exerted a uniquely powerful influence, the inspiration for the volume simply called *Paris* (1997). Other France holds, as in *Visiting Picasso* (2007), most notably the Provence of Vauvenargues, Arles and La Ciotat, closely worked personal observation within the silhouette of encompassing larger cultural reference. A retrospect, with additions, is to be met in *Sundown Explains Nothing: New and Selected Poems* (2019). In all, the international span of Oklahoma, Oregon, Missouri, Italy, Switzerland, Germany and France, the sense of site, America or Europe, has been of the essence.

***

But another desideratum has equally always held for Barnes, the call for and to craft, a deliberated force of compositional style, and whether for his own writing or that of others. Citing his longtime editorial experience at *The Chariton Review*, he berates in *On Native Ground* all contemporary tendency to "pretentious self-absorption," the absence of regard for "complication," "irony," "vantage point" and "tone." This need to be concerned with "the art of making," he has gone on insisting, serves as the prophylactic against being "doomed to have only subject to work with." A contribution to the Dictionary of Literary Biography's *Contemporary Authors Autobiography Series* (1997) amplifies on "form and structure" as literary prerequisite, the need for the "true sentence" within "this world of Po-biz."[5]

Beginning from two slim and soon out-of-print verse collections, *This Crazy Land* (1980) and *The Fish on Poteau Mountain* (1980), these concerns of craft, the close, deliberated working with image and voice and with the pathways of memory and forms of unsentimental cultural nostalgia, have clearly been acted upon in his own writing. Each subsequent collection adds confirmation, whether *The American Book of The Dead* (1982), *A Season of Loss: Poems* (1985) and *La Plata Cantata: Poems* (1989) – the three re-issued in a single volume as *On A Wing of The Sun* (2001) – or *The Sawdust War* (1992) along with the publication of *Paris* and *Visiting Picasso.*[6] There needs to be added story-writing like his personal favorite "The Reapers," and the considerable span of anthology and international journal publication from *American Poetry Review* to *Paris Review, Kenyon Review* to *Poetry Wales, Ploughshares* to *Italian Americana*. Barnes, throughout, has fused a commitment to verse as both "life" and well-wrought urn, the drama of the one or another site but always within an idiom assiduously honed to match.

In a general sense Barnes's poetry might be thought to belong somewhere inside a long elegaic tradition threading forward from the Horatian Ode. That has links to the late-Augustan English poetry of Gray and Collins with, in their wake, Wordsworth (whose "Nothing can bring back the hour/of Splendour in the grass …" he cites in his memorial World War II poem "Decades," *On a Wing of the Sun*, 144). The cautionary pastorals of Thomas Hardy and Robert Frost can be added, along with the language-play of Dylan Thomas. The wry-cautionary poems of the veteran Munich writer Dagmar Nick in volumes such as *Summon and Sign* (1980) and *Numbered Days* (1998), for which Barnes has acted as admiring and deservedly prize-winning translator, equally come into play. The monograph which arose from his doctoral thesis, published as *The Fiction of Malcolm Lowry and Thomas Mann: Structural Tradition* (1990), strikes a shared note. The emphasis falls on how both authors explore the destructive element in human affairs, life interpreted, not to say magnified, through a glass darkly. Nor, for a moment, is this to overlook other shaping influences from a Native sense of word, be it spoken or written, or an array of other European, British (to include Welsh) and American literary sources.

None of this, at any point, is to lessen Barnes's own strong personal distinctiveness of vision or style right across, to date, his ten or so published volumes of poetry. But a number of shared perspectives can be discerned: the contemplative temper, the recognition of the ironies and sway of time, the care for exactness of image. All necessarily act, and interact, as markers in his poetry's engagement with its different sites.

***

On Native Ground, at once life-writing and credo and typically meticulous in its voicing, supplies Barnes's own sense of career. The sitings in play each are given their recognition, whether Native America, the Oklahoma and Missouri of his upbringing and professional career, the Pacific Northwest, or the successive locales of Europe. For immediate purposes, one begins with indigenous legacy less to identify Barnes as some exclusively Native author than to emphasize how that aspect of his heritage has richly, and movingly, drawn his imagination.

Few do more so than the poem invoked in the opening chapter, namely "Contemporary Native American Poetry" (*The American Book of The Dead*). Therein Barnes offers a species of ironically titled, yet respectful and admiring, witness. For the poem's speaker, Native history may look fugitive, a one-remove from his own time and place. That history, however, lies wholly, and inescapably, engrained in his consciousness. The stanzas bear re-quotation:

For one thing, you believe it:
the skin chewed soft enough to wear,
the bones hewn hard as a totem
from hemlock. It's a kind of scare-

crow that will follow you home nights.
You've see it ragged against a field,
but you seldom think, at the time,
to get there it had to walk through hell. (*Wing*, 80)

The imagery gives off the perfect memorial resonance. The buffalo leather acts as a mnemonic for both food and clothing. Bones, hemlock-hard like a "totem," call up tribal ceremony. The well-judged hyphenation, and then the line-break, of "scare-crow" summons the crow as both warning emblem and trickster icon. As to "Native poetry" itself, that, indeed, and in its every inclusive implication of culture, has been to keep Native word, Native meaning, vibrant against history's nightmare. How, by implication, not to think of "relocations" such as the 1838 Cherokee Trail of Tears or 1862 Navajo Long March? These, and other enforced marches, literally were "to walk through hell" and to seek survival against odds of disease, each and every act further of dispossession. The history implied has its one-sided encoding in Manifest Destiny or the winning of the West. However so, Barnes, at the same time, far from implies simply loss, or even evisceration. This is Native continuance against all of history's field line. Little wonder the opening line gives the certifying assurance of "For one thing you can believe it," testimony to "Native poetry" as intimately felt and dwelt-in history.

With "A Song for All of Them" (*A Season of Loss*) Barnes again blends a dual sense of place and time, the poem's first-person voice pitched as though to speak to remembered tribal voices. An immediately met with Nature, likewise, doubles with Nature as the continuum of bones, bodies, ghosts, dust, sky, song and name:

Hills where my father hid the bones
lie dark about me. I look for
trails hacked hard in trees and lined
in stones all years war with. I am
here this one night to find the farthest
corner of the sky, to place my body
one with earth, sky, to talk with ghosts
long silent, long dark .....
Bones beneath my feet, I make
a song for all of them. My name,
earth name, is sacred as the sun.
My name goes with me out of this world. (*Wing*, 132)

The sense of land, "hills," as the tribal repository of both body and spirit, has long been a feature of Barnes' poetry. The "trails" of the poem thus point to entry into both past habitation (flint knife, bears, hunters) and unfolding time (ghosts, bones). These fold into the speaker's sense of his "earth name," its signification of arrival, existence, and future exit from the world. A one name, as may be, it is linked by the poem into the many, a "sacred" tribal sense of being bound up in the encompassing larger inscription and inerasability of all Native nomenclature.

"Ghost Fog" (*A Season of Loss*, *Wing*, 164), a species of reverie set in Palo Duro Canyon, summons the dying of Poor Buffalo, hunted nineteenth-century Comanche fighter. The "false dawn" of a present-day Tule Creek camp (near to Texas's Prairie Dog Town at the fork of the Red River) locates the poem inside the one time scheme. But another presses close from behind, one of "ancient campfires," the pitch of "an eagle-bone whistle," the "flap of sacred owl-skin," and the bones both of Poor Buffalo and his Tonkawa enemy K'ya-been. Within the immediate "dark dawn" reverie, confirms the poem, a "hundred years flowed back," present and earlier time, together with site, intricately joined. The "heavy smell of a prairie dog town," thereby, abuts a "shadow world," the uneasy cohabitation down through history of white settler and tribal Texas. But as memory steps back from the campsite into a ceremonial "place to die" for Poor Buffalo so, once more, present-time noisily intrudes:

Then out of the pitch black west
a low and rumbling thunder set me straight.
Here was now: a trucker, damn his tunneled eyes,
Barreling-ass down the Amarillo-Lubbock run. (*Wing*, 164)

"Here was now" indeed runs the accompanying, and accusing, cryptic gloss. A historic tribal death, a sense of land, the playback of memory, have all become inhumed within, or beneath, modernity's speed, the "low and rumbling thunder" of the truck upon the oil-fumed Amarillo-Lubbock highway. The camp serves as both location and chronology, two specifics of place and time and, at least by implication, all the human inter-layers between.

With "In Memory of a Day Nobody Remembers: September 26, 1874" (*A Season of Loss*, *Wing*, 114) Barnes looks to actual history, the attack under Colonel Ranald Slidell Mackenzie (1840-89) of the Fourth United States Cavalry upon peaceably encamped Kiowas and Comanches in Palo Duro Canyon and the next-day slaughter of more than a thousand of their horses at Tule Creek. MacKenzie had fought as a Union officer, led black troops in the Civil War, and in the wake of the so-called Red River War and the defeat of southern Plains tribes like the Comanches, Kiowas and Apaches eventually taken over regional command of the Black Hills down to Texas in the wake of George Armstrong Custer's death at the Battle of Little Big Horn in 1876. It is not Mackenzie, however, who is the subject of this dirge, but rather Poor Buffalo, Kiowa leader, and those like him prejudicially designated "Indian raiders." His death, as that of his comrades, remains ethereally in the air, spirit remainder in the face of all the Texas-Oklahoma land grab.

Barnes opens "In Memory of a Day" on a note of "ubi sunt?" but one colloquially pitched – "Who is left to recall the sacred earth/where Poor Buffalo bit the dust?" (*Wing* 114). He works back to the historic skirmish, and then the killings, through the local spectacle of "Town Indians drunk on Chock and Thunderbird." These addled tribal descendants have become lost to the hollow log creation story of the Kiowa (famously imagined in Scott Momaday's *The Names*), to the life ritual of the sun dance, and above all, to "the massacre/of men, and horses dead." The word *massacre* is fittingly deployed for what has occurred, the brute white-military assault on both warriors and steeds. Invoking yet other figures of tribal resistance, Isatai, Maman-ti and K'ye-been, the poem enjoins them to ghost-dance their way into the mellowing, almost Keatsian, autumnal leaves. For a moment the tribal dead might thus live again, their presence caught in Nature's own evanescent beauty:

> Dance, ghosts, among the yellow leaves
> Before they turn to dust. (*Wing,* 114)

Almost all of Barnes's Native-referenced, or perhaps more accurately, Native-shadowed, poems in *A Season of Loss* make use of this associative imagery of bones, runes, stones, flint and, most notably, glyph. The poetry, thereby, offers as much a temporal as physical topography, an implied tribal scale both of chronometer and site. "Bone Yard" (*Wing*, 106) operates exactly, and engagingly, in this way. Two contrastive images of a "hundred" buffalo, their bodies seemingly "live" though slowed by sludge, and then truly remnant and skeletal as though having become a graveyard, give the poem's opening:

> A hundred buffalo
> knee-deep in sludge.
>
> Bones bleached to pebbles
> and white sand. *(Wing*, 106)

This might almost be haiku, the totemic buffalo slowed, destroyed, bone-exposed and whitened, and finally reduced to "pebbles/and white sand." Yet within the "long-spent bones," "this dried waterhole," and "the land's cracked hide" – a nice elision of buffalo hide and earth – and the dead trees, sounds can be imagined to echo from earlier herd, and so tribal, life. At a prior time man and beast have met within a shared order of Nature, a shared chain of being. The poem speaks of the tramping "ghosts of hoofs," "hot wind," the remembered live stillness of the beasts in the "dead of winter." The dynamism of these animals persists even as they are seen through their present desiccation. The prairie's memorial "bone yard" notwithstanding, the poem winningly insists upon the re-embodied and hovering buffalo spirit of life.

"Paiute Ponies" (*Wing*, 107), using a shared contrast, looks to these tribal horses as ancestral energy, beauty or physique, and yet to be set against the arriving contemporary diesel truck. Their silhouette stands sharp against "a ringed moon." The ancient "tracks" may have become yet another modern highway, but one which leads into Nevada's tribally named Winnemucca. No explicit Native allusion is used other than in the title but the implication is unmistakable, the perennial within the given moment, an old power of site within the new. The middle stanza suggests precisely this overlap, almost as though a haunting:

> Mane and tail hanging vertical as ice,
> they sleep dead centuries,
> or if ponies dream they dream. (*Wing*, 107)

Not unlike W.B. Yeats's swans at Coole, or Wallace Stevens' thirteen blackbirds, Barnes's Paiute ponies carry time in their very composure. Even the truck fails to impede their continuance:

> The diesel warns again, begins its roar, passes.
> They raise their heads like automatons, blink,
> then drop once more into centuries or dreams. (*Wing*, 107)

These closing lines, roaring diesel truck set against ponies, give the perfect synopsis. Modernity's engine speed is almost mocked by the Paiute-ancestral timeline, each pony its own law of motion, full of enduring dream and even insouciance. The impact borders on the magical.

An implicit Native seam similarly runs through two Barnes poems of the Arkansas-Oklahoma border, both with settings tied into the Ouchita Mountain range. In "Trying To Hide Out on Rich Mountain" (*Wing*, 120), the poem opens with a mixed report on the mountain's history: a well-known Dutch inn flattened to bedrock, "lightning" lizards, ruin, "rotting moss and fresh crap," "a Caterpillar's track." These provide the backdrop for the speaker's own parlous emotional or psychological condition, be it the lies which have made up his life, or the hope to fool "the woman that you love this late" with a "phoney suicide," or his retreat to the mountain as escape or camouflage. The panorama, however, does not stop there. It looks to the "weekend tourists out of Tulsa," their calling cards spent beer cans and the bar-room music of "hard rock about mountains they will/never have to climb." But from beyond this wry complicity of commercially intruded-upon mountain, or of the speaker-self as against the weekenders, the eye opens to the wider vista of day and sky:

> The day stays open.
> Wide. Wide as all the skies your forebears watched
> eagles in. You wonder if you'd know their kind.
> But it's too hot to pray Indians out of stone. (*Wing*, 120)

The allusion to a domain in which "your forbears" saw soaring eagles signifies an altogether greater, and better, field of vision, one of implied grace and sweep of spirit, in all the perfect counter-balance. The closing notion, even so, of a Southwest heat torpor to inhibit "pray[ing] Indians out of stone" acts as both a sense of self-loss (the irony, surely, caught up in the name "Rich Mountain") and self-reprimand.

"Stopping on Kiamichi Mountain," from *The American Book of The Dead* (*Wing*, 95-6) offers a companion piece in which the one kind of outdoor hunting shadows the other. The speaking voice is all latter-day business: his Mustang driven past the sign for Sulphur Spring, the canyon below with its "snakes and tarantulas as fierce/as fire in jack pines," the desultory trail, the spring reduced to a trickle and full of bad sulfur smell, the incoming thunder and the tornado it portends, and the beckoning further sign for Antlers (the Oklahoma township in Pushmaha County). The scene is one of impending threat, a possible tornado or twister. Can the prospect of a beer, or even a binge-like "drunk," ease the sense of foreboding and "put a handle on the wind"? The transition is once more into other time, an Oklahoma of shared dangerous "wind" but whose indigenous name bears the necessary warning. The point, the contrast, is brought to the closing sequence:

> You head the Mustang straight into
> the dark and pray the only times you ever
> do that you know the wind by Indian name. (*Wing*, 96)

To the one degree or another the "Native" poems throughout *A Season of Loss* work in this manner, indigeneity or at least its remembrance, as a kind of collaborative and working substratum. A few, undoubtedly, are more explicit. "Song of I-see-o" (*Wing*, 113), told as though in the voice of a celebrated Kiowa warrior scout, invokes Rainy Mountain as pathway into the Fourth World. "Four Things Choctaw" (*Wing*, 121-2) – *Nashoba* (wolfsong), *Isuba* (horse), *Baii* (oak) and *Abukbo* (feather) – act, as Barnes offers them, as the passed-down Choctaw inventory of self within nature, the touchstones of tribal culture`s equilibrium. "Reading Santa Fe" (*Wing*, 126-7) looks to "the drummer drums," "the angles of this land" which, almost mysteriously, compel the speaker to contemplate a site beyond the invitations to give poetry readings, visit the city's museum, gaze upon the cathedral historic statue of Bishop Lamy, or assuredly, take part in the New Mexico of tourist razzamatazz. "Choctaw Cemetery" (*Wing*, 123) speaks beautifully to the one and many tribal deaths, each as always with its own timeline, but also to be memorialized through the ancestral emblem of the "four winds" as a right mode of situating self within the universe:

> Stones,
> hand-hewn symbols
> touching four winds. (*Wing*, 123)

Barnes knows, too, that a complex animism has always held in that same Native universe, from trickster coyote to turtle creator. "Crow" (*Wing*, 160), a prose-poem, contains no explicit Native markers, but it would be hard not to have in mind the bird's familiarity in tribal lore as variously wiseacre, clown or scout. At the same time, and undeniably, a Wallace Stevens blackbird again can plausibly, and fairly, be invoked, or any of the avian imagery in creature poems by, say, Gerard Manley Hopkins or Ted Hughes. But the unspoken Native provenance is hard to avoid. Each step in the interchange of voice and eye, the "conversation," more than hints of such. The crow`s caw, however closely imitated by the speaker, fails to fool the bird. Three times repeated, it causes the bird merely to ascend to the higher tree branches from where it looks down with "sidewise looks." It then lowers itself to immediate "eye level," twanging the lower limbs of the tree. In an exchange of mutual sightings the poem's self observes with no little irony "I can see the world behind me in his black pupils." The crow's eyes act as perfect reflector, man and bird, self and world.

***

La Plata Cantata yields further freshness of sight imagery, especially its allusions to "glyph" as recurrent Barnes metaphor. "Trying To Read The Glyphs" (*Wing*, 195), told as the climbing of a vertical cliff face, highlights "hand chiseled glyphs" each respectively "abstract," "open," or "riddled." Climbing upwards towards the glyphs the speaker meets spirals of wind rising from hidden caves, "cold stone," a want of footholds, the tumbling reflection of a waterfall "a thousand years dead," his own sweat, and the echoing inward sensation that "my mind is full of bones." The lines become a gathering ode as much to time as place. The river beneath is likened to "a glacier hunting for/the sea." The shadow of a pivoting hawk implies timeless avian habit. The setting sun completes this day as it has all others before. The poem's voice, synoptically, speaks of the consciousness of "bones I never knew I was heir to." This is Nature as alive in the present, immediate and kinetic, yet also a site to be understood through a wholly more ancient lexicon.

"Paraglyphs" (*Wing*, 218-20) reads in shared manner, a seven-part verse sequence given over to signs registered as though again past inside present, the older "language" borne down from Native to modern America. A Missouri cave so yields:

> Two fish,
> definitely carp,
> picassoed in stone:
> Holiday, Missouri. (*Wing*, 228)

The seaming of Picasso as modern art's ranking name into an ancient cave wall does symptomatic service, Nature's continuity of visual marking. Each ensuing section adds its confirming specificity. An "arc of moon," "this scythe," with a "shining" hawk overhead in its light, is seen etched on sandstone as though eternal configuration ("What's lost concerns me/more than was may be"). A similarly engraved "red ochre snake" suggests both "enemy" and "vein of life." A sea turtle is said to bear "a road map on its back." Holson Creek, after rain, yields three arrowheads, a spearhead, the axe-like adze, and the clay pot and human shinbone fragments amid the riverbank's oak fruit – a collage, as it were, of old and new habitation. Big Sur, seen from an overhead plane flight, becomes a tropic California of love and radicalism. Cuzco, Peru's fabled city to which the Incas are supposed to have descended from Lake Titicaca, is remembered from traditional Native cosmography as the place where sun and earth "stood still." Taken together Barnes's vivid, imagist vignettes build into a serial of markings, the linked diversity of human signature preserved upon an unfolding scroll of sites.

***

The Sawdust War yields four sequences. As a run of title poems "The Sawdust War" (3-32) takes its direction from childhood and war memory. "After The Great Plains" (35-57) looks to landscapes and their histories spanning Oklahoma, Missouri and Montana. "Elegies for John Berryman and Others" (61-83) develops literary tributes not only to the Berryman born in McAlesker, Oklahoma, and for whose *Mistress Bradstreet* (1956,) *77 Dream Songs* (1964) and *His Toy, His Dream, His Rest* (1968) Barnes has long shown admiration, but also to Malcolm Lowry and Ernest Hemingway. "In Another Country" (87-116), Hemingway's story-title the apt footfall, takes on different scenes and habitations in Italy.

Of these "After The Great Plains" (35) gives the strongest focus to the America he calls "this long land" (35) of Native and settler, which he also develops in a poem like "Wolf Watch: Winding Stair Mountain, 1923" (36-43). The panorama invoked embraces meadow, pine, cattle, sheep, fish, quail, crows and, centrally, the wolf, with a human quotient in a scene of preacher and flock, a waiting wife, and a dead herder. The note is one of shared American time and space, Native and settler, prairie and homestead.

In "Crow White" (51) and "Crow Firesticks" (52) Barnes writes two canny avian vignettes. Both enact myth-fables suitably told in speaker-trickster voice, the one to do with the origins of the bird's crow-black color and the other with Nature's chance ironies of fire and water told as the bird trapped inside a whale. "Postcard to James Welch in Missoula" (56) can be thought to work a shared vein, one of the many "postcards" Barnes has made over into poems. Cast in the form of a verse epistle it suggests, teasingly, how an "Indian" sense of rain and sound, sky and river, eludes the modern "inner ear." The old weather rain-dance has gone, the bass refuse to bite, and the rivers and corn have become dry and dust laden. The poem closes ruefully, and as though in shared affectionate envy with Welch, of other understandings of a day's forecast:

> Remember when you were here, how the sky
> Was right with clouds and the winds scalped
> us down to the skull. You told us in a glance
> the moving days are best, when sounds strike
> the inner ear from places only the hawk
> can name and some wild damned Indian,
> eyes full of rainbows and fast jacks. *Achukma!* (56)

The closing *Achukma!*, the Choctaw term for "It is good" or "I am fine," strikes just the right note. Two mixed writer-heirs to Native history, fellow American moderns yet with their respective pathways into American indigeneity, look to heritage, legacy. How, for either, to belong completely to the present-day world while actually, and residually, always conscious of Nature's sights and sounds seen or heard by "only the hawk" or "some damned wild Indian" (56) whose eyes give off a vision of "rainbows and fast jacks"? The personal and shared ancestry of site could not be more evident, self and place, self and time.

With "Fourche Maline Bottoms" (47) Barnes nicely, and economically, fuses his natal Oklahoma with Native heritage. Fourche Maline, French for "Dirty fork or path" (though here "river" or "bottoms") acts as the site for memory-within-memory. In childhood the speaker is told by "raucous neighborhood boys" that "*you won't find nothing down in them bottoms/worth a shit.*" In fact he finds a massive plenty, albeit a private plenty, at once a lift to the spirits and the sustaining link into his own memorial past:

> The joy
> Of finding arrowheads beneath the crumb-
> ling leaves was something I could never come
> to trade for any neighbor's game. (47)

The affection for the arrowheads, and through them once again the accompanying sense of entering Native American time as well as place, the poem summarizes exactly in its closing quatrain:

> For seven years I sifted coal-black dirt,
> found arrowheads so keen I knew I'd seen
> into my own ancestral past where hurt
> and harm stood taller than neighbor boys had been. (47)

"Coal-black dirt," "arrowheads," "ancestral past." Together they supply just the right collocation, a Native past-into-present as necessary and correlative larger context for the speaker's boyhood-into-adulthood. The images are precise, and appropriately temporal and physical, those of a burrowing into the American earth for both artifact and self-meaning.

***

The further repertoire of sites in Barnes's poetry, whether America, Europe, Japan and other Asia, deserves matching recognition. Selective poems do duty for the larger round, each given to a site sharp in particularity yet within shared register of place. In a well-taken recent appraisal of *On a Wing of the Sun*, for *Sewanee Review*, Sam Pickering speaks of "letting [Barnes's] poems ferment through darkening nights. The names of places reverberated across lines: Tom Fry Hollow, Big Piney River, Goats Bluff, Horsefly, Marshalltown, Pyramid Lake and Winding Stair Mountain."[7] Selecting these picture-like, mosaical names points in the right direction, an America-sited contemplative poetry precisely inviting of the reader's "fermentation."

This sense of site, a much traveled Southwest and West heavy in mulled-over feeling, recurs. "The Cabin on Nanny Ridge" (*The Sawdust War*, 11) calls up halcyon Oklahoma boyhood ("Time/ backed for us"), even as "Europe burned." By contrast "Military Burial, Summerfield Cemetery: A Late Eulogy" (19) recalls the European war actually carried into Oklahoma – "An honor guard brought the gray box down from/Tinker Field." The note is one of sad respect, a remembrance of death in the skies ("For all who had the will/for wings I have only words I wish were more"). In "At 39: The View from Sycamore Tower" (*La Plata Cantata*) a sense once again of boyhood life past ("scrub oak /or sparse pine where I stepped barefoot/on my first rattlesnake") joins with the adult present ("I came/ too many miles and from a woman/I could have been drinking bourbon with"). Within the perimeters of Buffalo Mountain and the Tower both supply memory sites for self-enquiry. Little wonder the air of the mountain is said to be "chock-full/of ghosts and insects" and home "always ten thousand miles away."

"La Plata, Missouri: Clear November Night" (*A Season of Loss, Wing*, 108) sees the Mid-west township under "an avalanche of stars," "snowing light," a heartlands at once literal yet preternaturally illuminated. "Driving through

Missouri" (*A Season of Loss*), a mid-autumn night vista, prompts thoughts of love and its call. The site to hand, at once close to hand and yet far away, is cast as wistful, real enough yet distant with hope and desire:

I gather all my light love

into an artifice of now, see a snow
  drifting at the bottom of my eye, although

I am contending with the real, the road.
I'd like to clap my hands and sing the woods

rich in rainy, salmon leaves and new light,
set a course for stars deep in softer night,

a night I could make a song on. Out of
this pale time there's still a thing or two to love. (109)

"On the Beach at Manzanita, Oregon" (*The American Book of The Dead, Wing*, 6-7) casts its gaze to the further west with a vision of "cryptic stone faces seaward" and "the ageless Chinook." Yet these "chords of memory" bring back to mind the almost defunct Yuchis of Oklahoma.

As inviting a triumph as almost any of Barnes's America-sited poems is to be encountered in "Notes for A Love Letter from Mid-America" (*A Season of Loss, Wing*, 148-50), his four-part rumination with a Preface from Chief Seattle ("There is no death. Only a change of worlds"), and which blends remembrance of a past lover with a past mid-west. The missing object of affection is situated against "dead November," "glacial drift." A winter of heart and land contrasts with "white-water sounds" and "salmon mad with love." The runes of love, close-lived and lost, overlap with Nature's own changing seasonal and topographical runes. Locale is both the physical exterior of mountain, cornfield, moss and rapids, and at the same time, reverberatingly, the inward terrain of feeling ("I miss my breath/in your hair," "A sense of place/allowed us room to love"). The mutuality of both sites, here as so often in Barnes's poetry, supplies a wholly distinctive signature.

***

Europe has greatly supplied Barnes with working poetic terrain, nowhere more so than in the seventy or so poems which make up the collection *Paris*. Barnes's itinerary is busy, alive with appetite for the city beginning from "Les Invalides" (1) with Napoleon's bones "perpetually enthroned" and "*Le Métro*" (2) with its "air brakes wheezing on the rails" and each tunnel's "rupturous light"

"On Rue de Fleurus" (5) offers homage to Gertrude Stein and Alice B. Toklas ("a flowering, a shining."). "At The Tomb of Baudelaire" (6) echoes *Les Fleurs du Mal* ("Nothing about this place seems dull:/ the stone flowers have a luster that grows full/as day goes down"). "Rodin's Garden" (42-3) offers its museum of "praying hands and walking men/and lovers locked in time" and grounds where "a white and silent peace abounds."

Italy likewise exerts its pull, rarely to more imaginative good purpose than in a poem like "Above Bellagio, Looking North to Varenna" (*The Sawdust War* 89-90). Gulls are said to circle the lake where rocks, and even graves, have fallen into the waters. Nearby Tremezzo reminds of where Mussolini, Il Duce, was shot. Hydrofoil and ferry cross, the latter with foghorn at full blast. Switzerland just about hovers into view ("the waves reflecting Alps/in their white caps" 89). Pliny and Dante are invoked. And the poem ends with its own eulogy, a site of true place, true feeling:

> No cantos are large enough
> to hold the spirit of this place. The water is deep,
> and the Alps lean hard into Lombardy's shifting winds. (90)

It could not be more appropriate to link this Europe with Barnes's America. "Anasazi Rocks" (*Paris*, 21) strikes the right note, a vignette of purchasing "a crude necklace" from an old jewels and lace shop in the city's Rue St. André des Arts:

> We had no thought of buying things
> So far from home. On touch I felt the red
> Canyon de Chelly sand and the drumming
> Of dry thunder and dread.
>
> I felt my blood pulse slow and paid too much,
> as any tourist would. The stones were dull
> and real, their faces heavy to our touch.
> On quai d'Orsay we pulled
>
> them free of the German silver bases
> and threw them wide into the rising Seine
> to ride the earthy current into sea
> and home on wind and rain. (21)

The poem gathers many of Barnes's characteristic interests. The idiom is immediate though tinged with a certain reflective *tristesse*. Necklace, colors, the act of casting the stones into the Seine as connecting world river, and the linking of France's Quai d'Orsay with the Anasazi Canyon de Chelly, make for a deep, inward continuity of travel, heritage, time.

***

With *Visiting Picasso,* his ninth collection, Barnes establishes yet further life-and-imagination linkage of Europe and America, sites encountered and pondered first-hand and then made over into his own energy of image. "Waiting for Recognition" (6-7), the Native poet in Basel for a reading, makes the connection with a fine touch of irony:

> Mid February
> and we are standing
> in the railway station
> of Basel,
> waiting to be fetched
> by a stranger host. (6)

The title-phrase itself sets the running – "waiting for recognition," to be sure, between Swiss host and American literary visitor, but also implying whole other and larger realms of recognition. Is not Native, or even part-Native, identity also still waiting for its recognition and beyond stereotype or silhouette? The "stranger host" may attempt train station recognition but how about the poet's own self-recognition? The spare, circumstantial detail of time (Winter's February) and place (Basel station as transit and yet waiting-place), and in line-spacing to match, underscores the sense of different cultural spaces, the several different kinds of two-worlds met and yet not met.

Within Switzerland's own multi-language regimen ("four languages come and go") one more enters ("Choctaw ghosts/take my arm"). "You aren't him, are you?" ventures the host, "him" being the poet in whom, self-complicatingly, have coalesced Wales, Oklahoma, Mississippi, Muskrat, Coyote, and Crow. It is also the "him" caught up in assumed popular culture formula, be it feathered Brady daguerreotype, the drum-bearer, medicine–man or fire-chanter of movie or comic book. How best, amid the "talking, talking," to say truly who you are, or even more to the point *not* to say who you truly are – the self within "the silence of snow/the silence of blood"? The poem in no way suggests ungraciousness towards the Swiss host (even her allusions to "our lineage/and reservations"). But it does teasingly contemplate the nuance of historical identity within the monotone notion of "Indian poet," the one set-phrase which far from locates a whole syntax of life. That this "waiting for recognition" takes place in Europe, the continent (Switzerland as may be) which begot "the Indian" in the first place, could not better convey or indeed compound the irony.

Europe, even so, and from his first visits onward, for Barnes has been a special haven, the poet's own Another Country. The span in *Visiting Picasso* is considerable. Switzerland yields the Montreux of the author of *Pale Fire* ("Homage to Nabokov" and of Byron ("Leaving Chillon"), along with the "far below" Vevey of the silent screen's greatest genius ("Charlie and The Funicular" 4-5):

> If Chaplin were
> here, the line would break, the clog wheel
> slip from greased cups, and would take
> one hell of a ride back to where
> we started form alive and well. (4)

Provence summons Fitzgerald and Zelda ("Féria de Pâques, Arles 1996" 29-30). Munich is to be associated with Robert Creeley ("Picture of Creeley ..." 38). Mountain Stuttgart recalls World War II memory and storm ("Birkenkopf 2000" 60) in which the forest trees are ripped and "mother earth slammed/into upheaval." Provence calls up the corrida and Hemingway ("The First Féria of the Third Millennium, Arles Easter Monday" 72-3) where "ghosts that refuse to leave this place." Bellagio speaks to Barnes's own earlier habitation there ("Villa Serbelloni Revisited, February 2003" 91) in which he echoes Wordsworth – "Twelve years since the bells of Bellagio/ have rung for us" and looks back to "that time ago that threw/us headlong into poetry".

All, as it were, compound into memorial geography, Europe as the site of local and expatriate homestead caught under the sheen of close-worked recollection. The speaker in each poem clearly associates himself with this home-and-away tradition while, at the same time, keeping in touch with the America of lived-in western landscape – as in the volume's various intercalated poems like "Deputy Finds Dean's Tombstone on Highway" (48-9), set in "the deep Indiana fields," or "Heading East Out of Rock Springs" (58-9) with its Missoula and Kirksville backdrop and Wyoming place-name. This America, also, and throughout each of his sojourns, continues to exist inside Barnes's Europe, precisely the heritage he finds himself "reminded of " even as he relishes those to which he has arrived as poet-traveler.

"Visiting Picasso" (63) and the other poems in which Picasso serves as motif, supply a spine, a working fulcrum. In the title poem "Visiting Picasso"

(63) he sites Picasso within the ancient Roman v. Ambron battle-field, visual art's modernist himself the take-no-prisoner's virtuoso in his near-Avignon outpost of Vauvenargues ("He wanted no survivors"). But where Picasso personifies Provence, French light and color for his Spanish palate, he can also be invoked right in the heart of Oklahoma. In "Rondeau for a Shovelbill Catfish, at the Buffalo Hole, Fourche Maline River, à la Recherche du Temps Perdu" (84) Barnes invokes the paddle-like and flat-jawed shovelbill as unique with the rider – "*Picasso never caught these bones/on a dirty plate* ....". Like the Wallace Stevens-style title, this local freshwater fish and Picasso's fish-engraved display crockery makes for a perfect conjuncture of sites, Oklahoma and Provence. For all his attraction to Picasso's stunning dexterity, nor does Barnes lose sight of the egotism, even the cruelty. His "In Memory of Dora Maar" (89) speaks of how, in the case of Maar as muse-mistress and artist in her own right, "We saw her ghost/ mainly though Pablo's eyes, where not/ everything was not focused right" and of how Maar's decline joined "the others he had ruined by love/or use."

Nonetheless this is the Picasso admiringly remembered in "Monsieur le Marquis de Vauvenargues" (51-3) as the craftsman of the "potter's wheel," "ceramic toil," "a whole crop of sketches," "oils" and "his eighth decade of taking chances." His death is said to occur "among shards/of time he could never trust," the surreal time-space virtuoso to the end. "The Maestro kept the faith" (52) acts as summarizing apostrophe, with Vauvenargues the site not just of Picasso's house or even of France but of a singular, eddying imagination. The link to Barnes, however, can be said to go beyond just a choice of subject-matter: *Visiting Picasso* again, and yet further, vindicates Barnes as Oklahoma international, his poetry of sites real and imagined and their peopling one of lasting distinction.

Notes

1 Jim Barnes, "A Song for All of Them," *A Season of Loss/On a Ring of the Sun*, West Lafayette: Purdue University Press, 1985, 32.

2 Jim Barnes, "In Another Country: A Suite for the Villa Serbelloni," *The Sawdust War*, Urbana and Chicago: University of Illinois Press, 1992, 101.

3 Jim Barnes, *On Native Grounds: Memoirs and Impressions*, Norman: University of Oklahoma Press, 1997, 259.

4 Jim Barnes, "Surveying Near Ellsworth, Kansas," *La Plata Cantata*, West Lafayette: Purdue University Press, 1985. Reprinted in *On a Wing of the Sun*, 180.

5 "Jim Barnes," *Contemporary Authors Autobiographical Series*, Vol. 28, 17-32, Farmington Hills: Thomson Gale, 1998.

6 For ease of reference all subsequent page references to *The American Book of the Dead, A Season of Loss, and La Plata Cantata* are to their inclusion in the one composite volume *On a Wing of the Sun*, Urbana and Chicago: University of Illinois Press, 2001.

7 Sam Pickering, "Time Ever Slow and Long," *Sewanee Review*, CXII, 3, Summer 2004, 468.

Works Cited

Barnes, Jim, *Sundown Explains Nothing: New and Selected Poems*, Nacodoches: Stephen F. Austin State University Press, 2019

_____, *Visiting Picasso*, Urbana and Chicago: University of Illinois Press, 2007.

_____, *On a Wing of the Sun*, Champaign-Urbana and Chicago: University of Illinois Press, 2001.

_____, Translator, *Gezählte Tage/Numbered Days: Poems by Dagmar Nick*, Kirksville, Missouri: New Odyssey Press, 1998.

_____, "Jim Barnes," *Contemporary Authors Autobiography Series*, Dictionary of Literary Biography, Vol. 28, 17-32, Farmington Hills, Michigan: Thompson Gale, 1997.

_____, *Paris*, Urbana and Chicago: University of Illinois Press, 1997.

_____, *On Native Grounds: Memoirs and Impressions*, Norman: University of Oklahoma Press, 1997.

_____, *The Sawdust War*, Champaign-Urbana and Chicago: University of Illinois Press, 1992.

_____, *The Fiction of Malcolm Lowry and Thomas Mann: Structural Tradition*, Kirksville, Missouri: Thomas Jefferson University Press, 1990.

_____, *A Season of Loss*, West Lafayette, Indiana: Purdue University Press, 1985

_____, *The American Book of the Dead*, Urbana: University of Illinois Press, 1982. Reprinted in *On a Wing of the Sun: Three Volumes of Poetry*, Urbana: University of Illinois Press, 2001.

_____, *The Fish on Poteau Mountain*, Stillwater, Oklahoma: Cedar Creek, 1980.

_____, *This Crazy Land*, Flagstaff, Arizona: Inland Boat Series, 1980

_____, Translator, *Summons and Sign: Poems by Dagmar Nick*, Kirksville, Missouri: Chariton Review Press, 1980.

_____, ed., *Five Missouri Poets*, Kirksville, Missouri: Chariton Review Press, 1979.

17

Two Handed: Self and Habitat in the Poetry of Linda Hogan

I don't remember when
the girl of myself turned her back
and walked away, that girl
whose thin arms
once held this body
and refused to work too hard
or listen in school,
said the hell then
and turned
that dark child,
that laugher and weeper,
without shame, who turned
and skipped away.

Linda Hogan, "The Lost Girls," *Savings* (1988)[1]

As an Indian woman I question our responsibilities to the caretaking of the future and to the other species who share our journeys....It is clear that we have strayed from the treaties we once had with the land and with the animals. It is also clear, and heartening, that in our time there are many – Indian and non-Indian alike – who want to restore and honor these broken agreements.

Linda Hogan, *Dwellings* (1995)[2]

It takes little time reading Linda Hogan's poetry to become acutely aware of the emphases indicated by this chapter's title. Given her mixed Chickasaw and European heritage she recurs, often movingly, but also defiantly, to the composite theatre of identity that has run through her life. Early collections like *Calling Myself Home* (1978) and *Daughters, I Love You* (1982) draw closely on rite-of-passage, the self in the making – gender, marriage, divorce, motherhood as well as ethnicity – and the poet within that making.

Other volumes, *Seeing Through The Sun* (1985), *Savings* (1988), *The Book of Medicines* (1993), through to *Dark. Sweet: New & Selected Poems* (2014), share the focus but also develop her abiding attention to the necessary wisdom, and yet precariousness, of the "living earth."[3] Earth, season, species, climate, plant, root, cave and forest, and insistently her perceived spirituality of Nature, prevail as epicenters in her writing. Across her collections, poem upon poem, moreover, Hogan as often intertwines the two, self and habitat symbiotically bound the one into the other. That can elicit celebration but where the subject of damage intrudes call for appropriate repair.

***

One of her best known poems, "The Truth Is" in *Seeing Through the Sun* (4-5), speaks directly to identity, wry, aslant, a soliloquy that ponders mixed heritage in the image of contrarily paired hands.[4] The opening lines turn anatomy into figuration:

> In my left pocket a Chickasaw hand
> rests on the bone of the pelvis.
> In my right pocket
> a white hand. (4)

Serious tease ensues. The white hand is not to be taken as some kind of ethnic stolen goods, Indian from white ("Don't worry. It's mine"). That it, and its companion hand, also belong to "a woman who sleeps in a twin bed" nicely extends the seeming bifurcation. But Hogan adds complicating imagery. The speaker walks along "with hands/in her own empty pockets/even though she has put them in others/for love not money" (4). Her reality, on this reckoning, is assuredly lived in pocketed ambiguity, the given and the taken, and always beyond any hand-me-down binaries. This touch of the quizzical extends into and through the next stanza.

The poem's voice so might be a kind of salvo ("About the hands, I'd like to say/ I am a tree, grafted branches/bearing two kinds of fruit" 4). Apricots or pit cherry, as they are named, the choice is immediately countermanded with "It's not that way." Rather, these antinomies "knock against each other," as though searching in a well-chosen word for "amnesty." The speaker imagines herself "taped together," pockets variously empty or jangled by coins and keys. Linked and competing "pockets" hold sway, at once raveled, and actually beyond unraveling. The resort to vernacular fits to a tee ("Linda, girl, I keep telling you/ this is nonsense/about who loved who/and who killed who" 4, and "Girl, I say,/ it is dangerous to be a woman of two countries" 5).

Under this regime, and given the allusions to past loves, historic indigenous and all race killings, and the ominous night-time knock on the door from authority, she admonishes herself to "relax." Other metaphor, the poem itself avers, can be brought into consideration, shoes for instance, again left and right, and again indicative of the linking nexus of indigenous and white. Teasingly, and in the closing lines, the shoes invite being considered "the true masks of the soul" – moccasins perhaps, or other footwear. The implication is one of walking, mobility, moving-on. Negotiation of the self's always itinerant unfolding persists, the kinetics of identity well beyond any binary. The ruminative tease of the poem's ending ("there are other things to think about") exactly implies identity's unending. Perfectly engaging in its own right "The Truth Is," at the same time, gives an important marker for Hogan's yet wider range of "identity" poems.

"Heritage," in *Calling Myself Home* (18-19), invites being thought an exercise in family elegy. The speaker's mother bequeaths mixed fare, the passed-down mirror in which she sees her own wrinkling "lines," the remembered warming smell of "baking bread," the impeding weight of her inherited "large white breasts." Her father conjures up not just "brown eyes" but association with buzzard-like locusts that devastate the crops. Her uncle, a veteran whittler of wood, reminds of houses long ago and "old chants" delivered in a Native tongue forbidden to her father. Her grandfather paradoxically "speaks" silence, the silence she fears as though snake-like.

The grandmother, blue-eyed yet brown-skinned, a snuff-user who spills "black saliva" on "my white shirt," assumes still greater force of memory. The tobacco this grandmother once used as snuff, a chew, and even fed into her son's mouth, likens impressionistically to Oklahoma as at once Indian Country and the "stain" of oil. Ancestrally, however, the tobacco has served as "medicine," a mythic-shamanistic purge or resort more efficacious than "stones and knives/ against your enemies." Its mysteries amount to "the dark night that covers me." The grandmother also passes down other indigenous belief: deer meat to aid swiftness and a compass-stick to give pointers west and east. The sum of all the speaker's corridor of remembrance the poem locates in the final two lines:

> From my family I have learned the secrets
> of never having a home. (19)

Identity from family evidently matters but there is also the secreted self in whole or in part of a home that is also an un-home.

Turn to "First Light" in *Savings* and Hogan writes a disarming cameo of self-identification (12). The poem, invoking dawn clarity, bids to forget the legacy of "Crooked chiefs/who make federal deals" in favor of "singing birds and blue sky." The one landscape yields to the other, illumination of spirit over the politics of sell-out. The self she posits knows interiority, wealth of temperament, even when constrained by demands of time and job. The creative pluralism within her beckons:

> I know I can bathe and stretch,
> make jewelry and love
> the witch and wise woman
> living inside, needing to be silenced
> and put at rest for work's long day. (12)

A full quotient of indigenous ritual follows. Her offers of tobacco and cornmeal at daybreak make for communion. The "hello" to ancestors links her to the encompassing spiritual universe. That it is voiced also to birds under the eaves and those under newly budding plants, signals invigoration and renewal. With the closing stanza the first person "I" transposes into "us":

> I know the old ones are here.
> And every morning I remember the song.
> about how buffalo left through a hole in the sky
> and how the grandmothers look out from those holes
> watching over us
> from there and from there. (12)

The poem's scale enlarges through this Native-inflected vision of guardian "old ones," the song of buffalos ascending despite un-Indian slaughter, and grandmothers maternal in their sky-hole watching and showing care. The self Hogan creates to offer her witness unmistakably draws upon "Indian" parameters. She does so, however, and at the same time, in an imagist loop of her own insistent making.

"Tear," in *The Book of Medicines*, adds another striking perspective in thinking through the nature of identity in the metaphor, and the reality, of Chickasaw tear dresses which also are to be associated with the Cherokee (39-40). The poem uses, but does not overuse, the tear/tear word-play, needlework and eye, to create reference to Oklahoma and the vexed Native history it encodes. The "I" this time takes on the implication of synecdoche, one woman's self the trope of others in the history of Trail of Tears displacement, poor soil, scant cloth, the ongoing losses and survival struggle. "Lightning split open the sky" reads an early line. Indeed it did.

Beginning from "the time before" her birth the poem invokes iconic mementos, wagon wheels and soldiers. Only needles were permitted to the tribal women for fear that scissors or knives would be used in reprisal. Torn cloth becomes "tears" in the double sense, "our weeping" and linen or calico made into colorful full-length dress in the face of loss. Remembrance transitions back to the treks, the black dogs, the children, the heavy horses, and the worn-out men. These collectively the speaker internalizes ("They walk inside me"). The tropes turn graphic, whether "The blood/is a map between us" or "I am why they survived." The past lives on in the poet ("All around me are my ancestors"), the future in "my unborn children." The final couplet joins time into the one holding identity:

> I am the tear between them
> and both sides live. (60)

The selections that make up *Dark. Sweet* afford a yet wider bounty. "Leaving" (24-5) turns upon ironic would-be moving-out from heritage ("I'm saying goodbye/to that person behind me"). Father or uncle become the past. Coyote, turtle, bone beads belong to "old skin." Has she not "burned all my brown sticks" for seeming new departure, adventure, but also regret? A similar bid for self-resolution presses from within "Watch Me" (83). "This year I was suddenly old," runs the testimony, advance of years but also sense of herself as though dispossessed Indian woman, "a mother, and without a single cow to my name." She vows no more weeping in home or cowboy bar. Rather the reader or listener is enjoined to "watch me" as she dances "the story of my life." Hers, by resolution, will now be bones of vitality over those of despair.

Hogan has always been careful not to risk sounding merely self-obsessed, identity edging toward narcissism. "The Lost Girls" (107-8) speaks affectingly of transition ("I don't remember when/the girl of myself turned her back/and walked away"). She equally, however, sees the wider reach. Her memory turns to "inner women" and "all the girls and women/I have always been" with their liberated "loose hair" and "dancing shoes." "The Grandmother Songs" (172-4) situates the poet under matrilinear auspices ("The grandmothers were my tribal gods"), their songs of sleep, divination, health, sunlight, and recovery of health, given internal retention. "Walking with My Father" (355-6) looks again to parentage and the grandmother of her "old house," a poem precise in allusion to early beginnings and later "losses" and which gives memorial circumstance to her very making both as daughter and poet.In tackling identity as a pivot in Hogan's poetry it would be wrong to imply rote. To the contrary. Her poems are at once shrewdly accessible and oblique, identity as enactive, a shifting process, and always nuanced by emphases of memory and sensation.

***

Habitat, its animal and bird life, vegetation, waters, caves, roots, trees, climate and topographies, has been a prevailing interest from the outset.[5] "Breaking" (*Dark Sweet* 103-4) typically articulates Nature's force of life, its "seed" and "grain" the essences from which to learn. This is "the ringing earth" of irresistible growth, the earth from "before our tribes…before the Americans/from broken worlds" yet ever "looking for the next world." The poem's imagery reads appetitively, the summons to relish and sight:

> In the dark field
> yellow squash is growing,
> bones are filling up the arms
> with new life,
> gourds are climbing fences. (104)

Accentuation falls upon the natural-order's benign breaking and entering, yellow squash "growing" and gourds "climbing fences." Both embody riposte to "politics" or temporary drugstore and barn. Hogan's vision of Nature as growth-cycle over death, "new life" from "bones" applies not only in this poem but gives working idiom across her oeuvre.

This environmental panorama, whether avian, arboreal, animal, marine, amphibian or arachnic, is as extensive as it is vivid. "Crow Law" (157) enacts the process whereby the crow rules as scavenger, its menu that of left-over rib particles and blood from the wolf's assault on a moose. "The oldest war" the poem calls it, prey and preyed upon ("where we are still afraid") as necessary ritual. "Tree Woman" (315-16) sees in "the largest tree I have ever seen" a figuring of Nature's own genealogical body. Its "rings" endure as markers of "time," "rain," drought, "the ice age," "mammoth," "science," and comfort against hunger or fear. "This great woman," serves as mothering refuge, evolutionary grace, and wholly and by dint of comparative age and beauty due its homage from "humans only half formed."

"Elk Song" (105-6) pays its due to an animal full of graceful brawn, speed, and in particular for the poet "the red running one/like thunder over hills." The notion of song as celebration extends to the companion round of deer, otter, fish, yelping dog and wolf, amid which, or whom, the elk is also mythic – "a saint with its holy hoof dance." Antlered, powerfully hooved, the elk "whistles" in its throat as it accelerates "on the earth's tight skin" and "from the other side of the forest." Watching and listening the poet-watcher imagines it a "train full of danger," a plane breaking the sound barrier. Above all, in her eye, this elk and others "have pulled the hide of earth/tight," its run a drumming of woodland and grass back to "days we were equal/and strong." The elk so holds domain at once for its own state of being and as avatar, dynamic body and inspirational spirit.

"Whale Rising" (219-20) goes the distance in capturing this cetacean mother who has "navigated the world/by whale map." Her "large dark eye" is said to act as mirror in which to "see ourselves," the Melvilleian trace one of many in the poem. Poised in a boat "for hours now" the poet-watcher this time ponders how the whale surfaces not only for air but risks meeting "enemies." The majesty of the creature, and for sure its ocean mystery, lies in having swum in the "blue, infinite/light" of deepest water. "No one returns unchanged" from navigation of these depths we are to understand, the whale's eye privy to secrets that "fixed us in its gaze." Whale song, "beautiful" from "beneath this world," takes hold of the boat's passengers, the folds and mists of breath a privileged invitation to hear the sound of unique sea-language. Poets both, whale and human, meet in shared colloquy, Hogan's poignancy unmistakable.

"Language of the Frogs" (378) bridges voices, amphibian "love language" to contrast with the poet's own travails of love ("I soak in the waters of loneliness"). Their coordinated sound of desire and mating gives an ironic chorus to the speaker's many losses, along with love, children, happiness, "maybe the heart." Nor are the frogs the only purveyors of life, amour. They have company in a bird's nest of "feather and horse hair" in which "five speckled eggs" guarded by their mother give promise of birth. Yet it remains the frogs who "praise the arrival of rain," amid swimming tadpoles and even as their pond shrinks. The imagery of chorus, larval promise of growth, and rain, plays against not just the shrinking pond but the speaker's shrinking heart. When the poem concludes with "I step outside in all the sound/and step outside" the implication gathers flawlessly: Nature's sound over silence, motion over stillness.

Hogan's ecology, it can take re-stressing, resists mere adulation, easy or coy deference. "Scorpion" (126-7), for instance, laments how this arachnic has largely lost habitat, its sting as it were drawn. "She was a god" in time gone by apostrophizes the poem, corn and silk monarch, a "sister to the heat waves" and "crony of red sky." But time, commerce, housing, has "exiled" her to "cupboards" and "stoops," the pestiferous insect. Her reduced status leads to a will to destruction ("she wants to sting herself/to death"). No longer can she assume prehistoric godhead, mythic crown. Rather she has been "exiled to brown shoes and porches," mere quotidian nuisance. But the keener eye can still discern in the scorpion "fiery life," a time when Nature's own dynamic pique was better known and felt. Ecology alive underwrites the poem, the scorpion but one of its heralds and champions.

***

For all of their interaction self and habitat far from make separate constituencies in Hogan's verse. Assuredly their interaction in the poems already cited is not to be missed. *Dark. Sweet*, however, when read through in sequence, leaves little doubt of how emphatic has been the relationship. Three examples serve, each characteristic in vision.

"Deer Dance" (236-7) has the poet implicated in her own private deer scene, the young deer having left their sleep imprint on the snow, the herd to which they belong having left hillside tracks. Ritual human, likely tribal, Spring dance comes into remembrance, the assumption of deer identity with flowered antlers as token of the new seasons of birth. Other animal-myth transformations press, whether Circe and pigs, women-bears, or wolf children ("none of them wanted to go back/to being human"). So compelling the thought of these metamorphoses the poet sleeps "outside my door last night" to exist in identity with the animals.

A later evening has her watching the deer shed their antlers, giving gaze at their dance, hearing their breath, and sensing their apprehension at her watching. The familiar road of her walks, however, allows her distance from which to see them, their grey-brown fur "never quite straight,/as if they has just stepped into it." The latter trope does greatly relevant service. For it is the poet, their fellow being, who has stepped into identity, self, earth's other life forms, "brush" and "crooked river" all in the one sweep joined and inter-transposed.

"Turtle Watchers" (226), in kind with "Turtle" in *Calling Myself Home*, situates the poet simultaneously in both Nature and called to one of the great indigenous myths. A Native "old mother" bows to the sight of returnee turtle mothers having swum to their birthplace for egg-laying, the arena in turn seen by the poet ("I'd seen it all") and at the same time Nature's "hungry watchers" keen to seize the eggs. The scene transitions into the poet swimming alongside a sea-turtle, the two of them caught in the shared current, both of them dipping and then rising for breath while at the same time mutual watchers. She thinks of ancestry, the tribes who call turtles "keepers of doors" with the shoreline "a realm to other worlds." Herein lies "the deep shift of life," turtle and poet, earth's waters and poet's self, "truly" met, the vista of the encompassing animate world into which "I am rounding the human corners."

"Our Song, Winter" (399-400) gives grounds to be thought a kind of summa, winter's moonlight ("The voice of the moon/is singing over land") the setting for a return to Nature's "song." Hogan does a careful imagist/iconic reckoning in the vision of "a prayer woman," her sightings in turn "primordial ocean," "germinating/ancient seeds," "sisterhood. The night sky becomes "horse dance," "turtle song," even "the tick song, and the duck." Given this visionary roster, and implication of wider planetary reach, poet and listener are synoptically enjoined to remember "every morning."

To that end the summarizing last lines of the poem offer memory and then benign prescription:

> our ancient home,
> the places ancestral shadows have been the
> germinating instance,
> have been our ecology, our language,
> and so we have this to recall,
> so step outside. Watch, Listen. (400)

"Our song," "our ecology," "our language," "our ancient home." Each inscribes, or better re-inscribes, the major environmental threads in Linda Hogan's poetry as in life. Her title poem "Dark. Sweet. The Full Eclipse" (361-2), the eclipse an imagining of galactic mystery and for her its "dark, sweet moment," speaks of "splendid planetary breathing." Hogan has rarely deviated in her poetry: the "breath" of her own mixed Native being pledged to the habitats of its inspiration not in doubt.

Notes

1 "The Lost Girls," *Savings*, Minneapolis: Coffee House Press, 1988, 31.
2 Linda Hogan, *Dwellings: A Spiritual History of the Living World*, New York: Simon & Schuster, 1995, 11.
3 In "Dedications," which prefaces *Dark. Sweet, New & Selected Poems*, Minneapolis: Coffee House Press, 2014, Hogan writes "May you remember to care for the earth, all we have. The living earth will care back." It will also be seen that "breath," "breathing," in relation both to the earth and to poetry, recur as motifs. See both the Introduction and the closing paragraph of this chapter.

4 "The Truth Is," *Seeing Through the Sun*, Amherst: University of Massachusetts Press, 1985, 4–5.
5 These and all subsequent poetry citations are again all taken from *Dark. Sweet.*

Works Cited

Hogan, Linda, *Dark. Sweet: New & Selected Poems*, Minneapolis: Coffee House Press, 2014.
_____, *Dwellings: A Spiritual History of the Living World*, New York: Simon & Schuster, 1995.
_____, *The Book of Medicines*, Minneapolis: Coffee House Press, 1993.
_____, *Savings*, Minneapolis: Coffee House Press, 1988.
_____, *Seeing Through the Sun*, Amherst: University of Massachusetts Press, 1985.
_____, *Daughters, I Love You*, Denver: Loretto Heights College, 1981.
_____, *Calling Myself Home*, Greenfield Center: Greenfield Review Press, 1978.

18

Electronic Computer and Stub Pencil: The Writing-in of Ralph Salisbury

> On an electronic computer's memory chip I am writing about myself as a writer – a dog chasing its own tail … Most of my poetry and much of my fiction has been composed with a stub pencil. The pencil a one-legged skater, trying not to stumble.
>
> *So Far, So Good* (2013)[1]

The merest first reading of *So Far, So Good*, Ralph Salisbury's autobiography deservedly awarded the River Teeth Literary Nonfiction Prize, can leave little doubt of a life early to negotiate frequent challenge. The tough farm upbringing at the edge of Depression-era subsistence, for him as "third child of an Irish American mother and an English-Cherokee-Shawnee father" and for his siblings in Fayette County, Iowa, meant the very challenge of survival – undernourishment, a dead child brother, winters, devoted parents and aunt but occasional paternal drink and gun violence. It makes a near paradoxical point of departure for a writer whose ambit increasingly would become transnational.

World War II enlistment in the US air force as specialist gunner, and which he joined under-age, not only promised to expose Salisbury to aerial bombardment of Germany (his war-service ultimately remained that of trainee) but made war a kind of persisting engram for him. The chance mis-registration that saved him from taking part in USAF missions in Korea acts as related touchstone. An adulthood pledged to peace, Vietnam to Iraq, together with ecological activism, further put him on the line as did bouts with pneumonia and later with cancer and heart problems. Increasingly the imperative to come to terms with the war and peace within his own life augments into confronting that of the world.

Although these factors situate Salisbury in the one unfolding of his life, so, as quintessentially, do connecting others. First has to be his "mixed race" legacy in all its Old and New World spiral, its pride and yet vex. Although tribally unenrolled, Caucasian (a term he favors) in appearance, and small of physique, he returns with self-aware frequency to his situating Native identity. "My immediate family's last-ditch Indian survivor" he designates himself. "We Indians" he says when writing of the 1992 quincentenary of Columbus's "discovery" of America. Yet for all the references to his sunrise prayers or to Cherokee traditions of sacred tobacco and respect for the seasons, and to his ancestral Cherokee grandmother, he has the honesty to ask "Am I still an Indian?" In this he shares status with, say, Louis Owens or Jim Barnes, writers to whom indigenous legacy supplies reference and locale but who remained outside tribe. In an interview with the Danish scholar Bo Schöler in 1985 Salisbury speaks, perhaps tendentiously, of Native "regional" authorship:

> Native American writers are part of the new regionalist movement. Thus we will be grouped with, for instance, Scandinavian Americans who are coming up more in awareness of their regional cultures, as are all ethnic groups in America.[2]

The other factor lies in the call to literary authorship for the world. The recall of boyhood creativity, the jottings and small drawings, point to the eventual larger resolve of "my writer's urge to tell the truth," aided in kind by his Kentucky father's itinerant stories and five-string banjo songs and by fondest second marriage to his writer-wife Ingrid Wendt. Contemplating the course of this personal pathway in the light of a re-found photograph he observes with some poignancy:

> A nineteen-year-old bomber crewman, only a year from beginning his writing career, yields to an eighty-two-year-old writer of poetry and prose. (265)

Other way-stations related to acts of writing equally feature, whether teacher training at the North Iowa Teachers College, study on the GI Bill and for an MFA in 1951 at the University of Iowa with Robert Lowell as one of his mentors, or the follow-on into different professorships but most of all in English and creative writing at the University of Oregon (1960-94). Likewise the Rockefeller-Bellagio award and residency by Lake Como adds its weight, as do Fulbright professorships in Norway and Germany and each further European trip. There can be added the USIS lectureship in India, editorship of *Northwest Review* (1965-68), co-translations with Harold Gaski of the Sami poet Nils-Aslak Valkeapää, and each public and campus reading.

Computer or stub pencil, prose or verse, Salisbury acknowledges authorial possession of his life's trajectory to have been an abiding impetus. Authorship, even so, was not to mean some mere exercise in self-reflexivity, though there would be self-reflexivity involved. That holds across the eleven poetry volumes, for which *Light from a Bullet Hole: Poems New and Selected 1950-2008* (2009) acts as representative anthology, and the three story-collections for which *The Indian Who Bombed Berlin* (2009) and its title-piece especially provides a trove. Each major fold of event finds address in the life-writing of *So Far, So Good.* So, inerasably, does the overlap with how and why he becomes the poet and story-writer for whom the larger dimensions of worlds beyond America becomes a necessary impetus.

***

The process of "re-authoring" the timeline from birth to war marks the very opening page of his autobiography:

> Bullet-shattered glass clattering onto my baby bed. I awake and cry, into darkness, for help.
>
> Do I remember this? Or do I remember being told? I will feel it, whichever it is. I will feel it, chill bomb-bay wind buffeting my eighteen-year-old body, a mile above an old volcano's jagged debris; feel it, seeing photos of Jewish concentration camp children, huddled together for warmth, photos of Korean orphans, huddled together, homeless in blizzard after American bombing – bombing in which, twenty-five, I had refused an order to join. (1).

If the self-queries given here link childhood to adulthood, drive-by Iowa shooting to Nazi camp and wartime Korea, they also reflect the author taking hold of his creative latitudes and longitudes ("Do I remember this … or being told?"). How, runs the implicit accompanying question, to assume authority of word, coordinating literary voice? The issue of the *figura* of Salisbury as the writer behind, and within, his own body of texts, clearly operates, as much his way of situating himself as "mixed" Native and Midwestern farm-boy or airman or even professor. *So Far, So Good*, for all the plentiful life-history it supplies, also incorporates full indication of his literary calling.

Salisbury also registers the detail of his life, especially the emphasis he gives to his boyhood, in terms wholly aware of how life-writing like *So Far, So Good* creates its own kind of fiction. Self-interrogation enters early when he speaks in his Prologue of starting "most days for most of my life … trying to write. Why?" He alleges *So Far, So Good* best be understood in the teasing phraseology of "a hop-skip-and-jumps-and-maybe-some-dancing memoir" (4). "Imagination" is to be apostrophized as "shield," the solvent for "free association, spontaneity, a wholeness of moment, a union of past and present." In other words if this is to be a line-graph of actual autobiography it is equally to be responded to for its performative sleights. The risk could have been of over-consciousness. In fact it makes for considerable density and layering.

Ruminatively, and with *So Far, So Good* as his "not-too-soon-to-end Cherokee-Shawnee Death Song," he ponders his English name-heritage and pitches himself as "the Shakespeare of pig-food bearers," "a post-Elizabethan word magician." As though in ancestral affiliation and a reflection of his own call to word he equally gives praise to Sequoia for his Cherokee "written symbols." Working repairs to his present-time house cause him to remember the electricity-less family farm and the "several books written with pencil" in anticipation of those composed on computer-screen. Avian reference, with its implication of literary flight, aligns bird and bomber, air and earth ("I can't remember when I began to dream of exploring Earth by flying"). He profiles himself as "fifteen-year-old bookworm" whose youth-time rescue of two drowning girls links to "what compels me to write," namely life-saving as though linked in literal and figurative senses.[3]

Even one of his severest dramas, that of the eighteen-year armorer precariously helping save fellow crew-members from likely death when an in-flight bomb slips its casing, comes under his self-circling "have I exaggerated?" The question plays into the creative awareness of deploying keyboard and pencil:

> By now I am so modern I have become addicted to a computer keyboard for creating prose, but for poems, elusive as deer among dawn mists, my rifle is a stub pencil, like those with which I first drew cowboys and Indians and other combatants and like those with which my father recorded the days the bull was observed in the act of creating calves. (240)

So Far, So Good gives a full enough repertoire in situating Salisbury within mixed Native and white identity, along with the economics of class, Europe and Asia war, university and its customs, peace activism, and always the ancestry of Cherokee and fellow tribes. Markers range from the Sand Creek Massacre to Hiroshima, *Huckleberry Finn* to *The Red Badge of Courage*. These, Salisbury concludes in sum, constitute "my memories of life flowing into the computer screen." They do so, however, in a way that refracts his rite of progression into poetry and authorship, the outrider determinedly written-in by his own insider. They also mark his every expanding grasp of world histories and politics.

***

To turn from *So Far, So Good* to the poetry is to become sharply aware of how much of this pattern of self-figuration inheres for Salisbury, whether in the context of his take on Native identity, or early family Iowa, or war, or ecology, or the role of poetry in the world. The voicing of each, allowing for how they inevitably also filter the one into the other, links always into the image of himself as the writer under near destined summons. Each poem, in kind with his storytelling, bears this kind of hallmark as if always the writer is to the one degree or another yet without over-intrusion writing him- or herself.

Salisbury's Native-white genealogy, incontestably, gives a major pivot to this writing-in, especially in "A Declaration, not of Independence" which opens *Rainbows of Stone* (2000). There he summons birthright in the wryest of terms:

> Apparently I'm Mom's immaculately-conceived
> Irish-American son, because,
> Social-security time come,
> My Cherokee dad could not prove he'd been born. (3)

This is Salisbury as mock-Jesus, the bureaucratic de-legitimization of his Native father the shrewdest taunt. One suspects, too, the implied wider irony. Tribal peoples not able to offer paper certification of birth obliquely shadows the Indian Citizenship Act of 1924 with its almost surreal conferring of their "right" to Americanization. In life and writing Cherokee signature for Salisbury, whatever the family attenuations and acknowledgment of Anglo and Irish roots, recurs for him as an inescapably situating point of reference. It may well have done so the more given his ability to pass for white. At the same time, and again self-situatingly, *So Far, So Good* serves to remind of his insistence on the inadequacy of versions of himself as somehow un-whole: "I am a Cherokee/Shawnee-English-Irish person, not part this part that but all everything, whatever that is."

"A Declaration" profitably segues into "An Indian Blows Up Mt. Rushmore and Indianizes What Cannot Be Resanctified," another opening poem, this time drawn from *Like The Sun in Storm* (2012).[4] Salisbury conjures up the imagined dismantling of each "Father of Their Country" presidential head carved by Gutzon Borglum, white supremacist Klan supporter in his time, from Black Hills granite. This is settler history's "Rushmore" word-inverted into "Rush Less. Not More" and "Thanksgiving" likewise into "Thanks-taking Day." Jefferson has become "marble-wigwamed," Lincoln emancipated by "Indian-Giving generations." It is also a poet's riposte. Teddy Roosevelt as Rough Rider gives way to Salisbury or his persona as "Rough Writer." "Vanishing American" may have become cliché but "Native American" contests, and repudiates, that cliché through "tongue petroglyphs" and "pow-wowing ears." Salisbury manages a deft contra-dance, "Make Peace Not War" becomes his requiem to tribal dispossession ("the shadows of desecrated peaks"), and yet at the same time tribal continuance and to which through his own scripts and its reader-listeners he envisages his shared and globalizing contribution.

The gallery is as various as frequent. "Being Indian" (5) in *Rainbows of Stone* focuses attention on the evolving complication of mixed Native heritage. The opening of "Who we were seemed simple when gun/dropped meat onto plates" yields to the poet's father provoked into a killing and probable life imprisonment "if a lawyer had not convinced the governor /to pardon an Indian." A personal shelf of memory gathers of a Cherokee grandparent ("Granny's apples and tales"), of "road snow, mud or dust, from my parents' farm," and of the library-learned "colonial tyranny." Each, on the poem's evolving disclosure, has played its part in his mixed-blood entry "into the 20th Century." Little surprise, perhaps, that Salisbury's closing line asserts "being what I was [was] not ever simple again."

"A Rainbow of Stone," the collection's near-title poem, brings a yet fuller Native diorama into view, the universe of "Thunder's home" and "Creation" to be remembered against "factories smoking guns," "a bomber." One order of planetary being has incriminatingly yielded to another, that of "my Cherokee people's buffalo, deer/plantations, even our holy town,/Echota" to "crime, monoxide, disease, and other city uncertainties." For right balance to be restored there needs be a four directions full human ecology before, in the poet's eye "the whole earth will be toe-to-toe/rainbows." Thunder God and "your home" so again can phase into Nature's right equilibrium. The poem situates Salisbury in visionary mode, modern versifier yet also aspiring indigenous seer.

A similar ambition of scale holds for "A 20th Century Cherokee Farewell to Arms" (26-7). Child fantasies of becoming a tribal warrior supply a juncture, disconcertingly, with the allied World War II bombing of Dresden and follow-up in atomic Japan. The poem then veers back from what might have been "oxygen" or "cherry blossom," the end to "killing skills" whether past or still in prospect:

> the screams of victims to be
> the screams of Cherokee tortured and massacred – and
> of all the people who have ever been or will be
> lovers or killers. (27)

The lines convey Salisbury's wary lamentation born out of his own emplacement within modern war, and as equally, within the haunt of Native history. Self, lineage, world war again filter the one into the other.

***

The first years of Salisbury's life serve his poems as a form of lattice, not only actual self-history but as the very genesis of his vocation as poet. The Preface to *Rainbows of Stone* (2000) gives a succinct gloss:

> I need to recall the vanishing farming and hunting traditions
> with which I was raised. They are the landmarks I need if I am to
> keep to the Medicine Path I feel is mine. (i)

These beginnings supply requisite footholds and echoes throughout the volume. In "Of Pheasant and Blue-Winged Teal" (10) alimentation becomes its own drama ("Dad's killed/buffalo, deer and bear, respectfully"). Prairie homestead and weather presides in "Without Thunder" (8) in the recollection "Twelve, I was shocked out of dreams by what/whatever makes thunder had done to the barn"). Farm animals and their role are remembered in "Unloading" (21) which looks back to "two huge geldings hauling home, easily, the mountain of hay my aching arms had raised." The killing of a predatory weasel presages later war-killing in "Frost Baby Harp Seal Pelt" (96-7) in the lines "blizzard-drift shape I clubbed/ And pried out of trap-teeth baited /With guts of victim-chicken" 96). The poetry wholly un-sentimentalizes the legacy. Farming and hunt emerge as indeed the family's spare terms of survival with Salisbury the real but also figurative presence of the boy-poet put to steer his way through, and beyond, them.

One of Salisbury's most affecting poems in this regard is to be met in *Rainbows of Stone*'s "A Harvesting" (117) with its link between seasonal just-about subsistence and the poet's own imaginative crop from his past.[5] Taking its point of departure from an image of growth in the shape of a fern frond ("Curling around a finger of air") the poem moves on to the poet's dead musician father "strumming/iced vines" above his grave and his "English, Irish and Cherokee tunes." This is the father whose "trigger-finger" and "hunt/ for food, for generations" embodies life-will, the refusal of defeat. One almost thinks of Breughel's "The Hunters in the Snow," dogs, snow, light. For if the lines bespeak a starker world, that of under-nutrition and necessity, they also point to the poet's "harvesting with tongue, then pen" and to "feasting, dancing, courting again begun." The balance is finely struck, the two kinds of crop "harvested" and celebrated with the poet as mediating presence.

Emphasis, however, falls time and again upon remembered eat-or-die survival in the face of odds and which will through the course of Salisbury's writing segue into his anti-war life ethos. A poem like "For my Daughter, 10 Then and Now 11" in *Like the Sun in Storm* (78) gives voice to exactly those connections. Set "on this farm/my home/I've returned to" it conjures back from past time "wild dogs tearing sheep/to self-sopping rags/when I was ten" and "our dog fleeing from a rabid skunk/around and around our yard/until Dad's shot." The prevailing memory, however, lies in helping birth the calf "I pulled out of the heifer's gene-narrowed young withers." This scene of utter life, even if the obstetric calf is likely destined for the butcher's blade "no doubt rusted to dust by now," and bombers supposedly keeping the peace but gnawing the air like "enormous rats," links to life's contrariety. However vital, or necessary, life ("like leaves of corn/ growing towards ripening"), precarity is always close, whether its threat to his "safe-for-now daughter" or himself.

Immediate ancestry finds memorial idiom in "Family Stories and the One Not Told" (29) from the 2009 collection *Light from a Bullet Hole* ("Our Irish mother's tongue," "Dad's … pipe smoke tethering in our ears," "Great Grandmother … her Cherokee-Shawnee braid loosened at last"). It does again in "To My Mother's Father" in *Rainbows of Stone* (108) as chronicled by "Your grandson, his family visiting done,/on his way home." "For My Sister" in *Like the Sun In Storm* (34-5) has him thinking of her at the family homestead in later age, her "hair gray as the shingles of the farm." Whether the voices of family, or scant mealtimes and farm accidents to his brothers, or plough horses and seedtime, or rabbits and gophers, school-going and winter snow, Salisbury's beginnings press hard. The imaginative force of writing himself in from early family life seized from farm and hunt can be little doubted: it bespeaks the very fibers of his formation as person and poet, his situated-ness in the specific and world order.

***

War and peace, as "Green Smoke" in *Rainbows of Stone* (28) underscores, conjoin in the B-24 bomb episode that continues to haunt him:

And yes, eighteen, I saved eight men.
Nine if I count myself,
Corralling a bomb banging wild like a colt
Against our own bomb-bay, and now I'm a poet
And try to save everything
I love. (28)

The framing oppositions do immediate figurative duty. "It's World War Two again" Salisbury tethers to "now I'm a poet." The black death-threat of the "bomb-bay" grates against the regenerative green growing around the "graves of some friends." The poet, awakened at "six in the morning" by long distance phone-news of a downed crewman who shares his own exact name and who has been saved by The Rescue Squadron, tracks back to his own near-destruction aboard the training plane. The one happenstance meets another. Time-present tracks back into time-past. East Coast Atlantic gives way to Oregon Pacific. The poet, arisingly, sees himself the by-chance rescuer of the living. Humane, custodial, un-clichéd, it can be thought symptomatic of Ralph Salisbury's insistent stance for life over death.

This same event again finds remembrance in "A Bomber Crewman's Dance Around the Dead" (38), one of the highly personal war poems gathered in *Blind Pumper at the Well: Poems From My 80th Year* (2008) and whose section-heading Salisbury entitles in upper case WAR: DECLARATIONS, EVOCATIONS AND CONDEMNATIONS. The poet's precarious "18-year-old self," dangling "from a catwalk two miles/of freezing air about peaks" seeks to un-jam a wayward shackle with its bomb-load attached. The detail is insistently physical, raw hands on steel, the chilled body poised over a bomb that "could instantly kill eight,/including me." Were the "safety wire – a copper cobra" to rip those, too, at ground-level below might die. The task, however, its altitude and daring once negotiated, brings back into view the plane's basic purpose:

> … bomb
> and bomber were joined in unholy matrimony,
> not to be put asunder, until
> divorce would tell
> a story, with no ending. (38)

Salisbury's metaphor of marital joining and breakage, the prospect of bomb released from bomber, acts as both memory and forewarning. The poet himself may well have dangled, but so does humankind in its sundered "story" of un-ended war.

These poems have their company across the Salisbury oeuvre. Family and war finds its outlet in "War on, One Brother, Sixteen, and I, Try to Be Men" (82). Harking back to the farm's "corn-stalk-cutting machine," and its ability to "slice me into bacon strips" as he works the land with the brother who will become his "soldier-brother," he creates a contrast of not one but two kinds of machine.

The earlier, culled from "68 years" of back-memory, invokes "planting," albeit itself dangerous with horse-reins gripped and mud underfoot. The other, with his brother in military service, invokes the un-planting implicit in a "war-besotted world." Both kinds of hazard count but rarely more so than in the willed condition of armed conflict.

Salisbury may well query so-called "Indian Wars" in poems like "Canyon de Chelly" (48), be it in frontier America's "name of civilization" or in conquistador Spain's "name of the Virgin." But his poetry alights just as persistently on modernity's unrelieved penchant for military violence. A quartet from *Blind Pumper at the Well* bids for consideration. "Old German Woman, Some Wars" (40) envisages an aged American poet helping an even more aged German "survivor of bombs" as she descends from a tram. The both of them carry war-history: he in his remembrance of bomb revenge for Britain's World War II Coventry, she of the Reich's marching soldiers. He ends literally askance at his own once-again writing-in ("my fate to live to write to be/ignored, or read, by all/I would love to save"). The contrast of two different sites accrues, in "A Cherokee Airman Remembers Two Wars," one the Trail of Tears forced removal of the Cherokee in the 1830s, and in a time-leap forward, the bombing of Laos and other Asia in the 1960s. Salisbury writes as though inside his own double or even own double-double, his vision of a once tribal warrior of the Mississippi basin and a future high-tech warrior embroiled in the Mekong predations ("the moment's shade").

"My Country Again Threatening Aggression (This time, for oil in Iraq.)" 29) shifts into more recent terrain. "Our crusaders" have become corporate bankers whose Middle East appetite has again led into war and with it the desecration of "the union of women and men –and children – with earth." Natural resources have become unnatural, oil as ultimate "ocean" available only as war currency and to go un-thanked and un-uncelebrated "in cathedral/or temple or mosque." "A Nightmare After 9-11" (46) has the poet indeed caught up in dream-terror, the evisceration of the tribes into "Vanishing Americans" and the process whereby "imperialism's wronged" have "turned planes, and themselves, into bombs." He imagines himself a would-be stay against both "Columbus's invasion" and an inheritor of the "poetry" of moon and tides each in natural motion "aeons" before the New York attack. As war-poet, his writing spans Europe to Asia to the Middle East to the ever-present danger of global nuclear calamity. In his poem "Night Sky, Indian Ridge" (27) he speaks of "our, nuclear target, home." 27). It gives voice to yet another writing-in.

***

International ecology, manifestly, holds sway in Salisbury's poetry. Rarely can that have been more emphatic than in the four-poem oil sequence in *Rainbows of Stone*, his environmentalist alarm at sheer reckless pollution imaged with characteristic vibrancy. "Around the Sun, the Alaskan Oil Spill" (68), tracing the *Exxon Valdez* calamity in Prince William Sound, Alaska in 1989, opens with the streak as "Space-capsules-globules." Born of ancient evolutionary process ("ghost lizard-birds' coevals"), its modern abuse has led oil's having become the pollutant of seabirds ("re-entering the atmosphere/in the nostrils of terns"). Wings, dark and saturated, have turned into "witch-wings." Nature's balance has been unbalanced. "Each tern is sacred" insists the poem. The oil itself, equally, "formed from the dead – is sacred." Likewise "each moment of life is sacred." This is sun-given life as the poem's title indicates, a gift of "breath" wholly the opposite of the oil spill and "not to be wasted" (68). A second stanza links the poet's flow of blood inside his own arteries to the earth's oil ("I understand my blood,/its cargo vegetable and animal"). In self-acknowledging "words" he sees fatal endangerment in either spillage.

"Oil Spills, 1966, 1989" (69), given over to the *Torre Canyon* reef collision off Land's End, Cornwall, the worst in UK history, and again to the *Exxon Valdez*, connects Salisbury family history to each disaster. The poem looks back to Roman England, where the name Salisbury with its meaning of salt-storage originates, and then sideways to the 1966 of the Vietnam War, Israel's defeat of the Arabs, and the civil war of Biafra. The contrast arises between animal killing "to keep my Indian people from extinction" and the arbitrary killing of habitat and people. Salt preserved and Native-consumed meat invites a truce "with the creatures whose lives we'd made ours." But modernity's glut lies far in excess of required subsistence. The closing stanza acts as summary:

> OIL SPILLS, MORE CARS, OIL, WARS
> and SUICIDAL MURDERS'S BULLET HOLES
> IN CHILDREN'S CHILDREN'S CHILDREN'S
> OZONE PROTECTION, our literature
> today, tomorrow's page. (69)

The mien is sardonic, 1966 or 1989 as a "literature" of crude-oil tanker spill, car, bullet, ozone or child, and with the "page" of the future likely more of the same. It then remains for the poet "fed/by a grant (conceived to prevent poets' extinction)" to issue written and written-in warning.

"Ocean Enough: Exxon's Alaskan Oil Spill" (71) avails itself of more closely Native-referenced bearings. It uses a deft avian contrast, oil-impaired bird and Salisbury's own possible membership of the Cherokee/Yunwiya "Bird Clan." Reports of "spilled tons" have been accompanied by the headline cant of "THE PRICE OF PROGRESS." The poet thinks back to the extinction of prairie chicken "that/ kept us from starving during The Great/Depression" as necessity but also guilt. He also thinks of Tsk-skwa, the Cherokee for mating, birds sprung from prehistoric pterodactyl but become "ghost-fledgling" in the wake of desecration of ocean and "corpse-poisoned shore."

"Oil Spill Spreading" (72) shares this vision. Time-scale has meant centuries of "oil put under pressure." Opportunism has led to the lure of "Black Gold," a "Siberia" of "imprisoning Indians" and "oil company guns." The upshot, courtesy of *Exxon Valdez*, has been "ink-black/fossil-blood on a white/Alaska shore" (the inserted scriptural or writing trace not to be missed) and yet more ominously under hunger for exploitable resources the "danger of being, forever,/the night of nuclear-winter." The "I" of the poem, Salisbury in persona, gives himself no exemption in the chain of exploitation ("I'm a killer, a carnivore"). His writing-in, albeit minute in scale, so links into the always immensely greater cost, the earth's vulnerability ("hurling towards extinction") in the face of each act of environmental predation.

***

Writing and its actuation in its own imaginative right assumes a defining importance throughout each Salisbury poetry-collection. Even so, in "Personal Poem, Perhaps in the Manner of Tu Fu," from *Like the Sun in Storm,* Salisbury is not above affecting the off-hand as though himself the merest good-luck poet:

> I drift in a poem an apple tree,
> Ripening before first frost, throws off,
> Without apparent thought. (28)

In fact there can be little mistaking his skills, the fine-tuning of metaphor, the adeptness with periodical line-sentence. Across all the domains which draw him it is always the poetry that dictates, however consequential the matter at hand. "Without apparent thought" may give off an impression of Zen-like osmosis. In fact it exactly belies Salisbury's summoning of self to craft.

"Words Concerned with Words" (4), the second poem in *Blind Pumper at the Well,* approaches something of his writer's credo. How best to keep language oxygenated, free of political or other sham? For him the answer lies in literary fraternity, that of the transnational poet above all. To that end he invokes a column of writers whose work has been preserved against odds: the great Jewish Hungarian writer Miklos Radnoti killed by the Nazis but whose work was saved by his wife ("The years of love in her husband's words" or the intervention of Robert Bridges in preserving the poetry of Hopkins, or Max Brod in the case of Kafka's "lifetimes of words." The final stanza takes its swipe at the pretend-truth of "millions of words/of leaders" as against, in a sharp paradox, "the betrayals of faithful friends, who saved loving and deathless, words"). Alluding to the "fidelity" in this respect of his own wife, he looks to his best fortune in anticipating the prospect of so being further written-in.

A whole concourse of shared self-allusion invites notice. In "For Years and Years" (*Rainbows of Stone* 114-15), a poem given to dreams of death by accident, the first of them recalls himself in childhood with "legs no longer than pencils." "Slitting the Tongue, so That Crow Should be Parrot" (*Light from a Bullet Hole* 137) Salisbury's remembrance of cutting his wounded crow's tongue in the name of having it "sing," he links it to his eventual bardism ("age bends my trigger-finger on pen"). "Caring for the Soon to Be Born" (*Light from a Bullet Hole* 140), glossed as "a final heartbeat likely to leave /grandchildren and poems not yet formed," offers the very synopsis of the poet at work with "stub-pencil sharpened on trigger-finger nail" and bound "to scribble the times/ of destinies, which would – war not yet nuclear – be born."[6]

Salisbury's fellow-writer tributes and affinities each add to the writing-in, whether "For Octavio Paz" ("This magician"),"Jim Barnes, Choctaw" ("Jim Barnes is trading the world"), "For Simon Ortiz" ("his words circle the world"), or "Two Poems in Memory of Nils-Aslak Valkeapää" ("remembering the Chernobyl disaster year, when Nils-Aslak and I first exchanged poems").[7] Perhaps verse like "Green Cows" in *Light from a Bullet Hole* (170) serves to draw the threads together. Late-written, aware of pressing mortality ("Alive, still"), Salisbury gives thanks for maple trees and their leaf-sugar ("seventy foot tall green cows") and beech trees (their squirrels and the gathered nuts "to bag and crack"). These are trees that yield "Growth ring/on growth ring – a poem." The allusion commands attention. It would be fitting to think Salisbury's lifetime writing-in his personal species of growth-ring, the poem within his poetry.

Notes

1 Ralph Salisbury, *So Far, So Good*, Lincoln: University of Nebraska Press, 2013, 186.

2 "I would save the cat: An Interview with Ralph Salisbury," Bo Schöler, *American Studies in Scandinavia*, 17, 1985, 33.

3 This episode is again summoned in "Swimming in the Morning News." The lines read of his awakening and remembering "the day I awkwardly swam/and saved two young women from drowning," as against "today, the somber wing of poetry so many's/sole chance to survive." *Like The Sun in Storm*, 65.

4 Ralph Salisbury, "An Indian Blows Up Mr. Rushmore and Indianizes What Cannot Be Resanctified," *Like The Sun in Storm*, Portland: The Habit of Rainy Nights Press, 2012,4.

5 Ralph Salisbury, "A Harvesting," *Like The Sun in Storm*, 62.

6 Ralph Salisbury, "Caring for the Soon to Be Born," *War in the Genes*, 2006. Reprinted in *Light from a Bullet Hole*, 140.

7 Ralph Salisbury, "For Octavio Paz," *Going to the Water*, 1983, reprinted in *Light from a Bullet Hole*, 63; "For Simon Ortiz," *Rainbows of Stone*, 78; "For Jim Barnes, Choctaw, *Rainbows of Stone*, 81; "Two Poems in Memory of Nils-AslakValpeapää," *Blind Pumper at the Well*, 65-6.

Works Cited

Salisbury, Ralph, *So Far, So Good*, Lincoln: University of Nebraska Press, 2013.

_____, *Like the Sun in Storm*, Portland: The Habit of Rainy Nights Press, 2012.

_____, *The Indian Who Bombed Berlin and Other Stories*, East Lansing: Michigan State University Press, 2009.

_____, *Light from a Bullet Hole: Poems New and Selected 1950–2008*, Eugene: Silverfish Review Press, 2008.

_____, *Blind Pumper at the Well: Poems from my 80th Year*, Cambridge: Salt, 2008.

_____, *Rainbows of Stone*, Tucson: University of Arizona Press, 2000.

Epilogue: Native, North American, Authorship

Native. North American. Authorship. Each of these terms possesses a deceptive innocence. Do they not simply mean "Indian" writings in the USA? Yes, it might be said, but then, and almost immediately, also no. For all three bear complex, even contradictory, implication: identity, geography, script. Their challenge to altogether more nuanced definition, or to unknotting them, gives departures, prerequisites. Until recent decades often assigned to the periphery, an assumed maybe interesting but lesser by-way, Native and First Nations writings in truth have created not some by-way but a full history of literary voice. That, too, may well have meant shared stocks of tribal myth or remembrance but no one univocal register. A plurality of compositional style holds, fiction, verse or discursive text.

Such, in fact, was always likely from the start given the vast language repertoire of the tribes, histories early to contemporary, regional and cross-border, reservation centered and citied, and gendered one or another. In few respects has that become the more evident than in the ways the Native-written page enters modern, and in a number of cases postmodern, styling. The exploratory range of invention across the genres has grown exponentially.

***

Native. How, best, to construe the use of Native as composite naming? It evidently has a role as catch-all, some ease-of-hand category. But that goes only so far.[1] Equally "Indian" continues to hold as usage, a geographic misnomer at the outset yet long installed by rote. Yet other generic terms have long won currency. In *So You Want to Write About American Indians?* (2005), for instance, Devon Abbott Mihesuah, Choctaw historian and previous editor of *American Indian Quarterly*, expresses a preference for Indigenous. Rightly, and equally, she calls for tribal particularization of naming.

If recognition of the full idiom of Native civilizations is to count one might begin with those of the Olmecs, Mayans and Aztecs. Other demography summons awareness of the Algonquin peoples, or the Navajo, the Anishinaabe, the Laguna and Acoma Pueblo, the Sioux, Cherokee, Comanches, Arapaho, Hopi, Apache (whether Mescalero, White Mountain, Jicarilla or San Carlos), Chickasaw, Osage, Zuni, Blackfeet, Salish, Nez Percé, or Seminoles. Native self-naming, often meaning simply the people, contests extraneous, and often wildly prejudicial, "Native" nomenclature. That embraces the *Diné*, the Navajo word for themselves, *Numa* for the Paiutes, *Apsaloka* for the Crow, *Tsis-tas* for the Cheyenne, and *Oceti Sakowin* (or Seven Fireplaces) as the different branches of the Sioux know their range of clan.

As to tribal languages themselves, they at first could indeed be construed by New England's Puritans as the Devil's Tongue, or, just as exotically, and a frequent assumption, some diasporic Lost Tribe's Hebrew. Translation led into every kind of impasse, literal misunderstandings to be sure, but also, as in the case of many missionary syllabaries, vernacular and especially sexual usages either changed or frequently censored. As the first "Indian" texts began to appear in print, themselves often twice or even three-times made over from oral sources or adapted from pictomyth, histories that once had been delivered in performance, full of live improvisation, became linear, a sequencing reassuringly western.[2]

For just as the Columbian conquest and 1492 began a seizure of land and body in the fifteenth-century, so the principal colonizing idioms of English, Spanish, French, Portuguese and Dutch seized, and in an always vexing term, *translated*, "the Indian" into their own preemptive writ. Indian/savage, indio/piel roja, peau-rouge/sauvage: these, and their like, whether in New England or Mexico's Nueva España or Canada's Nouvelle France, became the lexical pair bondings of Euro-colonialism. Othering by linguistic means actually begins early, whether Middle Ages or Renaissance locutions of "the primitive." Matters would grow into greater complexity given eventual demographic overlaps, the language in use often pejorative to describe the mix of Native with Europeans and Euro-Americans, notably Native with Spanish – hence Latino/a or as of now Latinx, or Native with African American and Asian American. Looking back to these histories the Mexican-Chicano performance artist, Guillermo Gómez-Peña asks with considerable pertinence: "How can the five hundred million *mestizos* who inhabit the Americas be called a 'minority'"?[3]

"Native," even so, and with "Indian" in alliance, can even now still carry the vexing ancestral tag of savagism, on the one hand noble in the terminology of Rousseau or on the other diabolic with Shakespeare's Caliban as half-ancestor to the image. Both versions plait into each other in the Puritan settlements of New England in seventeenth-century Algonquin-named Massachusetts and the Virginia settlements of Jamestown and thereafter in the territories of the Powhattan Confederacy. Other prejudicial terms, notably "Chief," "redman," "squaw," continue to be a source of provocation, the latter in a place-name like California's Squaw Valley. In his short-piece essay and story collections *Funny You Don't Look Like One* (1997) and the sequel, *Further Adventures of a Blue-Eyed Ojibway* (1999), Canada's Drew Hayden Taylor (Curve Lake Chippewa-Ojibwe) takes shrewdly comic aim at all and any essentialist versions of First Nations and Native peoples

Natives as Vanishing Americans has also increasingly met repudiation. The usual version holds that Native America largely bows out after the massacre at Wounded Knee in 1890 with a follow-on in both reservation and off-reservation poverty or drift. Versions of the West, rather, become mainly white settler frontierism, the saga of valiant homesteader and cowboy. But that, too, comes under scrutiny as the internal colonialism of Manifest Destiny. Increasingly Native activism has sought to right the balance. Politics, latterly, has found energy in the American Indian Movement (AIM), begun in 1968–9 as pan-tribal radical cadre under leadership like Clyde Bellecourt (White Earth Chippewa-Ojibwe), Dennis Banks (Leech Lake Chippewa-Ojibwe), Russell Means (Oglala Lakota), Ward Churchill (Muscogee-Creek-Cherokee), John Trudell (Santee Dakota) and Eddie Benton-Banai (Chippewa-Ojibwe). In them, and theirs, and despite murmurs of radical chic, Red Power enters modern currency.

There have also been the Tribal Councils, the National American Rights Fund (NARF) founded in 1971, the different sovereignty and resources movements, and the rise of tribally owned casinos in Connecticut, California, New Mexico and Minnesota. Political spectaculars like the 1969–1971 AIM occupation of Alcatraz Island and 1975 Pine Ridge shoot-out made media headlines. Canadian media likewise found itself reporting the politics whereby the country's Supreme Court in 1973 upheld the Niska people's land claims in British Columbia and in 1999 the recognition of Mi'kmaq fishing rights in Nova Scotia.

Given that *Native* necessarily implies plurality as against the one collectivized fiction the need for historical embedding is essential. In the case of North America selective way-stations serialize the process, pre-Columbian to modern. Columbus himself speaks of his proprietary encounter with the "gentle" Arowaks in the 1490s. Pope Julius II decrees that "Indians" can be thought to possess souls and are thereby to be elevated above animals in 1512. Cortés defeats the Aztecs in 1521. Anglo-America's early "Indian Wars" include the 1622–44 Virginia colonial conflicts with the Powhatan Confederacy, the 1630s conflicts with the Pequots in Massachusetts, King Philip's War in 1675–76, the Pueblo Revolt in New Mexico against Spanish colonization in 1680, and the British, French and Indian Wars of 1754–63 (notoriously involving the smallpox-infected blankets attributed to Lord Jeffrey Amherst). The New World "discovery" narrative shields that of the Americas as appropriated tribal habitation and terrain.

England establishes a Board of Commissioners in 1675 in Albany to handle "Indian Affairs." Andrew Jackson's war against the Creeks in 1814, the Indian Removal Act he signed in 1830, and the forced expulsion in 1838 of the Cherokee from Georgia to Oklahoma and known in Cherokee as *Nunna dual Tsuny* or the Trail of Tears also inaugurated by Jackson and pursued by his successor Martin Van Buren into the 1850s, makes for symptomatic memory. Following the inauguration of the Bureau of Indian Affairs, the BIA, in 1824, "Indians" in 1849 are revealingly put under the War Department, later the Department of the Interior.

One core event remains the Battle of Little Bighorn, Montana in 1876, the defeat of Lieutenant-Colonel George Custer and the 7th Cavalry by an alliance of the Northern Cheyenne and the Lakota Sioux under Sitting Bull. Frequently it is taken to be one of the Native triumphs against Manifest Destiny, the unremitting press of white-colonial and military encroachment. Even so, removal, and each wave of disease from pneumonia and TB, especially in the 1920s, to reservation alcoholism and FAS births, makes for a depleting litany.

The reversals look back to the infamous killing of 500 or so Shoshone by Federal troops at Bear River, Idaho, in 1863, the Sand Creek Massacre in 1864, the murder of peaceably encamped Cheyenne and Arapaho under the leadership at the Battle of Washita in 1868, the army attack on the Blackfeet at Marias River, Montana in 1870, and the culminating massacre of more than 250 Lakota Sioux adults and children camped at Pine Ridge's Wounded Knee, South Dakota, by the US 7th Cavalry, in 1890. The Dawes General Allotment (or Severalty) Act of 1887 and successor legislation in kind finagles Native land rights and head-title. Understandably the damage involved would mean not only literal but spiritual dislocation. The 1890s Ghost Dance, along with other revivalist movements inspired by the visions of the Paiute shaman Wovoka (1856–1932) known as Jack Wilson, were far from atavism. Rather they amount to a way of handling the cut of history.

It has, too, to be the richest historical irony that the Indian Citizenship Act of 1924, also known as the Snyder Act, made citizens of those descended from first inhabitants. To follow, the Wheeler-Howard/Indian Reorganization Act of 1934, supposedly re-assigns degrees of sovereignty. The IRA, sometimes called the Depression era's Red New Deal, also attracted opprobrium and rather to be thought the Raw New Deal. Without acceding to history-as-victimry the cost of this will to dominance has been grievous. It embraces white triumphal conquest by fort and cavalry, covered wagon, homestead, farm, oil-scatting, cattle-herding and the use of barbed wire (first patented in 1867), fur and other trapping in the Northwest and Canada, Missions in the Southwest and West, trophy-hunting of bison and buffalo, the "iron horse" locomotive, and the various kinds of legislative fiat.

As upshot the nations lost access to ancestral space, seasonal food-stock like the buffalo and rice, freedom of movement and continental horizon. *Native* becomes ever more a term to imply lesser or subjugated humanity and often enough in need of de-Indianization and Christian conversion. Eclipsed or lost is a due sense of lived time-space and calendar, creation and vision myth, art, dance, wordplay and humor, cedar burning, childrearing, and even foodways, whether wild rice, cornmeal, maize, game or fish cooked over mesquite. How, then, indeed to meet in its historicity, old and new and in every variety, a Native America and First Nations Canada whether tribally enrolled or not, full-blood or more likely mixed-blood, reservation and reserve (in the Canadianism) or city-urban, and for sure, modern?

Dips of population, much poverty, there undoubtedly have been, lowest at the transition into the twentieth-century. But today's estimated Native population of four million (some estimates speak of ten million when augmented by the First Nations peoples of Canada and the indigenous Pacific and Caribbean) bears witness to the radical fact of survival or in the increasingly used term *survivance* as deployed by the voluble Gerald Vizenor. *Survivance*, adapted from French, is to signal more than mere utilitarian *survival*, rather the continuity of un-static cultural vigor.[4]

In *Manifest Manners: Postindian Warriors of Survivance* (1994) Vizenor offers an encapsulation of obstacles to the writing of this America:

> The Indian was an occidental invention that became a bankable simulation; the word has no referent in tribal languages or cultures...Native American Indians have endured the envies of missionaries of manifest manners for five centuries. The Boy Scouts of America, the wild simulations of tribal misnomers used for football teams, automobiles and other products. Western movies, and the heroic adventures in novels by James Fenimore Cooper, Frederick Manfred, Karl May, and others are but a few examples of the manifold envies that have become manifest manners in the literatures of dominance.[5]

Shari M. Huhndorf's *Going Native: Indians in the American Cultural Imagination* (2001) adds astutely to this long spiral of "Indian" or "Native" simulation. Early World Fair exhibits supply manikin and cartoon. Forrest Carter's Young Adult but faux-Cherokee *The Education of Little Tree* (1976) becomes a best-seller. Robert J. Flaherty's silent movie documentary *Nanook of the North* in 1922 wins commercial success as "realism" while in fact staging many of its scenes. Kevin Costner adapts Michael Blake's novel *Dances with Wolves* (1988) in 1990 which despite Academy Awards and the use of Sioux language and actors dismayed any number of Native viewers for its gratuitous wolf symbolism, white-woman savior ethos, and final decamping into the mists. However beguiling, text or screen and from childhood's Cowboys and Indians forward, Native authorship has long had to negotiate, often enough rebut, the persistence of these silhouettes and charades.

Fortunately there has been restorative perspective at the hands of Native professional historians. Among them, most notably, ranks Vine Deloria (Yangton Sioux), historian, lawyer, holder of a theology degree, and University of Colorado professor, whose *Custer Died for Your Sins: An Indian Manifesto* (1969) and *We Talk, You Listen: New Tribes, New Turf* (1970) continue to win widespread status for cultural ground-clearing. Selective other Native authored histories include Rupert and Jeannette Costo's *The Missions of California: A Legacy of Genocide* (1987), Philip J. Deloria's *Playing Indian* (1999), Ned Blackhawk's *Violence Over the Land: Indians and Empires in the Early American West* (2008), and Jodi Byrd's *The Transit of Empire: Indigenous Critiques of Colonialism* (2011). These align yet on occasion contrast with studies like Angie Debo's *A History of the Indians of the United States* (1970), Dee Brown's *Bury My Heart at Wounded Knee* (1970), Peter Matthiessen's *In The Spirit of Crazy Horse* (1983), Robert M. Utley's *The Indian Frontier of the American West, 1846-1890* (1984), or Bruce Fox's *Native People, Native Lands: Canada's Indians, Inuit and Métis* (2008). Cumulatively the gains have been the altogether more complete account of the origins and continuity of Native presence.

Native and First Nations literary texts not only carry but are wholly constitutive of these histories. Whether they draw on specific tribal history, or shared creation and trickster lore, or take wholly new inventive bearings and so qualify for Vizenor's naming as *postindians*, the consequence has been to remember and at the same time transpose legacy. In the light of each arising body of fiction and verse, life-writing, theatre, and discursive text, it leaves little to doubt that Native (and First Nations) as presiding terms have undoubted shorthand uses but also their limits in the face of the human complexity that lies within them.

In *There There*, when Tommy Orange pauses the narrative for an Interlude, it is to enumerate all the reeling nomenclature that has gathered around the term Native:

> We are Indians and Native Americans, American Indians and Native American Indians. North American Indians, Natives, NDNs and Ind'ins, Status Indians and non-Status Indians, First Nations Indians and Indians so Indian we either think about the fact of it every single day or we never think about it at all. We are Urban Indians and Indigenous Indians, Rez Indians and Indians from Mexico and Central and South America ... We are full-blood, half-breed, quadroon, eighths, sixteenths, thirty -seconds. Undoable math. Insignificant remainders.

Taxonomy, mock-taxonomy, and even selected in part, the list does service, as does his accompanying contrast of Western and Native last names. Both riffs, virtuoso reckonings, throw light on the processes of "Native" othering.

***

Native North America. "America," in general parlance, overwhelmingly has come to signify North America. Yet in a necessary comprehensive sense it gives reason to call up all the Americas and Canada with full cognizance of indigenous locales reaching from Alaska's Bering Strait to Argentine's Tierra del Fuego, the Caribbean's Barbados and Jamaica to the Pacific of Hawai'i 'Oahu, Maui and Guam, and embracing each "Latin" country whether Spanish- or Brazilian-Portuguese speaking, or one of the many Amazonian and other indigenous languages. More nuanced cartography was always in order,

Native North America as formulation needs every particularization, habitations (and migrations) of Plains, Woodland, Rockies, Coast, Pueblo, Sea and River, and in due course the reservations, the reserves, and the cities. Almost all the nations internalize a profoundest sense of place, whether derived from memorial creation-myths, sightlines of land and mountain, past dynastic and settlement patterns, food-gathering and hunt, or even from imposed re-location. Of late there has been increasing critique of the ways settler-colonial America and Canada dominated the geographic narrative, settler-metropoles from New York to Vancouver. Ownership of continental space, and its cities, has rarely allowed for the full account, rather the New (old) World awaiting discovery and that in turn delayed by Native intransigence.

Native time-space, however, has its own sequence. Symptomatically it looks to Illinois's pre-Columbian Cahokia Mounds with their reminders of settlements and sophisticated earthen construction. It bequeaths Colorado's Mesa Verde with its mature Anasazi cliff and ledge dwellings. Algonquin peoples may have been made over into Atlantic past calendar as in James Fenimore Cooper's *The Last of the Mohicans: A Narrative of 1757* (1826). But it hardly reflects the historic reality of Mohegans and certainly not the fact that their far-from-last wholly present-day descendants continue and thrive. They are centered in the Mohegan Reservation by Connecticut's Thames River in Uncasville.

The Northeast's peoples, whether New York's Abenaki or Maine and New Brunswick's Passamaquoddy, likewise have continued through time, un-extinguished, actual, and with their own traditions of tribal law and self-governance. The south, again typically, can look to the Seminoles in Florida or the Choctaw and Chickasaw in Mississippi. The southwest besides the Navajo and Hopi vaunts the Pueblos, New Mexico's Laguna or Acoma, a tapestry of canyon, mesa, art, maize, pine, light and color. The upper mid-west has the Chippewa or Ojibwe whose Anishinaabe language (*Anishinaabemowin)* supplies the naming of the Mississippi as America's great arterial river (*misi-ziibi* or *gichi-zibi*), and whether the Red Lake Reservation of Minnesota and Ontario, Minnesota's White Earth, or the Oneida Reservation in Wisconsin. Spanning Canada and North Dakota and Montana are the Cree, currently the largest Native tribal population at 200,000 to which can be added the Cree-métis population.

North and South Dakota, the latter with its Black Hills, yield the Lakota and other Sioux, a people of historic resistance to frontier encroachment. Nevada, with its deserts, has the Paiute. Montana, with its imposing stretch of the Rocky Mountains, looks to the Flathead and Blackfeet peoples. The Pacific northwest of Washington and Oregon, with their forests, glaciers and coastline, besides the Salish, count the Coeur d'Alene, Blackfeet and Makah. California, coast to sierras, embraces the descendants of the Mission Indians and tribal peoples like the Pomo, Chumash, Yurok, Shoshone, and Yuki. Alaska, the Yukon, with their arctic tundra and seasonal round of fish and seal, has peopling in the Tlingit and

Inuit. Canada geographies likewise carry continental span, East to West Coast, more than 600 nations on land from Mohawk Ontario to the Inuit Arctic.

Always, pivotally, there is multi-tribal Oklahoma, Choctaw-named and the heart of "Indian Country" as it was once known with its more than sixty tribal clans and peoples, twenty-plus Native languages, and to include either by origin or forced relocation the Cherokee, Osage, Choctaw, Kiowa-Apache, Wyandot and Shawnee. Statehood was granted in 1907. It can justly be asked which, not to say whose, America, or Americas, are these.

One further sphere involves a yet more inclusive Native geography, that registered in scholarship like Philip J. Deloria's *Indians in Unexpected Places* (2004) and Jace Weaver's *The Red Atlantic: American Indigenes and the Making of the Modern World, 1000-1920* (2014). Both studies give weight to "place" in early and later Native lives. Few do so more than the Wahunsenacawh-born Powhatan captive Matoaka who passes into history as Pocahontas (1596–1617), bride to John Rolfe, who voyages to England and early death and burial in Gravesend, Kent, in the UK. Tomochichi (1644–1739), leader of Georgia's Tamacraw people, acts as intermediate with the British and appears with fellow Creeks to George II's court in Kensington, London. Paul Cuffee (1759–1817), mixed-blood and Quaker-abolitionist born of Wampanoag and Ashanti parentage, becomes a mariner, acquires a shipping fortune, and enters Sierra Leone and other Africa in the quest to end enslavement.

Deloria extends his coverage to the Custer circuses through to Native portraiture on the silent screen and Hollywood talkies. Weaver, with a nod to Paul Gilroy's *The Black Atlantic, Modernity and Double Consciousness* (1993), includes in the hemispheric reach not only voyagers, captives, soldiery, diplomats and celebrities but makers of literary texts. Unexpected places, the Red Atlantic: Native texts, as Native lives, have been written ever more globally be it Britain, Europe, Asia, or the Antipodes.[6]

***

Authorship. Literary inscription, from the outset, has had counterparts, alliances of vision and image in the visual arts. Native/First Nations authorship has always had creative company, the spectrum always larger than any one expressive art. Whole inter-dimensions of narrative go missing where there is inattention to the picturing of creation myth, belief system, powwow, potlatch, healing, through to life in "the urban reservation" of the cities. In specific terms this can mean Anasazi clay and habitation design, Chippewa-Ojibwe bark pictographs, Osage or Tlingit blankets, Pueblo pottery, Hopi basketwork, Zuni katchina carving, or Navajo sand painting, silverwork and turquoise coral jewelry. The same creativity of sign presses from behind San Gabriel's southern Californian petroglyphs and rock art, the Osage Picture Cave polychrome glyphs in the Osage country of Warrenton, eastern Missouri, and the vivid red-and-black Haida engravings of British Columbia. To these one adds the historic cedar and other wood heraldic carvings of thunderbird, salmon or bear by the Kwakiutl, Tlingit, Nootka, and again the Haida, in the Pacific Northwest, British Columbia to Alaska, These signify Native worlds, a sumptuous variety of analogous "authorship," again fully alive even in the very process of memorialization.

Galleries now hold a vast body of Native ancestral and modern artwork, painting, beadwork, jewelry, video and even graffiti. The National Museum of The American Indian opened in Washington D.C. in 2004. More single-tribally centered are the Wampanoag National Museum in Plymouth, Massachusetts, the Navajo Tribal Museum in Window Rock, Arizona, and the Makah Cultural Center in Neah Bay, Washington. Shared displays of artefact can be met in the annual Santa Fe Indian Market or the First Peoples Cultural Festival in Vancouver.

Indigenous curation has been a major development. Instances include the Monument Heritage Center of Minnesota's Grand Portage Ojibwe Band in conjunction with the National Park Service opened in 2007. Latterly New York's Metropolitan Museum has its first Native curator of indigenous American Art in Patricia Maroquin Norby, of Mexican-Purépecha descent and appointed in 2020. In Canada the MacKenzie Art Gallery in Regina has appointed John G. Hampton of Chickasaw descent as director with a brief to help decolonialize exhibition spaces and practices.

Visual legacy exerts its increasing calendar in these and like outsets, whole forums of image. Who best to pick? Allen Houser (Chiricahua Apache) creates hugely popular graphics. Expressionism has its exponents in George Morrison (Chippewa-Ojibwe). Modernism looks to T. C. Cannon (Kiowa) and Fritz Scholder (Luseño). Wit and story-panel speaks in David Bradley (Chippewa-Ojibwe). Map-drawing takes its impressionist turns in Jaune Quick-to-See Smith (Salish-Kootenai). Futurism has contemporary idiom in the canvases of Andrea Carlson (Chippewa-Ojibwe). Sculpture has long celebrated a First Nations master in Bill Reid (Haida) whose *Haida Gwaii*, his jade-bronze canoe sculpture with its human and animal world crew, stands as welcome in Vancouver Airport.

Film-work of consequence likewise increasingly gains ground. Chris Eyre (Cheyenne/Arapaho) directs *Smoke Signals* (1998), with its adaptation of Sherman Alexie's antic reverse-capture story "This is What it Means to Say Phoenix," a pioneer full feature. Sydney Freeland (Navajo) creates *Drunktown's Finest* (2014) which explores Navajo city life at the margins and uses a full Native cast. Ella-Máijá Tailfeathers (Blackfoot), with co-direction by Kathleen Hepburn, brings *The Body Remembers When the World Broke Open* (2019) to the screen, two First Nations women negotiating abuse and then friendship in East Vancouver. Modern Native photography might take in the currently ongoing portfolio of Russel Albert Daniels (Navajo-Diné) in *The Genízaro Pueblo of Abiquiú*, with its New Mexico documentation, or Tailyr Irvine (Salish-Kootenai) in *Reservation Mathematics: Navigating Love in Native America,* her model photojournalism. Both have displayed, gallery and website, at the National Museum of the American Indian (NMAI).

This formidable body of art from across the genres gives companion strength to Native/First Nations textual tradition. Canvas, screen, sculpture or other visual expression, the effect is to keep best company with the literature explored in *Native North American Authorship: Breath, Text, Modernity.*

Notes

1 See, in this respect, Deborah L. Madsen, ed., *Native Authenticity: Transnational Perspectives on Native American Literary Studies*, Albany: State University of New York Press, 2010. In her Introduction, "Contemporary Discourses on 'Indianness'" she writes a succinct account of the debates involved.

2 For overall guides see Franz Boas, *Race, Language and Culture*, New York: Macmillan, 1940; Lyle Campbell and Marianne Mithun, eds., *The Languages of Native America: Historical and Comparative Assessment*, Austin: University of Texas Press, 1979; William Bright, *American Indian Linguistics and Literature*, Berlin: Mouton, 1994; and Ives Goddard, *Native Languages and Language Families of North America*, Lincoln: University of Nebraska Press, 1999.

3 Guillermo Gómez-Peña, *The Graywolf Annual Five: Multicultural Literacy*, eds., Rick Simonson and Scott Walker, 1988.

4 Gerald Vizenor has long become identified with the term "survivance." An overview of its implications for Native authorship is to be found in Gerald Vizenor, ed., *Survivance: Narratives of Native Presence*, Lincoln: University of Nebraska Press, 2009.

5 Gerald Vizenor, *Manifest Manners, Postindian Warriors of Survivance*, Hanover and London: Wesleyan University Press, 1981, 11, 31.

6 Besides Deloria and Weaver, other studies which speak to this context include David E. Stannard, *American Holocaust: The Conquest of the New World*, New York: Oxford University Press, 1994; Jack Weatherford, *Indian Givers: How the Indians of the Americas Transformed the World*, New York: Random House, 2010; and Roxanne

Dunbar-Ortiz and Dina Gilo-Whitaker, *"All the Real Indians Died Off": And 20 Other Myths About Native Americans*, Boston: Beacon Press, 2016.

Works Cited

Blackhawk, Ned, *Violence Over the Land: Indians and Empires in the Early American West*, Cambridge: Harvard University Press, 2009.

Blake, Michael, *Dances with Wolves*, New York: Fawcett, 1988.

Brown, Dee, *Bury My Heart at Wounded Knee: An Indian History of the American West*, New York: Holt, Rinehart and Winston, 1970.

Byrd, Jodi, *The Transit of Empire: Indigenous Critiques of Colonialism*, Minneapolis: University of Minnesota Press, 2011.

Carter, Forrest, *The Education of Little Tree*, New York: Fawcett Gold Medal, 1988.

Costo, Rupert, and Costo, Jeannette A., *The Missions of California: A Legacy of Genocide*, San Francisco: Indian Historian Press, 1987.

Debo, Angie, *A History of the Indians of the United States*, Norman: University of Oklahoma Press, 1970.

Deloria, Philip, J., *Indians in Unexpected Places*, Lawrence: University Press of Kansas, 2004.

_____, *Playing Indian*, New Haven: Yale University Press, 1998.

Deloria, Vine, *We Talk, You Listen: New Tribes, New Turf*, New York: Macmillan, 1970.

_____, *Custer Died for Your Sins: An Indian Manifesto*, New York: Macmillan, 1969. 2nd Edition, Norman: University of Oklahoma Press, 1995.

Fox, Bruce, *Native People, Native Lands: Canada's Indians, Inuit and Métis*, New York: Oxford University Press, 1988.

Gilroy, Paul, *The Black Atlantic, Modernity and Double Consciousness*, Cambridge: Harvard University Press, 1993.

Howe, LeAnne, Markovitz, Harvey, and Cummins, Denise K., eds., *Seeing Red, Hollywood's Pixeled Skins: American Indians and Film*, East Lancing: Michigan State University Press, 2003.

Huhndorf, Sheri M., *Going Native: Indians in the American Cultural Imagination*, Ithica: Cornell University Press, 2001.

Matthiessen, Peter, *In the Spirit of Crazy Horse*, New York: Viking, 1983.

Mihesuah, Devon Abbott, *So You Want to Write About American Indians? A Guide for Writers, Students, and Scholars*, Lincoln: University of Nebraska Press, 2005.

Morris, Irvin, *From the Glittering World: A Navajo Story*, Norman: University of Oklahoma Press, 1997.

Taylor, Drew Hayden, *Further Adventures of a Blue-Eyed Ojibway*, Penticton, British Columbia: Theytus, 1999.

_____, *Funny You Don't Look Like One*, Penicton, British Columbia: Theytus, 1997.

Utley, Robert, *The Indian Frontier of the American West, 1846*-1890, Albuquerque: University of New Mexico Press, 1984.

Vizenor, Gerald, ed., *Survivance: Narratives of Native Presence*, Lincoln: University of Nebraska Press, 2009.

_____, *Manifest Manners: Postindian Warriors of Survivance*, Hanover: Wesleyan University Press/University of New England Press, 1992.

About the Author

A. Robert Lee, formerly of the University of Kent, UK, was Professor in the English Department of Nihon University, Tokyo 1996–2011. He has held visiting appointments at the University of Virginia, Bryn Mawr College, Northwestern University, the University of Colorado, the University of New Mexico, and the University of California, Berkeley. His publications include *Designs of Blackness: Mappings in the Literature and Culture of Afro-America* (1998, 25th Anniversary Edition, 2020), *Multicultural American Literature: Comparative Black, Native, Latino/a and Asian American Fictions* (2003), which won the 2004 American Book Award, *Gothic to Multicultural: Idioms of Imagining in American Literary Fiction* (2009), *United States: Re-Viewing American Multicultural Literature* (2009), *Modern American Counter Writing: Beats, Outriders, Ethnics* (2010), ed., *Native American Writing*, 4 Vols. (2011), ed., *The Routledge Handbook of International Beat Literature* (2018), *Writer Directory: A Book of Encounters* (2019), *The Beats: Authorships, Legacies* (2019), and ed., *The Joan Anderson Letter, Neal Cassady* (2020). Among his creative writings are *Ars Geographica: Maps and Compasses* (2012), *Imaginarium: Sightings, Galleries, Sightlines* (2013), *Password: A Book of Locks and Keys* (2016), *Written Eye: Visuals/Verse* (2017), *Daylong, Nightlong. 24 Hour Poetry* (2020), *Suspicious Circumstances* (2020), *Time Travels* (2022), and *Outside In: Hinges and Swivels* (2022). He currently lives in Murcia, Spain.

Index

www.ingramcontent.com/pod-product-compliance
Lightning Source LLC
Chambersburg PA
CBHW071747110726
47908CB00006B/1725

* 9 7 8 1 6 3 6 6 7 0 4 8 5 *